# THE GREAT
# REFORMS

# THE GREAT
# REFORMS

**AUTOCRACY,**
**BUREAUCRACY,**
**AND THE POLITICS OF CHANGE IN**
## IMPERIAL
## RUSSIA

*W. Bruce Lincoln*

NORTHERN ILLINOIS UNIVERSITY PRESS    DEKALB, ILLINOIS
**1990**

© 1990 by W. Bruce Lincoln
Published by the Northern Illinois University Press,
DeKalb, Illinois 60115
∞ Manufactured in the United States using acid-free paper
Design by Julia Fauci
Typeset by Deborah Thomas

Library of Congress Cataloging-in-Publication Data
Lincoln, W. Bruce.
    The great reforms: autocracy, bureaucracy, and the politics of
change in imperial Russia / W. Bruce Lincoln.
        p.    cm.
    Includes bibliographical references (p.    ).
    ISBN 0-87580-155-2. — ISBN 0-87580-549-3 (pbk.)
    1. Soviet Union—Politics and government—1855–1881.
2. Soviet Union—Politics and government—1881–1894.
3. Soviet Union—Politics and government—1894–1917.   I. Title
DK220.L56   1990
947.08—dc20                                                    90-7186
                                                                  CIP

*For Marc Raeff*

# CONTENTS

# PREFACE

Although the interpretation of much of Russia's past remains the subject of debate among historians, few would dispute that the Great Reforms of the 1860s marked the broadest attempt at social and economic renovation to occur between the death of Peter the Great in 1725 and the Revolution of 1905. In just over a decade, imperial reform acts freed Russia's serfs, restructured her courts, established institutions of local self-government in parts of the empire, altered the constraints that censorship imposed upon the press, and transformed Russia's vast serf armed force into a citizen army in which men from all classes bore equal responsibility for military service.

As the new institutions of the Great Reform era evolved, policymakers seemed prepared to encourage Russians to assume a more active role in their own—and their nation's—affairs. Yet, because this involved serious political and economic risks, many Russians ventured upon this new course only with the greatest reluctance. What was later fondly remembered as the "Era of the Great Reforms" was for many of its contemporaries a disquieting time in which longheld assumptions fell by the wayside and the manner in which men and women viewed their social and economic environment was forever altered.

Life no longer had the certainty of earlier times. If the promise of the Great Reforms was to be fully realized, Russia's government had to surrender some of its most cherished prerogatives, for, if Russians were to take more control of their lives, the government had to relinquish its ubiquitous paternalism. A space for public involvement in public affairs had to be opened between government and governed. Where the line between the two would be drawn and how wide the space for private initiative ought to (or needed to) be were questions about which neither government nor *obshchestvo*—the educated classes destined to become active in Russia's civic life—could agree. Nor could they answer them in the same way, for government and governed had ceased to share the common set of values that had guided them in earlier times. Uvarov's profane trinity of Orthodoxy, Autocracy, and Nationality no longer commanded Russians' allegiance as it had in the 1830s. As Russians' visions of their nation's course became more diverse and complex, the common ground shared by governed and government grew less solid and their footing less sure. If men and women now had more chances to shape their destinies, they also faced greater risks.

Both government and *obshchestvo* therefore moved slowly. The openness of *glasnost'* meshed poorly with the secrecy of the autocratic legislative process, and the renovation of Russia's society and institutions moved with many painful starts and hesitations. Each step forward took the nation's autocracy and its increasingly independent-minded polity onto new and uncertain terrain where neither knew for certain where a path once taken might lead. Only later did Russians begin to lavish praise upon the Great Reform era as a time of promise during which their nation could have taken a different course, followed the path taken by the constitutional monarchies of Western Europe, and prevented the divisive social and political conflicts that rent the fabric of Russian life as the nineteenth century neared its end.

Although they remembered the Great Reform era as a time of unique opportunity, Russian historians of the late nineteenth and early twentieth centuries insisted that its promise had not been realized. This rare moment had been irretrievably lost, they argued, because the autocrat had refused to honor the promises he had made in the 1860s, because the Great Reform legislation had suffered from serious shortcomings, and, most of all, because Russia's rising revolutionary movement made it impossible for autocrat and government to make common cause with responsible citizens to mend those failings. Especially among those Western scholars who, for several decades after 1917, longed to find in the twilight years of imperial Russia's history reflections of the West's democratic experience this view proved to be extremely durable. Those who were inclined to challenge it found it difficult to do so until the rich holdings of Soviet archives became more readily accessible.

Although from different perspectives, scholars in the Soviet Union and the West reexamined the Great Reform era and began to rewrite portions of its history on the basis of careful archival research during the 1960s. No longer did its beginnings seem to lie so certainly in the crisis of confidence among progressive Russians that had been brought on by Russia's Crimean defeat (as turn-of-the-century historians had thought), and a broader, more balanced, more complex perspective began to replace that view. Soviet historians, especially Iu. I. Gerasimova and others associated with M. V. Nechkina's symposium on the revolutionary situation in Russia during the early years of Alexander II's reign, argued that a broad crisis, brought on not only by the Crimean defeat but also by a rising wave of serf revolts and the failings of Russia's serf-based economy, forced the emperor and his advisers to embark upon a course of renovation and reform.[1] P. A. Zaionchkovskii, perhaps the greatest Soviet specialist on nineteenth-century Russia until his death in 1983, argued somewhat differently, and more plausibly, that there was no single explanation for the beginning of the Great Reform era and that it was the consequence of diverse and complex factors.[2]

In the West, the first new studies based on research in the archives of the U.S.S.R. tended to accept one or the other of these explanations or to combine the two in some way. Alfred Rieber therefore argued that the Crimean defeat, with its attendant fiscal crisis, convinced Alexander II that Russia must have a modern military establishment patterned on the Prussian design and, because such an army required a large reserve component, it could not be established until the serfs were emancipated.[3] Others saw the beginnings of the Great Reforms, as Zaionchkovskii had, more in terms of domestic issues. "There are two overriding considerations to be perceived in the state's motivations for undertaking emancipation: concern for economic development, and a desire to ensure social and political stability," Terence Emmons, one of Zaionchkovskii's most distinguished American students, explained in what was to become the first major rethinking of the reforms' beginnings. "Both," he concluded, "were directly related to the experience of Russia's defeat in the Crimean War."[4] A decade later, Daniel Field, another of Zaionchkovskii's leading American protégés, would

add that serfdom fell "by stages" as a consequence of the imperial legislative process that went forward because "nineteenth-
century Russian serfdom lacked supporting ideological and political structures."[5]

To answer the broader question of whether such factors as
serf revolts, economic crisis, and the Crimean failure actually
impelled Alexander II and his advisers to initiate the process of
social, administrative, judicial, and economic renovation remained a more difficult problem. For, although the Crimean
defeat and serf revolts made Russia's statesmen more aware of
the need for reform, there was not much evidence to indicate
that they felt any acute urgency about launching a dramatic
program of change. In 1855, no one in Russia, and Alexander
II least of all, had any sense that the Great Reforms would
become an accomplished fact in less than a decade. At the end
of the Crimean War, Russia's statesmen had begun to search for
the causes of their nation's defeat and were prepared to ponder
solutions to the problems that their searching revealed. But there
seemed to be no inclination among them to seek hasty answers
to those complex questions. Alexander II's creation of what
would be the last secret committee on peasant affairs at the
beginning of 1857 certainly projected no sense of urgency; nor
did the plan of action that the committee proposed. Russia's
senior statesmen at the beginning of 1857 shared much the same
view that their predecessors had thirty years earlier, when the
famous Committee of December 6th responded to the crisis
posed by the Decembrist revolt by recommending "not the full
alteration of the existing order of government but its refinement
by means of a few particular changes and additions."[6]

How, then, was the complex, far-reaching, and multifaceted
Great Reform legislation, which paved the way for the renovation of Russia's social, judicial, and economic order, produced
by a bureaucracy whose consistent record of glacial slowness
had shown it to be virtually incapable of dealing with much
less complex tasks? Looked at another way, the Great Reform
legislation simply was too complex to have been generated in
so brief a span as that which separated Alexander II's famous
speech to the Moscow nobility in March 1856 and late 1862,
when the bulk of the draft legislation for the emancipation, the
judicial reforms, and the reform of local self-government (*zemstvo*)
had been completed. Russia's senior statesmen simply were not

prepared to move that quickly; nor did they have the knowledge and foresight needed to do so. What, then, were the roots and origins of the Great Reforms?

Almost a decade ago, I suggested that, to answer more satisfactorily the questions about how the Great Reform legislation was produced and why it assumed the shape it did, it was necessary to look more carefully at the era of Nicholas I, especially at those years that historians had for so long characterized as one of the most reactionary periods in Russia's modern history. Beginning in the late 1830s and throughout the 1840s, a group of young officials whom I identified as enlightened bureaucrats took shape in St. Petersburg's chanceries. These were the men who would exercise a decisive influence on the content of the Great Reform legislation starting with the Emancipation Acts of February 19, 1861.[7]

Although the question of emancipation engaged their attention most readily as they began to reexamine the Great Reform era, historians in the 1960s cast their net much more widely. Although a discussion of the many impressive studies that have been written on other aspects of the Great Reforms during the past quarter century cannot detain us here, we need to note, at a minimum, the work of Garmiza and Starr on the *zemstvo* reforms,[8] the research of Wortman and Kaiser on the judicial reforms,[9] and that of Orlovsky on the Ministry of Internal Affairs in the Great Reform era.[10] Zaionchkovskii wrote on the military reforms as well as the emancipation and, soon to be followed by Zakharova, Chernukha, Pirumova, and Orzhekovskii, led the way in placing the Great Reform era against the backdrop of internal politics in the 1870s and 1880s.[11] To understand better the forces that shaped Russian politics and society as the empire moved toward the twentieth century, these scholars looked deeper into the bureaucracy and probed the autocratic legislative process (until then extremely poorly understood in the West) to show better the sources of the Great Reform legislation, the manner in which it was produced, and the way in which it was implemented.

More recently, Western scholars have looked in much more depth at the question of how the Great Reforms were implemented, tested, and developed and they have considered their broader social, political, and cultural implications in an impressive series of studies that are only now beginning to appear.

Supplemented by recent and immediately forthcoming volumes of essays on the *zemstvo*, the professions, and the problems of middle-class identity,[12] Eklof's work on Russian peasant schools and village culture,[13] Frieden's study of Russian physicians,[14] Robbins's work on the provincial governors,[15] Kassow's examination of the relationship between higher education and the state,[16] Seregny's study of the Russian teachers' movement,[17] Sinel's examination of educational reform,[18] Whelan's work on Alexander III and the State Council,[19] and Pearson's very recent book on autocracy and local self-government[20] mark only the beginning of what promises to be an impressive new wave of scholarship on Russian life and politics during the quarter century before the Revolution of 1905.

Although these and other efforts have gone a long way toward clarifying our understanding of the way the major legislation of the Great Reform era was produced and the impact it had in Russia, no one has yet used them to shape a synthesis of the Great Reform era. Nor has anyone seriously tested those conclusions about the Great Reforms' ultimate success or failure that have endured for the better part of a century against the evidence that is now available. Outside the widening circle of historians mentioned, too many continue to view the 1860s as a fleeting moment in history when a fortuitous combination of men with unusual talent and foresight glimpsed a new path for Russia and her people but failed to transform their vision into reality.

My chief concern here is to produce this long-needed synthesis of the Great Reform era on the basis of the impressive body of scholarship that has come forth in the Soviet Union and the West since Zaionchkovskii wrote his pioneering study on the military reforms more than thirty-five years ago and to supplement it where possible with additional materials from Soviet archives. Although they were not carefully planned from the beginning and, in fact, were drafted piecemeal, the Great Reforms nonetheless comprised a body of legislation designed to renovate ancien regime Russia and to create the framework for a *grazhdanskoe obshchestvo* (citizen society) in place of the rigidly defined *sosloviia* (society of classes) in which autocratic politics and aristocratic class interests ruled the lives of Russians. This was to be a renovated society in which an increasing number of men and women would shoulder those responsibilities for their lives and their society that the government no longer could continue to assume in the increasingly complex world created by Russia's industrial revolution.

Given its breadth and the complexity of the problems to be considered, certain cautions must apply to this study from the beginning. Perhaps most important and most obvious, in examining the Great Reforms in historical perspective, one cannot label as part of the Great Reforms everything progressive or innovative that transpired in Russia during the first two decades of Alexander II's reign. There seems to be a tendency to discover more "great reforms" as access to the rich materials in Soviet archives increases; although some of these were important, even vital, to the success of Russia's modernization, they were not all a part of the process of creating a citizen society and establishing the institutions needed to do so.

My purpose here is not to write a history of the legislation of the Great Reform era but only to bring into sharper focus the conclusions that more than three decades of research into politics and society in Russia during the reign of Alexander II have made possible, suggest answers to some yet-unanswered questions, and indicate some directions for further research. This book therefore will deal only with the Great Reforms as defined in the limited sense suggested above. It will not examine church reforms, education reforms, financial reforms, banking reforms, joint-stock company legislation, or a variety of other similar and important topics. Clearly, this is not the only book that could (or should) be written with these ends in mind. In addition to more detailed studies of the reign of Alexander III, the Great Reforms still have to be studied from the broader perspective of the two decades that separated the death of Alexander III from the beginning of the Great War. Only then will we begin to know where Russia really stood on the eve of the twentieth century, what the promise of the Great Reforms really was, and how much of that promise was (or could have been) realized.

# ACKNOWLEDGMENTS

It would require a great deal more space than can be taken here to thank the many people and institutions who have helped me while I have been writing this book. My greatest intellectual debt is to Marc Raeff, longtime Bakhmeteff Professor of Russian Studies at Columbia University, whose prodding and encouragement have been a major factor in shaping my understanding of Russia's historical experience. It has been a quarter of a century since our first meeting in Leningrad, and during the years that have intervened, Marc has been a persistent but generous critic, challenging assumptions I thought unassailable and encouraging me to rethink conclusions that I thought firmly established. Much of what is worthwhile in this volume I owe to him; where it falls short of the mark, I suspect that it is because I should have listened to his counsels more carefully. As a token of my gratitude, I have dedicated this book to him.

Others have played an important part in my work on this book as well. Jacob Kipp and Christine Ruane read an earlier draft of the manuscript, and their comments and criticisms, written from very different perspectives, helped me to sharpen its focus and to correct a number of flaws in its argument. I also owe a great debt to Petr Andreevich Zaionchkovskii, who guided my first research efforts on the Great Reforms many years ago and who, until his death in 1983, continued to offer generous advice and support during four of my extended research trips to the Soviet Union.

Among the people here at Northern Illinois University who have helped me, James Norris, Dean of the College of Liberal

Arts and Sciences, an accomplished historian and a much valued colleague, has helped to make the writing of this book easier and more pleasant by his dedication to supporting research among his faculty. Jerrold Zar, Dean of the Graduate School and Associate Provost for Research, has come to my aid with much-needed financial support on several occasions, and my colleague George Gutsche has continued to be a source of wise counsel and quizzical criticism.

I owe much more than I can hope to express here to my wife, Mary, who has made my life so much richer than it would have been without her. Her critical judgment and generous spirit have helped me to shape this book; her gentle but persistent urgings had a great deal to do with convincing me to write it in the first place.

Institutions, too, have been generous in supporting my efforts to write this book, and I should not have been able to complete it without their financial and logistical support. The following are among those to whom I am grateful for help rendered over a long period of years:

The Academy of Sciences of the U.S.S.R., Leningrad

The American Council of Learned Societies, New York

The Bakhmeteff Archive, Columbia University, New York

Bibliothèque Nationale, Paris

The British Museum, London

The Bodleian, Oxford

The Central State Historical Archive, Leningrad

The Central State Archive of the October Revolution, Moscow

The Fulbright-Hays Faculty Research Abroad Program,
　　U.S. Department of Education, Washington, D.C.

The Harriman Institute, Columbia University, New York

The International Research and Exchanges Board, Princeton,
　　New Jersey

The John Simon Guggenheim Memorial Foundation,
　　New York

The Kennan Institution, Woodrow Wilson Center, The
　　Smithsonian, Washington, D.C.

The Lenin Library (and its manuscript section), Moscow

The Library of Congress, Washington, D.C.

The National Endowment for the Humanities,
  Washington, D.C.

Northern Illinois University, DeKalb

The Regenstein Library, University of Chicago, Chicago

The Russian and East European Center, University of Illinois
  at Urbana-Champaign

St. Antony's College, Oxford

The Saltykov-Shchedrin Public Library (and its manuscript
  section), Leningrad

The Slavonic Library, Helsinki

The Sterling Memorial Library, Yale University, New Haven

Beyond the acknowledgments listed here, the University of
Illinois Library deserves a particular added note of thanks. Without access to its outstanding Slavic Collection I would have
found my task much more difficult. There have been many
among its dedicated staff who have helped me over the years,
but, on this book, I have to thank Helen Sullivan above all
others for the immense competence and amazing good humor
with which she met my frequent requests for assistance.

To all of these people and institutions, and to the many colleagues in this country and abroad with whom I have discussed
this book over the years, I owe a debt that formal thanks such
as those rendered here cannot begin to repay.

DeKalb, Illinois
Christmas Eve, 1989

# THE GREAT
# REFORMS

# I

## AUTOCRACY, BUREAUCRACY, AND REFORM

*A*great cultural and technological gulf divided Russia from Europe when Peter the Great came to the throne. During the two hundred years that had passed before, European ship captains had discovered the New World and circumnavigated the globe. The hardy handful of men and women they had carried across the Atlantic had built colonial empires whose civilization had put down deep roots, while those who had remained behind in Europe had made discoveries in technology and science that would change forever the course of human history. Men's thinking had moved resolutely from the contemplative medieval world into the dynamic Age of Reason. That their children would live in a world different from their own now seemed inevitable and desirable to the men and women who watched the brilliance of the Sun King's court at Versailles radiate across Europe. As the struggle for national greatness took precedence over ruling kingdoms for the glory of God, kings and statesmen grappled with new dilemmas of state economy and politics and devoted their leisure hours to music, literature, and haute cuisine, not to prayer and contemplation of life in the world to come as had their medieval forebears.

By contrast, life for Russians toward the end of the seventeenth century differed very little from what it had been at the end of the fifteenth. Desire for change and a quest for progress had not yet touched the lives of men and women who believed that the future would be like a present that differed very little from the past. Peasants lived and died within the limits of the isolated hamlets into which they were born, while the vision of their noble masters remained confined to the narrow world encompassed by their lands. Illiterate, superstitious, and unadventurous, Russia's lords and peasants differed from each other mainly in their ability to gratify personal wants and enjoy creature comforts. Only among that comparative handful of men who served the tsar had life begun to take on larger, more dynamic, dimensions. For them, the tsar's service had begun to open broader vistas that carried them to Moscow and, on rare occasions, to the foreign capitals that lay beyond Russia's frontiers.

Although it remained narrow in comparison to the world of Europeans, the frame of reference within which the tsar's servitors lived and worked expanded very quickly in the seventeenth century. As the tsar's agents gathered precious furs to finance their nation's reconstruction after the devastation wrought by the Time of Troubles, Russia's fur frontier moved four thousand miles eastward from the Ural Mountains to the Pacific between 1585 and 1650. Russian furs adorned men and women from Canterbury to Cathay in those days, and, until their newly settled American empires began to yield similar quantities of pelts in the eighteenth century, Europeans had no other source of furs. Siberia's furs, of which the tsar received only a tenth of the annual harvest, therefore drew ever-greater numbers of Europeans to Russia as they competed to purchase the rare pelts of sable, black fox, and marten at their source.[1]

By 1680, the domains over which the tsar's agents had to maintain control had grown more vast and the problems with which they had to contend more complex. Europeans had begun to move so resolutely into Russia that, by the middle of the seventeenth century, the English had built a cordage industry on the White Sea coast in the vicinity of Kholmogory and the Dutch had established mills to produce gunpowder, glass, paper, and lumber. At Tula, just two hundred miles south of Moscow, a Dutch foundry exported nearly a thousand first-rate cannon a year to Holland and sold only the inferior pieces to their Russian hosts.[2] To withstand this onslaught of avaricious men and nations, the tsar's servitors required more technological and political expertise than ever before. Therefore, while they continued to look eastward in search of more furs and greater wealth as the seventeenth century drew to a close, Russia's tsars and their counselors began to turn to the West for the know-how to resolve the increasingly complex problems they faced. At first, they did so timidly. Then, as the Russians crossed into the eighteenth century, Peter the Great transformed Russia's relationship with Europe more suddenly and completely than any of his predecessors had dared to contemplate.

Peter the Great wrought fundamental changes in the way that Russia's ruler viewed himself and his domains. The Tsar-Transformer thought himself no less an absolute monarch than did his predecessors, but, like his counterparts in Europe, he saw the state as an impersonal entity, not an extension of his private and personal domains. Like those who had ruled before him, Peter thought himself Russia's master; unlike them, he also considered himself the first servant of the nation and, as such, responsible for the general welfare of its citizens. "To labor for the general welfare and profit" of his nation's people, Peter insisted, must be a monarch's chief concern, just as *zakonnost'* (lawfulness) must eventually become the basis for his government.[3] Peter therefore never permitted his kingship to become the complex ceremonial office that his predecessors' had been. Nor was he the most pious, most gentle tsar whom his father, Aleksei Mikhailovich, had personified. Active, energetic, responsible for more—and more complex—tasks, Peter became Russia's sovereign emperor, a title conferred not by the church but by the Governing Senate that he had created. Once applied with reverence to Russia's ruler, the epithet "most gentle" disappeared.[4]

Whereas sixteenth- and seventeenth-century tsars generally had worked to insulate their land and people from Western influences, the dynamic Peter opened Russia's frontiers to diplomats, traders, adventurers, and technicians who brought with them the culture, ideas, and technology of Europe. Urged on by the relentless Tsar-Transformer, these men and the forces they represented carried Russia across the threshhold of the modern world. With their help, Peter built the army and navy that Russia used to force her way into the European community of great powers. He built factories, shaped instruments of government that allocated responsibilities more rationally and defined lines of authority more clearly, and turned Russia away from the inert, church-centered culture of Muscovy toward the energetic secular life of the West.

Peter transformed not only the technology, government, and

culture of Russia but also the role of the autocracy in national life. He demanded that the rules men lived by, the values around which they shaped their lives, and the way in which they viewed the world all must change. No longer dedicated to defending tradition and preserving Russia's religious heritage, the autocracy in Peter's hands therefore became an instrument for change, and Russia's autocrat became the nation's leading advocate of technological and cultural innovation. No one called for a more far-reaching transformation than did the tsar, who relentlessly demanded that Russians begin to look and work like the Europeans he so admired. Nor did anyone demand that the process move so rapidly.

Before his death in 1725, Peter had forced the Russians into military uniforms and administrative offices styled on the Western models and had begun to shape a crude replica of European society. Just liberated from the isolation of the *terem*, the special quarters to which they were confined in Muscovite Russia, Russia's noblewomen now donned Western fashions, coiffed their hair in the manner of their counterparts in Paris and Berlin, and danced the minuet and polonaise with men whose awkwardness fully matched their own. Of most importance, Peter built St. Petersburg, his "Window on the West," where, in response to his stern orders and incessant prodding, European palaces and government buildings arose amid the swamps of the Neva delta. This was to be "the city of Peter's creation," which stood "unshakable, like Russia," in Pushkin's words,[5] as a monument to the Tsar-Transformer's efforts to command nature's forces.

Peter's immediate successors disputed his political course, but the autocracy remained the leading force for change in Russia nonetheless. Even when child-emperor Peter II's courtiers turned their backs on Peter's city and returned Russia's capital to Moscow to escape the financial burdens of building Western palaces far away from the food and resources their estates could provide, they never challenged the Western cultural and technological innovations that Peter the Great had begun. None among them hurried to don kaftans, return their women to the *terem*, or spend long hours at prayer once Russia's government returned to Moscow in 1728. Before the end of Peter II's reign, enough young Russians had become sufficiently infatuated with things European that Prince Antiokh Kantemir made them the focus of his first satire. Such young men and women (the *petimetr* and the *shchegolikha*, in their Russian forms) shared none of Peter the Great's dedication to modernizing Russia. Yet, as these early satires showed, men like Kantemir had begun to take the West more seriously and to probe more deeply beneath the superficial cultural veneer that overlay the world in which the *petimetr* and *shchegolikha* lived.[6]

As in the time of Peter the Great, "reform" continued to mean "transformation" to the statesmen who tried to shape a new order in Russia according to the model of the West. Military technology and the industries that supported it, the forms of Russia's government, and the aristocratic society and cultural life of St. Petersburg and Moscow all changed during the first six decades of the eighteenth century, but their transformation continued to be more of form than of substance except in the case of the military, in which the two intertwined. For the most part, Russians had not yet begun to think as their European counterparts did, even though their institutions of government had been shaped according to European forms and their lives reflected European patterns. *Zakonnost'* (the lawful order that governed the behavior of men and rulers in the West) had not yet become a part of Russia's experience. Outside St. Petersburg and Moscow, powerful men used raw force to rule the Russian land in their own interests.[7] In 1760, the autocrat's authority still did not reach very far beyond Russia's capital cities.

Russians did not live by the law, in part because they found it extremely difficult to determine what the law was. Eager to move medieval Russia into the modern world, Peter the Great and his associates had defied tradition readily and ignored *zakonnost'* frequently, with the result that the thousands of hastily drafted decrees scattered through government offices in St. Petersburg and across Russia constituted the legal authority for the transformation they had put into motion. In their haste, these men had neglected to create a body of modern law to replace the traditional constraints they had so readily destroyed. As the Russians moved into the second half of the eighteenth century, it therefore became impossible to determine what the Petrine transformation had accomplished and what had been left undone. The best evidence indicates that even forty years after Peter's death most provincial Russians had no access to state officials, physicians, or teachers. The instruments of local government and the machinery of justice either functioned as

they had in the seventeenth century or, in those areas where
the old forms had been eradicated and new ones had not yet
been implemented, they did not function at all.[8]

Eager to appear as an enlightened lawgiver to the Europeans
whose favor she courted and certain that "any other form of
government [other than autocracy] not only would be harmful for
Russia but, in the end, would lead to her ruin,"[9] Catherine II
set out to create a lawful basis for Peter's transformation. Yet
her charge to the Legislative Commission, which she summoned
in 1767 to draft a code of enlightened laws for Russia, was not
to legislate but to debate how best to apply to the problems of
Russian life the principles she had set down in her celebrated
*Nakaz*, or *Instructions*, which she had prepared for their guidance. "Lawyers and procurators do not legislate here and never
will legislate while I am alive," she once wrote.[10] "There is
nothing so dangerous," she warned in her *Nakaz*, "as this general
rule: That one must consider the spirit of the Law, not the
letter."[11] Because she believed that only Russia's autocrat could
mediate between the self-interested social and economic groups
who would, by virtue of their origins and narrow interests, be
antagonistic to each other, Catherine sought to impose *zakonnost'*
from above. "The intention and purpose of autocratic government is the glory of its citizens, the state, and the ruler," she
explained in her *Nakaz*. "The object of autocracy," she concluded,
"is not to deprive men of their natural liberty, but to direct their
actions in such a manner as to achieve the greatest good for
all."[12]

Catherine endeavored to enlist the support of public opinion,
not only to aid her in imposing *zakonnost'* upon the Russians
but also to help clarify her own vision of the directions in which
the Petrine transformation should be broadened. Peter the Great
knew too well how many Russians opposed the course he had
chosen, and he therefore had never discussed state affairs
beyond that narrow circle of men in whom he had placed his
trust. Less acquainted with the Empire she had risen to govern,
and more naive in her belief that Russians could help to shape
their nation's destiny, Catherine encouraged limited public discussion of civic affairs—a prototypical form of what would come
to be called *glasnost'* in the nineteenth century—to broaden the
Westernization process in Russia and to deepen her own understanding of how that could be carried further. She therefore

directed the Legislative Commission to discuss how to moderate
serfdom and how to develop a sense of civic responsibility
among the nobility. Her well-intentioned effort revealed only
that she ruled a nation of men and women irreparably divided
by conflicting economic aspirations and antagonistic group loyal-
ties. Almost no one in the Legislative Commission would place
the welfare of Russia ahead of self-interest. Each particular group
or class hoped to win greater privileges by negotiating directly
with the autocrat and none would support Catherine in working
for such high-minded goals as the welfare of Russia and the
well-being of all the Russians.

When the Legislative Commission failed to draft the enlightened code of laws for which she had hoped, Catherine
concluded that before she could become an enlightened monarch she must first be an *enlightening* one. Modeled upon *The
Tatler* and *The Spectator* of Steele and Addison in London, her
monthly journal *Vsiakaia vsiachina* (*Odds and Ends*) satirized the
foibles of those self-interested Russian aristocrats who dressed
and acted as Europeans did but remained unconcerned about
the greater glory of their nation and the well-being of its people.
When Catherine invited others to follow her example, a half-
dozen privately published satirical journals—more than had appeared in Russia's entire history—were published within a
year.[13] Yet, just as Russians' self-interest and civic unconcern
had made success impossible for the Legislative Commission,
so Catherine's attempts to shape public opinion through satire
ran aground upon the shoals of ignorance. Very few men and
women looked for intellectual edification in what they read, and
the message of *Vsiakaia vsiachina* never reached those against
whose failings it was directed.

Catherine's effort to enlighten her subjects by establishing a
periodical press in Russia unleashed an awesome new force that
she could not control. While *Vsiakaia vsiachina* criticized the su-
perficiality of Russia's newly Westernized aristocratic culture,
the editors of other journals began to challenge some of the
principles and institutions that Catherine thought most vital to
her nation's welfare. None did so more persistently than Nikolai
Novikov, the publisher of four short-lived satirical journals that
came and went between 1769 and 1774. The first writer of consequence to question Russia's eighteenth-century social and economic order, Novikov criticized the absence of *zakonnost'* at every

level of Russian life. Russia's venal judges, her arrogant high officials, and, most of all, the moral indignity of serfdom were all subjects for his sharp wit and ready pen. "Everywhere I saw dire poverty and slavery among the peasants," he wrote while chronicling a journey through Russia's countryside, a device that Aleksandr Radishchev would use with even greater effect in his *Journey from St. Petersburg to Moscow* some fifteen years later.[14] All across Russia, Novikov found festering the sores of *proizvol*, the gross abuse of power that had eroded the Russian body politic for centuries. Thence oozed the infection that had tainted Catherine's efforts to convince the nobility that they must place their nation's welfare ahead of self-interest.

Although the evidence that Catherine forced Novikov to close his journals remains inconclusive, it was hardly coincidental that she established the first institutions of press censorship in Russia soon afterward.[15] Catherine's turn to secular censorship clearly indicated that Russia's autocracy had grown uncomfortable with the role that Peter's transformation had imposed upon it. At the same time, a small segment of educated Russian opinion had begun to demand a broader discussion of Russia's social and political ills than any autocrat dared permit. Throughout the 1780s, Catherine vacillated between continuing her effort to foster enlightenment and defending the integrity of autocratic authority. Then, in 1790, Aleksandr Radishchev's *Journey from St. Petersburg to Moscow*—a book "filled with the most pernicious philosophizing, destructive to civic peace, disparaging of citizens' respect for authority . . . and, finally, replete with insulting and frenzied remarks against the dignity and power of the Sovereign," in the words of the men who presided at his trial[16]— convinced her to take the latter course.

Ironically, Radishchev had been among a handful of talented graduates of the Imperial Corps of Pages whom Catherine had sent to the University of Leipzig to be trained as an elite corps of jurists to implement the enlightened code of laws that she expected the Legislative Commission to produce. Two decades later, in part because of the ideas he had absorbed at Leipzig and, quite probably, because he never had been given the opportunity to fulfill the dreams that his empress had nurtured in him, Radishchev became a bitter critic of the social amalgam and political order that Catherine had created.[17] Outraged at his criticisms, Catherine ordered Radishchev's book burnt and its author condemned to death, although she later commuted his sentence to exile in Siberia. Clearly, the Russian autocracy had begun to break the mold of transformer and innovator in which Peter the Great had cast it.

Catherine's violent reaction to Radishchev's call for the Petrine transformation to continue along the path taken by the West during the second half of the eighteenth century indicated the limits of her commitment to the Enlightenment and the dangers that even a prototypical form of *glasnost'* posed to autocratic authority in Russia. Radishchev's attempt to question the failings of autocracy as an advocate of innovation and modernization in Russia, she insisted, sought "in every possible way to disparage respect for power and authority and to goad the masses to indignation against their leaders and government."[18] For a quarter of a century, Catherine had put the final touches on shaping Russia in the image of ancien regime France that the Petrine transformation had begun. Then, when the French Revolution shattered that model in the West, Catherine concluded that, if her subjects insisted upon following the same path, and if the autocrat's personal example no longer could define the content of Russians' relationship with the West, censorship must limit the contact between the two. "It is necessary to throw all the works of the best writers, and all that which their words have spread throughout Europe, into the flames," she wrote.[19] As Radishchev began his exile in Siberia, she further abandoned the autocrat's role as the chief agent of the Petrine transformation and condemned Novikov to fifteen years of imprisonment in the fortress prison at Schlüsselburg.

If the experience of late eighteenth-century Europe required Russia's autocrat to be censor rather than modernizer and innovator, Catherine insisted that autocracy must retain the prerogative to moderate the censorship it imposed. This set a precedent that frustrated the course of reform and renovation in Russia in years to come at the same time as it complicated the nation's intellectual and political relationship with the West. At the height of the French Revolution, Catherine left the education of her grandson, the future Emperor Alexander I, in the hands of César LaHarpe, the Swiss Jacobin tutor she had chosen at an earlier time, and she allowed Alexander and certain of his friends to read and discuss the very works she forbade to other Russians.

In doing so, she established the principle that not even the most radical forms of Western thought and politics were *totally* forbidden for *all* Russians. Although her criteria for determining who could and could not read the most advanced writings from the West remained vague, Catherine made it clear that loyalty to the autocrat and to Russia must be the decisive factor. No longer was it a question of determining who was daring enough to have the most contact with the West as it had been in Peter's day. Which Russians were sufficiently "loyal" to their autocrat to be trusted not to use advanced European theories to criticize or attack the established order now became the chief test for determining their access to the West.

By the time Alexander I ascended the throne in 1801, young Russians had begun to turn away from those cosmic philosophical questions that had so occupied the minds of their eighteenth-century elders. As they elevated feeling above reason, thoughtful men and women abandoned the rationalism of the Enlightenment and the political activism it had engendered in favor of more contemplative ways of thinking about politics, life, and progress. Caution and passivity became noble virtues among the Russians as fathers' summons to action gave way to melancholic resignation among their sons. This allowed Alexander I and his counselors to set aside for a time the troublesome question of limiting Russians' access to European thought because the sentimentalist ideas they found most appealing carried no threat of political action. As Richard Wortman wrote some years ago, the sentimental ethos of Alexander I's reign made it possible for an educated nobleman "to abandon his rhetoric of struggle and substitute for it a manner of acquiescence." Even more, it "made the existence of irremediable injustice in a world that was supposed to be good not only tolerable but even pleasurable and uplifting."[20] In this new milieu, one commentator concluded, "social inequality could be tolerated because it was insignificant in comparison to moral equality."[21] Concerns for political and economic equality receded from the forefront of men's concerns for the same reason.

From such sentimentalist and romantic beginnings stemmed that body of nineteenth-century conservative thought that proclaimed Orthodoxy, Autocracy, and Nationality to be the fundamental truths that could guide Russia through a world that had been irrevocably transformed by the French and industrial revolutions. The belief that "in Russia the sovereign is the living law" and the conviction that "autocracy constitutes the main condition of the political existence of Russia" projected a view that the nation's greater glory could best be assured by strengthening the existing order, not by continuing to transform Russia along European lines as had eighteenth-century autocrats.[22] In contrast to Catherine II's firm insistence that "Russia is a European power"[23] and Alexander I's belief that Russia must not remain outside the course of European politics, Nicholas I and his counselors viewed East and West as two distinct and very different entities. "Europe" was evil; "Russia" was virtuous. "Europe" stood for revolution, "Russia" stood for stability, and the two stood in irreconcilable opposition to each other. "The East is not the West," one apostle of Russian conservatism explained in the 1850s. "Everything is different."[24] "Only two forces exist in Europe—Revolution and Russia," the poet Tiutchev concluded as Russia faced a new revolutionary challenge from the West in 1848. "The existence of one means the death of the other!"[25]

Although its caution and political passivity provided the foundations upon which nineteenth-century Russian conservatism developed, European romanticism displayed another side that cast its heroes as noble opponents of evil tyrants, not as men consumed by tragic resignation. Expressed most vividly in the German dramas of Schiller, such rebellion against tyranny longed for reconciliation with legitimate authority and was much more at home in the realm of fantasy than in the world of hard reality. "The poet of people who," as Martin Malia once wrote, "are condemned to dream about liberty but never to live it,"[26] Schiller and his writings stirred a responsive chord among young Russians as the obscurantist, militaristic regime of Count Aleksei Arakcheev tightened its grip on Russia toward the end of Alexander I's reign. "When will I see, O friends! The masses free?" Aleksandr Pushkin asked in one of his early poems. "When will that beautiful dawn of freedom so enlightened at last arise above our land?"[27]

In part a reflection of the political dissent connected with the early stages of nationalism in Europe, such passions in Russia produced the hopeless Decembrist revolt, whose flame flared for a single day on December 14, 1825. Then, even more than in the West, Russian romanticism soared away into Schiller's safer ethereal aesthetic realm, where men could compensate for

a lack of political freedom in the real world by dedicating themselves to a more elevated (and internalized) quest for friendship,
love, and beauty, while the Decembrists' failure to achieve their
revolutionary dream brought them to the dungeons of St.
Petersburg's Peter-Paul Fortress.

From their cells, the Decembrists spoke out with amazing
frankness about the injustices of the society in which they lived
and the failings of the government that ruled their lives. Russia
had no code of laws, her courts had become hopelessly clogged
with unresolved cases that stretched back into the previous century, her peasants stood bent beneath the weight of taxes they
could not pay while their lords arrogantly refused to take responsibility for their—and Russia's—welfare, and her officials remained as corrupt and self-interested as they had before Peter
the Great had launched his effort to reshape Russia's government
on the lines of the modern, rationalist West. Taken together,
these criticisms portrayed a nation abused by brutal and corrupt
men in which, as the official who compiled their testimony for
Nicholas I stated bluntly, "powerful men and informers flourish,
while the poor and innocent suffer."[28] Clearly, the Decembrists
looked to Nicholas to right those injustices by imposing from
above reforms that would bring Russian life more into line with
post-Napoleonic Europe. Yet, whereas Peter the Great and his
successors had been able to strengthen autocracy by imposing
innovations from the West upon Russia, Nicholas faced the certainty that the Western model now threatened autocracy's destruction.

In the context of the political course upon which Western
nations had embarked after 1789, autocracy stood out clearly as
an anachronism. For Nicholas to continue his eighteenth-century
predecessors' commitment to innovation and change threatened
to bring into Russia the political and social forces that would
demand the abolition of autocracy itself. Certain that he must
reject his predecessors' commitment to innovation in order to
preserve autocracy, Nicholas therefore tolerated change only in
the form of very gradual, careful, and cautious adjustments.
Ready to admit that the machinery of government required modest modifications to make it function as its creators had intended,
he nonetheless insisted that Russia's government and society
remained fundamentally sound.

More like a commander of an army than the ruler of an

empire, Nicholas I looked to trusted adjutants to accomplish the modifications Russia's government required. On December 6, 1826, he therefore formed a special committee to examine the state of imperial Russia's society and government. Called the Committee of December 6th and made up of three senior generals and six of Russia's most experienced statesmen, no body of senior officials in eighteenth- or nineteenth-century Russia ever received a broader mandate to renovate Russia.[29] Free to define the emperor's mandate in the way they thought suited Russia's interests best, these men chose to set a narrow, unimaginative, and timid course that left little room to pursue reform in any comprehensive fashion.

The framework within which the emperor's advisers cast their thoughts had undergone a striking change since the days of Peter and Catherine. Led by Mikhail Speranskii, the statesman who once had urged Alexander I to limit the power of the nobility, grant privileges only in return for duties responsibly performed, and moderate serfdom to the point of transforming Russia's peasants into a class of farmhands free to move from one estate to another, the Committee of December 6th insisted that its task could not be "the full alteration of the existing order of government, but only its refinement by means of a few particular changes and additions."[30] Reform in Russia no longer meant modernization and transformation as it had in the days of Peter the Great. Now it meant cautious renovations that could preserve the existing order while fearful statesmen searched for ways in which to make it function more effectively.

Obliged to confront the dilemma of how the Russian empire could meet the challenge posed by the nations of the West as they entered the age of the industrial revolution, Nicholas and his advisers endeavored to take from the West only those features that could be fitted into the framework of its ancien regime social order and serf-based economic system without sudden shifts of policy or abrupt changes of course. "Everything," Nicholas told the great lords who sat on Russia's State Council, "should be done gradually, and ought not and, indeed, cannot be done at once or suddenly."[31] Overwhelming concern to preserve the established order combined with cautious renovations to make it slightly more responsive to the new imperatives that now motivated Europeans thus became the hallmarks of the Nicholaevan system.

In Russia, where the difficulties of day-to-day administration had become so overwhelming that efforts to deal with them took on much greater significance than they ought to have, such renovations produced alterations in administrative form and procedure that had very little relation to the substance of government. When they had not understood Peter the Great's reform efforts, lesser officials in Russia's chanceries had held to the administrative procedures with which they were familiar, and their successors had acted in similar fashion when they had resisted senior statesmen's efforts to modernize Russia's administration. Such men, the historian A. N. Filippov once pointed out in an essay on ministerial government in Russia, "were hardly able to introduce a new spirit into the administration and, especially after Peter the Great, they almost completely failed to create that independent administrative body free from arbitrariness about which Peter and his closest associates had dreamed."[32] The passive resistance of petty officials thus condemned to failure any effort to introduce *zakonnost'* into Russian life and government. Unable to convince their officials to act in a lawful manner, Russia's autocrats had tried in vain to force them to do so. In that, they had violated the letter and spirit of *zakonnost'* just as fully as had the officials whose behavior they were trying to control.

Russia's eighteenth-century administration had not functioned very effectively outside the capitals, in any case. An acute shortage of trained officials had created such a desperate failure of communication between Russia's central government and its provinces that Catherine II had shifted her limited resources outward in the 1770s. As a result, all but three of Peter the Great's twelve administrative colleges had ceased to function before the end of the century,[33] and this had left Russia dangerously vulnerable to new challenges from the West. Just when Napoleon had begun to marshal France's national resources on an unprecedented scale, Alexander I had ascended the throne of an empire that, for all practical purposes, had no viable central administration.

Alexander's response had been to create a new ministerial government in which, in theory, ministers of state wielded sufficient monocratic authority to impose *zakonnost'* on the men and agencies under their control.[34] Yet, Russia's chronic shortage of trained, well-educated officials once again had crippled the autocrat's effort to substitute the predictability of *zakonnost'* for the uncertainties of *proizvol*. Because narrowly educated men trained to govern Russia according to rigid formulae and fixed procedures could not confront the problems of a rapidly changing world, better-educated officials had to be found before Russia's new administration could marshal its resources, enforce the sovereign's will, and serve its citizens' welfare.[35]

More, not better, bureaucrats filled imperial Russia's offices as the nineteenth century moved toward its midpoint. From approximately 16,000 in 1796, Russia's civil service personnel in the Table of Ranks burgeoned by more than 500 percent to 82,352 in 1855, and those figures did not include 32,073 petty *kantseliarskie sluzhiteli* (chancery clerks), who had not yet reached the Table's lowest grades.[36] At the same time, Russia's population increased by just over 60 percent, from about 36 to 59 million. In absolute terms, this bureaucratic force certainly was not large by European standards, for there were only about 1.6 officials per 1,000 inhabitants in Russia by the time of the Crimean War as compared to 4.1 per 1,000 in England and 4.8 per 1,000 in France. Viewed in more meaningful terms, however, Russia's bureaucracy was huge in comparison to those of the West, for most Russians, unlike their French and English counterparts, never encountered a government official from one year to the next. If we take into account only Russia's nobles, the men and women who encountered officials most frequently and who numbered approximately 886,800 in 1858, the ratio of officials to population rises to 12.9 per 1,000. And, even if we add to our calculations Russia's 400,000 merchants, the only others whose daily affairs brought them into regular contact with state officials, the proportion remains at a very large ratio of 8.9 officials per 1,000 people served.[37]

To better the education of Russia's growing army of officials, Alexander I's new Ministry of Public Instruction drew up a plan for building more district schools, provincial *gimnazii*, and universities soon after the nineteenth century opened. Although that grandiose scheme never took effect before the Great Reform era, Russia did establish new universities at Vilna, Dorpat, Kharkov, Kazan, and St. Petersburg.[38] No less important, Alexander presided over the opening of an elite lyceum at Tsarskoe Selo in 1811 to educate "those youths especially destined for important spheres of state service" in those areas that would be of greatest concern to Russia's government during the first half of the century.[39] Together, these institutions more than tripled the number of well-educated officials in Russia's service; the number of students in Russia's universities rose from 1,326 in 1825 to 3,141 by 1850.[40] Compared with the horde of men taken into Russia's civil service during the first half of the nineteenth century, those numbers remained paltry indeed. Very few men in Russia's civil service had the knowledge to resolve the complex domestic and international problems Russia faced during the second quarter of the nineteenth century. Fewer still had the breadth of vision to place those problems into the context of the rapidly changing world in which Russia found herself on the eve of the Crimean War.

In terms of the ability of the Russian government to function, the problem of too few educated men in the lower reaches of the civil service was worsened by the concentration of its handful of educated officials in St. Petersburg. So different from any other city in Russia, with its great brick, stucco, and stone buildings, wide avenues, and majestic canals, Peter the Great's northern capital exerted an irresistible pull on men born and raised in Russia's provinces, who felt that it stood at the hub of the political and cultural life of which they wanted to be a part. "We provincials somehow turn our steps toward Petersburg instinctively," Mikhail Saltykov-Shchedrin explained in his *Diary of a Provincial in St. Petersburg* some years later. "It is as if Petersburg, all by itself, with its name, its streets, its fog, rain, and snow, could resolve something or shed some new light on something."[41]

Others shared Saltykov-Shchedrin's sentiments. "I still do not understand very clearly why I came to St. Petersburg," one official confessed as he looked back upon a moment of youthful impetuosity from the perspective of middle age.[42] Yet he, like Saltykov-Shchedrin and many others, had made the journey to Russia's capital without a second thought. To all of them, it seemed that Petersburg's luster almost certainly would change their lives for the better. The salaries to be earned by junior officials were wretched but far better than in the provinces, and, if the chances of failure were great, the rewards could be even greater for those upon whom fortune smiled.[43] Few heeded the warning that Nikolai Gogol', a provincial who had allowed

Petersburg's glitter to draw him away from his native Ukraine, set down in an early story that bore as its title the name of the capital's main thoroughfare, the Nevskii Prospekt. "Everything's an illusion," Gogol' warned his readers. "Everything's not what it seems."[44]

However misleading its illusions and however many its disappointments, St. Petersburg offered the best opportunities for young officials to advance their careers in a government that judged men's stature by the significance of the matters with which they dealt and where complex patronage networks held the key to success.[45] In an administration already given to centralized decision making, Nicholas I's tendency to see administrative relationships in the context of a military command structure further concentrated authority at the top. At the same time, other forces worked to intensify centralization in Russia's government even more. Given officials' desire to serve in St. Petersburg, it was only there that even a relative handful of men capable of attending to the increasingly complex problems that the Russian government faced in the 1830s and 1840s could be found.

Concentration of talent and opportunity in St. Petersburg during the 1830s and 1840s left Russia's provincial offices more poorly staffed than ever. Officials who learned their tasks by repetition and performed them by rote were common in every provincial office, and the inept, corrupt town officials whom Gogol' described in *The Inspector General* too often proved to be the rule, not the exception.[46] The military governor of the great Volga entrepôt of Kazan reported in the 1840s that the city's public offices were staffed by untrained, often illiterate men, and reports from provincial governors in Saratov, Tula, and Poltava confirmed that the situation was equally bad elsewhere.[47] So great was the need for educated officials in Russia's more remote provinces that desperate governors hurried to recruit into their offices even men sent into exile for political crimes. The famous anarchists Mikhail Bakunin and Prince Petr Kropotkin both received government assignments while serving political sentences in the Russian provinces, and so did the radical Westernizer Aleksandr Herzen. But efforts to improve the quality of provincial officials on a broader scale produced very few results. An imperial decree that required all civil servants (beginning in 1839) to serve for three years in the provinces before they could accept an appointment in St. Petersburg or Moscow only forced talented young men to become provincial timeservers before they moved on to the capital.

Desperation carried to the point of assigning political criminals to government posts only dramatized the breakdown of administration that spread across Russia's provinces at midcentury. Poorly educated local officials who had learned narrow tasks through a crude apprenticeship system simply could not provide the services needed by the people for whose welfare they were responsible. Nor could they supply the data that the central government needed to make important decisions. Any nonroutine request for information from St. Petersburg's chanceries threw local bureaucrats into a panic, and they responded with silence because they feared that the central administration wanted to do them harm.[48] Even in the 1840s, central government officials found it difficult to learn the cost of basic goods and services in provincial capitals and county seats. To obtain through official channels information about the number of shops in a particular town or, even, to discover how many people lived in it proved beyond the ability of the central government despite the hordes of petty clerks who filled government offices.[49] "Clerkish rot and ignorance," one frustrated official wrote, was eroding Russia's government.[50] As midcentury passed, critical public services began to break down just as the emancipation was about to increase by more than a third the number of people for whom Russia's public administration was directly responsible.[51]

Effective decision making could not be concentrated at the center of Russia's government without rapid communications and without provincial officials who could provide the information required by policymakers in St. Petersburg. The first Russian emperor to do so regularly since Peter the Great, Nicholas made hurried journeys to inspect distant parts of his empire personally, but his efforts did little more than sharpen his sense of the diversity and complex vastness of the domains he ruled. Like his predecessors, he relied upon adjutants to connect Russia's capital and provinces, but he used them more frequently because the problems that confronted his government were more urgent and complex. Imperial adjutants hurried to areas suffering from famine, cholera, civil unrest, or, in many cases, simple governmental paralysis, to collect information and report back with recommendations about what course of action best suited local conditions. To supplement their emperor's efforts, imperial ministers sent out agents of special commissions on more complex fact-finding assignments that kept them in the provinces for periods that stretched from a few months to several years.[52] Such efforts to respond to local crises could not provide Russia with effective government, let alone bring about change. Nor could diligent service rendered by such adjutants and agents of special commissions counterbalance the broader failings of the administration they served. By the middle of the nineteenth century, the chancres of gross dishonesty and blatant unwillingness to serve the public welfare still blotted the face of Russian officialdom.

In the West, energetic advocates of public welfare supported by a public press that reported upon officials' misdeeds served to check corruption and inefficiency in government. In Russia, *nadzor* (surveillance), the administrative counterpart to public investigations of governmental failings, served the same purpose but worked less effectively even though agents of the Third Section of His Majesty's Own Chancery, the Imperial Gendarmerie that Nicholas created in 1826, served as the eyes and ears of the emperor and his government.[53] All across the empire, Third Section agents reported upon the state of public opinion, searched for malfeasance and corruption, and served as the moral guardians of Russia. Yet these men, whose sky-blue uniforms lit even the darkest corners of Russia from time to time, could not eradicate fear and ignorance or compensate for Russians' gross lack of civic responsibility. *Zakonnost'* could not be imposed from above upon officials who had no tradition of legality and lacked the moral fiber to take responsibility for the government of which they were a part.

To be effective, *nadzor* could not be separated from *proizvol*, the arbitrarily and abusively applied power that it was supposed to eliminate. For the *proizvol* that enabled inspectors general and adjutants acting in the name of the emperor to cut through one Gordian knot of red tape after another violated every canon of *zakonnost'*, the lawfulness that Russia's rulers had struggled to instill in citizens and officials since the time of Peter the Great. This, one thoughtful official warned, posed especially serious problems in Russia, "where public opinion stands mute, where citizens are not summoned to take part in the discussion of public affairs and where, finally, great statesmen frequently conceal their personal failings and mistakes behind the impenetrable shield of the autocrat's name."[54] Properly applied, *proizvol* could do good. In the wrong hands, it could do evil even more readily.

In a bureaucracy filled with timid men, *nadzor* made officials fearful of initiative and reluctant to press for change. The bureaucrats of Nicholas I's Russia sought refuge in complex procedures and ritualized routines that freed them from the burden of making decisions, created the false impression that a great deal was going on, and effectively blocked any renovation of their nation's increasingly ineffective administration. "Each agency had to direct its attention to refining the manner in which it functioned," one official remembered. "Beginning in the 1830s, every department concentrated upon improvements . . . in the details of its internal administrative apparatus."[55] Another lifelong bureaucrat recalled how "the administrative machine functioned with irreproachable harmony and elegance of detail" in those days and spoke of his superior's ability to project "either the awe-inspiring countenance of Jupiter or the fawning figure of an enchantress seeking to curry favor," depending upon who came into his presence.[56] The result was an overwhelming impression that, as Petr Valuev once wrote, "Everywhere, everything possible has been done, [and that] everywhere success has been achieved." A man who would one day rise to head the powerful Ministry of Internal Affairs and become one of nineteenth-century Russia's most effective statesmen, Valuev knew how deceptive that impression was. "On the surface it all seems splendid," he concluded as the Crimean War began to drain Russia's resources and energy, "but it is rotting away underneath."[57]

Even if Russia's administration was not rotting away as rapidly as Valuev feared at midcentury, it certainly was being buried beneath a mountain of unimportant forms, unnecessary correspondence, and useless information. "Here in Russia, the most simple and inconsequential matter, which is dealt with by a stroke of the pen elsewhere, generates a whole series of official papers," the noted Polish economist Ludvik Tengoborskii complained as the Crimean War drew to a close. "Records and letters," he added wearily, "seem to reproduce themselves in geometrical proportions."[58] That Tengoborskii's was not merely the complaint of a disgruntled Pole working among Russians was proved by the many times others echoed his sentiments. "The mechanical work of correspondence . . . surpasses the physical capabilities of the central offices of the provincial administration,"[59] Minister of Internal Affairs Count Lev Perovskii had warned Nicholas in a special report after he learned that his ministry had processed 22,326,842 documents in the course of his first year in office. When that figure had soared to 31,103,676 despite his best efforts to reduce it, Perovskii threw up his hands. "Bureaucratic formalities have reached the point of absurdity," he wrote to his emperor at midcentury. "Official correspondence absorbs all the attention and energy of those who execute policy and, instead of true supervision and administration, we have, for the most part, only record-keeping."[60]

Few men knowledgeable in the ways of Russia's administration would have disputed Perovskii's assessment, although some were known to think of each document that left the capital as "a new current of benevolence flowing . . . into the vastness of Russia."[61] Every document received in St. Petersburg had to be recorded in a ledger, copied out if necessary in that copperplate hand for which Russia's clerks were famous, and filed or passed on to another office. There could be no corrections, no smudges, no flaws of any kind, for superiors were known to order a document recopied because the spacing was too narrow or because the ink was too light or too dark. Sometimes dedicated clerks added elegant designs and tinted charts with watercolors when they prepared reports for senior officials, although few understood their contents or even cared.[62] No wonder, then, that one angry young official described Russia's administration as "a lot of arguments and passing official papers from hand to hand."[63]

The rising flood of reports and correspondence that threatened to engulf Perovskii's agency touched every level of government and administration in Russia. Fear of *nadzor* caused senior bureaucrats to impose new and more complex regulations upon their subordinates, and this concern with bureaucratic procedure entangled everyone in a morass of forms and papers from which none could escape. As officials saw administration in terms of producing documents, not solving problems, even senior statesmen found it difficult to get the proverbial forest into focus because regulations and bureaucratic routines required them to spend all their time pruning and cultivating each tree.[64] Everyone, from ministers of state to chancery clerks, spent his life reacting to the requests of the moment. Every year, some 165,000 documents (many of which actually dealt with nothing more significant than updating service records) passed through Ministry of Internal Affairs offices and, because they had been marked "URGENT," officials had to set regular business aside to deal with them.[65] Every year, provincial governors faced a hundred thousand documents that required their signature, and these, if they spent only a minute on each, promised to consume more than six hours of every working day.[66] Effective reform, a transformation such as Peter the Great had imposed upon Russia a century and a half before, simply could not be accomplished under such conditions. At best, officials could think in terms of minor renovations, of adjustments in the machinery of government, or, as Speranskii and his colleagues on the Committee of December 6th had said, the "refinement [of the existing order] by means of a few particular changes and additions."[67]

The problem of change in Russia during the 1840s was further complicated by the passive resistance of its clerkish legions, who feared that any change would burden them with tasks they could not learn or would find difficult to perform. At the beginning of the 1840s, a backlog of 3 million decrees and official requests waiting to be acted upon lay scattered through Russia's government offices to attest to the effectiveness of such passive resistance.[68] Even Nicholas himself waited for several months on some occasions for replies to inquiries sent to government offices that stood less than a mile from his study in the Winter Palace.[69] Russia's official world thus had become very different from that in which eighteenth-century autocrats had governed. So long as the empire's administration had remained relatively unstructured, the problems facing it generally uncomplex, and the bureaucracy reasonably small, Peter the Great and his successors had made policy as circumstances warranted and changed it as their perceptions of their empire's needs changed. But theirs had been a world in which the will of rulers and their loyal servitors could produce change. Now, as the nineteenth century approached its midpoint, it proved much harder to implement policy and even more difficult to alter its course.

Unable to change the existing system, and confident of its

fundamental soundness in any case, Russia's statesmen therefore concentrated on adjustments that could respond to the new conditions they confronted in the 1830s and 1840s but still preserve the ancien regime political and social framework to which they and their emperor remained committed. Such men saw a benevolent paternalism in the "Nicholas system" and the principles of Orthodoxy, Autocracy, and Nationality on which it was based, and they believed that their nation would be well governed if those precepts were diligently applied. Just as the Third Section became the moral guardian of Nicholas's Russia, so these men believed that the moral force of their creed of service, duty, and devotion to tsar and country could make Russia's increasingly ponderous bureaucracy capable of generating policy and applying it effectively.

A bureaucracy capable of generating policy and an administration efficient enough to implement it became the goal of at least four of the senior statesmen who served Nicholas I in the 1840s. Minister of State Domains Count Pavel Kiselev and Minister of Internal Affairs Count Lev Perovskii focused particularly upon building an institutional base that could generate meaningful policy changes; Count Dmitrii Bludov, Minister of Internal Affairs before Perovskii and Director of the Second Section of His Majesty's Own Chancery, which compiled and drafted Russia's laws, sought the means for formulating such changes clearly and precisely; and Minister of Justice Count Viktor Panin concentrated on producing true administrative efficiency rather than meaningless (and ineffective) routine. Perovskii and Kiselev therefore encouraged initiative among their subordinates while Bludov emphasized the virtues of voluntary submission to a higher order and Panin insisted upon strict subordination. Yet, because they shared a vision of efficient administration, of policies carefully developed on the basis of clear principles, accurate information, and a precise chain of command, these four statesmen became instrumental in shaping the institutional base out of which the enlightened bureaucracy would emerge to produce the broad renovations that became known as the Great Reforms some twenty years later.

Contrary to the generally held view among the emperor's counselors, Kiselev and Perovskii insisted that policy decisions must be based on complete and accurate data. Unable to reduce the flood of routine paperwork in Russia's governmental offices, they nonetheless encouraged senior officials to take a longer view, see problems in a larger context, and play a more active part in shaping policy. Bludov emphasized obedience and discipline as a means to the same end. Officials, he insisted, must study the "alphabet of service" that would instill in them the habit of subordination and, above all, respect. "Without respect," he once explained, "nothing great can be achieved, nothing durable can be established."[70] Count Panin shared Bludov's view and sought to translate it into "firm precision" in administration. For Panin, this meant complete subordination to higher authority. "He considered the will of the sovereign to be sacred," one of his subordinates wrote. "He fulfilled Imperial commands to the letter, without question, and demanded similar obedience to his orders from his subordinates."[71] Panin's view was too rigid to permit meaningful change, especially when mediocre senior bureaucrats replaced more thoughtful statesmen during the last years of the Nicholas era. Nonetheless, his call for "firm precision" helped to develop the administrative instruments that made it possible to draft and implement the Great Reforms of the 1860s.[72]

The administrative instruments that helped to produce the Great Reforms were a by-product of Panin's and Bludov's efforts, not their central focus, for it had not been their main purpose to do more than shape their ministries into efficient organs for implementing the conservative policies of the Nicholas system. Perovskii and Kiselev had gone a step further in their efforts to establish special bureaucratic agencies that cut across traditional lines of authority to assemble accurate data about economic and social conditions in Russia and bring that information to bear upon problems that needed to be resolved. This had enabled Kiselev's Ministry of State Domains to draft reforms that changed the way in which the government dealt with its state peasants, while Perovskii's Ministry of Internal Affairs successfully undertook detailed studies of administration and economy in Russia's towns and cities.[73] Yet the context within which both of these ministers worked remained necessarily narrow. The Nicholas system was not designed to confront effectively the very new and urgent economic, social, or political problems that Europe's industrial revolution posed for Russia. Although they strived to make government more efficient and effective, Bludov's "alphabet of service" and Panin's "firm precision" limited the ability of even energetic statesmen to respond to the political and economic realities of Russia's renewed competition with the West in the post-Napoleonic era.

Between 1775 and 1850, Europe had entered the industrial age in which England, her rural masses separated from the land by an agricultural revolution that had transformed her once-bold yeomanry from independent farmers into wage laborers, had taken a decisive lead. By 1850, France, Belgium, Austria, and parts of the lands that would become united into Germany and Italy a quarter century later had all followed England's path, and Europe, her people spread across the land for centuries, now became a continent of cities. As increasingly fewer men and women labored on the land, the economic and industrial resources at the disposal of European governments soared. But, as factories grew and wealth increased, the problems that kings and statesmen faced became more complex. Forced to rely on others to produce their food and dependent upon the government to provide desperately needed public services, the burgeoning urban working classes of Europe created social and economic dilemmas that seventeenth- and eighteenth-century statesmen had never foreseen.

No statesman or monarch could hope to possess the knowledge required to solve such problems. Only public participation in the business of government could provide the breadth of expertise required to address the economic and social dilemmas brought into being by the industrial revolution. And public participation in government set in motion political changes that proved fully as revolutionary as those that the industrial revolution had produced in Europe's economic and social life. The People, once dim figures in the calculations of aristocratic statesmen, moved aggressively toward center stage as Europe moved through the French Revolution of 1789 to the Revolutions of 1830 and 1848. Kings and statesmen began to speak not in the name of their nations but in the name of their people. Elevated to the throne by the Parisian crowd during the Revolution of 1830, Louis Philippe ruled not as the king of France but as king of the French.

In contrast to the rapidly changing life of modern Europe, Russia's industrial age still stood beyond the horizon in 1850. Although grain had become one of her most vital export commodities by that time, Russia produced only one-thirtieth as much agricultural machinery as the United States, and England's mills had more than twenty-two times as many spindles in operation as did hers even though the manufacture of cotton thread was her most highly mechanized industry by 1850.[74] Even though the number of industrial workers had risen from 210,568 to 483,542 during the second quarter of the nineteenth century and the smoky ring of factories that eventually would encircle St. Petersburg had begun to take shape, scarcely one Russian in a hundred worked in a factory, mill, or artisan workshop at midcentury. The empire that spanned a full sixth of the earth's surface still had less than 650 miles of railroads.[75] As in the time of Peter the Great, the overwhelming bulk of Russia's exports continued to be the raw materials that she exchanged with European merchants for the manufactured goods she could not yet produce.

Although she continued to escape them at home, Russia had to face the urgent problems of the industrial revolution in her relations with the West during the reign of Nicholas I. As industrial development and revolutionary movements in the West posed growing threats to his nation's security, Nicholas strengthened Russia's alliance with Prussia and the Habsburg monarchy to form a bulwark against revolution in Central and Eastern Europe. That revolution never penetrated Russia's lands in 1848, and that her armies marched to help the Austrians crush the rebellion of Lajos Kossuth in Hungary in 1849, seemed to indicate the success of Nicholas's system. But Russia's armies moved much too slowly in 1849. No railroads supported their advance and none of the military technology that had begun to produce longer-range, more accurate, faster-firing weapons for the armies of the West had touched them. Soldiers who advanced into Hungary in 1849 carried the same weapons that their forefathers had used against the armies of Napoleon in 1812 but used them less skillfully. Thirty-five years of training on the parade ground had taken a toll on the fighting abilities of soldiers and commanders alike, and very few of the men who went into battle on the plains of Hungary that summer had ever heard a shot fired in anger. Since army regulations allowed them no more than three charges of powder and ball a year, they knew very much less about marksmanship than they did about the manual of arms.

The Russians thus reached midcentury with a government,

society, and army on which the great economic and political changes that had transformed the West had made no significant impact. Their national life seemed comfortably stable and their system of government appeared commendably sound. Problems posed by incompetent ministers, corrupt officials, and administrative malpractices all seemed not so difficult to remedy by means of modest adjustments and improvements in procedures and regulations, and fundamental changes seemed unnecessarily dangerous. "Why change that political system that made [Russia] a first-class power in the world?" one Russian asked. "To undermine its foundations, everything that constitutes its strength and essence, is ill-advised and dangerous."[76] Very few Russians in 1850 sensed the depths of their nation's backwardness, nor did they realize that the Nicholas system had become almost completely unable to respond to any major crisis. They therefore did not anticipate the crisis that the Crimean War was about to bring upon them.

In a government in which regulation and routine had come to hold pride of place over initiative and good sense, the emperor's preference for counselors who, as he once said, were "not so much wise as service-oriented,"[77] meant that men of conspicuous loyalty and inconspicuous talent advanced to fill the places vacated by the once energetic, more capable men whom death and infirmity removed from Russia's service. Such replacements were too ready to observe the most fundamental of all bureaucratic principles: that it was unwise to advance talented subordinates to positions from which they might one day challenge a less able superior, and this support of mediocrity produced the inevitable negative consequences. "Why is it that we have so very few able statesmen?" one worried official asked his diary in 1855. "Because," he concluded, "not skill in fulfilling their tasks but [only] obedience is expected of them."[78]

By then, Perovskii had withdrawn from the Ministry of Internal Affairs into the less visible Ministry of Court Lands with its smaller problems and less urgent demands. Count Egor Kankrin, the minister of finance who had placed Russia's finances on a stable footing for the first time in more than a century, and Count Aleksandr Benkendorf, the chief of the Third Section who had seen the moral guidance of society as the main purpose of Russia's gendarmerie, were both dead. Count Uvarov had been forced into retirement by a stroke that came just in time to spare him from being driven from office by the allies of Count Dmitrii Buturlin's notorious censorship commission. In every case, men of lesser talent who were less willing to advise their emperor honestly and more ready to preserve the status quo at any cost took their places. In a government served by such statesmen as Kankrin, Kiselev, Benkendorf, Perovskii, and Uvarov, Panin's principles of "firm precision" and Bludov's "alphabet of service" held the promise of producing more effective administration in Russia. In the hands of such successors as Minister of Public Instruction Prince Platon Shirinskii-Shikhmatov, who once proudly stated, "I have neither a mind or a will of my own; I am the blind tool of the Sovereign's will,"[79] they only strengthened timidity and encouraged obscurantism. The censor Aleksandr Nikitenko concluded that the intellectual horizons of Russia's statesmen had shrunk "to the narrowest possible dimensions." Now, he wrote in 1855, "one only swims with the current."[80]

Timid ministers working within the increasingly rigid framework of the Nicholas system could not provide solutions to the multitude of problems that had arisen in Russia. The financial crisis that returned so readily once Kankrin's firm hands were removed from the strings of the public purse, Russians' growing difficulties in finding justice in their nation's courts, the deepening crisis posed by the empire's economic backwardness and undeveloped industry, and the continuing failure of the bureaucracy to provide effective government had to be dealt with. Serfdom, an anachronistic economic system that continued to hold nearly 50 million Russians in bondage to the government or to noble lords, lay at the root of these difficulties and posed dilemmas that none of Russia's rulers or statesmen had been able to solve. How could serfdom be abolished without destroying the economic life of the nobility, the traditional social base of autocratic power? If emancipated, how could almost 50 million newly freed serfs and state peasants be absorbed into the empire's outdated framework of local government, served by its overburdened courts, and integrated into its antiquated tax structure? How could abolition be accomplished without provoking massive peasant disorders all across Russia as the emancipated peasants shed their bonds and reveled in their first taste of freedom? "Educated serfowners," Perovskii had warned Nicholas, "fear the consequences of freedom [for their serfs], knowing the unbridled nature of the masses."[81]

The government of which Russia's senior statesmen were a part could not provide them with a context in which to find the answers to these questions, for theirs was a world where the artificially elegant functioning of the machinery of government isolated them from the reality of Russia. Officials always had found it difficult to report to their superiors information other than what they wanted to hear, but, beginning in 1851, civil servants had to live in greater fear of arousing their superiors' displeasure than ever before. "There has been a new decree about civil servants," Nikitenko wrote ominously in his diary at the end of that year. "A superior now has the right to remove subordinates from office for unreliability or 'for faults which cannot be proven.' "[82]

With their careers at the mercy of their superiors' whims, civil servants blatantly reported what they thought senior statesmen wanted to hear. "In all good conscience, I ought not to hold my tongue," one young man confided to his diary, "but they [that is, his superiors] can wipe me from the face of the earth, and thus, from necessity, one remains silent."[83] The result, Valuev wrote from his post as governor of Courland province toward the end of 1855, was "to perpetuate the official lie."[84] From the heights of a minister's office in St. Petersburg or from the vantage point of the imperial court, the chorus of accolades bestowed by fearful bureaucrats made it seem that, as one writer put it, "in Russia there exists everything necessary for national welfare."[85] Too many of Russia's statesmen continued to think of their country as an "awe-inspiring colossus" that towered over other nations.[86] Very few even cared to understand, as Valuev did, how mistaken that opinion had become.

Only a handful of Russian officials had begun to sense how important it was to break through the protective bureaucratic covering that lay so heavily upon Russian life in order to discover what really was happening underneath. Partly because of Kiselev's and Perovskii's efforts to recruit better-educated, more-independent officials and partly because of a fortunate combination of circumstances, a group of unusually able young men had come together in the Ministries of State Domains and Internal Affairs during the 1840s.[87] Led by Andrei Zablotskii-Desiatovskii in the Ministry of State Domains and Nikolai Miliutin in the Ministry of Internal Affairs, these young men viewed their role as government officials differently than did most bureaucrats. "Their ideal was the introduction of justice into all spheres of life," Zablotskii explained some years later. "In hard work they saw not only the means without which it is impossible to improve one's position in society legitimately, but also a necessary requirement for the full enjoyment of life. In the fulfillment of their duty," he concluded, "they saw a basic law of morality."[88]

Such men drew others of similar views to their departments in sufficient numbers that, when Nikolai Vtorov entered the Ministry of Internal Affairs in 1844, he found himself among "a friendly, like-minded circle of young men from the universities and lycées who dealt with administrative issues not from a paper-shuffling, purely formalistic or casuistic perspective, but who sought to see the heart of the matter at hand [and] tried, when possible, to . . . institute a clear-cut system under which . . . [they could reach] more solid and broadly based decisions."[89] Accurate and detailed information about conditions in Russia that could not be found in any ministry in St. Petersburg was needed to accomplish that purpose. Certain that they first must study how "[administrative] practice does not conform to the law" if they hoped to understand Russia's problems, these young officials began to use the Department of Economy in the Ministry of State Domains and the Economic Department in the Ministry of Internal Affairs as bases from which to launch broad statistical studies of life in Russia. Only in that way could they begin to "seek the means for a better organization of civic and economic affairs" in the empire.[90]

What made these enlightened young officials doubly unusual was their willingness to share information at a time when senior bureaucrats jealously guarded their agencies against all incursions from other departments and ministries. Young Aleksandr Shumakher explained his comrades' willingness "to exchange opinions and to consult with each other on more serious questions" as an effort to find solutions to difficult policy questions by establishing "clear principles based on reason and knowledge" to guide their work.[91] Even more important, they came to understand, as Konstantin Veselovskii explained in 1847, that "numbers [that is, raw data] alone cannot provide a full understanding of any given issue" and that "a qualitative evaluation of any problem also is necessary."[92] Well established as section chiefs and department heads by midcentury, these men had begun to understand that renovating Russia's stagnant social and economic system required more than collecting facts and figures, no matter how valuable those might be in elucidating the problems of their nation's life and government. That realization forced them to confront the most complex dilemma that modern Russian statesmen had yet to face. They had to find the means to change policy, not merely perfect the instruments to perpetuate the established order.

To change policy in a world that was beginning to be dominated by modern technology required information drawn from more diverse sources and participation of men of broader experience and more extensive knowledge than any single statesman or group of dedicated officials could possess. It was perhaps the most critical failing of the Nicholas system that it had not produced any of those politically or socially responsible groups to which European rulers and statesmen had begun to turn for advice and counsel in the post-Napoleonic era. "Our qualities as responsible citizens," Nikitenko wrote in his diary at the height of the Crimean War, "have not yet been formed because we do not yet have the essential elements . . . namely public-spiritedness, a sense of legality, and honor."[93] Aside from statesmen isolated from Russia's most pressing problems by mountains of bureaucratic paperwork and a handful of enlightened officials whose modest positions in St. Petersburg's official world did not allow them to influence the policy-making process directly, there was no one to whom a mid-nineteenth-century Russian emperor could turn for advice about planning reforms or upon whom he could rely to carry out any broad program of renovation.

Nor were there the means for communicating with any such group had it existed. Russia had neither a national assembly nor any national consultative body, for both were inconsistent with the premises upon which Nicholas I and his predecessors had built their autocracy. At the same time, the rigid censorship that the Nicholas system imposed on Russia's press excluded public debate and even public commentary about the empire's most urgent problems. A means to open dialogue between government and society while controlling it and keeping it within bounds acceptable to Russia's autocrat had to be found. Nicholas and his counselors had not been able to do so. Fearful that the new revolutionary wave that burst upon Europe in 1848 might spread to Russia, they had sought refuge in reaction. "Among our high officials and political figures," Valuev wrote not long after he had taken up his duties as governor of Courland province, "fear makes some silent . . . while others think only of finding a way to crush everything."[94]

This meant exercising the utmost caution at every turn. Censors now searched for the "inner meaning" in what authors wrote,[95] and Russia's new minister of public instruction proclaimed that "theology is the single strong foundation on which all useful education is based."[96] Unable to make common cause with educated society, to trust it, or even to communicate with it, the Russian government turned to crush it. Seventy-two young men, twenty-one of whom (including Dostoevskii) had been condemned to death and pardoned at the last moment, found themselves condemned to Siberian exile for taking part in naive discussions about utopian socialism at the lodgings of Mikhail Butashevich-Petrashevskii. The works of Tacitus and Plato and the published letters of Catherine II to Voltaire were suppressed. Censors even forbade the performance of Shakespeare's *Richard III* because it dealt with themes that were "dangerous in a moral sense."[97]

"A Holy War against scholarship and knowledge," Nikitenko wrote in despair, had begun.[98] Between 1848 and 1855, such mindless repression nearly destroyed some of Russia's greatest minds in physical, moral, and intellectual terms. Several prominent university professors and a number of leading writers sought refuge in the anonymity of government service;[99] others who had been (and would again become) some of Russia's most creative and brilliant writers set their pens aside and devoted their evenings to reading and writing erotic verse or to alcohol, cards, and whores.[100] As he drew parallels between the behavior of thinking Russians after 1848 and the way in which men and women had tried to forget the terrors of the plague by distracting each other with obscene anecdotes in Boccaccio's *Decameron*, the novelist Ivan Turgenev asked; "Wasn't the Nicholas oppression its own type of plague for educated society?"[101]

Journals that once had published serious literature and literary criticism now turned to bibliography and the narrowest forms of biography. "What house did a certain famous writer visit? What sort of tobacco did he smoke? What sort of boots did he wear? These are the favorite subjects of research, discus-

sion, and thought," the radical critic Nikolai Dobroliubov complained.[102] "Apathy in Petersburg has reached an extremely high
level of development," his friend and fellow critic Nikolai Chernyshevskii added as he spoke of the "pure pedantry" of literature in Russia in 1853.[103] Russians began to smell "the quiet of
a graveyard, rotting and stinking, both physically and morally"
in those days.[104] Some may have wondered whether the stench
of decay was rising from the European body with which Peter
the Great had endowed Russia and which now seemed on the
verge of decomposing. "Our government knows very well your
weak points and they are precisely the ones by which you are
tied to Europe," Count Reiset, a former First Secretary of the
French Embassy in St. Petersburg told a Russian acquaintance
at one point. "Let those ties be weakened," Reiset added, "and,
of your own accord, you will flow back towards the East and
you will become once again an Asiatic Power."[105] If Russia was
to remain a part of Europe and avoid being driven back into
Asia, some means of renovation must be found and autocracy
must once again assume a dynamic role in national life. Nothing
made that more certain than Russia's unexpected defeat in the
Crimean War.

# II

## THE IMPACT
## OF DEFEAT

*E*ver since the newly modernized armies of Peter the
Great had defeated the forces of Sweden at Poltava in
1709, Russia's military power had been her single, unchallenged
claim to status in Europe's community of great powers. At inter-
vals just frequent enough to be unsettling, Russia had reminded
Europe of that fact. Cossack cavalrymen had stormed into the
outskirts of Berlin at the end of the Seven Years' War and Russian
forces had paraded along the Champs d'Elysées in 1814. European politicians had feared the specter of Russia's influence all
across Eurasia and had spoken in worried tones of her "enormous power" after Napoleon's defeat.[1] There was no one alive
in Europe in 1850 who could remember a war in which Russian
arms had not triumphed. "No one has been more the master
of Europe except perhaps Napoleon," one diplomatic observer
wrote after Russia's armies had driven Louis Kossuth's rebels
from Hungary and dictated the fate of Germany at the Olmütz
Convention in 1850. Prince Albert, consort of Queen Victoria,
strongly seconded that view. "The Emperor Nicholas," he stated
flatly and simply the year before the Crimean War broke out,
"is master of Europe."[2] Backed by more than a million men
under arms, Russia's military power at that point seemed unassailable.

Admiral Prince Aleksandr Menshikov, personal ambassador
of Nicholas I and longtime chief of the Russian Admiralty, therefore approached the Ottoman Empire at the beginning of 1853
bearing a small olive branch in one hand and a very large sword
in the other. Well over sixty and longing for retirement, Men-

shikov was not the man to conduct sensitive negotiations in the best of times, but, when he arrived in Constantinople that February, he carried instructions that limited his freedom of action so severely that he had little room to negotiate at all. Confident of his power, Russia's emperor was not willing to consider compromise and moderation in those days, and the eight months that followed Menshikov's failed mission moved Russia and the Ottoman Empire inexorably toward the brink of conflict.

War began that October. Before the end of March 1854, France and Britain joined the Turks against the Russians and the armies of Nicholas I became locked in a test of strength they could not win. During the next two years, antiquated weapons, an undeveloped industrial base (there were only three weapons factories in all of Russia), and a primitive supply system (Russia had less than a thousand miles of railroads, and none in locations that could transport supplies and munitions to frontier war zones) highlighted the weakness of the Russians. At Inkerman in late 1854, superior rifled muskets enabled Allied infantrymen to cut down advancing Russians before they were close enough to use their antiquated smooth-bore weapons effectively. In the following year, the great Russian naval bastion at Sevastopol became a grave for defenders whom the Allies outgunned, outsupplied, and outmaneuvered at every turn. Allied gunners could fire their new rifled cannon more rapidly and hit targets at ranges that left the Russians shaking their heads in amazement. Newly invented telescopic sights mounted on modern percussion rifles allowed British and French sharpshooters to kill Russian officers at distances well beyond those at which riflemen in the Sevastopol redoubts could return their fire. Valor alone could not turn the tide as it had against the armies of Napoleon. As Russian soldiers went without boots and food and fought with empty guns because the General Staff could not supply them properly, the Crimean War became a prologue to all the tragedies of the First World War played out on a smaller scale. Clearly the Russian colossus could not stand against the technology of the newly industrialized West. In such a confrontation, defeat became inevitable.

Defeat in the Crimean War immediately challenged Russia's single claim to membership in the community of great powers. As the quality of armaments technology began to counterbalance the number of armed forces in determining a nation's power,

Russians began to debate how to prevent any further erosion of their nation's international standing. No one doubted that Russia must move decisively into the industrial age, for a nation without heavy industry and railroads could not hope to be counted among the great powers of the West. At the same time, the young Alexander II and his advisers knew that Russia no longer could afford to support an army of more than a million men in peacetime. European nations had begun to experiment with small standing armies that could be supplemented by a large system of ready reserves in time of war. Yet, as General Dmitrii Miliutin stated flatly in a memorandum in March 1856, no nation that drew its soldiers from a servile population dared to return them to bondage after training them in the use of arms.[3]

Dangerously weakened finances, a local administration that had failed to connect her people with their government, a premodern system of law in which semiliterate judges still presided over catastrophically backlogged law courts, the problems of developing modern industrial and transportation networks in a society that had not yet entered the industrial age, and an army in which a term of military service was akin to a sentence of penal servitude all had to be considered in plotting Russia's course after the Crimean War. Across all of these, serfdom continued to cast its retrograde shadow, for modern armies and modern industry required a free citizenry and a mobile labor force.

Serfdom's was not the only dark shadow that lay upon the Russian political and social landscape when the Crimean War ended in 1856. Although the army could not be modernized and industry could not be developed so long as serfdom remained, emancipation posed other problems whose resolution seemed fully as complex as serfdom itself. Emancipation would free Russia's nobility of its responsibilities for collecting taxes, assembling recruits, and administering justice to more than 20 million peasants. At one liberating stroke of the tsar's pen, these responsibilities would shift to the shoulders of the government, yet there were no current institutions that could integrate so many new citizens into the fabric of Russia's national life. Nor could the nearly bankrupt imperial treasury finance an emancipation.

Not only did the Crimean defeat challenge Russia's claim to

great power status but it called into question the principles that had directed her national life and government since the time of Peter the Great. To develop Russia's traditional institutions along the lines followed by Nicholas I and his predecessors—to bring them to the level of perfection implied in Uvarov's slogan "Orthodoxy, Autocracy, and Nationality" and proclaimed as truth by defenders of Official Nationality—meant, in fact, to weaken Russia, not strengthen her ability to confront the disconcerting challenges of the Crimean defeat. "Orthodoxy, Autocracy, and Nationality" articulated a political outlook that no longer had a place in Europe's experience, just as it described a social order that could not hope to survive among modern nations that had entered the industrial age. Even though Peter the Great had used them to win membership in the European great power community for Russia, such principles now could only carry Russia further away from the West.

Nineteenth-century Russian sovereigns had transformed the model of the well-ordered police state that Peter the Great and Catherine II had used to accelerate Russia's modernization into an instrument to resist change. In economic and military terms, Peter and Catherine had brought their country closer to the European standard by the end of the eighteenth century than she had ever been, but their failure to develop the social structure that had accompanied the emergence of a well-ordered police state in the West had deprived Russia of the economic and social dynamism that had set the industrial revolution in motion.[4] Without the social and political dimensions of the European experience, the continued defense of eighteenth-century principles by Russia's nineteenth-century monarchs had widened the gap between Russia and the West dramatically. The eighteenth-century institutional components of Russia's political and governmental experience—the autocracy and bureaucracy—remained strong enough to prevent nineteenth-century economic and political structures from developing.

Her eighteenth-century experience thus left Russia ill prepared to follow the West into the post-Napoleonic world. At the same time, the historical imperatives of international politics meant that she could not break away from competition with the West without forfeiting her status as a great power. Alexander II and his advisers therefore had to find a way to compete with Europe on a more viable footing while preserving autocracy and its

traditional instruments. By the middle of the nineteenth century
such instruments included, first of all, the bureaucracy, which,
in sharp contrast to the eighteenth century, offered the autocracy
a viable alternative to aristocracy as a social base of support.
Far more than the nobles, whose chief concerns had become
their declining economic and political position, Russia's bureaucrats now shared a commitment to autocracy's preservation. This
was true even of those enlightened bureaucrats and their allies
among the Russian intelligentsia who were soon to play a leading
role in drafting the Great Reforms. "I believe completely in the
necessity of absolutism in present-day Russia," Konstantin Kavelin had written to his friend Granovskii in 1848, "but it needs
to be progressive and enlightened."[5]

Although dedicated to preserving autocracy, the tsarist bureaucracy was too isolated from Russia and the West at midcentury
to resolve the dilemmas of modernization that the Crimean
defeat thrust upon them. In the West, modernization had created
social and economic problems, whose resolution had required
the concentration of individual initiative and specialized knowledge on such a vast scale that some form of dialogue between
government and society had become essential. In England, this
had taken an evolutionary traditional path in which merchants
and industrialists, who had played an active role in national
affairs since the days of Queen Elizabeth's merchant adventurers,
broadened their role in making policy after the Reform Bill of
1832 gave them increased representation in Parliament. In France
and parts of Central Europe, the dialogue between government
and governed had been established at least partly through revolution in 1830 and 1848, when the middle classes demanded a
voice in making those policy decisions that would determine
their destiny.

By contrast, Russia had no tradition of consultation between
government and society, and her instruments of state authority
remained far too strong for any revolution to overcome. Clearly,
the "public" must be brought into contact with their "government" if the nation were to follow the course of the West after
the Crimean defeat, but, in the minds of her policymakers, that
did not mean "public" participation in making policy. To open
a dialogue between government and *obshchestvo*—men and
women destined to become active in Russia's civic life—that

would not threaten the traditional pre-eminence of autocracy in making and changing policy, Alexander II, his advisers, and a number of senior officials tried to consult with educated opinion on a limited and informal basis. They regarded such consultations as a source of badly needed information about local economic and social conditions in Russia and as a means for clarifying the issues their government must resolve. None envisioned them as an invitation to public participation in policy-making.

To establish contact between government and *obshchestvo* required overcoming deep suspicions generated during the three decades since Nicholas I's stern suppression of the Decembrist revolt had shattered the self-confidence of thinking Russians and drawn a firm line between them and their government. Government and *obshchestvo* therefore began to live in isolation from each other as talented, thoughtful men disdained service to a regime they despised. "How could I be lured into government service under the political conditions that prevailed at that time?" young Boris Chicherin asked. "To become the instrument of a government that mercilessly suppressed every thought and any sort of enlightenment and which, as a consequence, I detested from the bottom of my soul, to inch my way up the civil service ladder, cringing every step of the way, trying to please my superiors, never expressing my own beliefs, and often performing duties that seemed to me especially evil," he continued angrily in memoirs he wrote many years later, "was the prospect that lay before me if I entered the civil service. I turned away from it," he confessed, "in indignation."[6]

To overcome such animosity was a difficult task, especially in a government in which senior statesmen attributed such views as Chicherin's to "the ruined and depraved segments of the aristocracy [or] foolhardy youth."[7] Partly because they worked too much in isolation from the people they governed and partly because they feared the revolutions they had seen in the West, not even the enlightened bureaucrats, who supported reform more strongly than Russia's senior statesmen at the beginning of Alexander II's reign, felt at ease with educated opinion. Nor did educated opinion feel comfortable with them. Some Russians disdained even the most progressive government officials as "unceremonious despots" and believed that true freedom had "nothing in common" with what one angry memoirist called the "stifling sphere of officialistic democracy" that surrounded them.[8]

If society disdained the government, the reverse was also the case. Such would-be reformers as Nikolai Miliutin thought that the nobility (and hence a very large segment of educated society in Russia) had become so unwilling to put national concerns ahead of narrow class interests that it would be useless to consult them about questions of policy or reform. "The nobility," he stated flatly in 1858, "is self-interested, unprepared, [and] under-developed."[9] Miliutin and men who thought as he did therefore turned to a modified form of bureaucratic co-optation to initiate a broader dialogue between educated opinion and government as they sought to clarify Russia's course in 1856 and 1857. They did so as a natural extension of earlier, more narrow discussions about reform and change that had occurred within their government agencies during the 1840s and early 1850s.[10] This modest beginning marked the first timid attempts to extend *glasnost'* beyond the narrow confines of St. Petersburg's chanceries since the days of Catherine the Great.

Officials groping to open a dialogue between government and *obshchestvo* sought to co-opt into their ranks men whom they knew personally and whose judgment they trusted. Konstantin Kavelin, who had retreated into the anonymity of the bureaucracy from his professorship at Moscow University during the repression that followed the revolutions of 1848, was perhaps the first to win the trust of Petersburg's enlightened bureaucrats during the last years of the Nicholaevan era, and the eminent Slavophile Iurii Samarin, who had served with Kavelin in Miliutin's Economic Department in the Ministry of Internal Affairs, was another. Literary circles that met at the lodgings of such distinguished journal editors as Ivan Panaev and Andrei Kraevskii, the well-known literary critic Nikolai Nadezhdin, and the eminent jurist Konstantin Nevolin provided additional points of contact between Russia's world of ideas and her world of government during the last decade of Nicholas's reign although these remained limited by the vigilant surveillance of the Third Section and the tightening grip of censorship.[11] Before any genuine interchange of views could begin, broader, more systematic contact had to be established.

Although a few circles and a handful of scattered individuals had made possible some dialogue between Russia's government and governed, the Imperial Russian Geographical Society became the broadest point of contact between them during the decade that separated the revolutions of 1848 from the beginnings of work on the Great Reform legislation in Russia. At a time when educated Russians dared not assemble to discuss political or social questions, this semiofficial body headed by Alexander II's younger brother, Grand Duke Konstantin Nikolaevich, provided men who supported autocracy but, like Kavelin, believed that it "ought to be progressive and enlightened,"[12] with an opportunity to follow a middle path between unquestioning acceptance of public policy and complete rejection of it. "Given the absence of any civic life among us at that time, the existence of such a center [as the Geographical Society] in which people interested in knowledge could gather for general discussions had a special value in the eyes of society," one young official recalled.[13] Many who favored progress shared that view.

In the Geographical Society, men who had become convinced that their nation's most urgent problems no longer could be stated in terms of bureaus that functioned ineffectively or officials who fulfilled their duties imperfectly began the demographic, economic, and statistical studies that became a vital element in laying the groundwork for the Great Reforms.[14] On the basis of detailed firsthand observation, Ivan Aksakov produced a complex study of commercial fairs in the Ukraine that assembled valuable information about domestic trade and manufacture never before available to the Russian government.[15] At the same time, as editors of the Society's *Etnograficheskii sbornik* (*Ethnographical Miscellany*), Kavelin and Nikolai Nadezhdin helped enlightened bureaucrats working in Miliutin's Economic Department and Zablotskii's Department of Rural Economy to broaden their studies of peasant life and economy. Most of all, their association in the Geographical Society during the difficult Crimean War years helped to cement common bonds among the men who eventually would draft the Great Reforms. With a bare handful of exceptions, every government official who helped to prepare the Great Reform legislation took an active part in the Geographical Society between 1850 and 1857.

Within the government offices in which they served, such officials pursued further the work they had set in motion in the Geographical Society. In the Ministries of State Domains and

Internal Affairs, they formed committees of "experts," many of whom they had come to know in the society, to study a widening range of economic and social questions. Organizing these committees across long-established and jealously guarded ministerial lines, they worked with more than mere administrative adjustments in mind.[16] Their deepening commitment to renovating Russia and their broadening sense of how that might be accomplished led them to speak seriously of *zakonnost'* and *glasnost'* just as the repression of the early 1850s reached its height.

In 1850, the Academic Committee in Zablotskii's Department of Rural Economy in the Ministry of State Domains had invited private citizens to submit "economic-statistical descriptions" of the farming techniques used in European Russia and had justified its decision to seek the opinions of men outside the bureaucracy by explaining that "only greater *glasnost'* can provide a solid basis for future measures for the improvement of this sector of national industry."[17] Although the committee drew back from following it up effectively, this was nonetheless a surprising early effort to draw public opinion into government work at precisely the moment when the political atmosphere in Russia seemed certain to preclude any such attempt. Perhaps even more surprising, a report that Zablotskii wrote the very next year spoke of the need for "gradually introducing new customs and *zakonnost'* in place of absolute confusion and *proizvol*"[18] and emphasized the advantages of private landownership to peasant life in Russia. Soon after the Crimean War, he developed that view even further. "The cooperation of private individuals, freely given, can be useful and valuable for the government," Zablotskii told Grand Duke Konstantin Nikolaevich. Russia's nobles therefore must be made to understand that "the abolition of serfdom is inevitable by ridding this idea of the phantoms and false notions formed by confused imaginations."[19]

Although the enlightened bureaucrats and their allies had begun to assemble some of the data needed to renovate Russia, they had not yet found the means to connect their committees of "experts" with the highest levels of their government's administrative structure in order to change policy. Their studies of economic and social problems had enabled them to see the dimensions of the renovation that would be required for Russia's modernization, but they had virtually no experience in translating their ideas on reform and change into law. During the Crimean War, some of them gained experience with the empire's complex legislative process in the very unlikely arena of the Imperial Russian Naval Ministry, where Grand Duke Konstantin Nikolaevich, whose thirtieth birthday still was more than a year and a half away when the war ended, was beginning to experiment with a type of *glasnost'* that allowed reformers to consult *obshchestvo* while allowing the government to retain full authority over making policy.

Konstantin Nikolaevich's appointment as honorary president of the Russian Geographical Society in 1845 had marked the beginning of an involvement with Russian internal affairs that eventually would make him a leading advocate of the Great Reforms and a prominent patron of the reforming bureaucrats who would draft them. His semiofficial protection helped to shield would-be reformers from the worst perils of Russia's capricious political climate during the last years of Nicholas's reign, and his efforts to draw some of them into reform work in Russia's Naval Ministry gave them much-needed schooling in legislative tactics. Five of the officials he recruited into his Naval Ministry during the Crimean War (Prince Dmitrii Obolenskii, Dmitrii Nabokov, Mikhail Reitern, Count Dmitrii Tolstoi, and Aleksandr Golovnin) would receive ministerial appointments during and after the Great Reform era. Together with a number of other talented young officials (all of them were under the age of thirty-five in 1850), they became known as the *konstantinovtsy*, the protégés of Konstantin Nikolaevich.[20]

Unorthodox training under the watchful eyes of the independent-minded sea captains who had been his adolescent mentors and comrades, his associations with the progressive officials he met in the Geographical Society, and his unique position as a grand duke in a ministerial office made Konstantin Nikolaevich more willing than other senior officials to delegate responsibility. Impatient to see results, he believed that energetic, honest, intelligent men could make a difference in government, and, unlike his father, he demanded "not fulsome praise, but the truth" from the men who served under him.[21] Intolerant of bureaucratic routine, he approached government and administration in a straightforward fashion notable for its belief that talent and virtue would triumph if given the opportunity. "If one separates the essential from the covering of paper—that which *is* from that which only *seems* to be—and sifts out the truth from the half-truths and falsehoods," he wrote in 1855, "then everywhere the brilliance will rise to the top and the rot will sink to the bottom."[22]

What distinguished Konstantin Nikolaevich's approach to Russia's legislative process from that of other ministers was his willingness to consult public opinion at a time when his colleagues feared it. The grand duke, one of his closest associates once explained, believed that, "in drafting legislation, it was essential to create, so to speak, artificial [iskusstvennaia] glasnost', to encourage debates and discussions and seek out the views of the entire group for which a law was being drafted rather than be satisfied with the opinions of a narrow circle."[23] As the Crimean War continued, Konstantin Nikolaevich shaped Morskoi sbornik (Naval Miscellany), the official journal of the Naval Ministry, into a rare and hitherto unseen instrument for broadening discussion between "government" and "society" about renovation and reform in Russia.

As the only Russian periodical permitted to publish details about the fighting in the Crimea, Morskoi sbornik assembled a more brilliant list of contributors than any other journal. Works by Ostrovskii, Goncharov, Pisemskii, and nearly a dozen other writers and playwrights appeared regularly in its pages as did the latest scientific work of Nikolai Pirogov, Heinrich Lenz, Karl Ernst von Baer, and Friedrich Georg Wilhelm von Struve from the famed Pulkovo Observatory. As the konstantinovtsy and their friends debated how to improve public education, abolish corporal punishment, and modernize Russia's courts and judicial system, Morskoi sbornik opened a discussion of reform that heralded the beginning of the Great Reform era. In late 1859, Pavel Glebov even questioned the foundations of the autocrat's long-standing insistence that jurists could never be interpreters of the law,[24] and the number of annual contributors to the unofficial section of the journal increased tenfold in the five years after the Crimean War began. At the end of the war, its list of subscribers stood at 5,565, nearly twice the 3,100 that the liberal Sovremennik (The Contemporary) had boasted in its heyday a decade before.[25] Morskoi sbornik became, in the words of the radical publicist Nikolai Chernyshevskii, "one of the most remarkable phenomena in our literature—perhaps the most remarkable in many ways."[26] As the censorship terror of Nicholas I's last years transformed Russia's periodical press into a miasma of bibliogra-

phy and obscure biographical notes, there were few thinking
men and women in Russia who did not share Chernyshevskii's
opinion.

After its timid beginnings among the enlightened bureaucrats
and the *konstantinovtsy*, the debate on *glasnost'* and *zakonnost'* in
Russia took on more serious and urgent dimensions as the Crimean War came to an end. The way was opened for that change
a year before the war ended when, at midday on February 18,
1855, Nicholas I breathed his last, and his son, the thirty-six-year-
old Grand Duke Aleksandr Nikolaevich, ascended Russia's
throne as Alexander II. The intense feelings stirred among the
Russians by that one day's events showed the imprint that
Nicholas and his system had left upon their lives. "It seems to
me that . . . the world has come tumbling down," a maid-of-
honor at Court confided to her diary. "I went to dine with my
parents," she added, "and Papa said 'it is as if we had been
told that a god had died.' "[27] At the other end of the spectrum,
the revolutionary emigré nobleman Aleksandr Herzen summoned his friends in far-away London, uncorked his best cham-
pagne, and showered silver coins "for beer and candy" upon
street urchins who, at his urging, ran through the streets shout-
ing, "Hurrah! Hurrah! Impernikel is dead! Impernikel is dead!"[28]

As Russians began to face the hard facts of their nation's
backwardness and searched for ways to overcome it, memories
of Nicholas's all-too-recent reign constricted their view of the
possible and the permissible. "I have not been able to collect
my thoughts," Kavelin wrote from St. Petersburg to his friend
Granovskii in Moscow. "If the present were not so strange and
clouded, the future not so dark and enigmatic, one could go
wild with joy and become intoxicated with happiness."[29]
Chicherin, whose writings on the peasant commune had driven
the final wedge between the Slavophiles and Westerners only
a few years earlier, shared Kavelin's happiness and uncertainty.
"No one could say what the future held," he remembered many
years later. "One felt a sudden sense of relief, as if a great
weight had been lifted from one's shoulders. One could breathe
more freely," he concluded. "All at once, one's courage returned
and so did brighter hopes for better times."[30]

"A sudden sense of relief" located in a "strange and clouded
present" combined with "brighter hopes" for a "dark and enigmatic" future combined to confuse the Russians as the Crimean

War approached its end. While Valuev lamented statesmen's efforts to "perpetuate the official lie" by concealing that Russia was "rotting away underneath,"[31] Chicherin bluntly condemned the "omnipresence of the official lie," which, he believed, had permeated civic life and government in Russia. "One can say without exaggeration," he wrote in 1856, "that every official statement is nothing but a lie. All reports and dispatches from our leading statesmen are lies. All reports and dispatches of governors and other regional authorities are, in fact, lies. All statistical data are lies [and] . . . even most patriotic statements are nothing but pure lies."[32]

Kavelin, who hated the memory of Nicholas's reign no less than Chicherin, counseled caution in word and deed and begged Chicherin to adopt "a gentler, more respectful tone toward the government."[33] Fearful that "everything thoughtful, everything enlightened, everything energetic, every desire to do good" had been destroyed by Nicholas's regime, Kavelin thought his fellow Russians needed to take at least a decade "without any reforms or transformation" just to recover their balance and regain a sense of direction before they embarked upon any new course.[34] As intellectual mentor of the enlightened bureaucrats, Kavelin struggled to restrain his more hotheaded countrymen. Moderation on the side of the intelligentsia, he thought, could help to win sympathy for reform in the new government.

As Russia's intellectuals began to consider their nation's course, they no longer thought in the theoretical, abstract terms to which the tightening bonds of the Nicholas system had confined them in the 1840s. The obvious failure of that system now focused their attention on the hard and urgent realities their nation must face in the 1860s, but, as they descended from the world of abstract ideas into the realm of concrete economic and political problems, they did not immediately find a solid footing in the shifting quicksands of Russian politics. The breakdown of the Nicholas system had left the limits beyond which they could not trespass more blurred than at any time in their history. There was, in N. Ia. Eidelman's apt phrase, "an indefinite, continually shifting line between 'Its all right' and 'Its not allowed,' between *glasnost'* and secrecy, between . . . fear of expanding the permissible and thinking about how to take advantage of that expansion."[35] Hopes for constitutional government, an aspiration to *zakonnost'*, and a sense of the inevitability of change stood in conflict with *proizvol*, the tyranny of bureaucratic procedure, and a longing to shore up the old order as *obshchestvo* and bureaucracy set new courses in the treacherous currents that carried Russia into the post-Crimean War world.

An episode that took place in the fall of 1858 perhaps best symbolizes the improbable sense of the possible that gripped the Russians in those days. Early one morning, while Alexander II was strolling in the park at the imperial summer palace at Tsarskoe Selo, the future revolutionary Nikolai Serno-Solov'evich, who was then serving as secretary to the chief clerk of the recently created Main Committee on Peasant Affairs, slipped past the guards and thrust into his amazed emperor's hands a lengthy memorandum that criticized the slowness with which the government was proceeding in its efforts to deal with serfdom. A few days later, Serno-Solov'evich received a summons to the office of Prince Aleksei Orlov, chief of the Imperial Gendarmes, who, after pointing out that the Emperor Nicholas "would have banished you to a place so remote that they would never even have found your bones," added: "Our present Sovereign Aleksandr Nikolaevich is so kind that he has ordered me to kiss you. Here," Orlov concluded as he moved toward the astonished young man who had come to the meeting with every expectation that he was about to be punished. "Embrace me."[36]

That the emperor should order one of the old regime's strongest defenders to embrace one of its new critics symbolized both the confusion and the new sense of liberation that were emerging in Russia. By no means confined to the serf question, the liberation movement that spread across Russia at the end of the Crimean War encompassed the emancipation of women and the liberation of society from an intricate series of interlocking bonds that had held it so closely during the Nicholas era. It was "a time of widespread euphoria and enthusiasm," the radical young critic Nikolai Dobroliubov remembered as he looked back upon the war's end. "Every breast swelled, and everyone's speech flowed sonorously and smoothly like a river that had been freed of ice," he wrote. "What a glorious time it was!"[37] Almost no dream seemed too absurd to be tested and no untried model too daring to be rejected out of hand. "Russian society," Nikitenko concluded, "is like a large lake in the depths of which underground fires are making bubbles that continually rise to the surface, break, and bubble up again."[38]

So divided during the last days of Nicholas's reign, when conflicting visions of their nation's past, present, and future had split them into bitter camps, Russia's intelligentsia now joined in a common quest for liberation. As they shed the fetters of the Nicholas system and turned to the question of national renovation, many thought that England and France, now the two greatest industrial powers in Europe, should become the models for Russia. That was so not only because those two nations had triumphed in the Crimean conflict but also, as one prominent Russian churchman insisted, because they were the receptacles of "the ideals of contemporary civilization."[39] Others, like the Slavophile publicist Iurii Samarin, called on his countrymen to look within themselves for the wherewithal to shape change. "We must turn inward on ourselves, study the fundamental reasons for our weakness, understand the true nature of our internal needs, and dedicate all our attention and all our resources to finding a solution," Samarin wrote. The road ahead would demand "no less bravery, persistence, and self-sacrifice" than the war just ended.[40]

Whether they reached beyond the ruins of the Nicholas system to search for something deeper within themselves, or whether they looked abroad for new principles that could replace their own discredited ones, Russians were at one in seeking new guidance and new directions. "There is not a single thought from yesterday," Nikitenko wrote, "that does not seem old today."[41] Looked at by an emperor whose traditional mission was to preserve autocracy, the danger in this situation was that Russia's once-fragmented intelligentsia might form a united front and demand political concessions that would transform his government into a more modern political system.

To prevent society from doing so, Alexander II attempted to integrate the artificial *glasnost'* that the academician Georg-Friedrich Parrot had urged upon his father in the late 1820s[42] with the mediating function of autocracy, about which the senior statesman Mikhail Speranskii had lectured him in his youth. In those days, Speranskii had insisted that the autocrat could promote orderly change only by balancing the political and economic aspirations of the empire's various elites against each other so that none could become too powerful and all would remain fragmented. Autocracy thus stood as the most important mediating institution in Russia, the only force capable of prevent-

ing the empire's corporate groups from extorting political concessions from the government. "When the hand holding the elements of supreme authority weakens, when it is not in a position
to lock the various 'aristocracies' within their prescribed limits,"
Speranskii had warned in 1836, "[they will] progress from
mutual competition among themselves to conflict with the supreme authority itself."[43]

Alexander therefore selected those segments of the nobility
and intelligentsia that he thought least threatening to his autocratic prerogatives and, taking advantage of the conciliatory
mood that pervaded *obshchestvo*, co-opted them into bureaucratic
bodies where they could be controlled through the natural (and
essentially limiting) forces of bureaucratic caution. This would
center the debate about reform within the confines of bureaucratic agencies and separate the co-opted elites from those
groups among the nobility, intelligentsia, and bureaucracy they
might have led in protest against the emperor's refusal to grant
the Russians the means of political expression that had accompanied the emergence of an economic and social order dominated by the middle class in the West. Once safely enlisted, these
men could become a source of public opinion that the government could consult about social and economic renovations without opening a full-scale public debate about policy. More aware
of the aspirations of nobility and *obshchestvo* and more familiar
with the complexities of local conditions than most central government officials, such carefully controlled sources of public
opinion could provide valuable information that government
offices had been unable to obtain. They might increase the government's points of contact without limiting its ability to decide
questions of policy in camera.

Much more than his predecessors, Alexander II understood
that accurate information about conditions in Russia must play
a crucial role in formulating any program for his empire's renovation. In early April 1856, some nine months before the Secret
Committee of 1857 began to discuss the dilemmas of improving
the conditions under which Russia's serfs lived, he ordered his
new minister of internal affairs, S. S. Lanskoi, to take charge of
all work related to serfdom and rural economy that was being
done by government agencies. This placed the enlightened
bureaucrats in a key position, for their concern to understand
Russia in statistical terms during the difficult last years of

Nicholas's reign had made them the guardians of a unique storehouse of knowledge about conditions in an empire so complex that no one could comprehend its diversity.

As the enlightened bureaucrats, led by Nikolai Miliutin, Andrei Zablotskii-Desiatovskii, and Iakov Solov'ev, began to assume the part for which their superior expertise about Russian conditions had prepared them,[44] they and those elements of public opinion that Alexander II had co-opted into the bureaucracy broadened their definitions of *zakonnost'* and *glasnost'*. Traditionally, *zakonnost'* had stood as a counterbalance to *proizvol*, the arbitrary authority that officials who had borne the personal commission of the autocrat often exercised in an abusive fashion. By the middle of the nineteenth century, progressive men had come to realize that there could be no rule of law in Russia without *zakonnost'*, yet that belief fit poorly with Russian tradition and experience, for, as we have seen, *proizvol* had a positive side that could not be set aside lightly. Not *zakonnost'* but *proizvol* had made it possible for Peter the Great to impose his transformation upon the Russians, and it had been the instrument his successors had used to overcome gross abuses by their subordinates.

*Proizvol* thus had been a key to implementing reform as well as a device by which unscrupulous officials had abused the Russians. To abandon *proizvol* therefore posed serious dangers to the success of any reform that might come from above in Russia. The efforts of Alexander I and his Unofficial Committee to draft a constitution for Russia at the beginning of the nineteenth century had run aground precisely on that dilemma, and the next half century had not produced a solution. "Many people in authority think that if their intentions are pure and their goal useful for society, then any means are acceptable so long as they lead toward the proposed end," Privy Counselor Nikolai Bakhtin wrote in 1856. "The need for *zakonnost'*," he concluded, "is rarely recognized by our officials."[45]

One historian wrote not long ago that *zakonnost'* was the "keystone" of the outlook of men who wanted "the further rationalization of the autocracy and supported the admission of responsible members of 'society' into the machinery of the Imperial government to help formulate state policy."[46] Yet to use *zakonnost'* to overcome *proizvol* without destroying the ability of well-intentioned officials to do good posed a fundamental dilemma for reformers in a government whose members too often planned change and made policy in secret. To eliminate corruption and arbitrariness required that the actions of public officials be held up to public scrutiny and that policy be made more openly. Only if *glasnost'* could be used as a check upon *proizvol* and corruption could *zakonnost'* become a reality in Russian life and government. *Glasnost'* therefore held the key to Russia's transformation from a society and government based on *proizvol* to a nation of citizens who lived and were governed on the basis of *zakonnost'*.

V. A. Tsie, schoolmate of the future reformist ministers Aleksandr Golovnin and Mikhail Reitern, had transferred from Russia's censorship offices to a civilian position in the Imperial War Ministry in the 1840s, and was perhaps the first to understand that *glasnost'* could serve as a fundamental guarantee for *zakonnost'*. By holding up the results of decision and policy-making to public scrutiny, Tsie argued, *glasnost'* could force the rank and file of Russia's bureaucracy to abandon its long-standing passive resistance to change and attack corruption at all levels of government. "*Glasnost'*," Tsie concluded at one point, "provides the oppressed with an opportunity to enjoy the protection of the law, and it alone, with its all-shattering power, can weaken and finally eradicate corruption, the most shameful ulcer of our society."[47]

If Tsie saw extreme centralization and the *proizvol* that it produced as serious impediments to effective government, others considered these faults to be even more pernicious and placed greater reliance on *glasnost'* as an antidote. Prince Petr Dolgorukov, a tempestuous figure during the first years of Alexander II's reign, regarded *glasnost'* as the single panacea that could uncover abuses of authority and hold corrupt officials in check. "Without the broad development of *glasnost'* the government will never have the opportunity to recognize all the abuses [in its administration] and thus will never have the opportunity to eradicate them," Dolgorukov insisted at one point. "*Glasnost'* is the best physician for the ulcers of the state," he added. "The wise use of *glasnost'* is the best weapon for destroying false rumors [and] secret schemes."[48] From Dolgorukov's perspective, *glasnost'* could weld Tsar, educated opinion, and masses into an instrument to overcome all reactionary and self-interested opposition to reform, a view that a number of radicals heartily endorsed. "*Glasnost'*," Aleksandr Herzen predicted in 1858, "will punish [the serf owners] long before the lash of the government or the axe of the peasant will reach them."[49]

Because neither held a position in Russia's government and both were violently antibureaucratic in their views, Dolgorukov and Herzen did not perceive the problems that *glasnost'* might pose for Russia's government. Neither Alexander II, his advisers, nor any of the enlightened bureaucrats thought in terms of abolishing censorship in Russia, and none envisioned the full and open public debate about Russia's needs that men such as Dolgorukov and Herzen had in mind. All agreed that *glasnost'* had to be kept within "reasonable limits" while Russians debated their nation's future course.[50] How broad the debate on public policy could be and how it could be controlled once it had been initiated, therefore, posed serious problems for even the most open-minded officials. Especially as it related to the press and censorship, this problem proved to be one of the most troublesome that Alexander II and his counselors faced. When they finally resolved it by narrowing the definition of *glasnost'* dramatically, their decision had very important effects on curtailing debate about Russia's renovation toward the middle of the 1860s.

Alexander himself articulated the dichotomy in the government's view of *glasnost'* in 1857 when he insisted that censorship must exercise "judicious vigilance" but that it ought not to "inhibit thinking."[51] Such a view presumed that everyone in Russia shared the government's values and believed that public debate about state policy ought to be confined to clarifying the views that the emperor and his advisers expressed, no matter how unclear or uncertain those might be. Censorship therefore was to be governed by moral imperatives, not administrative regulations, a view based on those precepts of official nationality that had shaped Alexander's education and early political experience. The institutional structure of Russia and, above all, the integrity of autocratic authority thus must remain unquestioned and untouched in any public debate about renovation or reform.

Perhaps no one stated that view more clearly than O. A. Przhetslavskii, a key figure in Russia's Main Censorship Administration. At the beginning of 1860, Przhetslavskii set down his views in a lengthy and unusually forceful memorandum, "On *Glasnost'* in Russian Journalistic Literature," in which he warned that, although *glasnost'* in theory "could have real value in stimulating discussions about serious issues within a framework permissible to the government," it in fact had produced the opposite effect. "Such *glasnost'* as has established itself in the Russian periodical press in recent years," Przhetslavskii stated flatly, "does not conform to our civic order, the peculiarities of our national character, the level of our present development, or our future requirements." *Glasnost'*, he insisted, must reflect a nation's character and take into account the level of education among its masses. It "must stand in inviolable harmony with the circumstances of time and place [and must] . . . conform to the bases and forms of the state and civic structure." *Glasnost'* must be a unique reflection of a nation's experience and heritage. "As it exists in one country," Przhetslavskii concluded, "*glasnost'* can never be fully and unconditionally transplanted to another."[52]

Przhetslavskii believed that moral imperatives could shape *glasnost'* so that it could preserve the prerogatives of autocracy and still encourage legitimate expressions of public opinion, which he defined as public support for government policy. Proceeding from the view that the loyal servitors of a benevolent autocrat would formulate and implement only policies that served the best interests of all Russians, he saw no need for public opinion to have a role in the policy-making process and expected the bureaucracy to chart Russia's future course. Przhetslavskii therefore hoped to use *glasnost'* to reshape Nicholas's system into a less repressive form yet keep the moral precepts that the government had imposed upon the Russians for the past half century intact.

The dilemma of the late 1850s, therefore, was whether *glasnost'* would open channels of communication between government and public opinion that would permit thoughtful Russians to influence policy or whether the government would treat public opinion merely as a source for officials to consult when they needed to supplement their inadequate sources of information. If Przhetslavskii's view triumphed, it would confine all debate on Russia's renovation to the inner reaches of St. Petersburg's chanceries.

What made it possible for Russia's blossoming public opinion to have any confidence that the debate of the late 1850s would not degenerate into inconsequential modifications of the Nicholas system was its belief in the renovating power of the autocrat. Certain that Alexander II could determine Russia's course and place their nation upon the path to reform, even such radicals as Nikolai Chernyshevskii, Aleksandr Herzen, and Nikolai Ogarev believed that a new era had opened after the Peace of Paris. "The blessings promised to the peacemakers and the meek crown Alexander II with a felicity which none of Europe's sovereigns ever achieved—the happiness both to begin and to complete the freeing of his subjects," Chernyshevskii wrote at the beginning of 1858. "With the reign of Alexander II," he concluded (a few pages after he had proclaimed that the era of reforms that lay ahead could, in its "grandeur and beneficence, be compared only with the reform achieved by Peter the Great"), "there begins a new era for Russia, just as one had begun with Peter's [reign]."[53]

From London, where he had no need to fear tsarist censorship or the tsar's police, Herzen greeted the opening of the debate about the consequences of Russia's Crimean failure in equally enthusiastic tones. "We are not only on the eve of a revolution, but we have already entered it," he wrote in an article that proclaimed "REVOLUTION IN RUSSIA" as its title in August 1857. The "will of the Tsar and public opinion," he explained six months later, now stood together in the cause of emancipation. Russia's serf owners, he predicted, could not resist such a powerful union.[54] "We have no doubt that Alexander II stands at the head of the masses," Herzen's friend and co-editor Nikolai Ogarev added a few weeks later. "We believe," he concluded, "that Alexander II stands at the head of progress in Russia."[55] Ogarev saw not the emperor, but the union of Russia's bureaucracy and noble serf owners—what he called the "serfowning bureaucracy"— as the major obstacle to renovation and reform in 1858. "Russia is thirsting for a transformation of the bureaucracy," he insisted. "Without that it will be impossible to take even one step forward."[56] Hopeful that *zakonnost'* would become a key element in this new era of openness between tsar and people, progressive public opinion remained briefly confident that the Emperor would not allow Russia's bureaucrats to violate the law in defining the course that lay ahead.

*Glasnost'* thus held out the promise of becoming the means

by which public opinion might provide the information Russia's reformers needed to shape the coming Great Reforms, while *zakonnost'* stood as the guarantee that tsar and reformers would not violate the law in the process. *Zakonnost'* and *glasnost'* thus became the reference points around which the Great Reform debate took shape as Russia's statesmen and intelligentsia struggled to come to grips with the dilemmas posed by the Crimean defeat.

Although the debate that followed Russia's defeat in the Crimean War eventually produced the Great Reforms, it began as a far less grandiose inquiry into the state of the Russian empire. In his manifesto announcing the end of the Crimean War on March 19, 1856, Alexander II expressed the hope that Russia's "domestic order may be strengthened and perfected, that justice and mercy may reign in her courts," and that, "under the protection of laws that are equally just for all," everyone in Russia might flourish.[57] He and Russian opinion had moved slowly during the first weeks of peace, each testing the virgin soil of reform in which they were about to cut their first furrows and both reluctant to cut too deeply too quickly. On the question of serfdom, Alexander spoke not of emancipation but of "improving the lot of the peasants,"[58] and he moved with equal caution with respect to the problems of administrative overcentralization and the need for renovating local government. Although committed to making justice more accessible to Russians and improving the effectiveness with which officials applied the law, Alexander did not set out to work fundamental changes in Russia's judicial system. "I completely share your opinion," he wrote in late 1857 to Count Dmitrii Bludov, who, as chief of the Second Section of His Majesty's Own Chancery, was responsible for drafting plans for improving Russia's laws. "We are still not mature enough for the introduction of public justice and lawyers."[59]

As they probed the dimensions of the Crimean defeat throughout 1856 and 1857, Alexander II and his advisers continued to think in terms of cautious renovations, not major transformations of Russian life. "The resolution of this question [of emancipation] is subject to many and varied conditions, the significance of which can be determined only by experience," the emperor wrote to his aunt in the fall of 1856 to explain why he continued to proceed with caution.[60] Even Count Kiselev, easily one of the most progressive statesmen of the Nicholaevan era, architect of the Peace of Paris, and Russia's ambassador to France, warned bluntly in mid-1857 that "to give *complete freedom* to twenty-two million peasants of both sexes is *undesirable* and *impossible*. It is *undesirable*," he continued, "because this huge mass is not ready for complete freedom. It is *impossible* because peasants without land would be placed in the most onerous dependence on the landowners imaginable and would become their complete slaves."[61]

In the meantime, public opinion had begun to race ahead in shaping new visions of the future. Prince Dmitrii Obolenskii, one of the enlightened bureaucrats whom Konstantin Niko-laevich had taken into Russia's naval ministry during the Crimean War, remembered how "proposals for railroads, memoranda about various financial reforms and improvements, about trans-forming the courts, emancipating the peasants, [and] reforming the army . . . began to pour into Petersburg from all sides,"[62] as timid suggestions for change turned into a flood of wide-ranging proposals for reform toward the end of 1857. Russians, the censor Nikitenko once had written, suffered from a "celerity of thought," an inability to "progress along the path of thought by firm logical steps," that caused them to "race at full speed with no clearly-defined goals."[63] As Russia passed the end of 1857 and turned toward the second anniversary of the Peace of Paris, this tendency to race ahead combined with the inflated hopes that the first days of *glasnost'* had stirred among the Russians to cause their aspirations to outrun the government's willingness to keep pace.

The responses of government and society to the debate on the dimensions of the Crimean defeat thus caused their paths to diverge just as serious work on the Great Reforms began. Once government and society embarked upon separate paths, they moved apart so rapidly that, by the fall of 1859, Chernyshev-skii and his tubercular young associate Nikolai Dobroliubov already had rejected any thought that a reforming tsar could direct Russia along the path to modernization and progress. "At the beginning of Alexander II's reign they loosened just a little the collar that Nicholas I had pulled so tightly and we began to feel that we were already free," "A Russian" wrote in an unsigned "Letter from the Provinces" that almost certainly came from the pen of Chernyshevskii or Dobroliubov. "You will soon see," the letter, which Herzen published in *Kolokol* (*The Bell*) "only after long debate" with his conscience, continued. "Alexander II soon will show his teeth just as Nicholas I did." The author's bitterness showed how wide the gap between government and radical opinion had grown in the year and a half since he had praised Alexander's "felicity" and had cheered the "grandeur and beneficence" of his reign. "Remember," he concluded, "that for hundreds of years faith in the good intentions of the Tsars has ruined our land."[64]

The virulence of the young radicals' rejection of the emperor as a key to Russia's renovation took even Herzen by surprise. "Have I been completely wrong?" he asked in his introduction to "A Russian's" letter. "Who of late has done anything sensible for Russia except for the Sovereign?" As Chernyshevskii himself had done a scant eighteen months before, Herzen emphasized the near-revolutionary force with which Russia's emperors had exercised their authority in the past; since the time of Peter the Great, he insisted, they had changed Russia more than the revolutionaries of 1792 and 1793 had changed France. The autocracy remained the force best able to overcome the self-interest of Russia's nobility. For that reason, he insisted, Russia's radicals must "render unto Caesar that which is Caesar's."[65]

On the more moderate side, those upon whom responsibility for drafting the Great Reforms would fall shed few tears as government and radical intelligentsia began to move along diverging paths. Once preparations for reform had begun and once they had established those groups of experts that they had chosen as their instruments for changing state policy, Russia's enlightened bureaucrats and their allies within and outside government abandoned the brief alliances they had made with radical opinion during the early days of Alexander II's reign. As it became their task to balance the caution of the government against the increasingly daring aspirations of *obshchestvo*, Russia's reformers again employed the time-honored bureaucratic technique of co-optation to draw only those segments of public opinion they particularly trusted into reform work. At the same time, for fear that they would become too difficult (or self-interested) to control, reformers tried to exclude the broader segments of Russian public opinion from any decisive influence on the content of the Great Reforms. Although dedicated to renovating and reforming the Russian empire, Russia's bureaucratic reformers, unlike the liberals and constitutionalists whom historians have too often thought them to be, remained autocratic servants of an autocratic master. That single characteristic dominated the manner in which they proceeded to shape the Great Reforms.

# III

## BEGINNING
## RUSSIA'S
## RENOVATION

*T*he debate that followed the Crimean defeat brought the
entire social and economic order of mid-nineteenth-
century Russia into question. A broad quest for liberation
stretched from the empire's land-hungry serf villages to the elegant boarding schools, where well-born young ladies dreamed
of reshaping their lives free of patriarchal authority. From the
rural nests of homespun squires who longed to be free of petty
bureaucratic constraints that, in the words of one nobleman,
had placed "the entire life of the people under governmental
tutelage,"[1] to the law courts, where the search for justice had
become so mired in formalism that sons and grandsons carried
on litigations begun by their fathers and grandfathers, the men
and women of Russia began to envision a renovated state and
society in which they would become responsible citizens of a
modern polity. "Russia," Herzen wrote in spring 1860, "had
emerged from that stifling time in which people could discuss
civic and public matters only in theoretical terms."[2] Now Russians had begun to think of public responsibility and civic action.

As never before, Herzen's countrymen sought real solutions
to real economic and social problems. Impatient for liberation,
the more radical among them posed the questions; "When will
the real day come?" (Dobroliubov) and "What is to be done?"
(Chernyshevskii) as they looked for "new men" to lead Russia
forward into a world without autocrats, aristocrats, or tyrannical
bureaucrats. Men of more moderate views thought of themselves and Russia as being *On the Eve*, to borrow the title of
Turgenev's 1859 novel, and continued to wait expectantly for

the reforms they now knew that tsar and ministers were in the process of bringing forth. There was worry, for this was a disquieting time when long-held assumptions fell by the wayside and the manner in which men and women viewed their social and economic environment was forever altered. But it also was a time of great anticipation, when no one knew what the future held but many sensed that they stood on the threshhold of an era that would carry them into the modern world. Some twenty years before, Alexander II's tutor, Vasilii Zhukovskii, had lamented that education had begun to move forward "like an onrushing train."[3] Now all of Russia seemed to be moving at that speed. "One senses an internal renovation in everything [and] one feels that a new era is beginning," one thoughtful nobleman wrote in 1858. "In the past two years civic opinion has achieved great successes in Russia," he continued. "From all sides, ideas and lucid views are gradually ousting the old routine which, taking pride in its ignorance and stupidity, was ashamed of nothing before and during the war."[4]

Between 1857 and 1864, reform legislation freed Russia's serfs, established institutions of representative government in key parts of the Empire, restructured the nation's law courts, introduced trial by jury, and placed justice in Russia for the first time in the hands of a judicial profession that could exercise authority over the law independently of the autocracy. Russia thus began her evolution from a nation of servitors into a nation of free men and women obliged to assume increasing responsibility for their destinies and those of their neighbors. The burden for Russians' welfare, public health, education, and the modernization of agriculture and industry began to shift away from the emperor and the bureaucrats who staffed Russia's central administration to elected officials and experts employed by local public institutions. This heralded the beginning of the greatest era of social and economic renovation to occur in Russia's history since the death of Peter the Great.

The key to opening this new era would be the emancipation of 22,558,748 peasants, whose enserfment to noble masters continued to be the chief obstacle to overcoming Russia's economic backwardness.[5] As in the American South, the majority served a comparative handful of masters. According to the Tenth Revision, which calculated Russia's serf population in 1857–58, slightly more than a fifth of the serf-owning nobility owned more than 80 percent of the serfs and, conversely, a little more than three-quarters of the nobility held a fraction less than a fifth of the serfs.[6] The gap that separated rich lord from poor squire in mid-nineteenth-century Russia was immense, for it required at least a hundred male serfs for a nobleman and his family to live from the proceeds of servile labor alone.[7] This meant that only one lord in five could live in reasonable comfort from the labor of his serfs if he stayed in the country; fewer than one serf owner in twenty-five (a total of 3,803 families in all of Russia) had enough bondsmen to live as absentee landlords.[8] Nonetheless, Russia's serf owners continued to believe that each among them benefited in some significant way from servile labor. For that reason alone, they supported its preservation.

Although mid-nineteenth-century Russia "was rich in devices for the enforcement and support of serfdom," as Daniel Field pointed out more than a decade ago, this institution, on which the life of lords and peasants was so firmly grounded, had no ideological or political structures to defend it.[9] At the same time, enough public sentiment supported emancipation *in theory* at midcentury to make it very difficult for the men and women whose lives had been built around serfdom to defend it. As early as 1841, Andrei Zablotskii-Desiatovskii, who would play an important part in the work of the Editing Commission that drafted the Emancipation Acts of 1861, wrote, "The question of the abolition of serfdom . . . now astonishes no one" and "everybody in one way or another is prepared to discuss it." That Zablotskii was not engaging in wishful thinking was confirmed just two years later when Baron August von Haxthausen reported in the three-volume *Studies on the Interior of Russia,* which earned him a European-wide reputation as an expert on Russian peasant life: "all sensible people [in Russia] agree that it is impossible to long maintain [serfdom] in its present state."[10] If on none other than moral grounds, it was not thought very respectable to defend serfdom publicly in mid-nineteenth-century Russia. "Educated, or 'enlightened' public opinion," Terence Emmons explained nearly a quarter century ago, "was, almost by definition, abolitionist opinion."[11]

Most educated Russians in 1850 would have agreed that, at some time in the future, serfdom must be abolished, but very few dared to call for its immediate abolition. Even Nicholas I had once told the State Council that serfdom was an "evil, palpable and obvious to all." But, he had continued on that occasion, "at the *present* time, any thought of [emancipation] would be neither more nor less than a criminal infringement on domestic tranquillity and the welfare of the state."[12] To move the question of abolishing serfdom from the indefinite future to the here-and-now, the emperor's advisers and Russia's policymakers would have to think that the need for reform was urgent enough to risk the danger to Russia's security that an emancipation might pose. Put another way, other threats to Russia's security would have to be seen as sufficiently threatening for these sober and conservative men to conclude that emancipation posed the lesser danger. When the Crimean defeat brought Russia's great power status into question and European statesmen began to talk about allowing her to flow back into Asia, that moment had come.[13]

### EMANCIPATING RUSSIA'S SERFS

The issues of serfdom and emancipation had never been far from the center of Russian policymakers' concerns since 1765 when Catherine II had asked the newly formed Free Economic Society to debate the question "Is it more beneficial for society for the peasant to have property rights to the land or only movable property, and how much should his rights to one or the other form of property be extended?"[14] Despite her readiness to pose the question about limiting servile labor and her willingness to allow the Free Economic Society to award their first annual prize to an essay that advocated its abolition, Catherine, in fact, had presided over the spread of serfdom into large areas of the empire where it had not existed before. During her reign, loyal noble servitors had received more than a million state peasants as gifts from their grateful empress and her son Paul I had added more than 50 percent to that number in the four years after her death.

Even as Catherine and her son had distributed human chattels to their favorites, sentiment for emancipation had begun to grow among foresightful Russians: Nikolai Novikov and the Moscow freemasons had advocated serfdom's reform in the 1770s and 1780s, and Aleksandr Radishchev had called for its abolition at the end of the decade. "Do you not know the peril in which we stand and the destruction that threatens us?"

Radishchev asked the readers of his *Journey from St. Petersburg to Moscow.* "The more dilatory and obstinate we are about freeing [the serfs] from their bonds," he warned, "the more violent their vengeance will be."[15] Thanks in part to Radishchev's work and in part to the impact of the French Revolution, the question of emancipation had become sufficiently focused in the minds of enlightened Russians by the beginning of the nineteenth century for Alexander I to put an end to the practice of rewarding loyal service with gifts of bondsmen.

Every autocrat after Catherine had considered limiting serfdom in some fashion, as had a number of their leading counselors, not the least of whom were the great Speranskii, his mentor Count Viktor Kochubei, and Alexander I's minister of finance, Dmitrii Gur'ev.[16] In 1804, the peasants in Russia's Baltic provinces had been emancipated and, the year before, Alexander had decreed a Law on Free Cultivators that allowed nobles to liberate Russian serfs under carefully specified conditions. Although both laws stipulated that serfs were to be set free with land, they both were altered (in 1816–19 in Courland, Livonia, and Estonia, and in 1807 in the case of the Free Cultivators) so that bondsmen could be liberated without it.[17] As the reign of Nicholas I began, the assumption remained that, if Russia's serfs ever were to be emancipated, they would be freed without land as they had been in the Baltic provinces and in England.

Mainly at the insistence of General Count Pavel Kiselev, courtier, imperial aide-de-camp, diplomat, and the minister of state domains who instituted far-reaching reforms in the administration of Russia's state peasants, that assumption changed in the 1830s and 1840s. A student of Chateaubriand, Jeremy Bentham, and Adam Smith, Kiselev insisted that Russia's serfs could not be freed without land, if for no other reason than the threat a landless rural proletariat would pose to the internal security of the empire.[18] "Emancipation with land not only is an essential economic condition but a vital political one," he would explain at one point.[19] Anticipating Stolypin's reforms by a good half century, Kiselev saw landowning peasants as a pillar to support the government and help guarantee the peaceful course of progress in Russia.

Between 1842 and 1856, the Ministry of State Domains assembled impressive quantities of data about life in state peasant villages that illustrated the importance of landownership among

the peasantry and supported Kiselev's insistence that Russia's
serfs must be freed with land. Directed by Zablotskii-Desiatovskii's Department of Rural Economy, these cadastral surveys
covered almost 11 million peasants and more than 65 million
acres of land in twenty-five Great Russian provinces. From them,
Zablotskii not only concluded that the peasants must have land
but (in contrast to Kiselev's view) argued that the peasant commune must be abolished. "Without the confidence of the peasant
in the continual ownership of those lands which he tills," he
wrote in 1851, "there never can be any successes in agriculture
and all other efforts at improvement will be rendered impotent."
Because the commune's abolition would not in itself eliminate
peasant poverty, Zablotskii looked for other ways to improve
rural life. "*Zakonnost'*," he wrote, must be introduced "in place
of absolute confusion and arbitrariness" in the government's
dealings with its peasants.[20] At the same time, his department's
Academic Committee added, "only greater *glasnost'* can provide
a solid basis for future measures for the improvement of this
sector of national industry."[21]

In his criticisms of serfdom, Zablotskii had moved well ahead
of his superiors. Neither *zakonnost'* nor *glasnost'* figured in the
thinking of most mid-nineteenth-century Russian statesmen,
and, although Kiselev had convinced Nicholas I that, in theory,
serfs must receive land in any emancipation that might someday
occur, he had not been so successful in winning his fellow
ministers to that view. None of the eight secret committees that
convened to discuss the problem of serfdom in Russia between
1826 and 1847 dared to propose emancipation, and all insisted
that the lands of Russia's estates must remain in the hands of
the nobility.[22] "It was the same old song," the historian Aleksandr Kizevetter concluded almost a century ago. "[They
wanted] to institute reforms so that no one would notice or feel
them."[23]

Although most educated men and women supported emancipation in theory at the end of the Crimean War, they stood
divided—Zablotskii from Kiselev, Westerners from Slavophiles,
and defenders of centralization from advocates of decentralization—on the question of the commune. At the same time, the
great lords who advised the tsar continued to insist that any
emancipation must be without land, whereas the men within
the government most knowledgeable about peasant life called

for emancipation with land and the introduction of *glasnost'* and *zakonnost'* to build a society in which private property and the fruits of one's labors would be protected by law. When Russia's senior statesmen took up the serf question in what would be the last of the secret committees in January 1857, the key question was whether they or the experts within the Ministries of Internal Affairs and State Domains would shape the course of the emancipation debate. The answer lay in the actions of Alexander II, who, for the moment, did not move only in one direction.

Within a week after he had told the assembled Moscow nobility on March 30, 1856, that "it is better to abolish serfdom from above than to await the time when it will begin to abolish itself from below,"[24] Alexander II had ordered Count Sergei Lanskoi, his newly appointed minister of internal affairs, to take charge of all work related to the "organization of the serfs of the nobility" that was being done in the central government and to determine what principles should be included in any reform of serf life.[25] That Russia's new emperor chose to assign this responsibility to what had, by midcentury, become the dominant institution of Russian domestic administration was no accident. Nicholas I already had ceded some of his jealously guarded legislative prerogatives to the Ministry of Internal Affairs so that it could deal with the empire's increasingly complex domestic problems, and, although still called "Most Humble Reports," many of the detailed documents that its senior officials prepared for the emperor and the State Council had become draft legislation by midcentury. Indeed, the dramatic increase in the number of circulars and instructions that Lanskoi's immediate predecessors had issued without their sovereign's direct approval during the 1840s and 1850s attested to their authority to make laws.[26]

If Alexander's purpose in centralizing all government work on the "organization of the serfs of the nobility" in the Ministry of Internal Affairs during the spring of 1856 was to encourage it to prepare draft reform legislation, Lanskoi was not content to take full responsibility without further guidance. Nor was he willing to face the inevitable opposition of Russia's great lords in the State Council alone.[27] In December 1856, he therefore urged Alexander to establish a small committee of senior officials "convinced of the need for passing to a new order without a moment's delay" to prepare a program for the emancipation work.[28] Less than a month later, the emperor acted on Lanskoi's advice.

That Alexander appointed a secret committee of great lords rather than the sort of men Lanskoi had suggested indicates that he may have been having second thoughts about emancipation or, at the very least, was not willing to move ahead very quickly. There were three princes and two counts among the secret committee's ten original members, four of whom held the rank of general. Four members each owned over a thousand serfs, and, when the emperor added General M. N. Murav'ev and Count V. N. Panin to the committee some months later, that number increased to six. Several of the committee's members were over seventy and some of them had served their emperor for more than half a century. None of them claimed any expertise on the complex subject of peasant affairs, although four had served on some of the secret committees that Nicholas I had appointed to discuss serfdom in the 1830s and 1840s. Count Dmitrii Bludov, for a quarter century the director of the Second Section of His Majesty's Own Chancery that compiled and drafted Russia's laws, had served on the famous Committee of December 6th, which Nicholas had formed in 1826.[29]

Composed of great lords whose rank, wealth, and long experience in Russia's service disposed them to look to the past rather than the future, the Secret Committee of 1857 quickly called for an emancipation "without any abrupt and drastic overturns." Like the committees assigned to study the problems of reform and change during the reign of Nicholas I, it set as its first task a thorough review of all previous measures proposed, discussed, or implemented by the central government.[30] Half a year of work produced such elevated platitudes as "no thoughtful and enlightened person who loves his country can be against the emancipation of the peasants" (General Ia. A. Rostovtsev) and "no man should belong to another" (again, Rostovtsev),[31] and had left the Secret Committee "positively convinced that it is not presently possible to undertake the general emancipation of the serfs among us."[32]

The Secret Committee therefore proposed a long-term, three-stage approach that would, in the foreseeable future, accomplish nothing more than "soften and ease the conditions of serfdom" in Russia without weakening the serf owners' hold on their bondsmen. Only at some distant (and unspecified) point would the second "transitional" stage begin to prepare the way for emancipation in the even more distant third.[33] In response to Alexander's warning that the emancipation question must "not be buried in the files under various pretexts," the Secret Committee had drawn what one high official called a "closed circle" around it.[34] Alexander piously penned, "May God help us to carry out this important matter with the necessary caution to the desired conclusion" in the margin of the Secret Committee's journal,[35] but he already had begun to look elsewhere for the leadership and ideas that would produce an emancipation.

Although it continued to meet and, in fact, received a new president in the person of Grand Duke Konstantin Nikolaevich, the Secret Committee's temporizing turned the emancipation question back to the Ministry of Internal Affairs. There, some three months later, the emancipation process took a decisive step forward when Lanskoi induced the nobility of the northwestern provinces of Kovno, Grodno, and Vilno to set in motion the chain of events that produced the famous Nazimov Rescript in late November 1857.[36] For the better part of a quarter century, the Russian government had been preparing to impose inventories, or precisely defined schedules of serfs' duties to their masters and masters' obligations to their bondsmen, that had the potential to remove some two-thirds of the estate lands of northwest Russia from the control of its Polish and Russian lords. By holding the imposition of inventories as a threat over their heads, V. I. Nazimov, governor-general of Kovno, Vilno, and Grodno, convinced these noblemen during 1857 to petition the tsar for permission to discuss emancipation as (in their minds) the lesser of two evils, since it might enable them to retain control over more of their lands. Their grudging agreement to discuss an emancipation without land as had occurred in the neighboring Baltic provinces a half century before set the stage for moving the debate from the quiet chambers of the Secret Committee and inner recesses of St. Petersburg's chanceries into the public domain. The government's response to their reluctant and feeble request thus marked an important milestone on the road that led from the fall of Sevastopol to the Great Reforms.[37]

On November 20, 1857, Alexander issued a rescript to the

nobility of Russia's northwest that authorized them to elect committees to draft proposals for statutes on the "systematic improvement of the serfs' way of life." Emancipation was not mentioned
and the rescript was very unclear on many crucial questions,
including when the "systematic improvement" (which had
served as a euphemism for emancipation for more than half a
century) ought to occur.[38] Nonetheless, the rescript made it
clear that the government would not permit the serfs to be
transformed into landless proletarians. "The peasants will keep
the right to remain on their household plots, which they will
acquire as property by means of redemption within a definite
period," the rescript announced. After promising that "the serfowners will retain the right to all land," it proceeded to qualify
that assurance by stating that "a quantity of land that will be
sufficient, in keeping with local conditions, for their subsistence
and for the fulfillment of their obligations to the government
and their landlords will be provided to the peasants."[39]

Only so long as their wall of silence remained unbroken had
it been possible for Russia's recalcitrant aristocrats to keep their
emperor waiting for their suggestions about how to proceed
toward emancipation. Alexander's publication of the Nazimov
Rescript, "completely approving of the intentions of the representatives of the nobility of Kovno, Vilno, and Grodno provinces
as corresponding with my views and wishes,"[40] therefore shattered the united front of aristocratic passive resistance and
opened the floodgates through which petitions from every province poured into St. Petersburg. During the next year or so,
forty-eight committees with almost fourteen hundred representatives began to meet to discuss the question of emancipating
Russia's serfs. Like their brethren in the northwest, most did so
unwillingly. The first rescripts, the novelist Ivan Turgenev wrote
to Herzen at the end of 1857, "have raised an unprecedented
alarm among our nobility. Beneath its outward readiness hides
the most obtuse obstinacy—as well as miserly meanness and
outright terror."[41] "The majority of the serfowners," the head
of the imperial gendarmerie reported a few months later, "regard
this whole business as an unjust amputation of their lands that
will ruin them in the future."[42] Some feared for their lives as
much as for their lands. "For the time being, everything is quiet,
but for how long?" a serf owner from the Volga River province
of Simbirsk wrote to a friend. The serf owners, Governor-General

A. A. Zakrevskii reported from Moscow, "fear not only for their property but for their persons."[43]

Such fears had little basis in fact. Although the number of serf disturbances increased from 40 in 1857 to 170 in 1858, the government itself was quick to point out that a substantial part of that number stemmed from local officials' greater readiness to report minor incidents and from peasant resistance to unreasonable new demands made by their masters. "In general," one police report stated flatly, "since the announcement of the [government's] intention to improve their way of life, the serfs have awaited the conclusion of this business with great patience and trust in the government and have not displayed any notable signs of hostility to their masters."[44]

During 1858, work on the emancipation of Russia's serfs moved ahead in the Secret Committee (renamed the Main Committee in January), the Ministry of Internal Affairs, and the committees of elected representatives that the serf owners organized in the provinces. All interpreted the emperor's commitment to emancipation differently, and each worked toward different ends. For the serf owners of Russia, the key issue no longer was whether serfdom would be abolished but what sort of settlement they could arrange in the forthcoming emancipation. None of the emperor's rescripts contained any hint of what financial arrangements the government had in mind, nor did they explain how the serf owners would "retain the right to all land" while the serfs would keep the right to remain on household plots that they would "acquire as property by means of redemption within a definite period."

Beyond stating that it was not intended to be "a detailed program for the committees' deliberations," the circular that Lanskoi issued on February 17, 1858, offered little more in the way of guidance. The solution to the "fundamental questions" that remained to be resolved and "their application to local conditions," Lanskoi announced grandly, "has been left by the Imperial rescript to the serfowners themselves."[45] Without clearly stated guidelines, some provincial committees began to prepare emancipation plans that, after the initial transition period, would return all lands used by the peasants to their former masters. Others schemed to obtain financial compensation for the loss of their land, and still others tried to find ways to include payment for the serfs themselves in that compensation.

In an effort to offer clearer guidance, Alexander told Lanskoi to prepare a "general plan" or a "general program" to guide the provincial committees in their work,[46] and Lanskoi assigned the task at the end of March to Iakov Solov'ev, head of the Rural Section of the Ministry of Internal Affairs, whose study of rural economy in Smolensk province had won the prestigious Zhukovskii Prize from the Russian Geographical Society the year before. A key figure in the growing circle of reform-minded bureaucrats that Nikolai Miliutin had been assembling in the Ministry of Internal Affairs for more than a decade,[47] Solov'ev combined his colleagues' typical emphasis on assembling accurate data before drafting reform legislation (a key point in his plan was that provincial committees should assemble detailed information about every estate in each province) with a form of the "artificial" *glasnost'* that Grand Duke Konstantin Nikolaevich had encouraged in the Naval Ministry. To the outrage of the Main Committee, he therefore arranged for a hundred copies of his proposed general program to be printed and distributed to government officials and private citizens whose judgment he respected.[48]

For that and other reasons, Solov'ev's were not the principles that were chosen to guide the provincial committees' work. The winds of reform seemed to be changing and, even before Solov'ev had set to work, his allies sensed that the initiative in the emancipation work was shifting into other hands. "Into whose hands are things passing now?" Miliutin asked Kiselev at the beginning of March. "It is distressing to call to mind *how* this difficult and important business is being carried forward," he added. "Self-interested, unprepared [and] undeveloped, the nobility is being left to its own devices. I cannot imagine what will come out of all this, without any guidance and direction, given the crude opposition of our great lords and the intrigues and unscrupulousness of responsible officials."[49]

The "April Program" that the Main Committee issued on April 21, 1858, to guide the provincial committees therefore showed little evidence of Solov'ev's work and relied heavily on suggestions that had been made by Mikhail Pozen, a great landowner from Poltava province who had the emperor's ear despite rumors of his corrupt dealings in the army. "A blank check for the provincial committees," according to one account,[50] the April Program left Russia's lords free to define almost every issue

related to the coming "improvement of the serfs' way of life"
as they thought best.[51] Most important, when Alexander II approved the April Program, it set him in conflict with the Ministry
of Internal Affairs, the one agency in the central government
that had men sufficiently expert in rural affairs to begin work
on an emancipation. "Recently, a reaction has begun to set in
and, of course, it will not end with a mere beginning," Nikolai
Miliutin sadly wrote to his elder brother. "It is hard to say what
will come out of all this," he continued, "but one can hardly
be optimistic." The villains, Miliutin insisted, were Pozen, Minister of State Domains Mikhail Murav'ev, and General Iakov Rostovtsev, who seemed to have fallen completely and uncritically
under Pozen's spell and had sponsored Pozen's proposals in the
Main Committee. Sober men who believed in emancipation
seemed to be losing faith in their government and their
sovereign. "You have no idea how this worries me," Miliutin
concluded, "but it is impossible to tear oneself away from it."[52]

The summer and fall of 1858 was a time of cautious testing
and precarious balancing as Russia's provincial committees
sought to discover the limits of the emperor's commitment to
reform and determine the extent to which the Main Committee
would limit an emancipation. Certainly, the reaction about
which Miliutin had worried in April seemed to be deepening.[53]
When members of the Main Committee toured the provinces
that summer, they were said to have told the nobles that the
government would settle for a nominal reform rather than insist-
ing upon full emancipation[54] and Alexander himself was obliged
to visit key provincial capitals to set the record straight. He
sought to reassure the nobility where possible, but he sometimes
spoke more harshly than any nineteenth-century Russian
sovereign ever had. He was perhaps most severe in Moscow:
"I have given you the principles and I shall not depart from
them," he warned his listeners after reminding them that he
again stood in the same chamber where, more than two years
before, he had urged them to be the first to take up the emancipation work. "Remember," he continued sternly, "all of Russia
looks to Moscow province. I am always ready to do whatever
I can for you," he concluded. "You must make it possible for
me to do that."[55]

Alexander's severity heralded new and surprising changes in

the emancipation program. Freed from what he called "the maelstrom of Petersburg" when the Main Committee recessed that summer, General Rostovtsev traveled to the spas of Central Europe to study the peasant question from a more detached and broader perspective. From Wildbad, Carlsruhe, and Dresden between August 17 and September 4, he wrote four letters to his emperor that were to have a profound impact on the course of emancipation in Russia. Now certain that Pozen's reactionary program must be set aside, Rostovtsev insisted that Russia's serfs must receive land to use immediately and must eventually receive title to it. Nor should they bear the burden of its purchase alone. "The government," he wrote, "ought to take part in the [peasants'] redemption of their land." Although Rostovtsev cautioned that "such help on the part of the government cannot be very large," he had injected a vital new element into the emancipation debate.[56] For the first time, a senior statesman who enjoyed the emperor's closest confidence had argued that, despite its near-bankruptcy from the Crimean defeat, the government must help the peasants to finance their emancipation.

Views such as those to which Rostovtsev converted late in the summer of 1858 were commonly held by a comparatively wide circle of enlightened officials, economic experts, and private citizens that included Lanskoi, the Miliutin brothers, Zablotskii-Desiatovskii, Solov'ev (and some two or three dozen other reform-minded bureaucrats), Provincial Governor V. A. Artsimovich, onetime imperial tutor and legal expert Konstantin Kavelin, Baron von Haxthausen, the leading figures of the Russian Geographical Society, the Slavophile salons of Moscow, Grand Duchess Elena Pavlovna, and Grand Duke Konstantin Nikolaevich. Although this impressive array represented some of the best minds in Russia, too many of them were regarded with suspicion by the emperor and his inner circle to be taken seriously. Kavelin recently had been dismissed from his post as tutor under circumstances that had stirred angry articles in Herzen's *Kolokol* and left bitter resentment among Russia's progressives. Nikolai Miliutin, Solov'ev, and Iurii Samarin had been branded as "reds" for coming to his defense, and most of the men who shared their views soon were tarred with the same brush by the emperor's inner circle.[57] Now an advocate of similar views, Rostovtsev set them directly before the emperor himself.

The importance of his "conversion" thus came not so much from the ideas he expressed as from the height at which he injected them into the emancipation debate.

Alexander II made clear his commitment to Rostovtsev's new views when the Main Committee reassembled in mid-October 1858. During the next six weeks, imperial orders dated October 26 and December 4 set down the main principles that must guide the emancipation work and clarified how the labors of the provincial committees would be evaluated. Both orders drew heavily from the letters Rostovtsev had written from Central Europe. Not only must the serfs feel "at once" that their lives had been improved by the emancipation, the order of October 26 stated in the bland language in which the government set down some of the most vital principles that would guide the legislation of the Great Reform era, but the provincial committees must explain "in detail" how they would accomplish that end when they submitted their drafts to the Main Committee for approval.[58]

If the order of October 26 eroded some of the procedural ground on which the nobility had hoped to build a defense against emancipation, that of December 4 wiped away some of the most cherished historical precepts on which the relationship between Russian lords and peasants had rested. Noble lands need no longer remain in noble hands, the order stated, nor would lords have control over their emancipated peasants. According to the principles incorporated into Alexander's order of December 4, the "improvement in the serfs' condition," as emancipation continued to be called euphemistically, would include civil rights and plans for enabling the former serfs to redeem their landholdings.[59] For more than two years, the emperor had avoided setting down firm principles for an emancipation in the hope that Russia's nobles would have a sufficiently generous sense of public responsibility to establish those principles themselves. In response, nobles in several provinces had advanced a liberal program, but, no matter how articulate, such men had comprised an impotent minority except in the province of Tver.[60]

The same had continued to be the case in the Main Committee, where all but Rostovtsev and Lanskoi had opposed any but the most insignificant concessions to the serfs. "If these opinions were accepted and brought together in one statute," Rostovtsev said of the views that had been set down by the majority of the Main Committee at one point, "what . . . would be left of the amelioration of the peasants' way of life, to say nothing of their emancipation?"[61] Rostovtsev, whom Herzen had cursed as a "new Arakcheev" and Kavelin once described as a "thick-tongued scoundrel," had begun to lead Russians toward emancipation and would continue to do so until his death on February 6, 1860.[62]

With a cavalryman's mustache that mirrored his emperor's, receding hair curled forward at the temples, and the epaulets of an adjutant-general in His Majesty's Own Suite flashing from his shoulders, Iakov Rostovtsev seemed an unlikely candidate for so complicated an assignment in civil affairs. Yet he was not the personification of the parade-ground officer from the Russia of Nicholas I that he seemed, for fate and fortune had played strange tricks on him as he had moved through life, and his destiny had been shaped accordingly. A man whose father had risen from merchant origins to a high position in the civil service, Rostovtsev had been trained for an army career at the Imperial Corps of Pages, where he had learned the unshakable loyalty to his Emperor that was the hallmark of successful military men. As a junior officer, he had been driven by that sense of loyalty to report the Decembrists' conspiracy in 1825, an act that had earned him the hatred of Russia's intelligentsia at the same time as it had made it all but certain that his career would flourish.

If fate had given Rostovtsev an unusual opportunity for advancement, it also had afflicted him with a stutter that rendered him useless on the drill field in an army known for its ability to execute precise maneuvers on parade. He therefore had been obliged to make his way as an adjutant to Grand Duke Mikhail Pavlovich, inspector general of Russia's military schools and perhaps the most narrow-minded and least pleasant of the emperor's brothers. As Mikhail Pavlovich's chief adjutant, Rostovtsev had no choice but to reflect the narrow outlook of the man he served until the grand duke's death in 1849. Then, as heir apparent, the future Alexander II had taken over Mikhail Pavlovich's responsibilities and Rostovtsev had become his mentor. In those days, Alexander had valued Rostovtsev's firm patriotism, his dedication to fulfilling his emperor's wishes, and his readiness to consider points of view other than his own. The stammering general's great influence on Russia's future emperor had begun at that time. His one weakness was that he tended not to be cautious in his choice of friends. That would become particularly evident in his friendship with Mikhail Pozen, the great serf owner whose self-interested proposals he unwarily sponsored in the Main Committee in spring 1858.[63]

While the Main Committee, Rostovtsev, and Alexander II had searched for the principles that should guide an emancipation, the committees of provincial nobility had struggled to come to grips with the idea of emancipation itself. Modest country squires at home on the land and uncomfortable in the city dominated their ranks, and few great lords sat among them. A sense of responsibility weighed heavily upon such men, for they saw themselves not only as defenders of their own property but as caretakers of the lands of the men who had elected them. "One must take a stricter stand on behalf of one who entrusts property [to one's care]," one deputy explained during a meeting of the Chernigov provincial nobility, "than on behalf of one's own." Many representatives of the nobility looked only for the means to exact the greatest personal benefit, to retain title to their lands, and to transform their bondsmen into a pitiful class of indigent farm laborers who could be hired to till the soil at wretchedly low wages. Was "systematic improvement of the serfs' way of life" really their purpose? a rare nobleman who did not share his comrades' self-interest asked of the committee in Simbirsk province. Or should they call themselves a committee for the improvement of the nobles' way of life?[64] In the vast majority of the provincial committees, most nobles preferred to place their interests ahead of any others.

Nobles who believed that their honor as the first citizens of the realm required them to find the means to transform serfs into full-fledged citizens composed a small minority among those who set down their views during the course of 1858 and 1859. In this respect, the lords of Tver province led the way, and they, in turn, were led by Aleksei Unkovskii and Aleksei Golovachev, two men who deserve places of honor in the temple of Russian liberalism. A young lord whose ancestors had lived close to the land for generations, Unkovskii had studied with Granovskii and Kavelin at Moscow University in the 1840s and had been a frequent visitor at those Sunday gatherings at which Kavelin had issued his well-known indictments of serfdom. Not long after he returned to his estate on the eve of the Crimean War, Unkovskii had become a spokesman for the Tver nobility.

He soon formed close ties with Aleksei Golovachev, a man older and wealthier than he, who shared his views on serfdom, emancipation, and politics. By 1858, both men decided that serfdom must be abolished, that the serfs must receive enough land to support themselves, and that the nobility must be compensated for the loss of lands and serfs by some sort of government-financed program.[65]

In their views on serfdom, emancipation, and compensation, Unkovskii and Golovachev agreed more with the ideas of such enlightened bureaucrats as Miliutin and Solov'ev.[66] Where they disagreed—and disagreed sharply—was on such vital issues as the future role that the nobility should play in local government and the extent to which the bureaucracy ought to direct Russia's course after the emancipation opened the way to other reforms. Because Unkovskii and Golovachev thought the bureaucracy too corrupt and incompetent, they urged that the nobility be entrusted with responsibility for directing local affairs after the serfs were freed and the lords' legal control over them was abolished. "Only the nobility, the most enlightened of all rural classes," Unkovskii insisted, "can direct and instruct the masses in fulfilling government decrees."[67] The passage of time only deepened the belief held by Unkovskii and his supporters that the bureaucracy could not be trusted to shape Russia's destiny. The government had "raised the question of emancipating the peasants but did not finally solve it," they concluded after the Emancipation Acts were promulgated. The government was "not capable of realizing" further reforms in Russian life.[68]

Before other reforms could be considered, serfdom had to be abolished. On that issue, in what the leading historian of the emancipation in Tver has called "a tour de force," Unkovskii and Golovachev convinced the Tver nobility to approve the most progressive plan for emancipation to be submitted by any provincial committee. Obligatory redemption of a substantial land allotment, immediate abolition of all control by lords over peasants, and a very brief period of transition before the former serfs would receive full civil liberties and control over their lives—all were a part of their program at a time when many nobles opposed giving the serfs anything but personal freedom.[69]

Although the program set down by Unkovskii and Golovachev remained the benchmark against which Russian liberalism would be measured throughout the Great Reform era, the Tver nobility were not alone among Russia's lords in supporting an emancipation that would transform their nation's servile population into responsible citizens. Minority reports submitted by progressive lords in the provinces of Kaluga, Vladimir, Nizhnii-Novgorod, Kharkov, Tula, Samara, and Riazan all embraced substantial parts of those liberal emancipation programs that had been circulating in Russia since 1855. A number of prominent advocates defended that position in hostile provincial committees during 1858 and 1859. Prince Vladimir Cherkasskii and Iurii Samarin, who moved easily in a circle that encompassed the salon of the Grand Duchess Elena Pavlovna, St. Petersburg's enlightened bureaucrats, and the Slavophiles of Moscow, spoke for the liberal program in Samara and Tula provinces. As a provincial governor, Konstantin Grot, a friend of Nikolai Miliutin and Zablotskii, helped Samarin to argue the case for a liberal emancipation program in Samara, while Aleksandr Koshelev, a longtime friend of Samarin and Cherkasskii, did so in Riazan. Dmitrii Khrushchev, a confidant of the Grand Duchess Elena Pavlovna, supported the program in Kharkov, and Dmitrii Rovinskii, an expert on jurisprudence who later helped to draft the judicial reforms of 1864, spoke for a liberal emancipation settlement in the hostile climate of Moscow.[70] Cherkasskii and Samarin soon appeared in even more prominent positions as members of the Editing Commissions that drafted the Emancipation Acts in 1859–60.

The men who defended a liberal emancipation program had no better understanding of rural economy or national economic interest than their opponents. More the product of ideas and education than of economic interests murkily perceived, their program incorporated what Emmons has called "a whole climate of opinion"[71] that drew on the teachings that Russia's best-educated provincial lords had assimilated while attending the universities and elite schools that their sovereigns had founded to prepare them for their nation's service. The program of Westernization that Peter the Great had imposed on his backward nation at the beginning of the eighteenth century finally had completed its mission. Serf-owning lords educated in liberal European thought now led the way in seeking to wipe away the institution on which the economic well-being of their class had rested for centuries. Except in Tver, the majority of their associates did not share their commitment to the ideas that had shaped modern Europe. Some preferred a landless emancipation in which they would exercise extensive patrimonial authority over their former serfs. Others favored freeing the serfs with land so long as they received adequate financial compensation. Most lords defended their interests as best they could, although very few knew enough about the productivity of their lands, the costs of production, and the comparative advantages of serf and free labor to make informed decisions. The emancipation proposals that they prepared therefore included widely divergent schemes, supported by data whose accuracy was completely open to question.

Russia was living through difficult times and faced an uncertain future. Although Alexander II at one time had indicated that different conditions could apply in different provinces, the imperial orders of October and December 1858 made it clear that he had begun to think in terms of more uniform legislation. Supported by Kavelin's eloquent pen, Miliutin and Solov'ev had been championing that view within the central government for the better part of a year and urged that the proposals drafted by the provincial committees should serve only as raw material from which a commission of experts and progressive officials would draft a single emancipation decree.[72] At Rostovtsev's urging, Alexander II moved decisively in that same direction at the beginning of 1859.

The key to this major shift in policy lay in the relationship that Rostovtsev had developed with Petr Semenov, a young and distant relative, who had just returned from two years spent as an explorer in the Tien-Shan mountains in Central Asia. A newcomer to St. Petersburg's world of bureaucratic intrigue and, like Rostovtsev, a man who believed that the emperor's will must be served, Semenov helped Rostovtsev prepare summaries and evaluations of the emancipation proposals that provincial committees had begun to submit to the emperor. Convinced of Semenov's rare ability to remain detached from the hotly contested issues of the emancipation debate while he applied his obvious talent for organizing and summarizing the complex materials that related to it, Rostovtsev had begun to rely heavily on him before the end of 1858.[73]

Thirty-one when he became Rostovtsev's assistant, Semenov had studied with some of the leading scientists at the universities of St. Petersburg and Berlin. He had explored the Alps and the volcanic craters of Italy and had translated Karl von Ritter's treatise (annotated from von Ritter's own lectures) on *The Physical Geography of Asia*. His fascination with geography had drawn him into the Imperial Russian Geographical Society, where he had grown comfortable in the company of Zablotskii (whose daughter he married), Kavelin, and the Miliutin brothers. Thanks to them and to his closest friend Nikolai Danilevskii, Semenov had moved freely in a broad intellectual circle that included the editor Kraevskii, the critic Belinskii, and the young writers Saltykov-Shchedrin and Dostoevskii.[74] During the early 1850s, he had studied serf life more closely and had concluded that Russia's provincial lords had developed "such base instincts that nothing could restrain them" when it came to exploiting their serfs' labor. The abolition of serfdom, he had concluded then, could only come about through "the will of the Tsar."[75]

The ideas that had led Russia's intelligentsia to urge emancipation thus were a part of Semenov's daily world, and, although he retained a scholar's detachment from the debate that they engendered, he brought them within Rostovtsev's reach. When Rostovtsev asked him to prepare a plan to shape the contradictory mass of emancipation proposals being prepared by Russia's provincial committees, Semenov therefore presented a view that was as much Kavelin's, Miliutin's, and Solov'ev's as his own. Like them, he recommended that Russia have a single emancipation statute and that an editing commission be organized with separate sections to deal with legal, economic, and administrative questions. Also like them, he urged that representatives of the provincial nobility be allowed to comment on the draft statute only when it could be presented to them in complete form.[76]

These views supplied the principles that Alexander II used to establish the Editing Commission under Rostovtsev's authority on February 17, 1859.[77] Because his life as an imperial adjutant and inspector of military schools had left him unacquainted with many of the middle and upper level personnel in Russia's central government, Rostovtsev turned to Semenov for recommendations about who could best serve as the commission's members. Only recently returned to St. Petersburg after more than six years of study in Europe and exploration in Central Asia, Semenov drew most of his nominations from the Geographical Society and the progressive intelligentsia, the two

groups in the capital he knew best.[78] Nowhere else in the central
government could men be found who knew life in Russia's provinces as did these men. Nor could men be found who were
more experienced in focusing the resources of separate agencies
on a common task in a bureaucracy in which most department
heads jealously guarded the resources under their control.

Led by Miliutin, Solov'ev, Samarin, and Cherkasskii, the quar-
tet whom Prince Dmitrii Obolenskii once called "the soul of the
Editing Commission," Semenov's nominees formed a bloc of
eighteen in the Editing Commission.[79] Supported by a satellite
group of five sympathizers, they dominated the emancipation
debate, especially when Rostovtsev divided the commission into
administrative, legal, and economic sections in April.[80] Only in
the Economic Section, the Editing Commission's largest and the
one that Semenov described as "the main laboratory designated
for deciding the most major and complex questions,"[81] can we
peer behind the curtain of silence drawn around what went on
in these meetings, but even the brief glimpse allowed by the
meager sources tells us that, although they sometimes differed
on details, these men unfailingly joined to defend the basic
principles that they believed an emancipation must include.

To accommodate Miliutin's habit of working until daybreak
and sleeping until midafternoon, the Economic Section usually
met after dinner and worked until dawn.[82] Mastery of bureaucratic procedure had taught the section's leaders the importance
of caution, precision, and consistency, and they acted accordingly.[83] This came naturally to Miliutin and Solov'ev. For Samarin, who had served as an official of special commissions in
Miliutin's Economic Department during the 1840s, this was, if
not natural, at least convenient. To Cherkasskii, an urbane lord
who knew the salons of Moscow and St. Petersburg but had no
experience in government, such tactics seemed awkward and
offensive. His nobleman's distrust of government officials made
him suspicious of the motives that guided Miliutin and Solov'ev,
and it was not until the summer of 1859 that the key alliance
between Miliutin, Samarin, and Cherkasskii that would domi-
nate debate in the plenary sessions of the Editing Commission
was cemented.[84]

When debate moved from the Editing Commission's separate
sections to its plenary sessions on May 4, 1859, Rostovtsev reminded its members that "the liberation of the peasants ought

to proceed from the serfowners as specified in the rescripts [that had called the provincial committees into being]."[85] That injunction proved to be more a matter of form than of substance as the supporters of an emancipation summarized the provincial committee proposals at the beginning of their reports to the plenary session, lamented their many contradictions, and then set down their own views on emancipation to settle conflicts that could not otherwise be resolved. In this way, and by voting as a bloc on key issues, the enlightened bureaucrats and their allies silenced the great lords of Russia who sat on the Editing Commission. "Here it is very difficult to express one's opinion even though it might be a very just and sensible one," Rostovtsev's onetime friend Mikhail Pozen complained at one point. "Taking the opportunity of free expression away from the minority of members," he added, "the economic section [where the Miliutin-Cherkasskii-Samarin alliance had centered its strength] does what it wants to do."[86]

By mid-1859, the lords on the Editing Commission had more to complain about than the fact of emancipation itself. As Stephen Hoch has shown in his startling recent study, the government's ill-advised decisions to finance Russian railroad construction and river steamship development with private capital had produced a banking crisis of such dimensions that the emperor's advisers had to rethink drastically their commitment to a government-supported redemption program.[87] The key expression of this new austerity had been the formation in the Editing Commission of a fourth section, a Financial Section, in April 1859. Led by Evgenii Lamanskii, Iurii Gagemeister, Miliutin, and the future finance ministers Reitern and Bunge, all of whom had worked together in the Geographical Society in the early 1850s, the Financial Section had quickly committed itself to the principle that the redemption of land for Russia's peasants must be a self-sustaining process. Russia's peasants would have to bear the entire cost of whatever funds the government advanced to their former masters to redeem their allotments.

These decisions placed a heavy financial burden on Russia's nobles by requiring that all loans for which serfs had been posted as collateral must be deducted from any sums the government advanced in the coming emancipation settlement. Over the next forty years, the Financial Section's decisions would place an even heavier burden on Russia's former serfs by requiring them to pay the entire cost of their land's redemption and by limiting their ability to acquire new holdings. Even in those cases in which Russia's lords were willing to grant larger allotments to former serfs, the Financial Section insisted that the amount of land for which government-arranged credit could be obtained must be limited in order to control the amount of redemption paper that would be put into circulation. Certainly this was the reformers' least attractive contribution to the emancipation settlement. Placing the interests of the state ahead of all individual or group concerns, they proceeded to impose this austere settlement on the reluctant lords of the Editing Commissions despite the complaints of Pozen and his allies.

Almost always prepared to subordinate differences of opinion among themselves to the higher purpose of defending the larger principles upon which they already had agreed, the men who followed Miliutin, Samarin, and Cherkasskii made it possible for Rostovtsev to declare on September 5, 1859, that the Editing Commission had completed a full draft of the Emancipation Acts and was ready to consider comments from deputies whom the provincial committees of the nobility would be invited to send to the capital. Certain that these comments would be hostile, and anxious to shield their work against such an attack, Solov'ev and Miliutin urged that the commission's consultations with the nobility be as perfunctory as possible. At a meeting to which Miliutin and Solov'ev invited only Samarin, Cherkasskii, and three others, they agreed to allow the provincial deputies to express personal opinions about only those questions on which Rostovtsev chose to seek their advice, and convinced Rostovtsev to present that view to the emperor.[88] Once Alexander had agreed to Rostovtsev's proposal, it came down to what one deputy called a "dialogue between the chickens and the cook."[89] To be summoned in two groups, the first in the fall of 1859 and the second at the beginning of 1860, the deputies could comment, consult among themselves, and testify before the Editing Commission whenever that body consented to hear them but their efforts seemed destined to have very little impact.

Although carefully laid, these plans went awry very soon after the deputies of the "First Summons" began their discussions with the Editing Commission on September 30. When Rostovtsev became critically ill that fall and could no longer preside at the commission's plenary sessions or continue his daily reports to the emperor, the emancipation's advocates lost their first and best defense against the flood of petitions that were pouring into the Winter Palace to condemn the proposed emancipation settlement. Grand Duchess Elena Pavlovna's efforts to arrange meetings between Miliutin, Cherkasskii, and the emperor at her salon helped to provide a stopgap defense of the Editing Commission's work, yet a man such as Miliutin could never replace Rostovtsev in Alexander's confidence. Alexander had accepted every major proposal about emancipation that Rostovtsev had made since the fall of 1858; Miliutin, friend of the "reds" Kavelin and Solov'ev, who, in the spring of 1858, had supported Herzen's attack on Rostovtsev, remained a red in his emperor's eyes.[90]

To Kavelin, Miliutin, Solov'ev, and their allies on the Editing Commission, Rostovtsev's death on February 6, 1860, from a gangrenous carbuncular infection in his neck cast a dark cloud over the future of the emancipation work.[91] Six days later, that cloud grew darker when the emperor named Count V. N. Panin as Rostovtsev's successor. One of the greatest lords in the empire, with vast estates and more than twenty thousand serfs, Panin was widely viewed as a reactionary who opposed emancipation in any form. "Count Panin's outlook is well known," Nikitenko wrote in his diary when he heard the news. "He has continually stood against all progress—intellectual, material, juridical, in general, everything. . . . One can't help feeling," he concluded, "that much that was splendid died with Rostovtsev."[92] Had Rostovtsev's death shaken the emperor's resolve to pursue the "systematic improvement of the serfs' way of life" to an emancipation? Had Rostovtsev's struggle during his last days of life to produce a final statement of principles to guide his emperor been in vain? To progressives and conservatives alike, Alexander's choice of Panin seemed to answer both questions in the affirmative.

Yet Panin had virtues that only his emperor and Rostovtsev (who evidently had recommended him as his successor) recognized.[93] Dry, cold, and dedicated to the bureaucratic process, Panin was known to believe in strict subordination and the complete subjection of imperial servitors to their emperor's will. "If the Emperor has a view different from mine," he once explained to Grand Duke Konstantin Nikolaevich, "then I consider it my duty to abandon my convictions immediately and to work against them with the same or even greater energy than if I were acting according to my own views."[94] Here was the quintessential bureaucrat who believed that every man must bow to higher authority. Alexander thought him the best choice to defend Rostovtsev's program against the attacks of Russia's self-interested lords. Panin, he explained to one of his confidants, "[is] an honest and devoted man who, I hope, will be able to bring the task [of drafting an emancipation statute] to its designated goal without paying attention to all the intrigues and vengeance, of which, unfortunately, there is no lack."[95]

Despite Alexander's hopes, Panin's dedication had its limits and his presidency brought renewed conflict to the emancipation debate. Panin did not remain entirely faithful to his pledge to defend the principles that Rostovtsev had put into place, and he questioned a number of key points in the proposed settlement just as the deputies of the "Second Summons" arrived in St. Petersburg. Quick to learn of the conflict between Panin and the supporters of an emancipation on the Editing Commission, these deputies organized what Daniel Field has called "the most coherent and powerful of all attacks" on the Editing Commission's work.[96] The emancipation proposals, the provincial delegates stated, "undoubtedly will destroy the fundamental principle of the inviolability of property, excessively and arbitrarily reducing the landed incomes of the nobles and . . . hindering the freedom of the peasants [by] tying them to the land."[97] Such statements were disconcerting for Alexander to hear, all the more so since Panin himself emphasized the economic damage that an emancipation would mean for Russia's first estate. As the emperor jotted "I also share these fears" and "How to escape the difficulty?" in the margins of a memorandum in which Panin reported his disagreements with the Editing Commission majority, it seemed that, without Rostovtsev, the emancipation might be in danger.[98]

Clearly, Alexander sympathized with the difficulties that emancipation might impose on Russia's nobility, but he held firmly to the principles upon which he and Rostovtsev had agreed. Once the Editing Commission completed its work in September 1860, the only hope that remained for its opponents was that the great lords on the Main Committee and the State Council would convince their emperor to modify its proposals.

To some, that still seemed a real possibility, for, although Alexander had committed himself publicly to Rostovtsev, he had not done so with the Editing Commission or the program that the men allied with Miliutin, Cherkasskii, and Samarin continued to champion. Indeed, in thanking the Editing Commission for its "enormous" efforts, Alexander added: "Of course every work done by man has its imperfections. You know this yourselves and I know it very well. Perhaps it will be necessary to change *much*. But, in any event, the honor of the first effort belongs to you."[99] Clearly such words conveyed the sense that, whatever its strengths and however well it reflected the principles to which Rostovtsev had adhered, the work of the Editing Commission had set nothing in final form.

Although none dared stand openly against him, bureaucrats, provincial squires, and great lords continued to set forth wildly divergent interpretations of their emperor's views about emancipation and continued to debate who could best fulfill his will until the very end. Only when Alexander rejected the last efforts of the State Council to make emancipation more advantageous for the nobility in early 1861 did he openly commit himself to the principles that the supporters of Miliutin, Samarin, and Cherkasskii had defended throughout the arduous debates in the Editing Commission. "Further delay can only arouse passions and lead to the most dangerous and disastrous consequences for the country in general and for the serfowners in particular," the emperor told the State Council then. "There is nothing more that we can do to protect the interests of the serfowners."[100] As word of the great lords' failure to turn the emperor from his path seeped into the countryside, a number of fainthearted squires left their estates and fled abroad for fear that the emancipation would provoke a great serf revolt.[101]

On February 19, 1861, Alexander signed the Emancipation Acts that lifted the yoke of serfdom from 22 million Russian serfs. Everyone expected the worst that day. Soldiers with loaded muskets and with six charges of live ammunition in their cartridge cases patrolled St. Petersburg's streets. Four battalions of infantry, six and a half squadrons of cavalry, and two dozen field guns stood ready to take up positions on the Winter Palace Square at a moment's notice, and the emperor spent the night at his sister's palace with horses and carriages ready in the courtyard. The government so feared a peasant uprising that it did not announce the emancipation until March 5, the first day of the forty-day Lenten fast during which all Orthodox believers were supposed to refrain from alcohol. The manifesto of liberation was first read to Russia's peasants in Vladimir on March 7. Its last reading was in Kishinev, in Bessarabia, on April 2.[102]

Made up of twenty-two enactments published in a large volume of 361 oversized pages, the Emancipation Acts that Alexander signed were bafflingly complex and by no means the panacea for which Russia's apostles of liberation had hoped. During the last stages of the Editing Commission's work, the pressure of Russia's mounting banking crisis had led the Financial Section to insist that only non-*barshchina* estates be included in the first stages of the emancipation's land redemption process, and their prohibition held firm until mid-1862, when serfs who paid *barshchina* (labor duties) rather than *obrok* (payments in cash or kind) were made eligible for the government's limited redemption program.

No longer subject to their lords, Russia's peasants became free to marry, acquire property, and engage in trade as their choice dictated. Yet, if they were no longer enserfed, they were not yet really free. For two years, Russia's former serfs were to continue their *barshchina* and *obrok* payments as they had in former times while the required land charters showing the lands to be occupied by former serfs and the amount of *barshchina* or *obrok* to be paid were drawn up. Then, for up to seven more years, the peasants could be required to remain on their allotments while a final settlement was worked out between former peasants and masters. Only after this had been reviewed by government-appointed rural mediators (*mirovye posredniki*) whose task it was to make certain that the lands occupied by the peasants met the norms established by the Emancipation Acts, would the government pay roughly 80 percent of the capital value of the peasants' allotments to the estate owners. If the redemption agreement met with the peasants' approval, then they were obliged to pay the remainder of the redemption directly to their former master. Otherwise, their former masters had to settle for the amount advanced by the government in the form of bonds and redemption certificates (which later were to be converted to bonds).

Individually, former serfs could accept a so-called beggar's allotment, which was roughly a quarter of the maximum norm and carried no redemption obligation. All other lands transferred to peasant hands were controlled by the peasant commune, which accepted mutual responsibility for meeting the redemption payments that would repay the government for its initial advance over a period of forty-nine years.[103] This saddled communities of former serfs with heavy payments for overpriced land allotments that, they believed, were theirs by right in the first place. At the same time, the preservation of the commune perpetuated the medieval agricultural methods (including three-field tillage and periodic redistribution of the peasants' landholdings) that would continue to retard the development of Russian agriculture into the twentieth century. Certainly, as Emmons and Zaionchkovskii have shown, there seems little reason to doubt that the peasants thought such an emancipation was unjust. Some protested, although very few turned to violence. "Heavy bewilderment and sorrowful disappointment," one provincial governor reported,[104] were the more usual response as Russia's former serfs continued to await the "promised hour" when the tsar's "Golden Charters" would, at last, grant them "real freedom."[105]

There remained the matter of liberating Russia's state peasants and those inscribed on crown lands, the personal estates of the imperial family. On March 1, ten days after Alexander had signed the Emancipation Acts and four days before their first public announcement, Minister of Imperial Crown Lands Count Vladimir Adlerberg prepared a memorandum recommending that "the economic and juridical situation of the crown peasants be made to conform to the Statute of 19 February."[106] Yet, the matter of emancipating the Romanovs' peasants did not move as rapidly as the emperor's comments about the urgency of emancipation for the serfs of the nobility in the winter of 1860–61 might have led observers to expect. Alexander did not announce the liberation of Russia's 1.75 million crown peasants until June 26, 1863, when they received outright ownership of slightly larger holdings of land at a moderately cheaper price. Unlike the Emancipation Acts of 1861, the decree of June 26 provided for the complete liberation of Crown Peasants in two years. Still, like the serfs of the nobility, they received less land than they had used before their liberation. Of the 4,259,833 *desiatiny** of land

---

*A *desiatina* is equivalent to 2.7 acres

they had farmed as crown peasants, they lost 148,158, or about one-tenth of a *desiatina* for each person emancipated.[107]

Although the liberation of the Crown Peasants was announced in June 1863, that of the state peasants did not occur until November 24, 1866. On the whole, state peasants received more land than either former Crown Peasants or serfs, but, for the first twenty years, they received only its use in return for a fixed yearly payment. On June 12, 1886, the government announced the beginning of a redemption program that would allow Russia's former state peasants to obtain full title to their lands in 1931.[108] Not yet willing to admit the absurdity of drawn-out redemption plans, Russia's government in 1896 actually extended the schedule of payments for former serfs into the 1950s in order to compensate for their failure to meet the original program. Only after revolution had lit the flame of revolt in Russia's dark peasant villages and cast the rebellious specter of Pugachev across the land did the government finally cancel all redemption payments on November 3, 1905.[109] By that time, a third of the peasants' land still lay fallow each year. The average yield of grain per acre stood at less than nine bushels while, in England, it had risen above thirty-five.[110] The result was all too predictable. "The poverty of the peasant establishment," a government report concluded in 1902, "is astounding."[111]

## THE *ZEMSTVO* STATUTES

The Crimean defeat and the prospect of emancipation forced the Russians to confront a crisis of undergovernment that had been building in their provinces since the seventeenth century. Collecting taxes, assembling close to a hundred thousand recruits for the army each year, and maintaining order outside the capitals of Moscow and St. Petersburg always had been very difficult for Russia's rulers and the officials who served them, but the post-Crimean pressure to compete with the rapidly industrializing nations of Europe, coupled with the impending need to take responsibility for 22 million about-to-be emancipated serfs, transformed that chronic malaise into an acute illness. How could a sparsely populated empire spread across some 8.5 million square miles of territory be governed when there were too few officials in its provinces and its people had no experience? How could millions of former serfs be incorporated into the Russian body politic and assured of fair treatment under the law? And how could Russia's government maintain its administrative ties with the masses to ensure adequate national defense and tax collection?

Plagued by a shortage of officials in their empire's provinces, Russian autocrats since the time of Peter the Great had relied on army units and local lords to assemble recruits and collect taxes. Such de facto officials had failed to confront the deeper political and economic crises brought on by chronic undergovernment and, during the middle of the eighteenth century, heavier tax burdens had led to more frequent peasant revolts. In 1773–74, these had culminated in the "peasant war" of Emelian Pugachev, during which more than a hundred thousand Cossacks, Old Believers, and serfs had rampaged across close to half a million square miles of lands in the southeastern quadrant of European Russia. For more than a year, a fearsome mass of Russians had raged out of control before Catherine II and her generals had found the means to contain them. Determined that the *pugachevshchina* must never recur, Catherine and her advisers knew that a means had to be found to strengthen the connections between government and governed in Russia.

Convinced that failed efforts to govern the provinces from the center had been the cause of Pugachev's success, Catherine had concentrated so much authority in the hands of fifty newly appointed provincial governors that large portions of Russia's central government became redundant. Beyond that, she had shifted much responsibility for rural affairs into the hands of local lords chosen by newly established district and provincial assemblies of the nobility. For the first time, as the leading authority on the well-ordered police state in Russia has explained, "the Russian provinces and countryside had acquired the means of keeping peace and effectively maintaining law and order."[112] Although this gave the central government the potential to touch the daily lives of provincial Russians as it never had before, it had neither the instruments nor the resources to do so.[113] Russia's provinces continued to be undergoverned and their administration understaffed. Only the fact that local nobles continued to take responsibility for the third of the empire's population that lived on their estates prevented the government from being overwhelmed by the burdens of administering its provinces.

Russia's new provincial institutions had only just been put into place when Catherine's son, Paul I, had begun to shift the balance of administrative authority in the other direction. Paul experimented with more effective central government institutions, removed some of the authority from the hands of his mother's governors, and replaced a number of key elected local officials with appointed ones. But Paul fell beneath the hands of assassins before these measures had much effect, and it remained for his son, Alexander I, to confront the problems that Catherine's provincial reforms had created at the center of Russia's government. As he concentrated on repairing the disorder that his grandmother's provincial legislation had produced in Russia's central government, Alexander carried his father's centralization further, but his effort produced mixed results. Although he weakened the authority of Catherine's governors by giving Russia's central ministries control over finances, police, education, and transportation in the provinces, Alexander did not give these newly established institutions sufficient resources to fulfill such responsibilities.

The problems of extending the autocrat's authority into Russia's provinces and finding a means to mobilize centralized resources to meet local needs thus remained unresolved when Napoleon invaded Russia in 1812, and there were few instruments in Russia's central government that could repair the devastation that the Grand Army left in its wake when it retreated at the end of the year. Then, as European affairs began to absorb Alexander's attention during the second half of his reign, neither he nor his advisers paid sufficient attention to the economic and administrative crises that were taking shape in the provinces. A number of Decembrists had spoken with particular urgency about those failings when they had testified before the Imperial Investigating Commission in 1826,[114] and Nicholas I had faced the problem of Russia's foundering provincial administration from the moment he ascended the throne.

Although the ideal of effective centralized decision making remained little more than a cruel delusion in a vast empire that had terrible roads, less than six hundred miles (at midcentury) of railroads, and a climate that left the land covered with snow or mud for almost two-thirds of the year, Nicholas had continued to emphasize centralization in all aspects of administration and government. His effort to develop a strong bureaucratic regime on the local level succeeded only in the formal sense of creating new hierarchies of provincial offices that slowed the process of government and left everything to be decided in the capital.[115] As everything flowed from the provinces toward St. Petersburg during the 1830s and 1840s, provincial government became paralyzed. When the governor-general of the Baltic provinces could not order a faulty flue in his office to be repaired on the spot but had to wait more than a fortnight for the necessary official documents to be processed in St. Petersburg, it was clear that the centralization of Russia's provincial government had gotten seriously out of hand.[116]

So had the flood of official documents that flowed between St. Petersburg and the provinces. It had required twenty-four reports to put the matter of fixing the governor-general's flue in Riga to rest,[117] but other undertakings required many more. Local and provincial authorities had to produce no fewer than 135 separate documents whenever a nobleman decided to sell a parcel of land,[118] and the fact that no public official could travel through the province in which he worked without a special pass meant that some 20,000 such documents had to be issued by local authorities in each province every year.[119] At midcentury, the Ministry of Internal Affairs requested 16,697,421 reports and communications each year from Russia's provincial offices. A sea of paper swirled around the desks of overworked clerks in understaffed provincial chanceries as frantic officials tried to comply with the central government's demands. In theory, everything worked according to fixed routines in these offices; in fact, provincial administration was chaotic, as desperate officials responded to the pressures of the moment without much concern for procedures or the long-term effects of their actions. Small wonder that, when Nikolai Miliutin's officials of special commissions went into the provinces to compile information about governing Russia on the local level, they found it all but impossible to sort out the files in local archives and unscramble their contents.[120]

Information simply was not available because no one could unravel the tangle of papers, misfiled documents, and improperly prepared reports that clogged local government files.[121] In some places officials had so long since ceased to try that, in one county in Kiev Province, the administration actually functioned for two decades without any office facilities.[122] Nor was the province of Kiev a striking exception. Aghast at what he found in Vladimir Province, whose capital stood less than 120 miles from Moscow, Senator Kastor Lebedev wrote that "it is a wonder that there is any government left here at all."[123] Even in Russia's capital, the authorities could not determine the assessed value of any particular piece of property in 1845.[124] No one could even state with certainty how many people lived in the province of St. Petersburg.

Although the lines of authority upon which local administration depended had become heavily centralized by the middle of the nineteenth century, Russia's central government could not supply even a bare minimum of the services that provincial Russians required. Large sums were allocated to build hospitals, repair roads, and construct public works, but there were bridges whose pilings were never constructed, hospitals whose walls never rose from the foundations, and roads that were never built even though the government collected more than 12 million rubles in local taxes annually at midcentury.[125] Fire fighting, education, public health services, and police all were grossly inadequate for the needs of Russia's provincials, but reprimands from provincial governors supported by stern directives from St. Petersburg could not improve them.

Made by men who had little understanding of the real problems the provinces faced, decisions about local affairs had become too far removed from the people they affected. "No question, however trifling, can be dealt with by the people themselves," Unkovskii complained in 1859 as he pointed out that provincial Russians "dare not repair a miserable bridge or hire an elementary school teacher" without permission from the central government.[126] The certainty that the emancipation would liberate Russia's provincial lords from responsibility for their serfs' care in addition to freeing the serfs from bondage to their masters made this situation all the more desperate. As Russia moved toward the 1860s, the central government had proved that it could not meet the responsibilities that the centralization of the Nicholas system imposed upon it, just as emancipation was about to increase those responsibilities by nearly 50 percent.

Perhaps none sensed the fearsome complexity of this dilemma more clearly than the officials of special commissions (some of whom Rostovtsev depended upon for advice about emancipating Russia's serfs) who had taken part in the studies of Russia's provinces that Nikolai Miliutin's Municipal Section in the Ministry of Internal Affairs had undertaken during the 1840s and 1850s. Known for their conviction that decisions must be made on the basis of accurate information rather than the whims of statesmen, some of these men boasted unparalleled knowledge of local conditions in Russia because they had worked in the provinces for years at a time. Miliutin's close friend Aleksandr Giers had spent over two years in Iaroslavl, as had his colleague A. K. Sivers. Konstantin Veselovskii had worked for more than a year in Mogilёv, young Count Dmitrii Tolstoi had spent two years in Voronezh, and Adolf Shtakel'berg, one of Miliutin's first recruits in the Municipal Section, had served for nearly all of the decade between 1842 and 1851 in the Baltic provinces.[127]

These men knew all too well that Gogol' had based his dismal portrait of provincial bureaucratic life on fact, and they knew the wretched state of the empire's communications.[128] It was no secret that a letter sent from Orenburg—on the western fringe of Siberia and only a quarter of the distance to Russia's Pacific shores—took six weeks to reach St. Petersburg,[129] but to men like Iurii Samarin and Shtakel'berg, who had waited for months to receive their pay and food allowances in the nearby Baltic provinces, the glacial slowness of Russia's communications was a matter of sad firsthand experience.[130] As Russia moved toward the opening of the Great Reform era, these men knew that the central government could never respond quickly to a crisis in an outlying region of the empire, and that it simply could not support the burden that 22 million liberated serfs would add to its responsibilities.

Such officials knew well the problems that provincial government faced in Russia, but they could not command a hearing in high places. What drew senior statesmen's attention more directly to the crisis of provincial government at the end of the Crimean War was the strong support that Russia's overworked, undersupported provincial governors themselves expressed for reform. "Which of our governors," Petr Valuev asked after he completed his assignment as governor of Courland, "can carry out properly and precisely all the duties entrusted to him?"[131] Without adequate staff or even enough clerical help, Russia's governors struggled in those days to coordinate the work of some eighteen agencies and prepare all the reports and communications required by the Ministry of Internal Affairs in St.

Petersburg through which, by midcentury, the staggering total of 31 million documents circulated every year.[132] "The essential work of a governor of a province disappears in a mass of details," wrote Viktor Artsimovich, whose call for reform rang out even more urgently from Tobolsk than had Valuev's from Riga. Details of centralized administration so thoroughly overwhelmed provincial government during the Crimean War that, in 1859, Governor-General Prince Ilarion Vasil'chikov calculated that he would need at least five hundred new clerks to stabilize administration in the province of Kiev.[133]

The governors' urgent calls for reform led Minister of Internal Affairs Lanskoi to press a program of limited decentralization on the emperor. On October 21, 1856, Alexander II proclaimed that Russia's governors were to have more autonomy and greater opportunity to exercise personal initiative.[134] That same month, Lanskoi began to consult some two dozen governors and five governors-general whose annual reports had shown an interest in improving provincial government, and he found strong support for further decentralization among them. These men repeatedly challenged the control of the Ministry of State Domains over state peasant affairs, the Ministry of Finance's over local treasury offices, the central Postal Department's over provincial mails, and the War Ministry's over local garrison commanders. Taken together, the governors' replies to Lanskoi's queries posed a serious challenge to the entire provincial system of Nicholas I.[135]

The hostile responses that Lanskoi received from his fellow ministers when he circulated the governors' remarks indicated that they were unwilling to consider limiting their authority in the provinces. Once the Secret Committee began to discuss emancipation, Russia's senior statesmen feared that any lessening of central authority might leave the government unable to control the "rural proletariat" that an emancipation without land (which most nobles and high officials favored at that point) seemed destined to produce. Certainly a concern for domestic security dominated the two proposals that Minister of State Domains Mikhail Murav'ev submitted to the Secret Committee (renamed the Main Committee in January) during winter and spring 1858.[136] That same concern to defend Russia against peasant unrest that, according to a number of estimates, seemed to be rising dramatically[137] accounted for Alexander II's support of Murav'ev's proposals, even though they went directly against the plans for decentralization that he had encouraged Lanskoi to explore with Russia's governors the year before.

The first of Murav'ev's proposals advocated dividing Russia into eight sprawling civil and military districts, each under the command of a military governor-general of the type that had been abolished in 1852 except in Russia's border regions. With power to overrule civil officials and provincial governors, such governors-general would have wielded immense authority and would have transformed the civil governors into impotent civil functionaries. At the same time, Murav'ev proposed that a *uezdnyi nachal'nik* (district chief) be appointed in each district of every province and that this small army of new officials report to the ministers collectively, not to the Minister of Internal Affairs. In both cases, Murav'ev's proposed officials would stand outside the regular structure of Russia's provincial administration and would undercut the authority of those provincial governors who had supported decentralization. With only Lanskoi to speak against Murav'ev's plans (Konstantin Nikolaevich was abroad at the time), the Main Committee approved them on May 16, 1858. Supported by the emperor, the Main Committee's action seemed to reverse the move toward decentralization that Russia's governors had cheered in their replies to Lanskoi's inquiries eighteen months before.

Standing at the very top of Russia's administrative hierarchy, the Main Committee saw little of what went on in the government below it, where other forces were working to undercut Murav'ev's triumph. Unlike his ministerial colleagues on the Main Committee, Lanskoi had a rare willingness to delegate authority to the educated men who were his subordinates, and, as Petr Valuev, his successor as minister of internal affairs and one of his leading opponents, once remarked, he readily drew such men directly into Russia's legislative process. "Of secondary status in terms of their service position," Valuev explained in his diary, "these officials outshone their superiors in intellect and ability, and they were not slow to make use of that superiority."[138] In the matter of reforming Russia's provincial administration, Valuev referred to the enlightened bureaucrats led by Miliutin and Solov'ev upon whom Lanskoi already had begun to rely for advice and support in peasant affairs. While Miliutin condemned the proposed governors-general as "pashas or satraps," Solov'ev insisted that the failings of provincial administration could be

corrected more easily by allowing provincial governors to exercise their authority than by creating new officials to usurp their
power.[139]

Aided by Viktor Artsimovich, who recently had resigned his
post as governor of Tobolsk to protest interference by the governor-
general of western Siberia, Miliutin and Solov'ev drafted a
memorandum in which they condemned Murav'ev's proposed
governors-general and urged the emperor to give Russia's provincial governors the personnel and resources needed to function
effectively.[140] This did not mean that they—or Lanskoi when
he accepted their views and presented them to the emperor as
his own—had greater faith in the ability of Russia's provincials
to govern themselves than did their opponents. Nor did it mean
that they were willing to place the destiny of Russia's provinces
in the hands of the nobles who inevitably would emerge to play
an influential role in any program of decentralization. In their
view, the central government's authority must remain uncom-
promised, but it had to be exercised in a different—and more
effective—manner. The increased resources and personnel for
which they called could enable Russia's governors to deal with
Russia's provincials more directly than ever before while the
Ministry of Internal Affairs would continue to deal with the
governors.

Convinced that only a careful reconcentration of administrative authority in the provinces could halt the breakdown of
provincial government in Russia, Lanskoi carried the views of
Miliutin, Artsimovich, and Solov'ev to the emperor.[141] He received a cool reception from a sovereign who had grown suspicious of Lanskoi's counselors and criticized the memorandum
he presented on August 1, 1858, as "a chancery view . . . completely at odds with my own."[142] Yet, when Lanskoi offered to
resign, Alexander retreated, asked him to remain, reversed his
position, and withdrew his support for Murav'ev's plan to place
Russia under the command of governors-general.[143] At the same
time, he turned away from Murav'ev's proposal to scatter *uezdnye
nachal'niki* across Russia, for Lanskoi's clever ploy of inviting the
provincial governors to comment on Murav'ev's plan had stirred
a hornet's nest of protest. With thirty-nine of forty-six governors
expressing "terror and alarm" at the Main Committee's plan for
subjecting Russia's districts to the rule of *uezdnye nachal'niki*,[144]
Alexander retreated from his support for Murav'ev's second plan.

When, on March 27, 1859, he announced the formation of the Commission on the Reorganization of Provincial and District Institutions, the debate about reforming provincial and district administration began to move along the lines that Miliutin, Solov'ev, and Artsimovich had proposed.[145]

As in the Editing Commission that Alexander had established six weeks earlier, enlightened bureaucrats figured prominently in the Commission on the Reorganization of Provincial and District Institutions. Working under Miliutin's chairmanship, Sergei Zarudnyi, Konstantin Grot, Nikolai Stoianovskii, Nikolai Kalachov, Aleksandr Giers, Artsimovich, and Solov'ev all shared a commitment to renovation and reform in Russia's central government, and all had been a part of the group that had been so prominent in the Russian Geographical Society during the early and mid-1850s.[146] These men dominated this commission even more than they had the Editing Commission, for their earlier experience had made them much more familiar with the dilemmas of provincial administrative reform than with the problems of serfdom. They knew that their emperor expected them to prepare legislation for new institutions of local government in Russia that could be promulgated at the same time as the Emancipation Acts. Given their familiarity with the problems that required their attention and their ability to control the commission, their prospects for preparing the legislation needed to reform provincial and district government in Russia seemed considerably brighter in 1859 than did the chances for an emancipation.

If the Editing Commission moved more quickly and successfully than expected under Rostovtsev's leadership, the Commission on the Reorganization of Provincial and District Institutions moved more slowly. That the Editing Commission claimed the first attention of Miliutin, Kalachov, Giers, and Solov'ev was one factor in slowing the provincial reform commission's work. Perhaps even more important, whereas Alexander had placed the Editing Commission outside the institutional structure of Russia's central government, he had placed the Commission on the Reorganization of Provincial and District Institutions firmly within the Ministry of Internal Affairs, where it had to contend directly with the empire's bureaucracy. It took more than a year for important materials from other agencies to be transferred to the new commission's control, and the Treasury did not even release the funds to pay its operating expenses until the middle of 1860. These were problems that the Editing Commission had been spared by virtue of its extrabureaucratic character.

Its key members finally freed from their responsibilities for drafting an emancipation, the Commission on the Reorganization of Provincial and District Institutions began to function more effectively during the second half of 1860. Then, just as its first major reform proposals, drafted mainly by Solov'ev and designed to take into account the administrative deconcentration that Governor General Prince Ilarion Vasil'chikov had instituted in the provinces of Kiev, Volynia, and Podolia were being prepared in the spring of 1861, the emperor summarily relieved Miliutin of his duties and sent Lanskoi into retirement. Lanskoi's successor, Valuev, insisted that the commission's work required extensive revisions if the new social and economic forces that the emancipation had unleashed were to be harnessed to ensure the survival of autocracy in Russia.[147]

Like Nikolai Miliutin, whose dynamism matched his own but whose stubborn independent-mindedness he could not tolerate in his ministry, Valuev hoped to co-opt the social and intellectual groups that formed the basis of the opposition's support. Yet, because Valuev was a more astute observer of Russia's government than Miliutin, he understood that new institutional instruments would be needed to accomplish that end. Whereas Miliutin hoped "to rally the elite of the country to the government" by means of "timely concessions,"[148] Valuev understood, as Miliutin did not in 1861, that some means must be found to allow the opposition an opportunity to participate in the autocratic political process if the government were "to seize control of the social movement" in the manner he thought necessary.[149] Therefore, in dramatic contrast to Miliutin's pious hope that a "center party" could be brought into being and to Kavelin's belief that only in the "fertile school" of local self-government could responsible citizens "prepare themselves . . . for further, broader political activities,"[150] Valuev advocated a "reform of the State Council on bases analogous to the Austrian *Reichsrat*." Representatives to Valuev's proposed consultative body would be elected mainly by those *zemstva*, those institutions of local self-government, that were about to emerge from the deliberations of the Commission on the Reorganization of Provincial and District Institutions.[151]

On the question of reforming Russia's provincial administration, Valuev believed that, although ministerial authority could be decentralized, the power of autocracy must remain undiluted and inviolable.[152] This meant that, although he might hope that Russia would one day have a "Congress of State Representatives," Valuev would not permit the nobility to preempt his ministry's authority over the Russian countryside even though Russia's nobles had made it clear that they expected to be compensated for their loss of economic control over their serfs by strengthening their influence in provincial affairs. For many Russian lords, such cooperation was simply a matter of self-interest, but few hoped to transform provincial life into a modern citizen society in which men from all classes would share responsibility for their destiny. The Tver nobility took that view when it met in its provincial assembly at the beginning of February 1862. "It goes without saying," these men had written in mid-1861, "that it is wrong to enjoy public rights without having any public obligations."[153] At the beginning of 1862, they had added that "only through the active participation of society through its elected representatives" could "a satisfactory solution" to the problems of district and provincial administration, "on which the welfare of the whole nation depends, be expected." Now, as they assembled at the beginning of February, they called for "the gathering of representatives from the entire people without distinction as to class."[154]

Coupled with conservative nobles' call for "the summoning of elected representatives from all the Russian land" into a national assembly and what Emmons has called the "Constitutionalist Campaign" of 1862,[155] such demands attacked those very foundations of autocracy that Valuev thought essential to Russia's survival. Yet he was not ready to replace nobles with peasants as the administrators of Russia's countryside. "The masses can be compared with sand, not solid ground," he later argued. "Only property in larger quantity, landed property that ties the owner to a specific region," he insisted, could make men responsible participants in local government.[156] Valuev therefore insisted on modifications in the new proposals for draft *zemstvo* legislation that Solov'ev and the Commission on the Reorganization of Provincial and District Institutions had submitted on March 9, 1862. Property qualifications for participation in provincial assemblies, he argued at two meetings of the commission in mid-March 1862, should be doubled in order to place Russia's aristocrats firmly in control of the empire's provincial and district institutions.[157]

Although the emperor supported his efforts to broaden noble participation in local government at the expense of Russia's peasants, Valuev faced strong opposition in a select committee chaired by Grand Duke Konstantin Nikolaevich that had been formed at the beginning of 1862 to discuss the commission's modified *zemstvo* proposals. Supported in his efforts to defend the peasants' interests by Mikhail Reitern, Aleksandr Golovnin, and Konstantin Chevkin, Konstantin Nikolaevich opposed Count Panin, Valuev, and Baron Modest Korf during the spring of 1862 in a series of debates that at first seemed to go in his favor, especially after Nikolai Miliutin unexpectedly returned to the capital that spring.[158] Ever since the emperor had sent Miliutin into retirement, Konstantin Nikolaevich, Golovnin, and Reitern had worked to return him to the battles that raged on Petersburg's bureaucratic front. There had been rumors during the Christmas holidays of 1861 that Miliutin would return at the beginning of the new year,[159] and, in April, Alexander had summoned him to St. Petersburg for the official purpose of discussing the possibility of appointing him director-in-chief of civil administration in Russian Poland. Miliutin thus returned to St. Petersburg just as the debate in Konstantin Nikolaevich's select committee reached a decisive stage.

In a memorandum written the next month, Miliutin defended Solov'ev's proposals for broad participation by Russia's newly freed peasants in the *zemstva*. "The most vital state interests . . . urgently demand that the new rural institutions . . . be given an effective and serious meaning," he insisted. Local self-government, in which "elected officials are empowered by law to undertake independent and serious activity," Miliutin argued, would free Russia's overburdened central administration of "moral responsibility for petty and distant abuses, a responsibility not in keeping with the true meaning and dignity of the state power." More than that, local self-government could "better serve to counteract anarchistic intellectual ferment" in Russia by offering a practical course of action and a legitimate means for developing a desperately needed sense of civic responsibility.[160] Soon after he wrote this defense, Miliutin returned to the West. A month later, the Council of Ministers supported a broader definition of the functions of the *zemstva,* and Alexander approved their position on June 2, 1862.[161]

The issue was by no means settled despite the apparent victory of Konstantin Nikolaevich and his supporters. In the next few months the grand duke failed to bring peace to Poland as the revolution that burst out in January 1863 signaled the failure of his moderate policies as that region's newly appointed viceroy.[162] Then, as advocates of aristocratic constitutionalism and those who feared the rising revolutionary movement in Poland attacked the draft *zemstvo* statutes, Valuev urged that the *zemstva* be connected much more closely to regular provincial government offices, that their executive powers be narrowed, that their power to tax be further limited, and that many of the more important administrative functions assigned to them by the draft legislation (including control over welfare and local grain reserves) be transferred to provincial authorities appointed by the central government.[163] Solov'ev, the architect of the draft *zemstvo* statutes, had neither the prestige nor the institutional power base to challenge Valuev in St. Petersburg, and Reitern, who now ruled the Ministry of Finance, was scarcely Valuev's equal in the politics of interministerial conflict.

Valuev faced more serious opposition during the summer of 1863 from Baron Korf, chief of the Second Section of His Majesty's Own Chancery. Once the preserve of Speranskii, the great codifier of Russia's laws, this office gave Korf, a man who viewed the emancipation of the Russian serfs as an act of supreme benevolence by the Russian nobility, a powerful base from which to pose as custodian of legality in Russia.[164] A devoted and dutiful servant of Russia's autocrats, Korf consistently criticized ministers who seemed to take too much power for themselves, and his treatment of Valuev in 1863 was no exception. He therefore prepared a lengthy criticism of the draft *zemstvo* statutes that attacked Valuev for seeking to "alter the most fundamental conditions of our system of local government, destroy its old bases and rebuild it on principles that are almost completely foreign to it—that is, decentralization and self-government."[165] Korf criticized Valuev's rigid distinction between noble and non-noble landlords and between city and peasant village in defining the *zemstvo* electorate. Most telling of all, he criticized his intention to keep the *zemstva* completely under the control of the Ministry of Internal Affairs.[166]

Clearly Valuev was more than Korf's equal in any political confrontation, but Korf's attack had given other opponents a wedge with which to open the way to further criticism. In the State Council's Combined Departments of Law and State Economy, Nikolai Bakhtin, whose call for *zakonnost'* in government in 1856 had been important in initiating the debate on decentralization and self-government,[167] now joined the attack, as did the former minister of public instruction, Egor Kovalevskii. In demanding that the *zemstva* be given control over education, public health, and local prisons, both men caught Valuev off guard. A suggestion by Kovalevskii and Reitern that provincial leaders be asked to comment on these questions enabled much of Solovev's proposals to become the basis for the amended *zemstvo* statutes that Alexander II approved on January 1, 1864.[168]

According to the legislation of January 1, 1864, each provincial and county *zemstvo* was to consist of an assembly, whose members would be elected by the local population voting in three separate bodies, one for individual landowners (including nobles, merchants, or members of any other social group so long as they were not peasants), a second for town and city dwellers, and a third for the peasant village communes. For all but peasants, the number of delegates sent to the county *zemstvo* assembly was determined by the amount of land held or, in the case of urban electors, the value of other property; delegates to the peasant electoral body were chosen by their village assembly according to a complex formula that varied from one county to another but was based on the number of allotments held by each peasant commune. County assemblies chose delegates to the higher provincial *zemstvo* assemblies. Delegates at both levels were elected for three-year terms and met once a year. When the *zemstvo* assembly was not in session, an executive board, elected by the *zemstvo* assembly, carried on the business of local government under a chairman whose tenure had to be confirmed, in the case of the district *zemstvo*, by the provincial governor. The chairmen of provincial *zemstvo* boards had to be approved by the minister of internal affairs.

Although the *zemstva* would emerge as an important political force in the countryside by the end of the century, they were brought into being very slowly. The first were established in 1865 but only in nineteen provinces. *Zemstvo* government was implemented in nine more provinces in 1866, and in six more between 1867 and 1875, bringing the total of provinces involved to thirty-four. After that, the organization of Russia's *zemstva* moved much more slowly so that on the eve of World War I, they existed in only forty-three of seventy provinces. Nonetheless, despite these geographical, property, and fiscal limitations, the statutes of 1864 brought into being institutions to replace the patrimonial power of the serf-owning nobility. As limited administrative deconcentration replaced the extreme centralization of the Nicholas era, another major breach in the crumbling edifice of the Nicholas system had been reconstructed with new and different bricks to reinforce the fortress of the Russian autocracy.[169]

### REFORMING RUSSIA'S COURTS

The Judicial Reform Statutes of November 20, 1864, constructed another major part of the edifice that eventually would house a modern citizen society in Russia. Certainly such a reform was needed after 1861 for if Russia's provinces were undergoverned at midcentury because of a shortage of officials, as Frederick Starr has argued, the dispensation of justice was even more poorly served. Left in the hands of serf owners and judicial officials who were untrained in the law, justice had become so capricious, one observer remarked, that Russia "resembled a lake, in the depths of which great fish devoured the smaller ones while, near the surface, everything was calm and glistened smoothly, like a mirror."[170]

Statesmen knew that Russia's judicial system urgently required fundamental renovations, yet that realization did not mean that the coming Judicial Reform Statutes would be so broad in scope or so far-reaching in their consequences. Richard Wortman made it clear more than a decade ago that Alexander II at first set out only to make the dispensation of justice more effective and did not contemplate any fundamental changes in Russia's judicial system.[171] That the Judicial Reform of 1864 accomplished much more and eventually created an independent judiciary that stood beyond the autocrat's control was the result of efforts made by a group of enlightened officials led by Sergei Zarudnyi, a senior official in the Imperial Ministry of Justice and a close friend of the Miliutins, Kavelin, and Zablotskii.

Trained in mathematics at the University of Kharkov, Zarudnyi had entered the Russian Ministry of Justice at the low rank
of *kollezhskii sekretar'* at the end of 1842, when his failure to find
a position at Russia's new Pulkovo Observatory had ended his
dream of dedicating his life to science. In the bureaucracy, Zarudnyi's analytic mind and scholarly talents helped him to rise
quickly. During the 1840s, he had served both Minister of Justice
Count Panin and Head of the Second Section of His Majesty's
Own Chancery Count Dmitrii Bludov with distinction and, as
senior juridical consultant in the Consultation Department of
the Ministry of Justice a few years later, he had organized what
one of his protégés described as "an entire school" for shaping
the skills of particularly talented young jurists.[172] Like Miliutin
and Zablotskii in the Ministries of Internal Affairs and State
Domains, Zarudnyi drew others to him and trained them
broadly in the law at a time when even the students at Russia's
newly organized elite Imperial School of Jurisprudence were
being taught only to administer the law, not to interpret it,
analyze its flaws, or change it.[173] A decade later, Zarudnyi's
protégés became the cadre that shaped the Judicial Reform Statutes of 1864.

The system of justice that Zarudnyi and his allies set out to
reform at the end of the Crimean War had been designed to
meet the needs of a static social order in which relations between
classes and groups were set firmly within a rigid framework.
Yet the *proizvol* that had marked all levels of administration and
social relationships under serfdom could not continue after its
abolition; something had to be done to enable Russia's judicial
administration to cope with the more fluid, rapidly evolving
society that the emancipation would bring into being. *Zakonnost'*,
"the first condition by which," Zablotskii once had said, "the
success of all administration is guaranteed,"[174] seemed to be
the key that could open the way to that important transformation. Certain that *glasnost'* stood as the chief support of *zakonnost'*
in the West, Zarudnyi and his associates thought that the time
had come to bring it to Russia. If *glasnost'* could attack *proizvol*
and establish *zakonnost'* in administration and government, a
number of enlightened officials argued, then it also could be
used to bring effective justice to the Russians after the serfs had
been emancipated.[175]

Just as the question of serfdom had not been far from statesmen's thoughts during the Nicholas era, so had the need to reform Russia's civil procedures held their attention. Count Bludov's Second Section of His Majesty's Own Chancery had taken up that question in the 1840s but had confined its efforts within the very limited framework of adjusting Russia's judicial administrative machinery.[176] The reform proposals that emerged from Bludov's Second Section during the 1850s did not envision a reform of Russia's judicial administration in broader terms, nor did Alexander II and the senior statesmen who discussed the question in the State Council think of separating the administration of law from the more general framework of government. An independent judiciary, with courts and procedures that functioned outside the state administration, lay well beyond what any of these timid, reluctant reformers hoped to accomplish.[177]

The question of broader judicial reforms came into focus when, as president of the Main Committee on Peasant Affairs, Grand Duke Konstantin Nikolaevich asked Prince Dmitrii Obolenskii to draft a critique of the proposals for judicial reform that Bludov's Second Section had submitted to the Combined Department of Laws and Civil Affairs of the State Council.[178] A graduate of the Imperial School of Jurisprudence who had directed preparations for the reform of judicial regulations in the Russian navy in the early 1850s, Obolenskii immediately called for broad reforms. "The transformation of the judicial sphere in Russia," he explained at the beginning of his report, "cannot be postponed, for the success of improvements in all other sectors of state administration depends upon this reform." Obolenskii warned that Russia could modernize no further without an independent judiciary. "If the lack of roads and, in general, good means of communications was, until now, the stumbling block preventing the development of the material forces of Russia," he wrote, "then the absence of a judiciary was, until the present time, an insurmountable obstacle which rendered futile all efforts of the government to improve the internal organization of Russia, to better the administration, to develop trade and industry, [and] to improve morality." The formalism of Russia's civil court system, the lengthy written legal processes that denied all illiterates access to civil courts, Obolenskii insisted, must be replaced by a more open and independent system that gave judges the freedom to interpret the law, not merely apply its provisions. "The most fundamental reason why a proper judicial order does not exist among us," Obolenskii concluded, "is that we have no lawyers."[179]

Obolenskii thought that the reforms he had in mind could be drafted only by men who had seen the conflict between law and reality "in all its scandalous nakedness."[180] A senior juridical consultant in the Ministry of Justice's influential Consultation Department for more than a decade and a member of the State Council's Department of Civil and Spiritual Affairs, Zarudnyi seemed especially suited to that task.[181] In 1858, he had gone to the West to study European judicial systems, and, after his return to Russia, had written several essays about how they had been reformed to fit the needs of a modernizing society.[182] Yet, even as he urged his fellow jurists to study foreign models, Zarudnyi understood that any reform must suit Russia's unique needs, not merely mirror Western patterns.[183] As work on the emancipation and the *zemstvo* reform drew him away from the problems of judicial reform toward the end of 1860, he left it to others to take up the debate.[184] The emergence of new, reform-minded leadership in the Ministry of Justice helped to make that possible.

That the path to the study of Western models that Zarudnyi and Obolenskii had blazed in the late 1850s became a well-worn trail was in large measure due to the efforts of Dmitrii Zamiatnin, who replaced Panin as minister of justice in 1862. A graduate of the Imperial Lyceum at Tsarskoe Selo, Zamiatnin had been a part of that elite circle of young men, including Baron Modest Korf and the Ministers of Justice Dmitrii Dashkov and Bludov, who had received their first practical experience in the law under Speranskii's tutelage. Zamiatnin had been named deputy minister of justice in 1858 and had taken over many of his superior's ministerial duties when the emperor appointed Panin to replace Rostovtsev as head of the Editing Commission. At that time, Zamiatnin's deep respect for expert opinion about questions of legal theory and judicial practice had led him to encourage a limited form of *glasnost'* among the ministry's officials in much the same way as Konstantin Nikolaevich had in the Naval Ministry.

The fresh atmosphere of openness and debate that Zamiatnin fostered in the Ministry of Justice led to the founding of a periodical press dedicated to interpreting the law and applying it to vital issues of the day.[185] This in turn formed the opinions of professional jurists, officials, and educated society into a united front that favored broader and more fundamental reforms of Russia's court structure and judicial procedure. Calls for more comprehensive reform came not only from such progressive noblemen as Unkovskii and Golovachev (both of whom had studied with Kavelin and those other Russian jurists of the 1840s who had been so deeply influenced by Hegel's view of civic society) but from conservative assemblies of the provincial nobility who now wanted stronger defenses of private property put into place. This endowed the issue of reforming the structure and procedure of Russia's courts with a conservative appeal that encouraged Alexander II to support a broader reform of his empire's judicial system than he originally had proposed.[186]

In October 1861, Alexander II therefore placed responsibility for preparing judicial reforms squarely in the hands of Zarudnyi, now a state secretary in the State Council's Department of Laws, who organized a special committee of men distinguished by their training in the law to draft legislative proposals.[187] This shifted the judicial reform work onto a plane very different from that of earlier Great Reform legislative preparation. None of the men who had drafted the Emancipation Acts had boasted similar expertise, nor could those who were in the process of preparing the *zemstvo* statute claim comparable knowledge of the complexities of local government. When completed, the Judicial Reform statutes would be the first of the Great Reforms drafted by men thoroughly and professionally trained in the field they were called upon to change.

The background and training of Zarudnyi's appointees showed an impressive breadth of judicial expertise. A hereditary nobleman, Nikolai Andreevich Butskovskii had been educated in the Central Engineers' School, had received an army commission, and had taught mathematics and bookkeeping at the School for Orphans at Gatchina. At twenty-eight, he had transferred to the Ministry of Justice, where, for more than a decade, he had applied the analytical talents he had developed as an engineer and mathematician to the study of European juridical literature. As an *ober-prokuror* (chief procurator) in one of the Moscow Departments of the Senate on the eve of the Crimean War, Butskovskii therefore combined a thorough knowledge of Russia's laws with a broad acquaintance with European models. Convinced of the backwardness of Russia's court procedure and an ardent opponent of the narrow formalism that constrained the empire's judicial apparatus, he was an obvious choice for Zarudnyi's committee and one of the first to be named to it in the fall of 1861.[188]

Unlike Butskovskii, Nikolai Ivanovich Stoianovskii, a nobleman from the province of Mogilëv, had studied law at the Imperial School of Jurisprudence and was one of three of the school's graduates whom Zarudnyi summoned to help draft the judicial reform statutes. As a professor of criminal court procedure at his alma mater at the height of Russia's censorship terror, Stoianovskii had composed a *Practical Guide to Russian Criminal Court Procedures* to help his students work their way through the maze of articles on criminal law in Russia's *Digest of Laws* only to have the censor reject it as "superfluous." As head of the Second Section, Bludov had ordered the *Practical Guide* published, but Stoianovskii had left his teaching post and transferred to Moscow to become an *ober-prokuror* in the Sixth and Seventh departments of the Senate. Miliutin had appointed Stoianovskii to the Commission on the Reorganization of Provincial and District Institutions, where he had championed an independent court system that would prevent police and state officials from interfering in the process of justice. Such experience made Stoianovskii a particularly effective advocate of an independent judiciary that would protect the accused from false witnesses and prevent police officials eager to solve crimes from using fraudulent statements to convict innocent defendants.[189]

Also a nobleman and serf owner, Dmitrii Aleksandrovich Rovinskii had entered the Imperial School of Jurisprudence a few months after Stoianovskii's graduation. Like Stoianovskii, he had studied criminal law and served in the Seventh Moscow Department of the Senate before he had become (in 1853) the Moscow provincial prosecutor with full responsibility for the oversight of all police activities in the province. Access to Moscow's prisons had shown Rovinskii the appalling manner in which the police operated outside the law during the last days of the Nicholas era. He had found prisoners who had been fed salt herring and denied water to extort confessions. On one occasion, he had discovered a special room in which prisoners were left to be attacked by voracious bed bugs if they refused to confess to the crimes of which they stood accused. Rovinskii's practical experience and his clear understanding of the abuses from which Russia's penal system suffered made him a strong advocate of humanitarian reforms in the treatment of prisoners, a champion of the jury system, and a dedicated opponent of corporal punishment.[190] Although Stoianovskii and Butskovskii could boast broader experience in administering the law at the highest level, Rovinskii brought to Zarudnyi's committee an unprecedented knowledge of the law's impact upon those who faced Russia's criminal courts and prisons.

Like Rovinskii and Stoianovskii, Konstantin Petrovich Pobedonostsev, the chief theorist on Zarudnyi's committee, had chosen to serve in Moscow after he graduated from the Imperial School of Jurisprudence. In the Eighth Moscow Department of the Senate, which he later called "the best practical school for juridical and administrative work,"[191] he had learned how unjustly Russia's laws were applied in practice. "There is no just case that cannot be lost," he wrote in dismay, "nor is there any unjust case that cannot be won, for there are no firm principles according to which the legal can be distinguished from the illegal."[192] Disillusioned by the *proizvol* his fellow bureaucrats exercised in judicial affairs, Pobedonostsev exchanged his post in the Senate for a position on Moscow University's law faculty, where he became convinced that European statutes could serve as models for judicial reform in Russia. When Pobedonostsev returned to St. Petersburg to tutor Russia's heir in law and history in 1861, Zarudnyi hurried to add him to his special committee.[193]

Of all the men chosen by Zarudnyi to draft the judicial reform legislation, Dmitrii Pavlovich Shubin-Pozdeev was his closest associate and, in an important sense, his protégé. A nobleman of very limited means, Shubin-Pozdeev had taken a degree in law at Moscow University and had served in Zarudnyi's department at the Ministry of Justice. He had followed Zarudnyi, first to the Ministry's Consultation Department and then to the State Council's Department of Laws. More than any of the others called on to draft judicial reforms at the beginning of the 1860s, Shubin-Pozdeev reflected the reform views of his mentor.[194]

Less prominent than Butskovskii, Stoianovskii, Rovinskii, or Pobedonostsev, Shubin-Pozdeev nonetheless stood well above the remaining members of Zarudnyi's special committee, all of whom played lesser roles in drafting the reform statutes. A nobleman from Mogilëv and a graduate of the University of Vilna, Aleksandr Plavskii had experience in drafting regulations and that qualified him to serve as editor of the committee's work. With an advanced degree in law from St. Vladimir University, Pii Danevskii had become a deputy state secretary in Russia's State Chancellery before he joined Zarudnyi's committee. A. P. Vilinbakhov, a chief clerk in the State Chancellery, as the youngest and least experienced of the group, played the most limited part in the committee's work.[195]

Two major obstacles slowed the efforts of Zarudnyi and his eight legal experts to draft the legislation that became the Judicial Reform Statutes of November 20, 1864. The first was Count Bludov, who, as chairman of the State Council's Department of Laws, could be expected to oppose their broader legal reform principles. Even more important, before Zarudnyi and his associates could begin to draw openly on European models in their work, they had to secure approval for such a radical departure from Russian legal practice at the highest level of government. The emperor removed the first of these obstacles when he named Prince Pavel Gagarin, best known for his unyielding opposition to the proposals of the Editing Commission, to replace Bludov as president of the State Council's Department of Laws in 1861. Now a "vocal and influential supporter of an independent judiciary" to defend the private property of the nobility against any further assaults such as it had sustained under the Emancipation Acts, Gagarin could be counted upon to support a thoroughgoing reform of Russia's judicial system.[196]

First as president of the Department of Laws and then as president of the State Council itself, Gagarin granted the approval that Zarudnyi's plan to draw on foreign judicial models required. When he issued a memorandum in January 1862 that instructed Zarudnyi and his committee to set forth "those basic principles, the *undoubted merit* of which is recognized at the present time as the *knowledge and experience of European states* and according to which the judicial sphere in Russia ought to be transformed,"[197] he opened the way for a fundamental shift in official attitudes about Western law and repudiated the long-held view that Russia's institutions were unique. "The Rubicon had been crossed!" the historian Dzhanshiev exclaimed when he wrote the history of the judicial reform statutes some four decades later. "The Chinese wall, which for forty-five years had isolated our legislative activity from the direct influence of European knowledge and contemporary progress, had been breached.

The principles of European public law and knowledge, reaching us until that point by an illegal route . . . finally gained free admittance to our legislative practice."[198]

Even when stripped of Dzhanshiev's immoderate praise, Gagarin's memorandum marked a critical watershed in the judicial reform work. Now free to explore the broadest contours of European experience, especially that of Hannover, where written court procedures had been abolished in the late 1840s and replaced by the procedures current in France,[199] Zarudnyi and his associates completed their memorandum on the "Basic Principles for the Transformation of the Courts" at the beginning of April 1862.[200] Although Russia's autocrat had always regarded his ability to dispense justice and interpret the law as being among his most cherished prerogatives, the "Basic Principles" proposed to create an independent court system in which independent and professionally trained judges would hand down verdicts at public trials. A just court, the memorandum's authors insisted, "spreads among the people that notion of justice and law without which there can be no prosperity and order in society." Zarudnyi and his reformers therefore called on the emperor and his government to use *glasnost'* to guarantee *zakonnost'* in Russia's courts and society as the best defense against the revolutionary movement that was rising among the nation's radicals. "A government that does not reject useful reforms for the perfection of state administration and the social order," Zarudnyi's committee concluded, "cannot but find support among the well-intentioned part of the public in its prosecution of ill-intentioned malefactors who strive for the destruction of the existing order."[201]

The emperor and his advisers proved to be more daring in dealing with the question of judicial reform than with either the emancipation or the reform of Russia's local and provincial government, and they turned aside from Zarudnyi's "Basic Principles" only on the extremely sensitive question of jury trials in political cases. In writing for a special volume published to commemorate the fiftieth anniversary of the Judicial Reform Statutes, the prominent twentieth-century jurist Dmitrii Nabokov described Alexander II's approval of the work of Zarudnyi's committee on September 29, 1862, as "the culminating point and most important date in the history of drafting the judicial statutes."[202] Some contemporaries spoke with even greater enthusiasm. "What unbelievable successes Russia has achieved in the present reign," the censor Nikitenko wrote in his diary when he first read Zarudnyi's "Basic Principles." "If during the Nicholas era anyone had even thought to dream of such things," he added, "he either would have been considered mad or been branded a state criminal."[203]

What remained to be completed was the painstaking labor of transforming the "Basic Principles" of Zarudnyi's committee into the statutes that would become the Judicial Reform Acts of November 20, 1864. For that task, a larger commission was established in the Imperial State Chancellery at the end of 1862. Unlike the Editing Commission, or even the Commission on the Reorganization of Provincial and District Institutions, the members of this body all had the expertise required for the task at hand. Of the commission's thirty-one members, at least twelve were graduates of the Imperial School of Jurisprudence and another twelve held university degrees.[204] Most prominent among its members were Zarudnyi and the men who had served on his special committee (except Stoianovskii, who, as Russia's newly appointed deputy minister of justice, now stood aside from its work). Aleksandr Knirim, whose essay "On Hanoverian Legal Procedure" had turned Russian jurists' attention to the example of Central Europe, played a key role on the commission, as did Nikolai Kalachov, editor of *The Archive of Historical and Practical Information about Russia* and the influential *Iuridicheskii Vestnik (Juridical Bulletin)*.[205]

The product of the special commission's labors comprised 1,758 printed folio sheets to which Stoianovskii added an additional 500 that he had prepared as Zamiatnin's deputy.[206] In December 1863, these materials went to the State Council, and, on November 20, less than a year after the *zemstvo* statutes had been issued, they were promulgated by the Senate. Based on the models of Western and Central Europe, the new statutes changed not the laws as contained in *The Complete Collection of the Laws of the Russian Empire* but the procedures of Russia's courts. These now separated the courts from Russia's regular state administration so decisively that even the new *okrugi* (circuits) transcended traditional provincial administrative divisions. Except on the local level, where the *zemstva* elected justices of the peace to resolve civil disputes and minor criminal matters, Zarudnyi's jurists had placed Russia's court structure entirely in the hands of professional jurists. Judges no longer held their posts at the emperor's pleasure but enjoyed life tenure. Incorporating Zarudnyi's view that *glasnost'* was the best guarantee of *zakonnost'* in legal proceedings, trials became public, and, although the State Council excluded political trials from juries' competence, the Judicial Reform Statutes introduced trials by jury in other criminal cases.[207]

The Judicial Reform Statutes of November 20, 1864, fulfilled Alexander II's wish to "introduce into Russia legal proceedings that are swift, just, merciful, and equal for all . . . and, in general, to strengthen in Our people that respect for the law without which civic well-being is impossible."[208] Yet they did far more, for they cut away the control over the dispensation of justice that had been one of the autocrat's most cherished prerogatives for centuries and began the transformation of autocracy into a more modern form of kingship. At the same time, the work of Zarudnyi and his associates laid the cornerstone for a modern society based on public justice and civic responsibility: Russians now had to judge their fellow citizens, defend their property, and secure justice for each other. Once the proposals of Zarudnyi's commission became law, Russians had to take control of their own destinies in ways that they never had been obliged to do before.

After 1864, Russia's citizens, not the emperor or his agents, had to secure the liberty that came with the Emancipation Acts and defend the freedom to shape their daily lives that came with the *zemstvo* statutes. No one could yet fully envision the shape of modern Russian society, for the meaning of these new laws remained to be tested. In a society being shaped according to the image of the more advanced West, the form of relations between former serfs and former masters was still to be determined, as was the relation of the newly emancipated peasants to their commune, the *zemstvo*, and national government. Questions of taxation, education, public works, and public health all had to be defined and clarified, and the dilemmas posed by juxtaposing the living remains of an ancient autocracy on the beginnings of a modern citizenry and industrial economy had to be resolved. None of these questions could be answered from above as they were in olden times, nor could answers come from below without a revolution. The definition and testing of the first wave of Great Reform legislation therefore had to come from within the body politic that was only beginning to emerge in Russia as the 1860s neared its midpoint. The new court system, which effectively separated autocratic power from the dispensation of justice and placed the defense of property and the definition of a citizen's responsibilities in the hands of the Russians themselves, became the key instrument for accomplishing that task. As no previous body of legislation had, the Judicial Reform Statutes institutionalized *glasnost'* and made it the instrument for ensuring that *zakonnost'* would govern the behavior of men and institutions in modern Russia.

By turning to *glasnost'* at the end of the Crimean War, Alexander II and some of his advisers had hoped to consult Russian public opinion without permitting it access to Russia's institutional policy-making instruments. Public debate about state policy, they had hoped, could be focused within the framework of the commonly held values of Orthodoxy, Autocracy, and Nationality, which, in turn, could help to chart the course that Russia must follow. Yet the nature of *glasnost'* conflicted with autocracy too sharply for such a policy to succeed and the expectations of private citizens quickly surpassed the willingness of autocracy to meet them. This situation created new tensions between government and governed that left the limits of *glasnost'* unclear until its institutionalization within Russia's new court system in the form of public trials conducted by independent judges began to define them.

Statesmen and citizens might debate whether the limits of *glasnost'* should be extended to include the formation of an elected assembly to discuss policy at the national level or if, as one senior official claimed, *glasnost'* had failed to "conform to our civic order, the peculiarities of our national character, and the level of our present development."[209] Such debates remained legitimate in the context of Russia's ongoing Great Reform experience. Yet, whether Russia's path moved to the Left or the Right, *glasnost'* itself had to remain in being, for it could not be obliterated without undercutting the judicial foundations upon which the renovations of Russian society and institutions were being constructed.

In time, this process could produce a new basis on which to shape Russian society. For, if Orthodoxy, Autocracy, and Nationality no longer sufficed to unite Russians, the aspiration to *zakonnost'*—to make the law's application "swift, just, merciful, and equal for all"—might do so. This possibility of reuniting Russian society was especially significant because, at least since the 1830s, some political theorists had seen the nation's body politic as divided into conflicting progressive and conservative groups, each striving to satisfy its own interests and aspirations at the expense of the other. It was the chief task of autocracy, the great statesman Speranskii had argued, to keep these groups in balance, thereby making it possible to achieve gradual progress. The autocrat had used this balancing of conservatives against progressives to help set the limits of the Great Reform debates at the beginnings of the 1860s, and that had been a reason for the ouster of Miliutin and Lanskoi in spring 1861. The aspiration to *zakonnost'* and the preservation of *glasnost'* as a means to define Russian political and social values after 1864 now offered new but untried instruments for reshaping Russian society as the Great Reform era entered its second decade. The debates of the late 1850s and the legislation of the early 1860s had built the basis for a society of citizens in Russia. The legislation that was to follow between 1865 and 1874 would oblige Russians to begin to act as citizens ought to act.

# IV

## THE
## GREAT REFORM
## ERA

*T*he time had come for Russians to take charge of their destinies rather than allow an all-powerful imperial master to shape their lives from above, for, in the complex world that their nation entered after the Crimean War, no government could continue to take responsibility for as many aspects of national life as had Nicholas I and his adjutant-ministers. Alexander II's government therefore needed to transfer some of the responsibilities for education, justice, and public services that the Great Reforms had created to institutions that could draw upon the untapped resources of Russia's citizens in ways that an autocratic government could not. In the West, this process had taken place gradually and, often, spontaneously, as local governments had assumed responsibility for dealing with increasingly complex social and economic problems. In Russia, neither the emperor nor his chief advisers dared to allow citizen involvement in public affairs to move so freely without first establishing controls to bar the men and the institutions they would inevitably create from the nation's political arena. Because Russia's statesmen defined "politics" very broadly, the limits they sought to impose from the very beginning slowed the growth of a citizen society. Equally important, these limits also sowed the seeds of conflict between government and citizens over matters that had been much less acrimonious—and sometimes even the focus of mutual cooperation—in the West. As the first Great Reform statutes began to shape the foundations for civic institutions in Russia that were similar to those that had helped to moderate the impact of the industrial revolution in the West, they also marked out lines of conflict that would bring government and society onto a collision course at the beginning of the twentieth century.

The roots of this conflict lay in the disagreements about where to draw the line between public and private activity that had divided governors from governed in Russia for the better part of two centuries. Beginning in the eighteenth century, Russia's statesmen had shaped their views about the relationship of subjects to their sovereign around the concepts of natural law that had dominated Central Europe, where, as Marc Raeff explained nearly two decades ago, greater stress was placed on the duties and obligations men owed to society than on the rights they derived from citizenship. Men in the world of the German *Aufklärung* (including the Russians) were not endowed with equal and inalienable rights; in the context of the community within which they lived, they received rights in return for duties well and faithfully performed.[1] Then, toward the end of the eighteenth century, some of the more radical members of Russia's emerging intelligentsia began to turn away from Central Europe's example to draw more heavily on the French Enlightenment and the experience of England. As they shifted their attention from Central Europe farther west, these men took up the Anglo-French belief that men had rights independent of their duty to the government that ruled their lives and the society in which they lived. This set the stage for a conflict that would emerge more sharply as Russia entered the Great Reform era three-quarters of a century later.

To such men and women, it seemed that a citizen state on the Anglo-French model must emerge in Russia after the Great Reforms. "The upper nobility," Bismarck wrote from St. Petersburg, "dreams of the position of the English peers and of the successes of Mirabeau,"[2] while the less well-to-do intelligentsia looked to the example of the House of Commons and the Chamber of Deputies. Such visions continued to attract Russians until after the February Revolution in 1917, and both would be very powerful in shaping the course of Duma politics in the early twentieth century. By contrast, those Russian statesmen and political theorists whose views remained firmly rooted in the precepts of Official Nationality thought that a citizen state modeled on the experience of Central Europe seemed the inevitable result of ideas about law and government that for so long had

been shaped within a German framework.[3] This view lay at the
root of the conviction (so often expressed by the councilors of
Nicholas I) that men in general were weak, perverse, inclined
to evil actions, and in need of stern guidance by a benevolent
supreme authority.[4]

Combined with the militaristic approach to government that
had flourished under Nicholas I, in which the emperor relied
on his adjutants to represent him in the provinces and to solve
problems in his name, the well-entrenched precepts of Official
Nationality meant that, although the Great Reform legislation
looked to Russians to take responsibility for their destinies on
the local level, senior statesmen intended to dictate the relationship of the tsar's subjects to the central government. Further,
they expected to impose a very broad definition of political
activity on the class of educated, professional men and women
that would develop over the next half century. What was thought
of as purely professional activity in the West therefore would
be condemned very often as political activity in Russia. The
process of training teachers, agronomists, and public health personnel, instilling in them a sense of their professional qualifications, and interjecting them into the arena of public affairs took
on much more aggressive political overtones in Russia than in
the West.[5]

Nowhere was this more clear than in Russia's provinces,
where governors continued to serve as personal representatives
of the autocrat during the 1870s and 1880s while *zemstva* officials,
elected representatives, and an increasing number of trained
professionals struggled to shape the institutions needed to serve
a growing body of citizens. "Masters of the province" in the
Empress Catherine II's words, independent of the authority of
all central government offices and answerable only to their
monarch, Russia's governors continued to be the direct agents
of the sovereign outside the capital throughout the Great Reform
era. The *Zemstvo* statutes, the Statute on Municipal Government,
and the Judicial Reform statutes all created new institutions that
challenged the governors' authority in local affairs, for these
made it possible for private citizens to act independently of a
governor and to challenge his acts in court.[6] Still, governors
remained, as they had been for nearly a hundred years, the
sovereign's personal representatives in the province. From the
1860s into the early twentieth century, the conflicts between

governors and governed therefore figured prominently in provincial life and played a major role in defining the nature and authority of a citizen society as it was beginning to emerge in Russia.

If the contours of a fully developed citizen society remained indistinct as Russia moved toward the 1870s, there were significant areas in which the government chose to impose the responsibilities of citizens on the Russians. Between 1865 and 1874, a second wave of Great Reform legislation obliged Russians to take responsibility for what they were writing and publishing, for shaping the urban centers in which modern life could flourish, and for defending Russia against foreign and domestic enemies. It was during this second decade of his reign that Alexander II abandoned a major element of the paternalistic outlook that had separated the system of Nicholas I from its contemporaries in the West. No longer would the emperor and his officials take responsibility before man and God for the Russians' behavior; Russians now must bear that burden themselves.

## THE CENSORSHIP REFORM

As men and women knew it in the mid-nineteenth century, censorship had existed for less than a hundred years in Russia. Secular censorship had begun late in the eighteenth century, when Russia's autocrats had first sensed the full dimensions of the threat that the ideas of the West posed to their authority. Censorship had tightened its grip on the Russians during the reign of Nicholas I, its purpose being to ban foreign books and to deter Russians from publishing works judged to be politically or morally dangerous. Yet censorship did not burden the Russians heavily during the 1830s and 1840s. As their emperor and his chief advisers had intended, most Russians saw the precepts of censorship as guiding principles set down to help them shape their moral and political attitudes. "The role of the censor," Sidney Monas once explained, "was conceived as that of an amiable legal guardian of letters, a foster father of the arts and sciences."[7] Many educated Russians in those days thought of censorship as a necessity. "What is right for London is early for Moscow," Russia's great poet Pushkin had written in 1830. Censors, he had concluded then, must "be strict but be intelligent."[8]

For some years at least, Pushkin's criterion held firm. Censors often were literary figures, journalists, or university professors, all dedicated to championing the written word in Russia. Certainly, there were Russians who considered censorship burdensome in those days, but the fact that intellectual and scholarly endeavor flourished on such an unprecedented scale indicated that most men and women found it possible to work creatively within its limits. Only after 1848 did censors become so capricious and repressive that they caused the last years of Nicholas's reign to be remembered as "the era of censorship terror." By 1850, no fewer than twelve government agencies dealt with censorship and, according to one contemporary estimate, the number of people working in the government's censorship apparatus actually exceeded the number of books published.[9]

Central to the dark era of censorship terror was the Buturlin Committee, whose creation on April 2, 1848, crowned the edifice of obscurantist, all-pervasive censorship in Russia. Chaired by Dmitrii Buturlin, a man remembered as an intelligent and charming dinner companion who was nonetheless despotic and strange,[10] this committee was composed of men anxious to read between the lines and to punish any author who stirred their suspicions. Even the loyal servant of Official Nationality Faddei Bulgarin had to bear their rebuke for writing in the long-favored semiofficial *Severnaia Pchela (Northern Bee)* that hackney drivers in St. Petersburg charged excessive fees in bad weather. "No criticism whatsoever of the activities or administration of the government and established authority [responsible for regulating hackney fees], even though it be indirect," Bulgarin was told, "will be allowed in print."[11] As censorship began to punish even the regime's most loyal servants, Russians' bitterness toward their government deepened. What was "most necessary of all at the present moment," Valuev confided to his diary as the Crimean War drew to a close, was "a transformation of censorship."[12]

The first breach in the walls of Russia's fortress of censorship regulations came suddenly and from a very unexpected source. Late in 1855, Baron Modest Korf, once one of the most energetic members of the Buturlin Committee, complained to Alexander II that pervasive censorship had given birth to a widely and clandestinely circulated body of manuscript literature in Russia over which the government had no control.[13] Alexander's abolition of the Buturlin Committee a few days later heralded the begin-

ning of a decade in which Russia's press flourished and nearly
ten times as many newspapers and journals made their debut
as in the last decade of the Nicholas era. Whereas only four
newspapers in all of Russia had been allowed to report (without
comment) their government's foreign and domestic policies before 1855, Alexander II granted all journals and newspapers
permission to do so before he had been on the throne a year.[14]
Yet the beginnings of a more active press created new dilemmas
for which neither Alexander nor his advisers could find easy
solutions. Most obviously and urgently, how could public opinion be expressed more openly but, at the same time, be kept
from exceeding acceptable limits? "The Emperor is deeply preoc-
cupied with censorship," Nikitenko remarked in his diary after
a meeting with Minister of Public Instruction A. S. Norov. "At
the moment he demands restrictions, but, at the same time,
does not want to inhibit thinking."[15]

How were such obviously contradictory aims to be accomplished? Powerful and loyal men took very different positions
on that question as they sought to reshape Russia's censorship
policies. Among Alexander's closest advisers, Prince Aleksei
Orlov (President of the State Council), Prince Vladimir Dolgorukov (Head of the Third Section), Petr Brok (Minister of
Finance), Konstantin Chevkin (Director of Communications),
and, above all, Count Panin stood firmly against moderating
censorship. So did O. A. Przhetslavskii, a key figure in the Main
Censorship Administration and author of an important memorandum "On *Glasnost'* in Russian Journalistic Literature."[16]
While Count Bludov, Aleksandr Norov, and Egor Kovalevskii,
Norov's successor as minister of public instruction, kept to the
middle ground, Grand Duke Konstantin Nikolaevich, Rostovtsev, Deputy Minister of Justice Zamiatnin, Nikolai Miliutin,
Zarudnyi, and Aleksandr Golovnin (who replaced Kovalevskii
in 1861) championed a more moderate censorship policy in
which they were supported by calls for "*glasnost'* within reasonable limits" by Baron N. V. Medem and Nikitenko from within
the Main Censorship Administration.[17] None of the men who
called for moderation advocated freedom of the press; all hoped
to foster controlled public debate about the critical issues Russia
must face in the 1860s. Like the emperor himself, all struggled
to find ways to prevent that debate from getting out of control
before it was allowed to begin.

The emperor's view that censors must exercise "judicious vigilance" but not "inhibit thinking" clearly expressed the ongoing dichotomy in official policy during 1858.[18] At the beginning of the year, Alexander announced that private citizens could discuss the peasant question in the press, only to insist less than two weeks later that all articles on peasant affairs must be approved in advance by the Ministry of Internal Affairs.[19] Then, in a passing fit of pique about the wide-ranging discussions of "progress" that were beginning to sweep across Russia, he instructed that the word *progress* "not be used in official papers" and overzealous censors hurried to apply that restriction to Russia's entire public press at the beginning of May.[20] Clearly, the emperor and his advisers were seeking to establish some limited contact with opinion outside official circles to help them clarify Russia's course. Just as clearly, any thought that such contact might require the easing of censorship made them extremely uncomfortable. "For the government," Nikitenko wrote at one point, "a union with the press is obviously more useful and safer than a war against it."[21] But, although Alexander and his advisers sensed that bureaucratic regulation alone could not bring such an alliance into being, they felt uncertain about how to apply the moral imperatives that had formed the core of Nicholas I's policies of Official Nationality in the more fluid conditions of post-Crimean politics.

On January 24, 1859, Alexander decided to institutionalize these moral imperatives by establishing the Committee on Press Affairs. Described by one of its members as "a special bureau that would concern itself with the direction of literature in moral, not administrative, terms,"[22] the Committee on Press Affairs, like the Buturlin Committee a decade earlier, reflected the government's realization that existing institutions had failed to respond effectively to the changing needs of censorship. With disagreement about principles at the highest policy-making levels still standing in the way of a clear policy,[23] Alexander II now proceeded, as his father had in 1848, to place censorship in the hands of men whom he could trust to serve as extensions of his own will. The Committee on Press Affairs of January 1859, not the Secret Committee on Peasant Affairs of January 1857, marked his last effort to apply his father's methods to post-Crimean problems.

The task of the Committee on Press Affairs, according to one official source, was to maintain "an *unofficial surveillance* over the trends of . . . literature in accordance with the views of the government."[24] Composed of Count Aleksandr Adlerberg (son of the minister of the Imperial Court and one of the young emperor's closest friends), Nikolai Mukhanov (Kovalevskii's deputy at the Ministry of Public Instruction), and General Aleksandr Timashev (chief of staff of the Corps of Gendarmes), the committee was no better suited to make judgments about political, moral, or literary questions than the members of the Buturlin Committee had been. All were bureaucrats steeped in the tradition and experience of the Nicholas system who thought that censors should coerce writers into submission. They therefore had no notion about how to encourage writers to support the government's reform program while preventing them from demanding more change than the state dared permit.[25] "They will direct writers, counsel them, discuss with them the most important moral, political and literary questions—they who have never discussed or read anything, and who do not read anything at the moment!" Nikitenko lamented when Kovalevskii first urged him to join the committee. "If one deliberately tried to find the people most unsuited for this role," he concluded, "one could not find better ones [than these]."[26]

The addition of Nikitenko, censor, onetime editor of *Sovremennik*, and associate of a number of reforming bureaucrats who shared with him an interest in the Russian Geographical Society, was a not very successful effort to provide the bridge between senior statesmen and educated opinion in Russia that Adlerberg, Mukhanov, and Timashev lacked the sensitivity to establish. "There are certain aspirations which are not in agreement with the views of the government," Nikitenko remembered the emperor telling him in the interview at which he so gingerly had agreed to join the committee. "It is necessary to restrain them," Alexander added, "but I want no oppressive measures of any sort. I very much desire," he concluded, "that important questions be examined and discussed in a learned fashion."[27] Believing that *"glasnost', zakonnost',* and the development of the instruments for teaching and educating the masses" were essential to progress, Nikitenko joined the Committee on Press Affairs at the end of February 1859. Convinced that, "as a mediator between literature and the Emperor," the committee needed to "see in literature a civic force which can do much good for society," he hoped that he and his colleagues "could act upon public opinion [and], by means of the press, lead it to the views and purposes of the government."[28]

As Nikitenko feared, Russia's press greeted the Committee for Press Affairs as a reincarnation of the Buturlin Committee, and the petty tyranny of Adlerberg, Mukhanov, and Timashev thoroughly reinforced that view. By late April, Nikitenko had begun to despair of seeing the committee exercise what he once had called "a wise influence upon public opinion" and resigned himself to its failure.[29] "What will I do with minds so petty that they strain out mosquitoes while they swallow camels?" he asked his diary as he lamented the overriding concern with which his senior colleagues addressed minor issues. "They rage about trivia," he concluded crossly. "They think they are rescuing society from a tempest when they succeed in mauling some phrase or brief article."[30] Convinced that "censorship ought to protect the fundamental principles of our state structure" but certain that less repressive means had to be found, Nikitenko knew that other instruments must be used to "rescue . . . the political principle of society . . . and strengthen [its] calm, equitable development."[31] After October, the Committee on Press Affairs no longer met. On its first anniversary, January 24, 1860, it slipped quietly out of existence.[32]

Two proposals—one for a Main Directorate of Press Affairs to serve as a ministry of censorship, the other recommending that responsibility for censorship be shifted from the Ministry of Public Instruction to the Ministry of Internal Affairs—emerged as alternatives to the Committee on Press Affairs between the end of 1859 and the beginning of 1861. The moving force behind the first was again Baron Korf. A dedicated practitioner of what Bludov once had called the "alphabet of service," Korf combined unusual diligence and rare efficiency with literary and political talents that placed him firmly in the center of St. Petersburg's social and political life.[33] Articulate, widely read, and, as director of the Imperial Public Library, a man whose contact with the world of periodicals and books was unrivaled among Russia's senior statesmen, Korf moved easily in a circle that encompassed the salons and dining rooms of such luminaries as Count Tatishchev, Count Kiselev, Count Uvarov, Countess Nesselrode, and Grand Duchess Elena Pavlovna.[34] Although some regarded him as an intriguer, none questioned his dedication to the emperor or his loyalty to the principles of Orthodoxy, Autocracy, and Nationality. Still, Russia's rulers had not felt entirely comfortable with Korf and they had elevated others to ministerial positions while leaving him to sit on the State Council and serve as a state secretary. Then, when Alexander announced that Korf would head a yet-to-be-organized ministry of censorship at the end of November 1859, it seemed that this loyal statesman's fondest wish lay within easy reach.[35]

In the draft decree that would have created a Main Directorate of Press Affairs to take control of all censorship in Russia on January 1, 1860, Korf promised more rationally organized censorship to reduce the capriciousness of outdated policies applied differently by different ministries.[36] In doing so, he moved too quickly, challenged the prerogatives of other agencies involved with censorship too directly, and, for reasons that still are not clear, announced his support for a more liberal censorship policy in a way that led Russia's other ministers to accuse him of currying favor with the press. Korf may have been thinking only in terms of the policy he had proposed when he had recommended the abolition of the Buturlin Committee at the end of 1855 and he may have designed his remarks to encourage writers to publish their work rather than circulate it in manuscript, but his words stirred a hornets' nest of protest among Russia's senior statesmen. "Korf sought popularity too quickly," Nikitenko concluded, "but his main error was that he showed his desire to obtain it."[37]

For a few weeks, Korf plunged ahead with plans to spend more than the proposed censorship ministry's entire yearly budget on purchasing and refurbishing palatial quarters[38] at a time when Russia's fiscal crisis had forced the government to abandon any attempt to assume a part of the cost of the forthcoming emancipation settlement.[39] Under such circumstances, Foreign Minister Prince Gorchakov remarked nastily, Russians were being asked to "pay dearly for the suppression of free speech,"[40] and Alexander abandoned his plan for a main Directorate of Press Affairs at that point. "The entire structure," Korf's proposed deputy wrote to his brother, "turned to ashes" in less than a week.[41]

As was the case with work on the *zemstvo* statutes and the judicial reforms, the final stages of the emancipation debates slowed efforts to formulate new censorship policies during 1860 and early 1861 and this increased the tension between *obshchestvo* and Russia's government. Certainly, censorship was less onerous in 1860 than it had been a scant decade before, yet the very possibility of commenting on government policy had caused Russians' aspirations to soar and had clouded their sense of how much the curtain of censorship had lifted since the Crimean War. Even though two out of every five requests to publish new periodicals were approved in 1860, the historian Kostomarov thought that censorship had "become murderously severe."[42] Safely abroad in Nice, the radical critic Dobroliubov echoed his words. "In Russia," he remarked to his friend Petr Kazanskii, "censorship rages ferociously."[43]

If such people thought that the relaxation of censorship had not gone far enough, Alexander II had begun to worry that it had gone too far. "Journals and newspapers . . . are finding room for such things as are impossible to tolerate in print even in a well-ordered state and even less so among us in view of the poorly-developed and immature nature of our civic education," he wrote toward the end of 1860.[44] Then, when a wave of disorders swept through Russia's universities in 1861, Russia's emperor tightened the reins on the press. As the irate students of St. Petersburg University boycotted classes within sight of the Winter Palace and the authorities faced demonstrations in the streets of the capital for the first time, Alexander called for stricter control of the press as well as the universities.[45] Convinced that Russia's youth had developed "an extreme hatred . . . for the entire existing order of things,"[46] he asked Minister of Public Instruction Kovalevskii (who had remained responsible for censorship after Korf's fiasco the year before) to resign and, for the first time since Admiral Shishkov's retirement in 1828, appointed a military man in his place.

Alexander's unfortunate choice to replace the moderate Kovalevskii was Admiral Count E. V. Putiatin, a capable naval officer whose ability to deal with the complex responsibilities of the Ministry of Public Instruction was sadly limited. "His ideas are in many ways very strange, if not outright absurd," Nikitenko confessed not long after his new superior took office.[47] Valuev thought Putiatin so inferior as to be "beneath any criticism," and a number of other senior statesmen shared that low opinion.[48] Perhaps too influenced by the intrigues of the metropolitan Filaret and the empress in making Putiatin's appointment,[49]

Alexander hurried to replace him less than six months later with Aleksandr Golovnin, a protégé of Konstantin Nikolaevich. He did not manage to do so before the admiral's stubborn dedication to the Nicholas system had deepened the tension between government and *obshchestvo* still further. Because Putiatin's repressive policies could not be continued, it became Golovnin's first task to produce a more workable censorship policy.

With the grand duke's confidence but without experience in either educational administration or censorship, Golovnin took over the Ministry of Public Instruction just as Russia's universities suffered new outbreaks of disorders. Sadly, he possessed neither the vision nor the sensitivity that these crises demanded. Valuev's estimate a few months before Golovnin took office had been that it was "impossible to expect much from him . . . [because] his methodical, complacently theoretical mind is unable to adjust itself to an era of rapid movements and upheavals."[50] Now, Valuev dismissed Golovnin as "intelligent, ingratiating, methodical, cold, egotistical, and not very pleasant." Although Boris Chicherin knew Golovnin much better than Valuev, he offered no more favorable an assessment, even in retrospect. "He [was] an honorable man of limited intellect, painstaking, diligent, obstinate, narrow in the extreme, and a pedant," Chicherin explained later. "In practical terms," he added, "he [was] completely unacquainted with the affairs [of the Ministry of Public Instruction]."[51]

At first Golovnin advocated a censorship policy that reflected views very similar to those Nikitenko had championed on the short-lived Committee for Press Affairs. Like Nikitenko, he believed in *glasnost'* and advocated "greater freedom, a lessening of that arbitrariness that formerly weighed so heavily upon society, [and] the introduction of greater *zakonnost'*."[52] In a more abstract sense, Golovnin believed that "a government that truly desires success in enlightenment should strive first of all for *complete* liberty and freedom . . . in the sense of that legitimate liberty that all citizens of England, the North American states, Belgium, and Switzerland presently enjoy."[53] Yet these were at best starry ideals, not programs that could be implemented in Russia. A senior statesman who still expected to dictate the relationship of the tsar's subjects to the central government while allowing them greater civic freedom in local affairs, Golovnin thought that Russians were not yet ready for those broader civic liberties enjoyed by the citizens of Europe. Convinced that revolution threatened Russia, he insisted that the government's first priority must be to deal with that menace. "Our major task is to struggle against the impending revolution," he wrote to Konstantin Nikolaevich in May 1862. "Only a blind man could fail to see its approach."[54]

Although Golovnin moved quickly to warn censors that they must enforce the regulations then in effect, his plans "to struggle against the impending revolution" did not involve outright repression. Rather, he struggled to find some means to lift the crushing work load with which the flood of new books and periodicals had burdened every censor in the empire. Even after he relieved Russia's censors from the terrible task of reviewing 4,721 issues of official journals every year, these men still bore an impossible burden. Assisted by twenty-three clerks in nine different cities, thirty-nine censors labored to review 6,669 issues of periodicals and newspapers in addition to 1,884 books during 1863, while another fifteen censors and six clerks had to take responsibility for reviewing thousands more titles imported from abroad.[55]

Golovnin therefore proposed to shift responsibility for what was published in Russia from the government to writers and publishers themselves by replacing "preventative" censorship, which had required that authors and publishers submit all materials to the censors before publication, with *karatel'naia* (postpublication) censorship, which, once the judicial reform statutes were completed, would oblige the government to argue its case for censorship violations in court.[56] This would relieve the government of a task it no longer had the resources to perform. For, just as Russia no longer could bear the burden of maintaining a million-man standing army in the post-Crimean era, so she could not support an adequate "preventative" censorship apparatus to oversee the large number of new periodicals that came into being during the Great Reform era.[57]

On March 8, 1862, two days before he freed government publications from preliminary censorship, Golovnin established a special commission under the presidency of Prince Dmitrii Obolenskii to draft a new censorship statute for Russia.[58] The prince had been the first of the enlightened bureaucrats invited into Grand Duchess Elena Pavlovna's circle in the late 1840s, and he had been among the first young officials whom Konstantin Nikolaevich had drafted into the Naval ministry a few years later.[59] Of the commission's other leading figures, Vladimir Tsie, recently named by Golovnin to chair the St. Petersburg Censorship Committee, was well known as a defender of *zakonnost'* and, on at least one occasion, had come very close to saying that *glasnost'* might serve as a substitute for *nadzor* (surveillance) and *perliustratsiia* (the reading of private correspondence by the police). A defender of *zakonnost'* and *glasnost'* like Obolenskii and Tsie, Konstantin Veselovskii also had been a part of the enlightened bureaucrats' circle in the Ministries of Internal Affairs and State Domains, had played a prominent part in their seizure of the Russian Geographical Society in 1850, and then had moved on to become the secretary of the Imperial Russian Academy of Sciences.[60]

Under Obolenskii's direction, these men examined Russia's censorship regulations, searched for European models that might be adapted to Russian conditions, determined how and under what conditions *karatel'naia* censorship might replace preliminary censorship, and considered ways to establish special courts to deal with press affairs. They agreed that censorship in Russia was arbitrary, coercive, and ineffective. And, although they still felt it necessary "to restrain literature within those limits necessary for the tranquillity of the state and private citizens . . . [and], by force of law and lawful procedures, to *chastise* those guilty of violating the established rules," they now considered it essential to establish institutions that would "function independently from arbitrary interference at the highest levels of government." Only in that way, they concluded, might it be possible to "weaken the mistrust with which even the most moderate segments of the press regard [the government]."[61]

Somewhat surprisingly, Obolenskii's commission took the position that Golovnin's stopgap attempt to mix preliminary and *karatel'naia* censorship in the Ministry of Public Instruction was "*completely bankrupt*"[62] and that only the Ministry of Internal Affairs could provide the "independence that censorship has lacked for twenty years."[63] Apparently even more surprising, Golovnin supported their recommendation to transfer censorship to Valuev's ministry in the report he presented to the Committee of Ministers on January 10, 1863.

In fact, Golovnin did not agree to support the transfer willingly, and the month that separated the completion of the commission's report and his support for its conclusions in the Committee of Ministers was punctuated by a series of unsuccessful attempts to defend what had long been one of the most cherished prerogatives of his ministry. Yet Golovnin could not stand against so powerful an opponent as Valuev, who believed, as he had told the emperor a few months before, that "in an era of civic awakening it is more important than ever for the government to seize control of the social movement and stand at its head." Then, Valuev had called for "notable boldness that will astonish the masses and impress them."[64] Now, he insisted that, if public opinion were to be shaped to support the government to preserve the bureaucracy's monopoly of what Daniel Orlovsky has called "legitimate politics," the Ministry of Internal Affairs must control censorship.[65]

With both Obolenskii and Tsie supporting the transfer of censorship to the Ministry of Internal Affairs and the emperor urging him to concentrate his efforts on education reform, Golovnin bowed to Valuev's demands.[66] "The role of the Ministry of Internal Affairs in censorship is clearer, more precisely defined, and simpler," he announced after explaining that censorship fitted poorly with his ministry's "obligation to act as a patron of literature." Therefore, he concluded, "its goal is more attainable."[67]

When preparations for Russia's new censorship law passed from the Ministry of Public Instruction to the Ministry of Internal Affairs on January 10, 1863, Valuev announced that a second commission under Obolenskii would complete the task that its predecessor had begun.[68] In June, he circulated the committee's draft of a new censorship statute to Russia's senior statesmen. Then, some eighteen months later in January 1865, he sent to the State Council the draft statute and commentaries from Golovnin, Baron Korf (as head of the Second Section of His Majesty's Own Chancery until April 1864), Panin (Korf's successor in the Second Section), and Minister of Justice Zamiatnin. Three months later, on April 6, 1865, the council issued the "temporary regulations" on censorship that were to remain in effect for the next thirty-eight years.[69]

The "temporary regulations" of April 6, 1865, made writers, editors, and publishers liable to criminal prosecution if they published material that the authorities considered dangerous. At the same time, the "temporary regulations" concentrated the tasks of Russia's censorship apparatus in a single ministry whose head had the option of imposing administrative penalties (including suspending a journal's publication for up to six months) as an alternative to prosecuting violators in the courts. The new regulations thus obliged Russians to take responsibility for what they published at the same time as they made it possible for the government to punish offenders more effectively. "Valuev has attained his goal," Nikitenko confided to his diary in mid-May 1865. "He has made himself the complete master of published work [in Russia]."[70] Valuev used his great power sparingly and the fears that he would abuse his authority proved to have little substance.[71] Yet it was not only Valuev's power to impose penalties on the press that worried thoughtful Russians, for the obligation to take responsibility before the law for what they wrote seemed perhaps even more fearsome. "Previously, the censor's shield freed publishers from responsibility to some extent," Nikitenko explained. "Now there is no censor [and] in his place the sword of Damocles hangs over the head of publishers and editors."[72]

For the first time, educated Russians had to face their responsibilities as citizens squarely and, to men and women unaccustomed to the civic duties that Europeans had borne for centuries, the experience was less edifying than some might have hoped. Russians' lack of civic tradition not only made them uncomfortable in taking responsibility for their actions but left them even more unsure about answering for the welfare of their neighbors and their communities. Perhaps nowhere was this more evident than in Russia's towns and cities, where, for a full three-quarters of a century, urban dwellers had been chronic evaders of the civic duties that Catherine II's Municipal Charter of 1785 had imposed on them. That Russia's government no longer could afford the wasteful luxury of overseeing every line published by the nation's authors in the rapidly modernizing post-Crimean era had been a key reason for shifting from preliminary to *karatel'naia* censorship in 1865. In the case of city government, the motivation behind reform once again was to lessen the many and complex responsibilities that the Nicholas system had imposed upon the central administration. In the *zemstva* and in city government, Nikolai Miliutin had written in 1862, "the most experienced and best people" must work to free the central government from the burden of minor local affairs that had consumed so much of its time and resources during the Nicholas era.[73] As work began on what would become the Municipal Reform Statute of 1870, Russians once again were about to be obliged to act as citizens ought. As in the case of the censorship reform, they were not entirely prepared to assume that new burden.

### REFORMING CITY GOVERNMENT

At the end of the Crimean War, about one out of every ten Russians—about 9 million in all—lived in the towns and cities of Alexander II's Empire. With a population of 490,808, St. Petersburg ranked fifth among the cities of the Western world and Moscow, with 368,765 dwellers, ranked eleventh.[74] As Russia stood at the brink of the industrial revolution, these cities faced rapid growth that would bring them all the problems that the urban centers of England, France, Central Europe, and the United States already had experienced. Coupled with new technology that made possible larger and more sophisticated buildings, machines and machine industries, structural steel, and modern communications helped to begin the transformation of Russia's cities as the nineteenth century entered its second half. In fifty years, St. Petersburg's population would triple and Moscow's would quadruple. The population of Warsaw would increase by a factor of five, that of Odessa by six, and Kiev by eight. Not even listed among the fifteen largest cities of the Russian empire in 1856, Tashkent, Ekaterinoslav, Baku, Kharkov, and Łódz all had joined that group by 1910, each of them with a population of more than 200,000.[75]

In 1856, Russia's cities had not yet begun to enter the modern world. Of 738 settlements that the government designated urban areas, 568 had fewer than ten thousand dwellers. In more than half of the 595 "cities" that lay within the geographical confines of European Russia, agriculture remained the population's chief occupation,[76] and the city's chief function continued to be the administrative tasks it performed for the imperial government. "With very few exceptions, our cities have had neither political significance nor importance as industrial centers," the editors of the Ministry of Internal Affairs' seven-volume compilation about *Urban Settlements in the Russian Empire* wrote in 1860. "Many settlements, which had been transformed into cities for administrative purposes," the editors concluded, "still preserve their former rural character."[77] Before the cities of Russia could take on the central economic and social role that their counterparts had claimed in Western Europe, their urban character had to be defined and established in law.[78]

Although the day-to-day administration of such "cities" was the responsibility of the elective institutions that Catherine II's Municipal Charter had created on April 21, 1785, urban government in Russia continued to be a haphazard affair. Most of the institutions specified in Catherine's charter were never established, and the handful of city officials who actually did take office simply failed to carry out the tasks that the central government delegated to them. Incompetence, ignorance, and malignant unconcern vied with outright dishonesty for pride of place as the sin that best characterized the conduct of city officials at midcentury. "Out of every hundred elected officials, two-thirds are swindlers," the Slavophile Ivan Aksakov reported to his superiors in the Ministry of Internal Affairs in 1850. "And, out of every hundred minor bureaucrats, one cannot find even two who are honest."[79] Reports from other parts of Russia complaining that because untrained, illiterate men staffed urban elective offices, control of public affairs went by default to a handful of corrupt clerks confirmed Aksakov's gloomy view.[80]

To be fair, elective officeholding in mid-nineteenth-century Russia was a burden that offered very few legitimate rewards. Minimal at best, salaries for public servants sometimes plummeted into a realm of absurdity that is perhaps best demonstrated by the appalling statistic that, in some towns of Russia, regular members of municipal fire-fighting units received two rubles, eighty-six kopeks (three day's pay for the poorest paid official in St. Petersburg), a year for their services![81] On the higher administrative level, the task of processing documents had become every bit as arduous as in the central government itself. Even without the army of ill-trained scribes that central government offices had at their disposal, St. Petersburg's City Council processed almost eighty thousand written communications in an average year.[82] The object of satire and ridicule, city administration in many parts of Russia had almost ceased to function by midcentury. Gogol' described Russia's urban crisis in openly grotesque terms in *The Inspector General*, but tales of real life fully matched his play. Certainly, Aleksandr Artem'ev's diary account of his visit to Myshkin, a county seat in Iaroslav

Province, rivals *The Inspector General* in terms of the obvious bad taste displayed by provincial town officials and the gross peculation in which they engaged.[83]

By midcentury, the breakdown of Russia's city government had reached crisis proportions. A timid response to a desperate situation, the Municipal Act of 1846 in St. Petersburg had improved the quality of day-to-day administration in Russia's capital but had failed to instill a serious sense of civic responsibility among the city's leading citizens.[84] If there was an area of Russian life where the need for reform was blatantly obvious as Alexander II's reign opened, it was in the towns and cities, where extensive preparation would be needed even to begin the reform process. "Before drafting proposals for the introduction of new principles of public administration [in Russia's cities]," one group of experts wrote, "it is first of all necessary to *define* the character of these settlements . . . so that the prescribed forms of civic administration can be fully in accordance with local needs."[85]

The studies that Nikolai Miliutin's Municipal Section had carried out during the 1840s and early 1850s provided enough data for the Ministry of Internal Affairs to assess the economic and administrative structure of Russia's urban settlements at the beginning of the 1860s, and Valuev used that as a starting point when Alexander II charged him "to seek the means for improving public administration in all cities of the Empire."[86] That Valuev's Ministry of Internal Affairs received full responsibility for drafting such a broad reform indicated the emperor's great confidence, yet, because Valuev could not separate the expressed needs and desires of Russia's many towns and cities from his ministry's larger mission to shape the contours of Russian domestic policy, it also indicated the limits within which the municipal reform process would have to function.

On April 26, 1862, Valuev instructed Russia's provincial governors to convene special all-class committees to prepare recommendations for municipal reform in Russia.[87] Their deliberations were to follow a detailed format prepared by A. D. Shumakher, an enlightened bureaucrat who had begun his rise in the Ministry of Internal Affairs under the tutelage of Perovskii and Miliutin.[88] Assisted by Nikolai Vtorov, a graduate of the University of Kazan who also had become a specialist on municipal government and economy under Miliutin's guidance, Shumakher was to play a key part in preparing the first drafts of the municipal reform of 1870.[89]

In his instructions about how the 509 local committees should proceed with their study of municipal reform in 1862–1863, Shumakher detailed the shortcomings of urban administration in Russia. The functions and responsibilities of municipal public institutions required extensive clarification, he explained, because citizens' eligibility to participate in the public administration of Russia's towns and cities had been defined too narrowly. To have "all municipal civic affairs concentrated in the hands of residents belonging only to those tax-paying or industrial classes who consider themselves alone to be true citizens," as Catherine's charter had decreed, Shumakher argued, now worked against the best interests of the state because it excluded some of the most able city residents from elective office. "Such a limitation," he insisted, was "harmful in the sense that many of the residents [excluded from elected office] . . . , especially those belonging to the nobility, are, by virtue of their education and acquired service experience, potentially the most capable in municipal public office." The poor quality of public administration in Russian towns and cities, Shumakher went on, could only be improved by encouraging a broader stratum of Russia's city population to serve in elected office. "*All classes* paying taxes in the city," he concluded, must be given a role in shaping municipal affairs.[90]

In response to Shumakher's instructions, the local committees called for representation of all classes in municipal elective offices and urged that Russia's central administrative authorities end their interference in city government. Their major concerns thus were to extend those principles of administrative decentralization that were about to be incorporated into the *zemstvo* statutes to city affairs, to reduce the interference of state officials in municipal government, and to broaden the authority of city officials beyond the limited economic and administrative functions set down in Catherine's charter of 1785.[91] Obviously, the efforts of the Ministry of Internal Affairs to stimulate a controlled debate about reforming municipal government had produced broad demands that Shumakher, Vtorov, and their associates would find difficult to satisfy. Despite their readiness to extol *glasnost'* and *zakonnost'* as antidotes to *proizvol* and secrecy in government affairs, Shumakher and Vtorov resisted efforts to eliminate state interference in city government just as Miliutin had in 1846. Valuev's belief that the government must take the lead in directing reform added a ministerial imperative to their own strong convictions.[92]

Many years of experience in the Ministry of Internal Affairs dictated the content of the draft legislation that Shumakher and Vtorov prepared in response to the demands set down by Russia's 509 all-class municipal committees.[93] They retained many of the features of Miliutin's reform of St. Petersburg's administration, insisted that municipal elective assemblies serve only as advisory bodies, and urged that Russia's city governments be subordinated to provincial governors and the Ministry of Internal Affairs in all areas of policy-making.[94]

Yet if they would relinquish none of the central government's prerogatives in making policy, Shumakher and Vtorov proved very willing to look to the West for models on which to base the electoral procedures that would create new city councils. Basing their recommendations on Vtorov's comparative study of local government in Central and Western Europe, they proposed three assemblies of voters, each of which would elect a third of each city council's deputies. Not class origin or occupation but taxes paid on real estate, business enterprises, or commercial activities would serve as the basis for election; those who paid the highest taxes would have a proportionally larger voice in city affairs.[95] This represented a serious effort by Shumakher and Vtorov to bring the best educated citizens into city government.[96]

As head of the Second Section of His Majesty's Own Chancery, Baron Korf had convinced Alexander II in May 1862 to give the Second Section the authority to review all draft legislation before it went to the State Council.[97] Since the initial ministerial recommendations had predated Korf's proposal, the *Zemstvo* and Judicial Reform statutes had been spared this extra level of bureaucratic scrutiny, but Second Section was destined to play a very important part in the municipal reform legislation. Now headed by Count Panin, the Second Section in 1865 proposed to modify Shumakher's and Vtorov's draft to increase the opportunities for local aristocrats to influence urban affairs. Real estate holdings, in addition to taxes paid, the Second Section insisted, must determine eligibility for city office. At the same time, D. M. Sol'skii, a protégé of Korf's who had risen to become

Panin's deputy at the age of thirty-two, urged that municipal governments be allowed to function more independently on a daily basis but that special Provincial Boards for City Affairs composed of the governor, marshals of the nobility, and three other high-ranking provincial officials be established to oversee their work.[98]

Vtorov's sudden death at the beginning of 1865 left Shumakher to face the criticisms of the Second Section alone, and he did not finish reconciling the proposals of Panin and Sol'skii with the principles he and Valuev thought needed to be preserved until the end of the year.[99] Yet, if Vtorov's death increased Shumakher's responsibilities, it also made compromise easier. Because it had been Vtorov who had argued that taxes paid should determine eligibility for membership on the city councils that the new law would establish, Shumakher found it a simple matter to return to his own earlier view that real estate as well as taxes should determine a citizen's eligibility to hold city office.

Although Shumakher would make concessions to increase the influence of the nobility in urban affairs, he would not permit them to occupy the commanding heights of municipal government on the basis of class alone. "The designation of municipal resident," he told the State Council at the end of 1866, "does not comprise a special class status within the state." He therefore insisted that the government of Russia's cities must be shaped upon nonclass principles. "Municipal society," he concluded, "is comprised of all permanent residents of a town or city who own real estate or pay taxes based upon trade or industry conducted within its boundaries."[100] As the State Council and its Department of Laws began to study his proposals for urban reform during 1867 and 1868, Shumakher continued to insist that not class origins but ability to contribute to the development of his community should determine a citizen's eligibility for public service. That he could not defend that position effectively indicated that Shumakher did not have the political skill of his mentors.

During his lengthy career under Miliutin's tutelage, Shumakher had come to know well the bureaucratic maneuvering that was a fundamental element of the legislative process in mid-nineteenth-century Russia. His mastery of the tactics of committee debate nearly rivaled that of such prominent reformers as Miliutin, Zablotskii, and Iakov Solov'ev, but, if he could hold his own with such men in the arena of bureaucratic conflict, Shumakher lacked their ability to see the broader contours of important social and administrative questions and shape draft legislation accordingly. He therefore left key questions about city government unresolved in the draft legislation that the Ministry of Internal Affairs sent to the State Council at the beginning of 1867, and this gave his opponents an opportunity to delay the publication of Russia's municipal reform statute for nearly three years by attacking his work.

Shumakher also suffered from arrogance born of controlling a body of data that was more comprehensive than any available to those enlightened bureaucrats who had drafted the first Great Reform statutes. Firm in his belief that the quantities of information about urban life that he and his colleagues had assembled under Miliutin's guidance in the late 1840s and 1850s could provide a full and accurate view of conditions in Russia's towns and cities, he had paid too little attention to the recommendations that the municipal committees had sent to the Ministry of Internal Affairs in 1863. That made it possible for Baron Korf, who, as head of the State Council's Department of Laws, demanded precision in draft legislation, to convince Russia's senior statesmen to return Shumakher's proposals to the Ministry of Internal Affairs for further work.[101]

Blame for delaying the municipal reform statute should not be laid at Shumakher's door alone. Such rivals as the Ministry of Internal Affairs and the Second Section could hardly be expected to work separately on legislation and have their recommendations fit neatly together. The draft legislation that these agencies sent to the State Council at the end of 1869 therefore disagreed on such crucial questions as electoral procedure, areas of municipal authority, and the extent to which the central government should control the affairs of Russia's towns and cities.[102] When Korf called for a special committee to resolve these disagreements, Alexander II summoned an imperial commission and instructed it to complete a final draft in ten weeks' time. As had been done with the Emancipation Acts and the *zemstvo* reform statutes, this method of establishing a special committee outside the control of any single government agency produced success where separate ministerial reform efforts had failed.

Prince Sergei Urussov (Panin's successor as head of the Second Section) opened the first meeting of the newly appointed imperial commission on January 7, 1870. As with previous commissions of that type, its early work was dominated by enlightened bureaucrats—in this case, Konstantin Grot, Konstantin Domontovich, and Shumakher—who had gained extensive experience under the tutelage of Nikolai Miliutin and Zablotskii during the 1840s and 1850s. Together with Koz'ma Repinskii, who had served in the Second Section since the days of Speranskii, these men settled most of the points of difference between the Ministry of Internal Affairs and the Second Section within a month, although they left unresolved the question of which central government agencies should control the administration of Russia's towns and cities.[103] Perhaps even more important than resolving specific conflicts, Urussov's special commission proposed to shape the municipal reform statutes in such a way as to make it easy to change them when experience showed it to be necessary.[104] At last, the rigid insistence of Nicholaevan officials on precise definition and regulation in draft legislation had begun to give way to the view that experience on the local level should determine the content of Russia's laws.

The first stage of the deliberations of Urussov's special commission ended on January 26, 1870, and the second stage began a fortnight later with ten "experts" being added to its ranks from among Russia's mayors and city council members. Of particular importance, their number included Prince Vladimir Cherkasskii, who had played such a key part in drafting the Emancipation Acts and helping Nikolai Miliutin to draft the reforms of 1864–1866 in Poland. As mayor of Moscow, Cherkasskii championed local authority against the central bureaucracy as Miliutin had done a few years earlier. Then, Mulitutin had argued that "moral responsibility for petty and distant abuses [was] a responsibility not in keeping with the true meaning and dignity of the state power."[105] Now, Cherkasskii called upon the central government to give Russia's mayors broader authority to deal with local problems. Along with Domontovich and Grot, with whom he had collaborated in drafting the Emancipation Acts, he urged that the municipal electorate be expanded to include those well-educated professionals who were beginning to filter into Russia's provincial towns as employees of the *zemstva* even though they held no property.[106] This would increase the expertise available to city governments as they faced the onset of the industrial revolution in Russia. It also would broaden the base from which they could draw elected public servants.

Along with additional recommendations from General Aleksandr Timashev, Valuev's successor as minister of internal affairs, Urussov's commission forwarded a final draft of the Municipal Reform Act to the State Council on March 31, 1870, and the council approved a municipal statute based on its recommendations before the middle of June.[107] Alexander II's approval of their work on June 16 marked the completion of the most lengthily debated of the Great Reforms and put in place more of the elements needed to shape a citizen society in Russia. Certainly, the Municipal Reform Statute placed limits on the development of municipal life and institutions that men such as Cherkasskii would have preferred to do without. As in the case of the rural *zemstva*, Russia's new city councils had to confine themselves to narrowly defined local questions and rely on agencies controlled by the central government for the executive power to enforce their decisions. Yet if Alexander and his advisers had been unwilling to relinquish much of their authority to Russia's towns and cities, they had shown themselves very willing to abandon responsibility for the tasks that had lain within the purview of civic society in the West for many years. Russia's city folk now had to shoulder responsibility for their own public works, public welfare, public health, and public services, and their effort succeeded more quickly than did similar efforts in the *zemstva*. Replacement of the medieval practice of dividing society according to class with divisions based on taxes paid and real estate owned opened the way for men who were more willing and better able to take part in civic affairs than their predecessors had been.

The result was more striking than many of the reform's planners could have imagined. In less than two decades, Russia's newly created city councils increased their spending on public education by an astronomical 760 percent. They spent 660 percent more on public welfare institutions and 540 percent more on public health. Only ten cities in the entire empire boasted annual budgets of more than two hundred thousand rubles in 1871; by 1889 that number had risen to forty, and the average city budget had increased by more than two and a half times.[108] As Nikolai Miliutin had hoped in 1862, the stage had been set for "the most experienced and best people" to be drawn into Russia's urban affairs.[109] The extent to which Russia's towns and cities could sustain that accomplishment would shape municipal society during the coming decades and determine the success of the government's attempt to make Russians responsible for the course of their daily lives while denying them any part in determining their destiny at the national level.

### THE MILITARY REFORMS

The reforms of the 1860s had heralded the end of the ancien regime in Russia. The Emancipation Acts had destroyed the absolute and arbitrary power that lords had exercised over their bondsmen, and the *zemstvo* reform statute had created institutions to govern the countryside in which Russia's newly freed peasants were assigned an important part. The judicial reform statutes had brought into being judges whose tenure no longer depended on the autocrat's whim, as well as public court proceedings in which lawyers spoke for plaintiffs and defendants. These undermined still more of the premises on which the anachronistic autocratic state had been based, for the new order, of necessity, endeavored to protect the rights of Russia's newly emerged citizens. For the first time, the law, not the emperor and his agents, dispensed justice in Russia.

In similar fashion, the law began to define the relationship between subjects and sovereign in different ways. Russia's autocrat still might insist upon directing the course of state affairs in St. Petersburg, but he expected his subjects to take more responsibility for their daily lives and for the economic and social problems that they faced in their communities. As the state began to set aside those burdensome public responsibilities that the old regime had assumed since the days of Peter the Great, Russia's citizens also had to answer for their nation's defense, for the reforms of the 1860s had destroyed the administrative and social order on which the old Russian army had rested. No longer could Russia maintain an armed force based on serfdom and aristocratic privilege. If Russia were to be a nation of citizens, she now required a citizen army.

The man most responsible for transforming Russia's army from a servile to a citizen force was General Dmitrii Alekseevich Miliutin, elder brother of Nikolai Miliutin and minister of war from 1861 until the beginning of Alexander III's reign. Unlike those enlightened bureaucrats who worked during the 1860s to transform the civilian sector of Russian life, Dmitrii Miliutin was not obliged to see his reforms implemented by men who violated their meaning and spirit, for he held the emperor's full confidence from the time he began to prepare Russia's military reforms until well after they had been put into effect. Indeed, Alexander II probably held him in higher esteem during the last year of his reign than he did at any other time in the twenty years Muliutin had served as Russia's minister of war.

Dmitrii Miliutin was the first of those young bureaucratic technicians who had risen to positions of influence toward the end of the Nicholas era to have an opportunity to begin work on reform after the accession of Alexander II.[110] This came even before the end of the Crimean War, when he was appointed to a special commission headed by General Count F. V. Ridiger, a Baltic German hero of Russia's wars against Napoleon and commander of the Guards and Grenadier Corps. An intimate of the emperor and his family for the better part of a quarter century, Ridiger became a sharp critic of the old Nicholaevan order as the Crimean War entered its final months. Russian officers, he warned his new emperor bluntly in June 1855, were blind instruments at the command of their superiors and it was "impossible to expect character, duty, or any sort of understanding of people or affairs from [such] puppets."[111] Two weeks later, Alexander appointed Ridiger to chair the Commission for the Improvement of Military Affairs, whose membership was as diverse as the problems it faced.[112] Ridiger's vice-chairman was the lackluster General P. A. Dannenberg, "distinguished," in the words of one expert, "by his complete lack of ability in military affairs."[113] At the other end of the spectrum stood Prince Aleksandr Bariatinskii, one of the brightest military lights in the new emperor's inner circle.

As a junior member of Ridiger's commission, Dmitrii Miliutin called for Russia to compress her vast standing army into a smaller peacetime force that could be expanded in time of crisis by means of a large reserve system and, perhaps too boldly, even implied that serfdom alone stood in the way of doing so.[114] His strong views stemmed from more than twenty years' experience—as a young line officer in the Caucasus in the 1840s, as a professor at Russia's General Staff War Academy, and as a

General Staff officer—in a military establishment that believed that every military force must function with machinelike precision. "Our officers are trained just like parrots," Miliutin had complained to his diary after he returned to St. Petersburg from fighting his first campaign in the Caucasus. "Until they receive their commissions they are kept in a cage and everyone shouts at them incessantly: 'Polly, Left Face!' and Polly repeats: 'Left Face!' 'Polly, Present Arms!' and Polly repeats this too. When Polly reaches the point at which he has learned all these commands precisely and by heart," he concluded, "they give him epaulets."[115] In the army of Nicholas I, precisely that sort of training was valued most, for parade-ground perfection counted above all else. To march on parade and to perform the manual of arms did not require a soldier to think. "I do not think there has ever been anything more splendid, perfect, or overwhelming since soldiers first appeared on earth," Nicholas remarked after a review in which his armies had performed particularly well. "O Lord, I thank Thee that Thou has given me such power," he added. "Grant me the strength never to abuse it."[116] Miliutin thought very differently. As a young officer on the Guards' General Staff, he had insisted that "it is not enough to use an army like a machine. [A commander]," he concluded, "must know how to manage men."[117]

Certainly 1855–56 was not the time for daring changes in Russia's armed forces, but Ridiger's recommendations for teaching common soldiers to read and write, upgrading their combat training, and teaching officers to be more independent in the field charted a course for others to follow in the years ahead,[118] even though Alexander II's appointment of General Nikolai Sukhozanet as Russia's new minister of war in April 1856 quickly blunted this first call for reforms. Almost certainly chosen because he could be counted on to exercise no initiative in the War Ministry, Sukhozanet responded to his emperor's instructions in the most cautious fashion possible. Although he spoke of "those substantive changes which were recognized as necessary in the organization and administration of the army in order to establish it on a level with current demands of military science and make it a worthy representative of the power of so mighty a state as Russia,"[119] he always identified them with the emperor's own directives and did nothing without specific instructions.

Uncertain of the role he would be called upon to play in a military establishment led by an officer who personified all the rigidity and rudeness of the Nicholaevan military establishment, Miliutin applied for extended leave a month after Sukhozanet's appointment.[120] Like a number of Russians from Pushkin to Tolstoi, he sought refuge in the Caucasus, traditionally a region of freer action and fewer conventional restraints. Yet his was no attempt to escape the obligations of service while Sukhozanet began his timid tinkerings with the administrative machinery of Russia's armed forces. For it was in the Caucasus that substantive military reform first would be tested as Alexander II followed the daring course (in view of Russia's crushing Crimean defeat) of launching a full-scale campaign against the natives who had resisted the Russians' best efforts to subjugate them for a quarter of a century. Over Sukhozanet's insistent objections, Alexander gave command of the Caucasus to Prince Aleksandr Bariatinskii, whom he appointed its viceroy in mid-1856. That fall, Miliutin accepted an appointment as Bariatinskii's chief of staff. With over three hundred thousand men and a sixth of the Empire's military budget at their command, the two men set out to eradicate native resistance to Russian authority and to test the principles of military reform they had discussed on Ridiger's commission.[121]

Much as his younger brother had used the patronage of Count Perovskii to broaden the resources for reform work in the Ministry of Internal Affairs,[122] so Dmitrii Miliutin worked with Bariatinskii in the Caucasus to shape his ideas on military reform. Basing his effort on Bariatinskii's preference for a reorganization of Russia's command structure along Prussian lines that would place greater authority in the hands of officers in the field, he first sought to rationalize the structure of military administration in the Caucasus and develop a plan of operations to defeat the native mountaineers. Together he and Bariatinskii decentralized the army's command structure so that officers could respond more directly to the rapidly changing conditions of battle, raised the standards for promotion, and instituted better combat training.[123] Combined with Bariatinskii's talents in the field, the result was the long-awaited capture in August 1859 of Shamil, leader of the mountain tribesmen in the eastern Caucasus who had eluded the Russians throughout the reign of Nicholas I.[124]

Although Alexander II inherited his father's "paradomania" and much of the Nicholaevan regime survived into the 1860s, there was freedom to test innovations in the Caucasus, and the talent for military planning and administration that Miliutin demonstrated there assured him of Bariatinskii's patronage in court circles. Envisioning a restructuring of the High Command in which the emperor would be commander-in-chief but leave real command of Russia's land forces in the hands of its chief of staff, Bariatinskii championed Miliutin as Sukhozanet's replacement with the idea that Milutin would deal with administration, supply, and logistics while he would take command of Russia's armies himself. Despite his close friendship with Alexander II, Bariatinskii failed to win the position he coveted, but his efforts to advance Miliutin as Sukhozanet's successor proved more fruitful. In August 1860, Alexander named Miliutin as Sukhozanet's deputy. Fifteen months later, on November 9, 1861, he appointed him minister of war.[125]

The ministerial portfolio that Miliutin took up at the end of 1861 was bulging with problems, many of them critical and all of them pressing. The imperial treasury had emerged from the Crimean War more than 1 billion rubles in debt, and that figure had risen at an annual rate of some 75 millions ever since. Sukhozanet had made crude efforts to reduce Russia's military budget by returning nearly a quarter million of its wartime forces to civilian life, by shortening terms of service, by delaying new recruit levies, and by abolishing military colonies and units of military cantonists, but Russia's military establishment still had well over three-quarters of a million men on active duty at a cost of nearly a 100 million rubles a year at the end of 1861.[126] None of this was a secret to anyone who moved in the upper reaches of Russia's military establishment. Nor was it a secret that the War Ministry's effort to replace the smoothbore flintlock muskets that her soldiers had carried since before the days of Suvorov with percussion rifle-muskets had required its ordnance officers to place large weapons orders abroad.[127] Rearming Russia's army with weapons purchased abroad would add millions of rubles to the military budget in the years ahead; men of vision, who could see that breech-loading weapons soon would make even the new muzzle-loading rifles obsolete, could imagine that the costly rearming of Russia's forces after the Crimean War soon would have to be repeated.

The high costs of keeping a huge armed force and purchasing expensive weapons needed for rearmament were only part of the problem Miliutin faced. Russia's army still bore too much the stamp of the Nicholaevan establishment, with its extreme centralization, parade-ground precision, and automaton-like training of officers and men. Broader education for officers; better training (including regular rifle practice); reform of the ordnance service and quartermaster corps to provide better supplies of food, uniforms, and ammunition; decentralization of command authority; and, above all (and the point to which Miliutin returned repeatedly), a need to transform Russia's standing army into a leaner peacetime force supplemented by a system of reserves—all had to be included in any serious reform program.

Much of what Miliutin would undertake during his two decades in office already had been anticipated on a smaller scale by the reforms of Grand Duke Konstantin Nikolaevich in the Admiralty, and the example of the grand duke's effort was never far from Miliutin's mind.[128] From the moment he took charge of Russia's military affairs, Miliutin introduced into the War Ministry the same sort of "artificial" *glasnost'* that Grand Duke Konstantin Nikolaevich had used in the Admiralty a decade before. In June 1856, Miliutin had urged that the War Ministry publish a journal that could provide a forum in which officers could discuss key military questions, and he clearly had in mind the widely read *Morskoi sbornik*, which Konstantin Nikolaevich had established. Although *Voennyi sbornik* (*Military Miscellany*) did not come into being until 1858, when Miliutin and Bariatinskii were in the Caucasus, it was a striking enterprise from its beginnings. Initially edited by none other than the radical publicist Nikolai Chernyshevskii and Captain Nikolai Obruchev, a staff officer who flirted briefly with revolutionary activism before rising to become imperial chief of staff in the 1880s, *Voennyi sbornik* had a circulation that soared to six thousand within a few months. Chernyshevskii resigned in less than a year, but the journal continued to attract important contributors and a large readership. As soon as he took command of the War Ministry, Miliutin began to use *Voennyi sbornik* as an instrument to encourage discussion of military reforms among Russia's officer corps.[129]

Although the opening of the reform debate in the late 1850s had found cadres of reformers already assembled and experienced in working together in several of Russia's civilian ministries, the experience of the War Ministry had been very different. Headed by conservative officers who were forever wed to the tried and true, its establishment tolerated no word of criticism or call for change. "The organization of military administration finds itself at the desired level of perfection and requires no essential changes whatever," War Minister General Prince Aleksandr Chernyshev had reported confidently each year between 1837–1852, and his successor General Prince Vasilii Dolgorukov made no effort to alter that view despite the strains of the Crimean War.[130] "Right up until the death of the Emperor Nicholas I," the author of the official history of Russia's War Ministry wrote at the beginning of the twentieth century, "not a single word of criticism was ever spoken about the organization of the military administration."[131]

Unlike Chernyshev and Dolgorukov, Sukhozanet had understood that change must inevitably come but had proceeded only on direct orders from his emperor and then with the greatest caution possible. Surrounded by men well known for their timidity, Sukhozanet gave no encouragement to officers who proposed reform or tried to move with the spirit of the times.[132] He therefore left no legacy of men experienced in confronting the dilemmas of modernization and reform as Kiselev and Perovskii had in the Nicholaevan Ministries of State Domains and Internal Affairs, and Miliutin's first task therefore was to create the cadre of reformers needed to modernize Russia's army that his conservative predecessors' stubborn discouragement of change had prevented from developing on its own.

In a bureaucracy known for its slowness in making decisions, Miliutin moved with remarkable quickness. Working closely with an inner circle of carefully chosen advisers, he organized conferences to discuss the problems of reform, formed special commissions to discuss how reform might be accomplished, and encouraged concerned officers to criticize the shortcomings of the Nicholaevan army in *Voennyi sbornik*. On January 15, 1862, he laid before the emperor his recommendations for the army in the typical form of a "Most Humble Report" that contained the blueprint of the reform program he would implement during the next twelve years. As might be expected from the work that his longtime friends among Russia's bureaucratic reformers already had accomplished in the civilian sector, Miliutin emphasized decentralization, *zakonnost'*, and a program of education that, by training recruits to be better soldiers, would make them better citizens.[133]

The difficulty that had to be addressed first, Miliutin wrote at the beginning of his report, was "the need to reconcile as closely as possible two mutually contradictory goals." Russia's military expenses must be reduced, but her armed forces must be kept powerful enough to maintain her status as a great power among the nations of Europe.[134] "The requirements of foreign policy," Miliutin stated flatly, "dictate, in large measure, the lower limits below which it is impossible to permit the Empire's military strength to fall."[135] Yet it would not be enough, he warned, for Russia to maintain her great power status among the nations of the West. The Russian empire consisted of far-flung territories that bordered states as diverse as Great Britain's Canadian territories, China, the khanates of Central Asia, Persia, and the Ottoman Empire. Inhabited by people who spoke more than a hundred different languages and dialects, many of whom longed for liberation from Russian domination, these lands remained wellsprings of chronic discord.

Fear of serf revolts and uprisings among these turbulent national minorities had long required Russia's rulers to garrison large numbers of soldiers across an empire whose territories required a full year to cross before the coming of the railroad. The manpower needs of Russia's armed forces therefore were dictated not only by the "requirements of foreign policy," Miliutin explained, but by the needs of domestic security. "Significant reductions [in the size of these armed forces] will be possible," he concluded, "only when the [newly emancipated] peasants become aware of all the benefits bestowed upon them by freedom."[136]

Convinced that, until other reforms had been accomplished, it was impossible "even to think of reducing [the size of] the army" below the eight-hundred-thousand-man force that it comprised at the beginning of 1862, Miliutin tried to reduce the cost of administering the large army that foreign and domestic needs required his nation to maintain by a thorough reorganization of Russia's military administration. Miliutin recognized that a major factor in the empire's bloated military budget was the extreme centralization of the Nicholaevan military establishment, which, he once had remarked, had reduced even the minister of war to a mere "secretary to the Sovereign for military affairs . . . [who] almost never took any personal initiative."[137] He therefore proposed that Russia's ponderous armies and corps, whose large and costly peacetime staffs had proved worthless in wartime, be replaced by fifteen military administrative districts whose commanders would take full responsibility for the troops garrisoned within them. By doing so, he hoped to make it easier to mobilize the army and free the War Ministry from tasks that had consumed the energies of too many staff officers during the Nicholaevan era.[138] "The most important advantage of the proposed organization," Miliutin explained to Alexander II at the beginning of May 1862, "is that only in this way will it be possible to eliminate the most basic flaw in our military administration—its extreme concentration in the War Ministry."[139] Looking further ahead, Miliutin's plan would create the administrative base that would serve the reduced standing army and modern reserve system he would establish a decade later.

To win support for the reforms he proposed, Miliutin circulated his May 1862 memorandum to more than two hundred senior commanders. "The most important shortcoming of our military administration is to be found in the extreme concentration of administration in the [War] Ministry," he wrote. "The best means for eliminating this failing is the organization of *local* military administrations, similar to those already in existence in the Caucasus, the Orenburg region, and Siberia, for the purpose of dividing the remaining area of the Empire into a number of military districts."[140] As his friends among the civilian officials who were preparing the *zemstvo* reform statutes learned from provincial Russians at about the same time, Miliutin found considerable support for decentralization among Russia's senior commanders. Opposition came mainly from those senior generals who preserved the outlook and values of the Nicholaevan military establishment.[141]

Miliutin's plans to decentralize Russia's military administration closely paralleled the introduction of similar measures in the empire's local government. On August 6, 1864, just a little over seven months after the *zemstvo* statutes were published, Alexander II established military districts in Russia. Four such districts already had been created in 1862 as part of Russia's efforts to quell unrest in her western provinces and, later, to crush the revolt of 1863–1864 in Poland. Thus, to the Warsaw,

Vilno, Kiev, and Odessa military districts, six others (St. Petersburg, Moscow, Finland, Riga, Kharkov, and Kazan) were added in 1864 and five more (Turkestan, Western Siberia, Eastern Siberia, the Caucasus, and the Orenburg region) were created a few years later.[142] This reorganization yielded dramatic results. Before Miliutin left the War Ministry in 1881, the number of officers and civilian administrative personnel assigned to Russia's army units outside its central offices had plummeted by more than a third.[143]

Significantly, much of Miliutin's military district system would survive into the Soviet Union of the 1980s, as would his program to reshape the General Staff into a center for military planning and war preparation. Beginning with the artillery and engineers in 1862 and finishing with the General Staff in 1867, Miliutin brought the central administration of the War Ministry into line with his new system of military districts and cut nearly a thousand positions from the ministry's tables of organization. During those years, perhaps for the first time anywhere in Russia's central government, he also stemmed the flood of official correspondence. Between 1863 and 1875, the number of official documents processed by the War Ministry fell by almost half, from 446,044 to 244,291 as Miliutin broke down the Nicholaevan procedures that had required all matters, no matter how insignificant, to be carried to the war minister himself.[144] This did not mean that Miliutin, himself more a military bureaucrat than a field commander, relieved his subordinates of paperwork. Indeed, accusations that he overburdened field officers with too many bureaucratic responsibilities were among the favorite charges that his enemies directed against him from time to time.[145] Still, among bureaucrats who regarded the production of official documents as a measure of achievement, Miliutin's effort to reduce correspondence between various staffs and the War Ministry indicated a shift in attitudes that most reformers had thought impossible to achieve. Although every progressive Russian statesman had tried to discourage bureaucrats' infatuation with paperwork since at least the early 1840s,[146] only Dmitrii Miliutin had achieved results.

If Russia were to transform her cumbersome standing army into a citizen force like those that defended the nations of the West, the rank and file had to develop attitudes more appropriate to citizen soldiers. The faster-firing breech-loading weapons being adopted by the armies of Europe and America that Miliutin soon hoped to place in the hands of Russia's soldiers made that transformation even more necessary, for commanders had to deploy smaller, more mobile tactical units to minimize soldiers' exposure to the more deadly fire that such weapons could deliver. Such a revolution in tactics required officers and men who could act independently rather than depend on tactical decisions made at the corps or army level, as had been the case in the Nicholaevan army. To achieve that transformation, Russia's officers needed better training. At the same time, illiterate peasant recruits had to be taught to read and write.

One of Miliutin's contemporaries once wrote, "the military reform compelled the masses to study just when [Minister of Public Instruction] Count D. A. Tolstoi was impeding the development of literacy."[147] Certainly Miliutin made unprecedented efforts to educate Russia's peasant recruits in the 1860s and 1870s. *Soldatskaia beseda* (*Soldier's Talk*), a journal similar to the volumes of *Sel'skoe chtenie* (*Village Reading-matter*) that Zablotskii and Prince Odoevskii had published in the Ministry of State Domains to educate Russia's state peasants in the 1840s, became the instrument that the War Ministry used to reach the one soldier in eleven or twelve who could read simple prose. To educate the illiterate mass of peasants in Russia's service, Miliutin developed new programs to teach the rudiments of reading, writing, and arithmetic. Conducted on the lowest command levels of the army—in infantry companies, artillery batteries, and cavalry squadrons that had been driven into winter quarters by the ravages of the cold—these programs produced striking results. By the end of the 1860s, almost half of the enlisted men in Russia's army could read; slightly more than a quarter could write as well.[148]

To train Russia's officers to lead a modern army required even greater effort. As is often the case with educational reformers, Miliutin proposed a program that reflected his perceptions of the strengths and weaknesses of his own education. Unlike many Russian officers, he had studied at the Boarding School for Sons of the Nobility at Moscow University before he entered the army, and the values he learned there him made him critical of the narrow training he received at the General Staff War Academy. In a memorandum written in 1862 for Grand Duke Mikhail Nikolaevich, Rostovtsev's successor as chief of Russia's military school administration, Miliutin argued that Russia's officers must be educated more broadly to prevent the rigid outlook that had been so common during the time of Nicholas. Convinced that the constraints of such extreme military discipline would cause "fundamental damage to the moral qualities of young men," Miliutin urged that "the education of boys and youths ought to be undertaken at home and in civilian [educational] institutions. Purely military institutions," he concluded, "ought to exist only for a single purpose: to provide special [military] academic education for those young men who feel themselves drawn to military careers."[149]

Beginning in 1862 and continuing into the 1870s, Miliutin therefore presided over the modernization of Russia's system of military education. Most notably, he reorganized the elite Cadet Corps into a group of specialized military institutions that were fed from below by civilian schools offering a broader curriculum. Young men therefore did not enter military school before the age of sixteen, and not until after they had completed a regular course of public school education.[150] Clearly the old days of training officers in the manner of parrots were passing but, as in the military services of any nation, tradition died hard in Russia. Certainly it can be argued that the elite, expensive, privilege-ridden Cadet Corps schools survived in the somewhat disguised form of special military *gimnazii* and that they continued to influence the attitudes of Russia's officer corps. Nonetheless, most of Russia's officers graduated from the new Miliutin schools on the eve of the twentieth century, and many of them were from very modest, even peasant, origins.[151]

During the 1860s, Miliutin broadened his reform program in an effort to humanize military justice, improve the quality of the enlisted men's rations and clothing, and raise the quality of medical care in Russia's armed forces. Most remarkably, Miliutin accomplished these broad reforms as well as a major rearmament program at reasonable cost during a decade when military budgets were soaring in the West. Germany had to increase her military budget by 164 percent between 1859 and 1874 to replace muzzle-loading muskets and cannon with with breech-loading rifles and modern field guns; under Miliutin's careful stewardship, Russia's military budget rose by less than a third of that amount.[152]

All of these efforts marked a turn in the direction of building a military force in which men took up arms out of a sense of duty as citizens to defend their homeland. Still, the old order of privilege was destined to survive so long as Russia's army continued to be one of peasant conscripts commanded by aristocratic officers for whom military service remained entirely voluntary. To transform Russia's fighting forces into a citizen army required all men to bear an equal obligation to defend their nation. That could be accomplished only if universal military service replaced the forms of conscription that Russia's absolutist government had employed during the days of serfdom. Before that could be done, Miliutin had to create a large pool of trained reserves so that Russia could expand her reduced peacetime forces in the event of war. To do so required time and careful planning. Beginning in 1862, Miliutin therefore had set the empire's annual quota of recruits, all of whom still came from the lower classes, at 125,000 men. These were to be sent on permanent leave after they had served only seven or eight years of their twenty-five-year terms so that, by the end of the decade, Russia would have a military reserve more than three times larger than when he had taken office. Such reserves then would make it possible to reduce the empire's standing army and institute the all-class citizen force that Western nations already had tested in the Austro-Prussian and Franco-Prussian wars.[153]

As the Franco-Prussian War neared its end late in 1870, Miliutin faced his most difficult challenge. His earlier reforms had angered powerful men whose personal animosity, ambition, or desire to defend the order that had bestowed high ranks upon them had set them against the changes Miliutin thought vital to Russia's welfare. If his earlier reforms had made such men uneasy, his proposals for an all-class citizen army now outraged them by challenging the very foundation of noble privilege in Russia. Conservatives saw in Miliutin's plans the most fundamental attack yet to be made against the nobility, which already had sustained assaults from the Emancipation of 1861, the *zemstvo* reforms, and the Judicial Reform Statutes of 1864. Not only such senior generals as P. A. Fadeev and Miliutin's former patron Prince Bariatinskii but also Minister of Public Instruction Count Dmitrii Tolstoi, Minister of Foreign Affairs Prince Aleksandr Gorchakov, and Mikhail Katkov and his ultraconservative journal *Moskovskie vedomosti* (*Moscow Gazette*) all formed a common front against his program.[154]

Such opposition could not be dismissed lightly. Nor could it be dealt with quickly. Still the apostle of reform and modernization in the imperial family, Grand Duke Konstantin Nikolaevich wrote of "terribly difficult" sessions in the State Council during which the supporters of Miliutin's draft universal military service statute failed to "move even one paragraph forward."[155] Against such opponents, it required a full three years of maneuvering before emperor and war minister were ready to announce on New Year's Day 1874 that "the defense of throne and homeland against foreign enemies is the sacred duty of every Russian subject" and must be borne by all men "without distinction of class."[156] The consequences of that single statement were tremendous and far-reaching; so much so that Alexander had insisted that Miliutin add the words *throne* and *subject* to his draft of the law's initial paragraph to moderate some of its most startling implications. For, without the addition of those words, the Universal Military Service Statute would have begun with the very clear implication that Russians ought to place allegiance to their country before loyalty to their sovereign. Such a view fit poorly with the concept of an autocracy in which men served the emperor, not the nation.

Even more certain—and this was fact, not implication—the publication of the Universal Military Service Statute meant that Alexander had rescinded the emancipation from compulsory state service that Russia's nobles had wrested from his great-great-grandfather, Peter III, in 1762. As of January 1, 1874, all Russian men bore an equal obligation before the law to defend their country. Every Russian male now had to register for military service between the ages of sixteen and twenty, although by no means all would be drafted. Those on whom service fell by lot faced a fifteen-year term, which was divided in varying proportions among the regular army, the reserve, and the militia, with those who had the least education serving the longest terms (up to six years) in the active forces and those with university educations at the time they received their call-up notices serving as little as six months. To these requirements there were many exceptions and exemptions, but none was based strictly on class origins.

Men whose fathers, grandfathers, or uncles had died in military service; who had a father or brother in the army; or could claim to be only sons—all could request exemption from the draft under Miliutin's new statute. So could hundreds of thousands of able-bodied young men whose family status allowed them to claim exemption as "breadwinners." Even those who did not qualify for such exemptions were by no means certain candidates for induction. Before the new statute had been in effect for a quarter century, a full 50 percent of those who received call-up notices appealed their conscription and nearly three out of every four won a release.[157] On the eve of the outbreak of the Russo-Japanese War in 1904, fifteen times as many Russians as Germans or Austro-Hungarians won exemptions from military service for family reasons.[158] "The army," cynics began to remark, "is an assembly of people who have failed to evade military service."[159] Still, none of these exemptions had class as its chief criterion. If shortages of available men forced the Russian authorities to draft more recruits with physical defects and poor health at the beginning of the twentieth century than did their counterparts in England, France, Germany, or Austria-Hungary, it was not because the empire's formerly privileged classes had been exempted from service.

The reform legislation that Miliutin drafted during the 1860s and 1870s thus transferred all of the social changes wrought by the Great Reforms in the civilian sector of Russian life to the army, traditionally the most conservative institution in the empire. Although it may be an exaggeration to claim, as some enthusiastic historians have, that "it was in the army, that stronghold of tradition and conservatism, that Russian democracy scored one of its first modest, yet real, successes,"[160] there can be no doubt that Miliutin's Universal Military Service Statute created the judicial and institutional framework for a modern army in Russia, elements of which would survive for more than a century. The dilemma that Russians still faced was that no one, from emperor to peasant, clearly understood what a citizen was and what constituted civic society. Who were Russia's citizens? Were they all equal in fact as well as under the law? How did one become a part of civic society? The Great Reforms had addressed these questions only in the most general terms, with none of the answers clearly stated.

At the same time, the institutions of civic society that the Great Reforms had tried to create on the local level had been kept firmly subordinate to the government and its bureaucracy.

Although the men who had drafted the Great Reforms had acclaimed *zakonnost'* and condemned the *proizvol* of government officials, they had not really faced squarely the hard fact that the autocracy was itself an institutionalization of *proizvol*. The conflict between *proizvol* and *zakonnost'* thus remained, whatever efforts the Great Reform statutes had made to institute rule by law in Russia. Until that fundamental contradiction was resolved, it remained unclear how power would be exercised, who would exercise it, and how policy would be shaped. Most of all, it remained unclear where the final source of power lay in Russia now that the Great Reforms had undercut the privileges of the nobility and the ancient precepts that permitted only the autocrat to interpret the law. As the 1870s neared their midpoint, the meanings of *glasnost'* and *zakonnost'* and their relationship to *proizvol* still remained unclear. Until those dilemmas were resolved, the meaning of the Great Reforms remained clouded and their significance not fully realized. A time of testing therefore lay ahead. During the thirty years after Miliutin issued the Universal Military Service Statute, the Great Reforms would be challenged from Left and Right to test their provisions and clarify their meaning. Only when that had been accomplished could the Great Reform society be defined and its full achievement measured.

# V

## TESTING THE
## GREAT REFORMS

*T*he Russian empire had entered the era of the Great Reforms with the creaking impedimenta of the Nicholas system intact. In this rigidly ordered society, in which extreme militarism had intensified the abusiveness of unchecked power, or *proizvol*, a hierarchy of authority had extended upward from manor houses to the imperial throne to enable lords to rule the lives of their serfs while the emperor and his high officials ruled them. Daily life in Russia's provinces thus had remained under the control of local lords at the same time as the authority to resolve all matters of administration and state policy was concentrated at the top. Russians had understood in those days that the key to action was to reach that point in the hierarchy of authority where decisions could be made, problems solved, and favors won. Those who could not reach that point had remained mired in the morass of inaction and indecision that held men of high and low estate in check while officials waited for decisions to be handed down from above. "The entire life of the people is under governmental tutelage," one bitter provincial marshal of the nobility had complained in 1859. "No question, however trifling, can be dealt with by the people themselves."[1]

Despite its failings, the Nicholas system had endowed Russians with a more complete system of values than any they had known since Peter the Great had shattered the precepts that had ruled life in Muscovite Russia. The profane trinity of Orthodoxy, Autocracy, and Nationality had told Russians what to believe, what they should and could not write, and what the higher purpose of their lives ought to be. Just as the *proizvol* exercised by emperor, high officials, and provincial lords had been imposed from above, so had Official Nationality imposed itself on the Russians, but the men and women who had drawn a sense of satisfaction from the certainty of this system of values had far outnumbered those who found it repressive. "This fortunate land of Russia," High State Counselor Aleksandr Kamenskii had written enthusiastically in 1850, "is blossoming under the sacred, beneficent protection of autocracy."[2] "Why change that political system which made [Russia] a first-class power in the world?" another high-ranking Russian had asked a few years later. It would be "ill-advised and dangerous," he had concluded, "to undermine [Russia's] foundations, everything that constitutes its strength and essence."[3] That life in Russia had taken on a certainty at midcentury that it had not known since the church schism of the 1660s was an accomplishment that many Russians had been prepared to attribute to their emperor and the system he had created. "During the lifetime of [the emperor] Nikolai Pavlovich, Russia had great and noble stature," one of them wrote wistfully from the perspective of the 1880s. "Everyone and everything bowed down before him and before Russia!"[4]

Followed in a year by defeat in the Crimean War, the death of Nicholas I in February 1855 had shaken the certainty of those Russians who had extolled the Nicholas system at the same time as it had shattered the complacency with which they had viewed the world around them. The Crimean defeat had cost Russia no vital territory and posed no immediate threat to her security, but it nonetheless had forced her statesmen to search for the causes of their empire's weakness and to ponder the failings that their searching revealed. None could escape the certainty that the Crimean defeat had called into question the military strength on which Russia had built her claim to great power status since the time of Peter the Great. Alexander II and his chief advisers therefore had to rethink their nation's foreign policy, gain a clearer sense of the resources they had at their command, and clarify the direction in which domestic affairs must move in the years ahead. Although they had approached the matter with considerably less urgency than often has been argued, Russia's statesmen and emperor soon had realized that resolute and far-reaching renovations would be required if Russia were to move resolutely into the second half of the nineteenth century.

If the need for change had not been difficult to recognize, its dimensions and implications had been much less clearly understood. Alexander II, Russia's bureaucratic reformers, and their supporters among the senior statesmen of the empire therefore had all experimented with using public debate about the problems of renovation and reform to clarify their views about the direction in which state policy ought to move. Although they had hoped to shape them around the familiar precepts of Orthodoxy, Autocracy, and Nationality and use them to build support for state policy, none had been willing to permit such discussions to evolve into open public participation in policymaking. Eager to preserve the integrity of the autocratic legislative process that had evolved during the second quarter of the nineteenth century, they had looked to some limited form of *glasnost'*, perhaps what the reform-minded Grand Duke Konstantin Nikolaevich once had called "artificial" *glasnost'*, as a means to consult public opinion without allowing it direct access to the decision-making apparatus in Russia's government. Since the government no longer could bear full responsibility for Russians' welfare as it once had, they also hoped to use *glasnost'* to induce Russia's newly emerging citizens to assume a greater role in shaping their daily lives.

The rigidity of autocracy had conflicted with *glasnost'* too sharply for that to happen. Far too quickly, the expectations of Russia's new citizens had exceeded the willingness of the autocrat and his advisers to satisfy them, and that had produced deeper and sharper tensions between government and *obshchestvo,* the educated classes destined to become active in the civic life of Russia. Moderate nobles called for a voice in national affairs while radicals condemned the emancipation as a new form of serfdom designed to replace the old one.[5] The government, the first illegal printed work of the 1860s had warned, was "leading Russia into a *pugachevshchina*," a massive peasant revolt of the type that had swept the empire in the 1770s. *Obshchestvo* therefore must "take the conduct of affairs into its own hands and out of the hands of the incompetent government." Only in that way would it be possible to "save the masses from such torment."[6]

During the days after the Emancipation proclamation, such sharp criticism of the government's first major step toward renovation left the limits of *glasnost'* unclear and its future in doubt. Offended and angry at what he considered to be its unwarranted trespass into the sacrosanct preserve of government activity, one senior official already had roundly condemned *glasnost'* as a force that stood "in opposition to the spirit and bases of state institutions, and to Russia's system of administration and legislation."[7] As radicals' criticisms of the emancipation deepened, and as conservative lords who once had stood with the government against all critics demanded a more decisive voice in the decisions affecting the regions in which they lived, other senior officials came to share that uncompromising and bluntly stated view. The *obshchestvo* that the government had hoped to co-opt during the days when Russians had reveled in their first taste of *glasnost'* now had begun to broaden. As its views became more diverse, it began to disagree more sharply with the government about the limits within which *glasnost'* ought to function. Could *glasnost'* serve the government as a source of public opinion? Should it function independently as a benchmark against which to measure the government's commitment to renovation? Or had it, as a conservative critic wrote, so failed to "conform to our civic order [and] the peculiarities of our national character" that it ought not to function at all?[8]

Among those who believed that *glasnost'* must be preserved if Russia were to rejoin the mainstream of European experience, the men who drafted the Judicial Reform Statutes had insisted that it must serve not only as an antidote to *proizvol*, but also as a guarantor of *zakonnost'*, the aspiration to lawfulness that held out hope for transforming Russia from a state ruled by the caprice of officials and landowners into a nation in which the law shaped the behavior of its citizens.[9] The Judicial Reform Statutes' institutionalization of *glasnost'* within Russia's new court system in the form of public trials conducted by independent judges thus had guaranteed the survival of *glasnost'* and begun to define the boundaries within which it could function. Government and governed now both faced what the great jurist Aleksandr Koni once called "a judge-man, not an indifferent machine who signed decisions prepared by the chancellery"[10] in defining the limits that were permissible in law, society, and administration.

Whether Russia's path moved toward the Left or the Right, public trials and independent judges meant that *glasnost'* itself could not be obliterated without shattering the judicial foundations on which the social and institutional renovations of the

1860s and 1870s were being constructed. In time, this process could produce a new basis upon which to build the society in which Russians were destined to live as they entered the industrial revolution and approached the twentieth century. For, if Orthodoxy, Autocracy, and Nationality no longer sufficed to unite the Russians, the aspiration to *zakonnost'*—to make the law's application "swift, just, merciful, and equal for all," as Alexander II had announced in the beginning of the Judicial Reform Statutes—might do so. This posed the possibility of reuniting those educated men and women whose diverging visions of Russia's future had forced them to take different directions since at least the end of the eighteenth century into a society that respected the law and allowed it to rule its actions.

Although the aspiration to *zakonnost'* might become a focus around which *obshchestvo* might one day coalesce, the *proizvol-zakonnost'* dichotomy continued to pose major problems for the Russians as the 1860s began to shade toward the 1870s. Partly because the framers of the Great Reform legislation themselves had not begun their work with a clear vision of what the Great Reform society ought to be, and partly because the full meaning of the legislation had yet to be tested and clarified, it remained uncertain where the line between government and governed would be drawn and how the authority of each would be applied. Because *proizvol* would remain a factor in Russian government and politics so long as autocracy survived and because the aspiration to *zakonnost'* would continue so long as *glasnost'* remained to defend it, the areas in which each could be exercised had to be defined. How paramount state interest ought to be and how far citizens' rights could be extended also had to be considered. To define the parameters of each required that the Great Reforms be tested in the manner of all bodies of social legislation, whose full meaning only could be determined by practical experience. This moved the Great Reforms from the realm of administration into the world of politics and social action. Only after the forces of Left and Right had probed their limits could the boundaries of the Great Reform legislation be clearly established.

Between the mid-1870s and the death of Alexander III in 1894, the Great Reforms therefore were tested from the Left and Right as the Russians sought to define the limits within which *glasnost'*, *proizvol*, and *zakonnost'* could function. Testing from the

Left began almost as soon as the emancipation was decreed as radical Russians pressed the government to broaden the limits of *glasnost'* beyond those that had produced the Emancipation debate itself. In *Kolokol*, Herzen and Ogarev proclaimed the serfs' liberation to be a fraud, a new form of serfdom, in which the government hoped to convince Russia's peasants "that black was not black and that two plus two does not equal four."[11] "The people need land and freedom," Ogarev insisted from London that summer, "land, freedom, and education."[12] "It is impossible to live this way any longer," *Kolokol* added that fall, "but things can't get any better so long as power remains in the hands of a Tsar." It was nothing more than "sentimentalism" to expect *obshchestvo* to provide leadership, the article continued, because its interests and the government's were one and the same. "*Obshchestvo* will never really oppose the government," *Kolokol* concluded in mid-September. "And it will never voluntarily give the masses what they need."[13] Well before the end of 1861, *Kolokol* had rejected autocracy, bureaucracy, and *obshchestvo* as instruments for renovation and reform. For radicals who cast their lot with the editors of *Kolokol*, the masses remained the only hope for true liberation and progress.

Within Russia, the year 1861 saw close to 250 peasant protests, including some that led to violence.[14] At Bezdna, a village to the southeast of Kazan, soldiers massacred some two hundred peasants[15]; at Kandeevka, two companies of infantry faced ten thousand peasants and, although the casualties numbered far fewer than at Bezdna, the sense of unease that the incident stirred was scarcely less intense.[16] In the middle of 1861, such incidents seemed to promise more disorders and young radicals seized upon their elders' forebodings as a starting point for their criticisms of the new course on which their nation had embarked. "Imperial Russia is in dissolution," the manifesto *To the Younger Generation* proclaimed that fall. "We do not need either a Tsar, an Emperor, the myth of some lord, or the purple which cloaks hereditary incompetence," its authors announced, as they called "the younger generation" to "move boldly forward to the revolution" in which a popular republic based on the communal institutions of peasant life would replace Russia's autocracy and bureaucracy.[17]

Although disappointed with the Emancipation and disillusioned with their emperor, most Russian radicals did not choose revolution as their preferred course at first. Certain that "if matters continue along their present course we must expect terrible upheavals," the authors of the first issue of *Velikoruss* (*The Great Russian*) summoned *obshchestvo* to "take matters out of the hands of the inept government." Convinced that even an "all-powerful sovereign" could not withstand the overwhelming force of bureaucratic formalism, intrigue, and deception," *Velikoruss* concluded that "only a government based upon the free will of the nation can complete those transformations without which Russia will suffer frightful upheavals." For such men, efforts by "the enlightened part of the nation" remained preferable to mass action. The hope still remained that *obshchestvo* could "curb the government and give it direction."[18] Only if that failed would they turn to the masses.

Attempts to call the government to account broadened in 1861 as Russia's university students turned onto a collision course with the authorities. The broadening liberation movement of the later 1850s had thrown the empire's universities into turmoil, and there had been clashes between the garrison and students in Kazan during the fall of 1856 and at Kiev a year later. In 1857, several students at Moscow University had suffered serious injuries in a scuffle with the police, and the next year had seen student protests recur in Moscow and break out anew in Kazan and Kharkov.[19] "The university became especially attractive," one student remembered as he recalled the appeal that radicalism had for him and his comrades in those days. "You were expecting something new, special, bravura. Everyone felt an irresistible longing to show his worth in some desperately courageous, heroic action."[20] There were rumors: rumors of a constitution, rumors of a revolution, rumors that the capital would be moved. That none of them had any real substance made them all the more exciting.[21] Tension mounted in classrooms, student eating houses, and on city streets. "The very air," another student remembered, "seemed alive with the thirst for progress and enlightenment."[22]

The storm burst in the fall of 1861, when, after several months of confrontations, students at the University of St. Petersburg moved into the streets to demonstrate against the authorities. A flood of arrests that filled the cells in the Peter and Paul Fortress and required the use of the nearby Kronstadt naval base for the overflow followed a bloody confrontation between students and police on October 12, and, for a brief moment, it seemed that *obshchestvo* and the students would coalesce in the cause of Russia's liberation.[23] "The mood of society was extraordinarily elevated," one student recalled. "The main thing was the general expectation that something of enormous significance was going to happen, perhaps even in the very near future."[24] By the end of the year the authorities abandoned any further effort at reconciliation. Although the emperor removed the inept Putiatin from his position as minister of public instruction just before the new year and installed Golovnin in his place, he left the university closed until August 1863, when the rising wave of anti-Polish sentiment that came in the wake of the Polish revolution of that year began, albeit briefly, to reunite *obshchestvo* and government.

Coupled with the fires of 1862 and the outbreak of revolution in Poland at the beginning of 1863, the university disorders of 1861 narrowed the middle ground on which Russia's government, *obshchestvo*, and radicals might stand and drove them toward both extremes of the political spectrum. "What can be smashed should be," the radical critic Dmitrii Pisarev wrote in presenting what he called "the ultimatum of our camp" in 1861. "What stands up under the blows," he continued, "is acceptable. What flies into a thousand pieces is trash."[25] Personified in the minds of many by Bazarov, the leading character in Turgenev's *Fathers and Sons*, nihilists began to replace those civic-minded members of *obshchestvo* who had hoped that "the enlightened part of the nation" could "curb the government and give it direction." The nihilist now became the idol of those who yearned to make their mark by some "desperately courageous, heroic action."

As defined by Pisarev in the essay "Bazarov" that he published in *Russkoe Slovo* (*The Russian Word*) in 1862, nihilism offered no positive vision, no plan for social or political action. Russia's "new man," Pisarev explained, recognized "no governing social force, no moral law, no sanctioning principle outside himself" and sought to act on nothing beyond himself.[26] But the radical youths who in 1862 turned away from tsar, government, *obshchestvo*, and such aging radicals as Herzen and Ogarev found Pisarev's cold admonitions not to "dream about orange groves and palm trees while standing in snow drifts on frozen tundras" too devoid of positive vision to revive the withered remnants of the dreams they had cherished during the halcyon days of the late 1850s.[27] Seeking a vision of a new society and a plan for its construction, they seized on *What Is to Be Done?*, the novel that Nikolai Chernyshevskii wrote in the Peter and Paul Fortress during the year after Russia's university disorders. When *What Is to Be Done?* appeared in 1863, the ascetic, rude, and humorless Chernyshevskii had been the idol of the younger generation for nearly a decade. Now, on the eve of his condemnation to penal servitude in Siberia, he summoned Russia's radical youth to establish artels and other forms of communal organizations to build a revolutionary new society of justice and equality.

While Chernyshevskii's book summoned young Russians to a new world of communal endeavor, other forces pulled the less radical portions of *obshchestvo* in other directions. During the second half of May 1862, a series of terrible fires had spread through St. Petersburg, striking terror among the lower classes and stirring suspicion among many of the men and women who had cheered the beginnings of reform. Wild rumors circulated about the fires' origins, and the most common belief among both groups was that radical students had set the city ablaze. St. Petersburg's lower classes treated the students as representatives of privileged society whose rude behavior and disdain for authority marked them not as champions in the struggle against the authorities but as ready targets for abuse.[28] As they rejected any sympathy with radicalism, the more moderate segments of *obshchestvo* treated the students no better. Even Konstantin Kavelin, whose sympathy with the students' cause had led him to resign his position as a professor at St. Petersburg University during the protests of 1861, now concluded that they had set the blazes that had ravaged so much of the city. "Can this be called progress?" he wrote angrily to a friend. "Such progress merits only buckshot and the gallows."[29] Others took an even more rigid stance. "It became improper to talk of reforms," the future anarchist Prince Petr Kropotkin remembered. "The whole atmosphere was laden with a reactionary spirit." Russia had entered a time, he added a fortnight afterward, of "reaction, full speed backwards."[30]

A few months later, the outbreak of a full-fledged revolution in Poland made the authorities and *obshchestvo* even less tolerant of dissent than Kropotkin had found them during the weeks after the Petersburg fires. To the Poles' declaration of revolution, Russia's statesmen and citizens responded as one, united in a common desire to crush an age-old enemy whose demands continued to stir unrest in the Russian land. The key issue no longer was whether Russia or Poland "will become mightier," wrote the once-progressive journalist Mikhail Katkov. The main question, he now concluded in a statement that heralded his debut as an apostle of Russian chauvinism, had become "which of them will exist."[31] As a tidal wave of patriotism swept across Russia, it swallowed the infant revolutionary movement beneath its crest. "Seven years of liberalism had exhausted the whole reserve of radical aspirations," Herzen later confessed sadly. "The force of public opinion, hardly called to life, [now] manifested itself as a savage conservatism."[32]

The wave of reaction that Herzen saw "elbowing the government into the debauchery of terror and persecution"[33] was only one consequence of the Polish revolt. During the 1850s and early 1860s, a shortage of career opportunities had alienated well-educated young Russians from their tsar and government. Now, as the stern regime that Russia imposed on her reconquered Polish lands took shape, numbers of lucrative new government positions helped to entice that recently alienated portion of *obshchestvo* away from radical idealism and into the imperial establishment by the promise of political prestige and material rewards.[34] Combined with the opportunities for involvement in local affairs offered by the new *zemstva* and the new professional careers in law, medicine, and applied science that the *zemstva* and the judicial reform statutes promised to create for educated men and women,[35] a larger portion of *obshchestvo* began to hope for a better opportunity for positive action within the framework of the established order.

Repeated calls for the abolition of the nobility as a class (and, therefore, an end to its special monopoly over local affairs) strengthened that sense of broader opportunity. In addition to a number of provincial assemblies of the nobility, such prominent aristocrats as Ivan Aksakov and Aleksandr Koshelev urged (to use Aksakov's words) "that the gentry be allowed to perform solemnly and before all Russia, the great act of abolishing itself as a class."[36] Such a summons to self-obliteration provoked opposition, of course. There were many who believed that the nobility already had sacrificed enough by relinquishing control of its serfs and that its members should be compensated as a class with broad political rights. Others, and Kavelin stood prominently among them in the 1860s, saw "the nobility and particularly the provincial nobility" as the "single source for the renovation of Russia."[37] Yet, men like Kavelin emphasized the importance of Russia's lords as a vital part of *obshchestvo*, not as members of a privileged class. As educated, able men, Kavelin insisted, the nobility must be integrated into Russia's provincial body politic on a broader, more equal basis. "Political rights for one class without political rights for all others," he stated flatly at one point, "are something unthinkable, something that should encounter unanimous opposition, not only from the government, but from the masses and every enlightened, liberal person in Russia."[38]

Kavelin thus urged Russia's nobles to take a leading role in encouraging the broader participation of *obshchestvo* in local affairs as an alternative to their former monopoly of corporate district and provincial administration. "Self-government, that treasured dream of every enlightened and liberal person in Russia, can only begin to come true in the provinces with the energetic assistance of the nobility," Kavelin wrote. "In this fertile school," he concluded, "the nobility will prepare itself for those broader political activities which, without such preparation, always will remain nothing but an unrealized fantasy."[39] Only by schooling itself in self-government could *obshchestvo* provide an alternative to continuing rule by bureaucracy. "I expect absolutely no changes for the better in the central government," Kavelin confessed in 1865. "Without political guarantees, it is impossible, unthinkable."[40] Until a renovation of provincial politics and government took place, Kavelin warned, the bureaucracy would continue to cripple progress in Russia.[41]

This seemed all the more probable because of the imperial government's deep-seated apprehension about the *zemstva*. "The word *zemstvo* stirs up fear in high circles," Grand Duchess Elena Pavlovna had confessed two years before the *zemstvo* statutes were promulgated,[42] and the government's tardiness in putting them into effect showed that these reservations had not been put to rest. Certainly Valuev worried about the elected element in the *zemstva*, and so did many of his colleagues in the Committee of Ministers, State Council, and Senate. "Opposition between local self-government and the central administration or supreme power is inevitable," the great statesman Witte explained some years later. "The latter is based upon the principle of the single and undivided will of the monarch, while local self-government . . . is based upon the independent activity of representatives elected by the people."[43]

Given imperial statesmen's determination to emphasize form not substance in developing the *zemstva*,[44] such hopes as Kavelin and his progressive countrymen had expressed for self-government were destined to be realized very slowly. Particularly during the 1860s and early 1870s, when the *zemstvo* men suffered from inexperience and the number of professionals in their ranks was particularly small, there was a growing sense that local affairs simply did not have much importance. "There was too much unanimity," the Scots observer Donald MacKenzie Wallace remarked when he visited a district *zemstvo* in Novgorod in 1870, "a fact indicating plainly that the majority of the members did not take a very deep interest in the matters presented to them."[45] With only the most limited financial resources and no fewer than fourteen different types of responsibilities that ranged from overseeing public health, public education, prisons, and philanthropy to fostering economic and agricultural development assigned to them,[46] the *zemstvo* had to choose its civic involvements modestly and carefully, especially because it had no enforcement or police power. Both of these key instruments, so vital to the proper conduct of local government everywhere, remained in the hands of the provincial governors and the bureaucrats who served them. To carry out its will, the *zemstvo* therefore had to rely on the very administration whose work it so often criticized.

Very much in 1864, and even more after a second, reformed *zemstvo* statute appeared in 1890, Russia's provincial bureaucracy held the *zemstvo* in a firm grip.[47] This meant that, no matter how committed individual *zemstvo* boards might be to self-government or how dedicated to civic progress the early *zemstvo* professionals might become, they all faced the bureaucracy at every turn. "The bureaucracy is a terrible, gigantic force, more powerful than anything else," Kavelin once wrote. "This is a real force, and one has to meet force with force that is equal to it."[48] Such a force would have to emerge from among the Russians themselves, and it would inevitably involve the time-consuming process of changing attitudes, values, and political outlooks. "By what miracle could our bureaucracy be better than ourselves?" Kavelin asked in 1865. "How could it be a model of thrift, honesty, enlightenment, self-sacrifice, and patriotism when we ourselves, at all levels, are ignoramuses, rude and stupid spendthrifts and thieves, and think only of the present moment?"[49]

Russia's political climate had begun to turn against any change that might weaken the time-honored principles on which the nation's government had rested for centuries. Not only the popular representation to which Valuev had referred but any extension of *glasnost'* or elevation of *zakonnost'* at the expense of *proizvol* made Russian statesmen especially wary during the days that separated the Polish revolt from Dmitrii Karakozov's attempt to kill Alexander II outside the Summer Gardens in April 1866. After that, reaction intensified. As Count Dmitrii Tolstoi, a man whose opposition to the Great Reforms had marked him as a statesman who contemplated "no dilution of the central power, no loosening of unity for the empire",[50] took command of the Ministry of Public Instruction, an era of much sterner government control began. "Already nicked by the two-edged sword of education," Allen Sinel wrote some years ago, "the autocracy in 1866 called on Tolstoi to make this weapon safer to handle without destroying its usefulness for the state."[51] At the same time, the Ministry of Internal Affairs moved to curb the authority of the *zemstva* in at least three important areas, all related to the ability of elected officials to assemble the economic resources needed to carry out their agencies' tasks independent of Russia's provincial government.[52] "They have published the new regulations concerning the institutions of local government," Nikitenko noted in his diary in July 1867. "Reaction is making very rapid strides forward."[53]

During the late 1860s and early 1870s, the rising wave of reaction in Russia suppressed the development of the revolutionary movement at the same time as it built a broader base of support for it. Stern men in command of the Ministry of Public Instruction, the Third Section, and the Military Governor Generalship of St. Petersburg made it all but impossible for the handful of young radicals who remained at large even to exchange ideas safely. This was all the more true because Karakozov's shot had indicated that they had committed themselves to a much more revolutionary vision than ever before.

No longer satisfied to renovate Russia through a far-reaching program of reform, they now called for a full-fledged transformation of their nation's government and society on principles very different from any that had been a part of the Great Reform debate. Not autocracy, not a renovated autocracy, not even a reformed autocracy had any place in the vision of Russia that the empire's revolutionaries carried into the 1870s. Disillusioned and bitter, they now declared war on the autocrat and the institutions that supported him.

The very fact of Karakozov's shot indicated how dramatically the revolutionaries' vision diverged from the principles of reform and renovation that had guided Russians during the first decade of Alexander II's reign. Ever since the Grand Prince of Moscow had risen to rule the Russian land half a millennium before, no commoner had attempted to murder the tsar until Karakozov's single badly aimed shot proclaimed that some Russians had crossed the line that separated radical criticism from revolutionary commitment. Convinced that freedom, social justice, and the destruction of bureaucratic tyranny could not be achieved by *obshchestvo* working within a framework defined by *zakonnost'* and *glasnost'*, Russia's revolutionaries now vowed to destroy autocracy and its instruments.

A variety of murky visions about how such a full-fledged transformation might be accomplished came to the fore at the beginning of the 1870s as Russia's revolutionary youth struggled to link the *obshchestvo* and the *narod* (Russia's peasant masses) after centuries of cultural, social, and political separation. Responding to a series of idealized visions that portrayed the masses as either fertile soil for revolutionary propaganda (Lavrov) or a source of pent-up anger and hatred for established authority that could ignite a revolutionary conflagration (Bakunin), Russia's revolutionary youth went to the people during spring, summer, and fall 1874. As they explored the possibilities for revolutionary action in hundreds of peasant villages scattered across European Russia, they began a final effort to locate the boundaries of the Great Reform legislation on the Left, to determine whether the society that the Great Reforms had envisioned could be reshaped to include the destruction of autocracy and its bureaucratic defenders.

The two waves of the Movement to the People that occurred in 1874 and in 1877–78 showed that the heritage of the masses diverged too far from the aspirations of the radical wing of *obshchestvo* to allow them to unite for common action. Neither the revolutionary youths committed to the teachings of Lavrov nor those intoxicated by the passionate, impatient urgings of Bakunin found a hearing among Russia's always apathetic, sometimes hostile peasants. "Scientific socialism, the socialism of the West," one of the *narodniki* lamented as he recalled the hostile reception he and his comrades had received, "bounces off the Russian masses like a pea off a wall."[54] Nor did those doctrines of recast revolutionary populism that focused more directly on the theme of liberty and land communally held strike a more responsive chord among Russia's masses. "Every peasant, if circumstances permit, will, in the most exemplary fashion, exploit every other," one *zemstvo* agronomist confessed after working among Russia's rural folk for many years.[55] The cultural and social chasm between *obshchestvo* and *narod* remained too vast and the visions too disparate to be bridged so easily. Language, culture, and stereotyped misunderstandings all continued to form an impenetrable wall between them.

Unwilling to abandon belief in the masses or relinquish their deep hope that they would one day become the bearers of revolution in Russia, Russia's revolutionary youth turned from populism to terrorism at the end of the 1870s only to find that the excesses of terrorism reduced the opportunities for useful social and civic enterprises even more surely than populism had. Culminating in their assassination of Alexander II on March 1, 1881, the activities of *Narodnaia Volia* (the Party of the People's Will) therefore narrowed the limits within which the Great Reforms would be shaped and reduced the extent to which the government would seek the participation of *obshchestvo* in their development. The dual failure of the Movement to the People and the terrorist assault against the autocrat also showed that Russia's revolutionaries could not define the Great Reform legislation in terms of transformation rather than renovation. Unable to replace Russia's twin yokes of autocracy and bureaucracy with some form of socialist-democratic polity, the revolutionaries of the 1870s faced near-paralysis in the conservative political climate that dominated the 1880s.

Perhaps nothing emphasized that fact more forcefully than the programs of General Count Mikhail Loris-Melikov, the Armenian-Georgian nobleman whose stern suppression of revolutionaries as acting governor-general of Kharkov province won him an appointment as Russia's minister of internal affairs in August 1880.[56] Loris-Melikov knew well the tensions that the *glasnost'*-*proizvol* dichotomy had created in Russia's legislative process, and he sought to end the paralysis of policy that had come in its wake by a series of proposals designed, in Daniel Orlovsky's careful judgment, to "revitalize the ministerial bureaucracy and transform autocratic law-making."[57] Loris-Melikov had sought to accomplish that end by preserving both *glasnost'* and *proizvol* and by controlling each in its turn. Using *proizvol* as his instrument, he therefore sought to institutionalize *glasnost'* at the center of Russia's government (in his famous project of January 28, 1881, to which Alexander II gave his approval on the morning of his assassination) by providing for special consultations with representatives chosen from among the most "useful and knowledgeable people."[58] Designed to function much as had the non-government "experts" in the special commissions that had drafted the Great Reform legislation, Loris-Melikov's proposed "useful and knowledgeable" representatives had been a carefully calculated response designed to accommodate the desire of the less radical portions of *obshchestvo* to participate in Russia's national political life.

The foundations of Loris-Melikov's scheme crumbled among the debris left by the terrorists' bombs that took Alexander II's life on March 1, 1881. Beginning in the 1880s, the social and political dimensions of the Great Reforms would be defined from the Right as those conservative forces that had been briefly checked by the development of the Great Reform debate between 1861 and 1874 reasserted themselves. Certainly, the Right had never ceased to challenge the Great Reform legislation and to demand that it be interpreted within very narrow limits. This had been the motivation behind the censor Przhetslavskii's belief that *glasnost'* could be used to reshape Official Nationality into a less repressive form. Public opinion, Przhetslavskii had insisted, needed no direct input in Russia's policy-making process because the loyal servitors of a benevolent autocrat would, by definition, formulate only policies that served the interests of all good and loyal Russians. Moral imperatives therefore ought to shape *glasnost'* in such a manner as to preserve the prerogatives of autocracy but allow the government access to legitimate expressions of public opinion, which Przhetslavskii defined all too readily as public support for government policies.[59]

For defenders of any such moderated version of Official Nationality, good citizens ought first of all to be loyal subjects. Such men and women continued to regard loyalty to the autocrat as the primary requirement of good citizenship because they continued to equate the Russian tsar with the Russian state just as their medieval forebears had. For that reason, when Dmitrii Miliutin had written (in the preamble to the Universal Military Service Statute) that "the defense of the homeland against foreign enemies is the sacred duty of every Russian," Alexander II had insisted that his words be changed to read, "the defense of the *throne and* homeland" was the duty of "every Russian *subject."* For Russia's emperor and the defenders of autocracy, the duties of a subject superseded the responsibilities of a citizen and, although a citizen might be expected to defend his country, Alexander insisted that the duty of a subject to defend the throne must come first.

Although such views had found advocates in high places throughout the 1860s and 1870s, the shock of the Crimean defeat and the certainty that Russia must be launched decisively on the road to modernization had kept them in check until the widespread successes of Russian arms and diplomacy in the Transcaucasus and Central Asia brightened the empire's tarnished international image in the late 1870s. This released the advocates of conservative renovation from the constraints that the Crimean defeat had imposed on them and allowed them to give freer rein to their hopes for narrowing the dimensions of the society that the Great Reform legislation must eventually produce. Combined with the more conservative political outlook of Alexander III and the widespread revulsion against radicalism that the terrorists' assassination of Alexander II had stirred, the 1880s—traditionally called the Era of Counterreforms—would see a strong resurgence of conservative values among Russia's *obshchestvo.*

"A whole regiment of Don Cossacks galloping in attack formation, their red lances shining brightly in the last rays of a crimson March sunset," one observer remembered,[60] had surrounded Alexander III when he had left his father's deathbed to begin his reign early in the evening of March 1, 1881. What one of the young women involved in the plot to kill Alexander II called the "White Terror" began that very day, shattering the revolutionary movement in Russia and condemning émigré revolutionaries to decades of frustrated isolation abroad. It would be almost a quarter century before Vera Zasulich, the young woman whose attempt to kill St. Petersburg's Governor-General Trepov in 1878 had given Russia's new jury system its most severe test, would set foot again on Russian soil. Fearful of reprisals from the tsarist police, Georgii Plekhanov, the founding father of Russian Marxism, would remain abroad for thirty-seven years before he returned to his homeland in 1917. Unwilling to compromise on principles whose validity he considered divinely sanctioned, Alexander III remained an unyielding opponent of such men and women. So long as he ruled Russia, revolutionaries would find it difficult to gain even an uncertain foothold among the empire's masses. Even those who dissented only modestly from the principles whose virtues he considered to be self-evident found little tolerance for their views.

Despite the staunchly conservative aura that surrounds the reign of Alexander III, it is misleading and inaccurate to portray the 1880s too simply as a time of crude reaction. Certainly the image of White Terror was justified from the perspective of Russia's broken revolutionaries, and the new emperor made it clear from the first that the cautious steps that Loris-Melikov had taken toward modernizing Russia's central government could not soon be repeated. But there was more to the so-called counterreforms of the 1880s than a crude effort to smother the Great Reforms beneath a blanket of raw obscurantism. As a broad and not unintelligent endeavor to shape a society that would be more in keeping with the contours of Russian experience, the counterreforms sought to define the Great Reform legislation in a more conservative fashion than its framers had intended. In that context, *obshchestvo* must assume more responsibilities but must not encroach on the prerogatives of the autocracy and its chief institutions. Statesmen of the counterreform era thought that Russia needed to be ruled by a stern, benevolent sovereign who would take authority into his hands to spare the Russians from the temptations that might arise from wielding it themselves. It therefore was for the Russian autocrat—paternal, all-powerful, stern, yet all-caring—to assume that "limitless, terrible strength of power, and its limitless and terrible burden" for the welfare and salvation of all Russians.[61] Acting as good subjects ought to act within this framework automatically would make Russians into good citizens.

These were the views championed by Konstantin Pobedonostsev, director general of the Holy Synod from 1880 to 1905, Alexander III's tutor, his close adviser at the beginning of his reign, and a man whose opinions played an important part in shaping the atmosphere in which the early counterreforms were conceived and launched. A young jurist who had been shocked by the injustice of Russia's legal system in the 1840s, Pobedonostsev had been among Zarudnyi's first choices to sit on the committee that had drafted the Judicial Reform Statutes. Yet, whereas many of the reformers of the 1860s had remained faithful to their cause during the 1870s and into the 1880s, Pobedonostsev soon abandoned his reformist views in favor of a static conservativism that was as frigid as it was brittle. Unlike those reformers who continued to believe, as did Grand Duke Konstantin Nikolaevich, in "the necessity of the progressive movement of humanity along the path of enlightenment,"[62] Pobedonostsev became what Robert Byrnes has described as "a believer in painful, slow growth."[63]

Such, at best, was Pobedonostsev's view of Russia's march toward the twentieth century. In sharp contrast to Mikhail Reitern, the protégé of Grand Duke Konstantin Nikolaevich who served Russia so ably as minister of finance during most of the 1860s and 1870s and who, as president of the Committee of Ministers during the first half of the 1880s, stood as one of the chief opponents of the conservative pall in which Alexander III's regime sought to envelop Russia, Pobedonostsev had neither faith in individual initiative nor belief in the free market economies that were developing in the West. Fascinated by the American experience, Reitern had persistently urged that Russia move away from a command economy to one in which the free play of market forces could bring the creative energies of its people into play.[64] Convinced that men would work toward evil purposes without proper supervision, Pobedonostsev stood a full 180 degrees to Reitern's right. "We grow up with infinite expectations, begotten of immeasurable vanity and innumerable artificial needs," he once wrote as he looked back longingly toward those bygone days when men had been satisfied with the condition in which God had placed them and "each was held to his place and to his work by a sentiment of duty."[65] Certain that even "the best of men are not free from low instincts and interested motives,"[66] Pobedonostsev believed that a good subject—and hence, a good citizen—must know his place and the limits it imposed upon him. Otherwise, the result would be chaos, in which "masses of men dissatisfied with their condition, dissatisfied with social institutions, blinded by the wildest instincts of their nature . . . [would] aspire to the realization of their wild ideals on earth."[67]

Whereas Reitern saw the belief that a person of talent need not be resigned to life in a lowly estate as a force that could raise Russia to new heights on the threshhold of the twentieth century, Pobedonostsev called it "the malady of our time," the "permanent and epidemic disease which has tainted all the younger generation."[68] This gloomy outlook shaped Pobedonostsev's view of life and determined the framework within which he believed that the Great Reform society should be shaped. The masses must not be flattered, nor must statesmen "pander to their basest instincts and tendencies," he insisted. The virtuous man, "he who, in the consciousness of duty is capable of disinterested service to the community," he warned, must approach the crowd only "to condemn its follies and expose its depravity."[69] This meant that the government must strengthen the control it exercised over its subjects. "I am a Russian living among Russians," he wrote. "I know the Russian heart and what it wants."[70]

Beginning at least in the early 1870s, Pobedonostsev had begun to view humanity through a misanthropic prism. He was, as Heide Whelan explained recently, "a critic, not a creator,"[71] and he believed that the first task of any government and any sovereign was to control the corrupt, base passions that ruled the lives of men. Although Reitern had long since rejected such a view in the belief that any effort to "restrain each person in his place" would "burden the administration with vast fruitless [tasks],"[72] Pobedonostsev insisted that any institution that was not directed toward the control of men and their passions could only produce more harm than good. He therefore considered the public press to be "one of the falsest institutions of our time," catering to "intellectual puriency of the basest kind," and he cursed parliament in similar fashion as "one of the greatest illustrations of human delusion."[73] Yet Pobedonostsev offered no alternatives to enable Russia to accommodate the changing world in which she found herself as she entered her industrial revolution. "He always knew very well what ought not to be done," one Russian statesman remarked, "but he never knew what should be done."[74]

Such views had serious, even crippling limits, for they confined Pobedonostsev's sense of the possible to the most narrow dimensions. In the government of Alexander III, he therefore became what the great jurist Aleksandr Koni called the "state pessimist" of Russia.[75] Pobedonostsev projected this negative view of men and progress into Russian politics so emphatically that even Alexander III himself once reportedly urged him to remember that "one cannot live by criticism alone" and must, at some point, move ahead.[76] "He is like a frost that hinders further decay," the conservative thinker Konstantin Leont'ev explained at the time. "He not only is not a creator, but he is not even a reactionary, not a regenerator, not even a restorer."[77] Pobedonostsev, in fact, saw himself in much the same fashion. "The continuation of the regime depends upon our ability to keep Russia in a frozen state," a grand duke heard him say at one point. "The slightest warm breath of life would cause the whole thing to rot."[78] This was criticism for its own sake magnified into a program of negative political action. "He had," Zaionchkovskii concluded almost a quarter century ago, "no positive program whatsoever."[79]

If Pobedonostsev's narrow outlook was more static than most, it was nonetheless a reflection of a conservative view that Alexander III shared with his closest counselors, the most notable of whom were Mikhail Katkov and Prince Vladimir Meshcherskii— the editors of the right-wing journals *Moskovskie Vedomosti* and *Grazhdanin (The Citizen)*—and Count Dmitrii Tolstoi, the statesman whose tenacious defense of autocracy led Alexander III to call him the "last of the Mohicans."[80] Like Pobedonostsev a cold, self-righteous man who, like Count Panin in the reigns of Nicholas I and Alexander II, preferred his emperor's favor to all else, Tolstoi disdained public opinion and despised statesmen who courted its favor. "I do not want popularity," he once told an assembly of university students in Odessa. "I despise . . . [those who seek] popularity." A man who gave petitioners who entered his anteroom at the Ministry of Education a mere two minutes to state their business, Tolstoi believed that only autocracy could serve as the instrument for orderly progress in Russia, and he thought it ill-advised and wrong for any autocrat to consider (as Alexander II had) relinquishing voluntarily powers that Western rulers had retained until revolutions had torn them from their grasp.[81] Loyal, ready to do his sovereign's will, dedicated to autocratic government, Tolstoi would serve Alexander III as Rostovtsev had served his father during the first "revolutionary situation" at the beginning of the Great Reform era and as Dmitrii Miliutin and Loris-Melikov had served him during the "second revolutionary situation" from 1878 to 1881.[82]

Yet, in contrast to Miliutin, Loris-Melikov, and Rostovtsev, whose broader perspectives had enabled them to envision long-term solutions to the crises Russia faced after the Crimean and Russo-Turkish wars, Tolstoi was a man who, as Boris Chicherin once said, remained "a bureaucrat to the very marrow."[83] He took comfort from the intricacies of the bureaucratic process and sought to project its artificial order onto Russian life. Order, he insisted from the moment he took office as minister of internal affairs, would be his chief concern.[84] Convinced that the Great Reforms had brought into being a "ruined, beggarly, drunk, and dissatisfied peasantry, a ruined, dissatisfied nobility, courts that continually get in the way of the police, and six-hundred zemstvo rumor mills that stand in opposition to the government," Tolstoi reportedly told Alexander III that the Great Reforms were "a mistake" and that Russia's countryside had to be brought more firmly under control.[85] He thought it absurd that Russia's uneducated, illiterate peasants should be expected to govern themselves on the basis of written law. The twenty years that had passed since the implementation of the first Great Reform statutes had shown that deepening impoverishment and increasing administrative disorder in Russia's countryside were the main result of such misplaced hopes. The best that could be expected from the empire's peasantry, Tolstoi concluded, was that they could provide information about local problems to a government that must retain a monopoly on political power.[86] Certainly, the government ought not to encourage the formation of administrative bodies that could provide an institutional base for opposition and dissent among the masses. "The task of the Minister of Internal Affairs," he insisted at the time of his appointment in 1882, "must be to paralyze all opposition to the government, not encourage it."[87] "The name of Count Tolstoi," Katkov wrote then, "is in itself both a manifesto and a program."[88]

For Tolstoi, opposition meant not only those who opposed the government but also any who did not share his vision that, although *obshchestvo* might advise the government, the government should relinquish none of its power in return. The Great Reforms had opened an area between government and *obshchestvo* in which the sphere of one did not quite directly touch that of the other, and where the division between the two should be drawn had been a subject of considerable debate throughout the 1870s. Alexander III's choice of Tolstoi to rule the Ministry of Internal Affairs now meant that order and autocracy would take precedence over all other concerns. Tolstoi's vision of returning to the central government responsibility for providing local administration and supplying peasant needs without any assistance from Russia's newly emerged peasant citizens made it certain that the space within which *grazhdanskoe obshchestvo*—the citizen society of which civic-minded Russians had begun to speak—would be allowed to function was narrowly focused and pragmatically defined. By definition, a good subject would automatically be a good citizen, but not necessarily the other way around.

What underlay this rigidity and narrow pragmatism on the part of Alexander III and his confidants was that the rise of the revolutionary movement and the need to use such extra legal means as the governors-general to suppress opposition and discontent during the political crisis of 1878-82 had shown Russia's central government that it still did not have the resources or the instruments needed to control its provinces.[89] Indeed, the dramatic political crisis, of which the rise of revolutionary terrorism was a major part, had diverted attention from an even more serious economic crisis that was building in the Russian countryside, where mismanaged tax collection had combined with acute shortages of land and grain to produce a massive tax arrears. In a government that took fiscal considerations seriously into account in formulating policy,[90] this had produced genuine apprehension. As reports on rural apathy, rural anarchy, rural hunger, and rural administrative confusion mounted, Russia's statesmen and high officials began to fear that the nation's peasants might lose all respect for authority unless some form of effective supervision could be established at the local level.[91] Some recasting of the self-government institutions that the Great Reforms bestowed on Russia's peasants therefore seemed very much needed.

Work on such a reform actually had begun in August 1880, when Alexander II had appointed four senators to investigate ten key provinces where the tax arrears were the highest and peasant land shortages greatest.[92] Submitted a few months after his death, their reports chronicled a mass of abuses, corruption, and outright indifference, in peasant assemblies on the level of the *volost* (the territorial unit that constituted each *uezd* [district]) and in village communes. Clearly, there was a very great distance between the ideal set forth in the legislation of 1861 and 1864 and everyday practice. "Not one matter is decided objectively since there are no assemblies where persuasion with vodka by the interested parties does not occur," one senator wrote. "The peasants are indifferent toward elections, believing that even if a good person were to be elected, he would be corrupted by the office."[93]

Vodka, of course, had been used by state officials to explain peasant recalcitrance, peasant indifference, and peasant corruption for a long time. Even in the 1830s, Zablotskii-Desiatovskii and Prince Vladimir Odoevskii, his colleague in the Ministry of State Domains, had made it a focus of their efforts to educate state peasants in elementary agronomy and the homely virtues of thrift and sobriety.[94] But even though they bore the tradition of peasant drunkenness in mind, the rough reality of village politics, so different from the vision of the reformers of the 1860s, clearly shocked senior officials from St. Petersburg. "This picture of inebriated peasants voting for the desires of their benefactors at the assembly," Thomas Pearson concluded in his impressive recent study of autocracy and local self-government after the Emancipation, "could only dismay officials who, two decades earlier, foresaw the imminent creation of genuine public self-government at the village level."[95]

Drunkenness and illiteracy, neither of them a surprise to men acquainted with life in Russia's countryside, were the chief curses that the senators who had inspected Russia's provinces in 1880 and 1881 had uncovered in the practices of village self-government. An even broader study conducted by the Ministry of

Internal Affairs showed that there were more than four times as many illiterate village elders as there were literate ones, and only a few more *volost* elders who could read than could not.[96] It was a sad commentary on the visions of the reformers of the 1860s that village education had made so little headway in two decades. It also meant that it had become almost impossible for Russia's central government to communicate with the men responsible for the empire's local administration.

While Russia's village and *volost* assemblies languished for lack of state supervision, the *zemstva* had to struggle against the increasing weight of bureaucratic interference. As they found it increasingly difficult to collect the meager tax revenues on which their efforts to improve public health, agronomy, and education depended, the *zemstva* began to languish. Clearly, the key institutions of the Great Reform legislation of 1861–1864 were not functioning in Russia's countryside. "From the administrator's point of view," George Yaney wrote some years ago, peasant local government in Russia had become "a chaos."[97]

From a regime committed to order and control, "chaos" demanded serious attention. On the recommendation of Count Nikolai Ignat'ev, Tolstoi's predecessor as minister of internal affairs, Alexander III had established a special commission under the chairmanship of Mikhail Kakhanov to study the problems of local self-government and to draft plans for its reform. A former provincial governor and Loris-Melikov's deputy during the last months of the preceding reign, Kakhanov had begun his assignment with the full endorsement of the Committee of Ministers. *Glasnost'* and *zakonnost'* were to be his guiding principles as he and the members of his commission's Special Conference set about translating the vision of the men who had drafted the Great Reforms into a series of village and *volost* institutions that could function, in Pearson's words, "as truly public organizations."[98] The result, completed in November 1883, was a comprehensive program for making Russians responsible for rural self-government, not as members of antiquated social estates but as full-fledged citizens, with peasants and nobles becoming equal partners in shaping the destiny of the communities in which they lived.[99]

But the atmosphere in which Kakhanov and his Special Conference completed their proposals for reform was very different from that in which they had begun their work. Immediately,

Kakhanov's recommendations stirred outrage among some of Alexander's confidants, especially Pobedonostsev. "The realization of such a project is inconceivable to me," he wrote to Tolstoi. "[Kakhanov's plan] is written," he concluded, "to destroy all authority in Russia, to splinter it into myriads of unconnected grains of sand."[100] Tolstoi, who had replaced the flamboyant and arrogant Ignat'ev in 1882, was no supporter of Kakhanov's proposals for a more open and more diverse society,[101] and his view of his work was scarcely more generous than Pobedonostsev's. "I have decided," he told State Secretary Aleksandr Polovtsev at the end of November, "to reduce the results of . . . [the Kakhanov Commission's] work to zero."[102]

Yet Tolstoi was not prepared to close the Kakhanov Commission and take upon himself the onus of having cut short its effort to come to grips with the chaos in Russia's countryside.[103] Supported by a large majority of provincial governors who, as a group, were among the most outspoken advocates of bureaucratic control,[104] Tolstoi looked for other ways to deal with the problems of rural lawlessness and administrative breakdown that stemmed, as one governor pointed out, from the peasants' "right to govern themselves according to their customs instead of the law . . . [even though] there are no firmly established customs."[105] As the governors called for officials to be appointed by the central government to oversee administration and justice in Russia's countryside and establish firm government control over the peasants, their very pointed and urgent criticisms gave Tolstoi the information he needed to shape a program for dealing with the crisis of rural self-government. "I know provincial life better than the Lycurguses of the Kakhanov Commission," he told Prince Meshcherskii in late 1884. "I will not allow the implementation of those liberal innovations and undertakings, which without a doubt are contrary to the needs of provincial life."[106]

By early 1885, Tolstoi had completed his evolution from what Pearson calls "a bureaucrat who simply executed his sovereign's will to a politician who sought to mold it."[107] Now secure enough in his emperor's confidence to dismiss even the imperial favorite Katkov as "a swine [as he once told Polovtsev] the likes of which I don't permit in my presence,"[108] Tolstoi recommended the abolition of the Kakhanov Commission and received the emperor's enthusiastic agreement. By that time, he also had found a willing ally and assistant in the person of Aleksandr Pazukhin, an obscure district marshal of the nobility from the Volga River province of Simbirsk, who had been one of the so-called experts on local conditions invited to work with the Kakhanov Commission during its final months. Although the key ideas would come from Tolstoi, Pazukhin, as director of Tolstoi's private chancellery, would provide the labor for drafting what became known as the Land Captain Statute of July 12, 1889, and the *Zemstvo* Reform Law of June 12, 1890.[109]

Drafted by Pazukhin in late 1885 and 1886, the Land Captain Statute involved more than three years of arduous negotiation and debate at the highest ministerial levels before a revised version of it became law. Central to the debate between 1886 and 1889 were other ministers' antipathy to Tolstoi's vision of centralization that would bring all elected and appointed officials in Russia's local administration under the control of the minister of internal affairs and, in effect, make him a prime minister of sorts. Another key element in the opposition to Tolstoi's effort was those aging enlightened bureaucrats and their allies who still sat in the State Council and saw the Tolstoi-Pazukhin plan as a crude attempt to destroy the principles of the *zemstvo* and judicial reform statutes of 1864. Yet, in this case, it was Alexander III, not Tolstoi, Pazukhin, their few allies, or many opponents, who played the key role in determining the Land Captain Statute's final form. Wearied of the ongoing State Council debate that had wrested a number of concessions from the now mortally ill Tolstoi, Alexander moved directly and decisively as his father never had, ignored the political maneuvering that had occupied his senior statesmen for the better part of three years, and returned the Land Captain Statute to something close to its original form.[110] "The basic principle of our government," Tolstoi once had said, "[is] imperial, autocratic authority."[111] Once again—and not for the last time—Alexander III had proved him absolutely correct.

Raw *proizvol* such as had not been seen since the days of Nicholas I thus abolished Russia's popular justices of the peace and placed control of judicial and administrative affairs in the countryside in the hands of the *zemskie nachal'niki* (land captains). Selected by the minister of internal affairs from a list of local lords prepared by district and provincial marshals of the nobility, endowed with the relatively high sixth rank in the Table of

Ranks, and provided with a substantial yearly salary of twenty-five hundred rubles, the land captains took responsibility for the financial, economic, social, and cultural destiny of what George Yaney has called "the unadministrable and unteachable village."[112] That the new law endeavored to return a large measure of local administrative authority to Russia's nobles is not surprising in view of Tolstoi's belief that they were the only group in the Russian countryside with the necessary education to carry out these complex tasks. What is perhaps more striking is that Tolstoi never envisioned reestablishing the permanent partnership between nobles and autocrat for which men such as Katkov longed so ardently. For him, Russia's nobles were not the first estate of the realm but loyal servants of the autocrat. As created by the law of 1889, the land captains were bureaucratic agents of a bureaucratic government whose task it would be to impose autocratic order on the (still unfathomable to central government officials) Russian countryside.[113]

By the time that the Land Captain Statute was promulgated on July 12, 1889, Tolstoi had been dead for ten weeks. Yet there was more to his centralization program than placing the local institutions of peasant self-government under state control. More visible and far more crucial in the minds of the men who represented *obshchestvo* was Tolstoi's effort—again drafted by the the diligent Pazukhin—to bring the self-governing *zemstva* under the direct control of the Ministry of Internal Affairs and, in so doing, to transform them into instruments of the central government. Certainly, a number of sound administrative reasons lay behind Tolstoi's plan to impose more control on the *zemstva*, for they had become an object of indifference and even disdain among Russia's provincial nobles at the same time as they had become a focus of distrust and occasional hostility among the peasantry. He therefore proposed that the government appoint *zemstvo* executive officials, that every *zemstvo* resolution be submitted to provincial governors for approval, and that elected *zemstvo* service be made obligatory. No longer could men with a desire for public service choose to serve in the *zemstva*. Those elected now would be required to do so under the threat of what Tolstoi called "appropriate punitive measures."[114] Oversimplified, this was the essence of the proposals for *zemstvo* reform that Tolstoi submitted to the State Council in January 1888.[115]

Discussion of Tolstoi's proposals did not begun until March

1890, almost a year after his death. Now Ivan Durnovo, onetime governor of Moscow Province and Tolstoi's longtime deputy, sat in his mentor's place to defend the unpopular program of so-called counterrreform that his former chief had prepared. Yet Durnovo's manner was not Tolstoi's, even though he had worked with him for nearly a decade. He had not won the confidence of Alexander III that his predecessor had enjoyed, nor did he boast Tolstoi's mastery of political intrigue at the highest levels of government. Pressed by his emperor to have the *zemstvo* reform statute passed before the end of the State Council's session in 1890 and unwilling, as a newly appointed minister, to press his senior colleagues too far, Durnovo made concessions that reduced Tolstoi's plan to control the *zemstva* from the center to a shadow of its former self. The *Zemstvo* Reform Law of June 12, 1890 therefore lacked many of the instruments for bureaucratic control that had been a part of the draft that Tolstoi and Pazukhin had prepared.[116]

Although branded as the second major piece of counterreform legislation to be issued during Alexander III's reign, the *Zemstvo* Reform Law had more virtues than historians have been willing to attribute to it until very recently. Far from being a narrow, reactionary effort to destroy the *zemstva*, the law of 1890, according to the best current estimates, helped the *zemstva* to become more effective by obliging provincial governors to assume some responsibility for their success. Certainly, the huge achievements of the *zemstva* in public health, education, and creation of food reserves in the 1890s were impressive compared to what had been done during the previous quarter century. And, the higher quality of personnel entering *zemstvo* service during the two decades before World War I marked another significant improvement.[117] Although the application of similar principles to Russia's city governments by the Municipal Statute of June 11, 1892 (a product of the post-Tolstoi-Pazukhin era), produced similar results,[118] none of these efforts resolved the growing crisis of administration and confidence that was building throughout the empire.

Russia was moving resolutely into the modern world and undergoing a dramatic economic transformation in the process. Yet her state administration reflected very few of those new directions, for the newly emerging middle classes were not inclined to take up positions in the bureaucracy[119] and their needs and aspirations were not expressed in its decisions. How power should be exercised in this rapidly changing environment, who (or what institutions) should exercise it, and how the new interest groups that were emerging should be accommodated within Russia's institutional, social, and political framework were vital questions that remained unresolved as the empire of the tsars approached the twentieth century. Ironically, these new groups often looked first to Russia's most traditional political and administrative instrument—to *proizvol* exercised by a benevolent autocrat and his chief deputies—to represent their interests most effectively.

The conflict between *proizvol* and *zakonnost'* thus remained unresolved, and both seemed more durable at the end of Alexander III's reign than at its beginning. Certainly, Alexander exercised his autocratic authority in a more unrestrained fashion on some occasions than his father ever had. Yet, even he, the most autocratic sovereign to rule Russia between the Crimean War and the Revolutions of 1917, could not exercise *proizvol* in the manner of such notable predecessors as Peter the Great and Nicholas I. The very existence of the law and the rapidly developing institutionalized defenses that supported it limited his ability to do so. Therefore, although Alexander III still could overrule his ministers as he had when he had imposed a more rigid version of the Land Captain Statute on his State Council, he could not now overrule the law in the manner of his eighteenth- and early-nineteenth-century predecessors.

By approving permanent tenure for judges in the Judicial Reform Statutes of 1864, Alexander II had surrendered exclusive control over the dispensation of justice and the interpretation of the law, two of the autocrat's most cherished and long-standing prerogatives. Clearly an attack against the institution of independent judges was high on Alexander III's list of priorities, yet, some two decades after permanent tenure for judges had been instituted, he found himself unable to do more than impose extremely modest limitations on it. At least in such vital matters as justice and administration in Russia, the law could so limit the autocrat's freedom of action that, aside from abolishing the popular justices of the peace as a part of the Land Captain Statute, Alexander III could not abrogate the Judicial Reform Statute of 1864 however much he wished to do so.

Nor could the men in Russia who were most eager to do

their sovereign's will. From the very first days of Alexander III's reign, Katkov and Pobedonostsev had willingly attacked the Judicial Reform Statute of 1864, as the emperor wished, but their attempt to undercut *zakonnost'* with *proizvol* had provoked deep-seated and stubborn opposition. The Western European sources from which Russia was trying to secure loans to finance her industrial revolution agreed with many educated Russians that an independent judiciary was a vital component of any modern state, and conservatives therefore joined progressives on the State Council and in *obshchestvo* to defend that principle.[120] A modern society, Russians and Europeans agreed, could not function effectively without *zakonnost'*; *zakonnost'* could not be assured without judges who could apply the law independent of the autocrat's wishes.

Although effective in stemming attacks against the Judicial Reform Statute, Russians' broad and wide-ranging defense of *zakonnost'* raised other troublesome questions. Among other things, a second form of *zakonnost'* was beginning to emerge from the process of Russia's modernization that did not entirely coincide with the one that had guided the framers of the Great Reform legislation. Clearly, the enlightened bureaucrats' view of *zakonnost'* as a moral force that, under the guidance of bureaucratic rationality, could be used to defend order and ensure orderly progress took little account of the needs of a modernizing economy and society in which the defense of private property and the rights of contract soon were to assume paramount importance.

Nowhere were the beginnings of this process more evident than in Russian Poland, where the interplay of market forces had begun the transformation of an eighteenth-century police state into a state ruled by law somewhat earlier than in Russia proper. Along with Poland's more highly developed civic society and traditions of public service, this process had produced bitter tensions between Poles and Russians that continued from the first stirring of conflict in the late 1850s, through the revolutionary struggles of 1863–64, and into the twentieth century. To the dismay of many tsarist statesmen, the development of banking and credit facilities as well as efforts to attract foreign investment capital to finance industrialization were in progress in Russian Poland by midcentury as the Polish Bank and the Warsaw Stock Exchange began to take the lead in shaping the nation's economic destiny. In Russia, such a "state within a state," in which men outside the government could influence and even control policy, continued to be viewed as intolerable.[121]

As one of Grand Duke Konstantin Nikolaevich's assistants in the Russian Admiralty, Mikhail Reitern had proposed in the late 1850s that Russia follow a course similar to Poland's[122] and had advocated that view even more energetically as Alexander II's minister of finance between 1862 and 1878. In this, he had received support from some of Russia's conservative nobles who, once the Emancipation had stripped them of their serfs and their rights to act as unchallenged police officials and judges in countryside, had to transform themselves from autocratic (although, in theory, benevolent) masters into responsible citizens. These men realized that they needed the protection of the law to complete that process. They also understood that not estate privilege but law that stood independent of the administration was needed to protect their property and allow them to begin to shape a market economy in which they might operate safely as entrepreneurs.[123] Ironically, it was Pobedonostsev who, in 1861, penned one of the strongest statements to support that position. "The first concern of the law," he had written then, "should be the *creditor*, for his legal interests are the interests of *property*, and the interests of property are inseparably tied with the internal security and internal prosperity of the state itself."[124] Yet it was not until the 1880s (when Reitern had left the Ministry of Finance to preside over the Committee of Ministers, and Pobedonostsev had long since reversed his position) that the transformation from a command economy to a market-oriented one had developed sufficiently in Russia to bring the questions of private property and contract rights so decisively into the forefront that they began to reshape the meaning of *zakonnost'* itself.

Thus, the development of an entrepreneurial society raised the specter of a conflict between *zakonnost'* as defined by free market forces and contract law, and *zakonnost'* that viewed law as a moral force to defend order and foster change in a gradual and controlled manner from above. To some extent, this conflict underlay the growing rivalry between the Ministry of Finance and the Ministry of Internal Affairs for control of Russia's economic destiny as the empire moved into the 1890s, for these definitions of *zakonnost'* dictated the way in which these two key ministries would approach problems of administration, social change, and politics as the new century approached. Equally—or, perhaps, even more—important, they also helped to focus the participation of *obshchestvo* in Russia's civic processes. For, whether they viewed *zakonnost'* as a moral force for social control or as a means to protect entrepreneurial activity determined the way in which Russians defined their place and their responsibilities in the citizen society that was beginning to emerge on the eve of the twentieth century. This was particularly evident in the growing participation of *obshchestvo* in public affairs and in the rise of voluntary associations that pursued broadly defined social, cultural, and civic goals independent of the government and outside its control.[125] At first centered mainly in the cities, these were becoming an obvious part of Russian life at the end of the 1880s. At the beginning of the 1890s, they broadened their role and their influence as the great famine of 1891 and the cholera epidemic of 1892 drew attention toward the starving, disease-ridden Russian countryside.

# VI

## AT THE
## TURN OF
## THE CENTURY

*A*s the stirrings of a new sense of civic responsibility had drawn educated men and women toward the countryside and inspired their efforts to build the foundations of a new order among Russia's liberated serfs, *obshchestvo* had broadened its participation in Russian life from the few hundred of the 1860s to the several thousands of the 1870s. Yet, Russia's rural masses had not proved to be the malleable raw material from which the more radical segments of *obshchestvo* had hoped to fashion a new society. Obdurately self-interested and stubbornly conservative, Russia's peasants had continued to seek refuge from the forces of change in the shelter of tradition. Custom, not the law of the empire, still ruled Russia's peasant villages in the 1870s, and, as judicial and administrative chaos spread across the countryside, the dream that *obshchestvo* one day would unite with the *narod* and guide them toward social, political, and economic transformation had clouded very quickly. The 1880s therefore had seen *obshchestvo* retreat into an era of small deeds in which it had sought to build a more modest base for change and progress in Russia.[1] Following on the heels of the tumultuous Movement to the People and the daring act of terrorism that had taken the life of the tsar on March 1, 1881, Alexander III's reign had been a more quiet time of seeking to build a Great Reform society in a more conservative, balanced way.

Disillusioned by the peasants' refusal to respond to their preachings in the 1870s, and with the institutions that could bring Russia's masses into the modern world still not firmly fixed and fully developed, *obshchestvo* had turned away from the *narod* to regain its earlier urban focus during the 1880s. The beginnings of serious efforts to improve public health, education, and welfare therefore were centered in Russia's cities during that decade as municipal governments became increasingly dominated by the representatives of *obshchestvo* who focused their attention more directly upon the well-being of the poor and began to confront urban poverty in more modern terms. The day of the workhouse and almshouse was passing quickly. Although the problem of urban poverty could never be solved, responsible citizens now began to think it their obligation to confront the deeper causes of lower-class misery, not merely to distribute alms as they had in decades and centuries past. The antiquated notion that philanthropy must be done for the salvation of the donor's soul began to shift to the more modern view that the welfare of one's fellow man was an important concern for every responsible citizen. Especially among the class of entrepreneurs who had begun to shape Russia's industrial revolution, the belief took root that responsible men and women were obliged to return to society a portion of what they had taken from it.[2]

The industrial revolution over which such men presided in the 1880s required vast sums of capital, much of which had to be found in money markets outside Russia. Ivan Vyshnegradskii, a humble priest's son who has been called an "aggressive and unrepentant conservative,"[3] played a key role in assembling the billions of rubles that Russia's new industrialists required. Vyshnegradskii's conservative fiscal policies as Russia's minister of finance won him many supporters among the capital-rich bankers of Berlin, London, Brussels, and, especially, Paris. French investors poured in so much capital that, by 1900, an amazing one-quarter of all French foreign investment was in Russia and, by 1914, the French stake in Russia would rise to more than three times that of the Germans, British, and Belgians combined.[4]

Vyshnegradskii's policies required a betterment in Russia's balance of trade, and, in a nation whose nascent industries produced little that could be marketed abroad, the best plan seemed to be to increase the value of grain exports. Proclaiming in 1887 that "we may not eat enough, but we will export,"[5] Vyshnegradskii had manipulated imperial taxation policies to force Russia's undernourished and impoverished peasants to sell more of their crops than ever before and had increased grain exports by an amazing 30 percent in the process. As Vyshnegrad-skii turned Russia's budget deficit into a large surplus in a mere three years' time, it seemed for a moment that he had found the magic formula for which so many of his predecessors had searched in vain to solve their nation's economic difficulties. Russia's gold reserves rose by more than 300 million gold rubles during his six years in office. At the same time, the government of Alexander III was able to pour more than 50 million rubles into new railroad construction every year.[6]

Despite their apparent success, Vyshnegradskii's policies had a dark and dangerous side that began to show itself toward the end of his fourth year in office. Too reckless in trimming the slender margin of subsistence that sustained a rural population that consumed only a quarter as much food as their American counterparts, Vyshnegradskii had left nothing to cushion Russia's countryside against any sort of adversity.[7] As unusually hard frosts followed by drought and scorching heat struck the empire's central agricultural region during the winter, spring, and summer of 1891, the specter of famine began to loom very large very quickly. "No one should know of this—[or it] . . . will spoil my rate of exchange [in Europe's money markets]," Vysh-negradskii reportedly told the department director who first warned him of the danger in May. "Your notes," he said, as he locked the offending report in his desk, "will never come out of this drawer."[8] Yet evidence of the approach of such a major disaster could not be concealed very long. Nor could it be ig-nored without great risk. Even though Minister of Internal Af-fairs Ivan Durnovo allocated some 30 million rubles, nearly four times the government's entire relief fund, for famine relief in September 1891, close to 36 million peasants scattered over al-most a million square miles in European Russia were on the verge of starvation before the end of the year.[9] As hunger and typhus spread across Russia that winter, the needs of her people seemed almost without limit although the government's capacity to meet those needs had very severe limits indeed.

In retrospect, some saw the government's unprecedented will-ingness to permit public participation in famine relief as an attempt to "deflect the energy of *obshchestvo* from a struggle with the government to a struggle with famine."[10] Certainly, the famine of 1891 and the typhus epidemic that followed it in 1892 turned the attention of *obshchestvo* back toward Russia's peasants, and, as private charity began to play a small but important part in famine relief, it drew concerned citizens into the countryside. This contributed to a revitalization of public life—to the "energizing of *obshchestvo*," in the words of one observer[11]— as work among the *narod* revealed to civic-minded Russians the depths of peasant want and worker poverty, the extent of their nation's backwardness, and the massiveness of the social and economic traumas that Vyshnegradskii's policies had produced. Clearly, the shocking breadth and depth of poverty in Russia intensified the social and economic ills that the industrial revolution inevitably brought to every country. Public response to the revelations of the men and women who worked among the *narod* at the beginning of the 1890s would transform the nature of Russians' civic involvement in the decades that lay ahead.

A period of increased social activism and heightened political consciousness followed as broader, more effective participation in local affairs by *obshchestvo* made the *zemstva* a more significant force in provincial life than ever before. Those *zemstvo* physicians who struggled to alleviate suffering during the famine and then took up the even more desperate task of quelling the cholera epidemic provided dramatic evidence of this new activism,[12] and so did the burgeoning numbers of teachers who entered the countryside once the government and the *zemstva* began to commit increased funds to education after 1890.[13] Such growing involvement of *obshchestvo* in public health, medicine, and education was notable, but the heightened sense of civic awareness that entered Russian public life in the 1890s was even broader. Especially under the leadership of Dmitrii Shipov, the chairman of the Moscow *zemstvo* board who has been described as "a man capable of uniting persons of the most various views in comradely work,"[14] Russia's *zemstvo* leaders began to work together for the first time to influence the direction of the government's domestic policies.

Nowhere was the emergence of Russia's new citizen society more evident than in the growth of voluntary associations, as the members of *obshchestvo* organized themselves into societies for professional, occupational, philanthropic, educational, and cultural purposes during the 1890s and the early twentieth century.[15] In sharp contrast to the 1870s, when a broader segment of *obshchestvo* had supported social and political radicalism or, at least, had sympathized with the efforts of those who did, civic opinion in the 1890s turned away from revolutionary activity. The very concrete tasks associated with building Russian industry and dealing with the problems that process created emphasized sober and constructive activity that allowed little scope for the utopian dreams and revolutionary visions of earlier times. Men and women therefore began to live more practical lives than ever before. "If I were offered a choice between the 'ideals' of the celebrated sixties and today's poorest *zemstvo* hospital," the great writer Chekhov (himself also a physician) wrote to a friend, "I'd take the latter without the least hesitation."[16]

A deeper sense of responsibility for the welfare and good order of the society in which they lived thus led civic-minded Russians to seek change within the institutional framework of Russia, not outside it. To be sure, the government continued to deny any political dimension to the individual initiative and independence of mind that its policies encouraged in the economic sphere. But the many opportunities for practical work among the masses in town and country that the processes of industrialization and urbanization had created enabled *obshchestvo* to pursue its chosen tasks effectively without politics for the time being. The tsar's domains remained immensely far-flung and their many parts extremely diverse, but, as modern technology began to tie the Russian empire more closely together, responsible citizens began to see its problems on a broader, national scale. As they began to think in terms of all-Russian problems, they began to envision all-Russian solutions that would break down the regionalism that had been so much a part of Russian life at the beginning of the Great Reform era.

*Obshchestvo* also developed a broader perspective at the turn of the century because its professional segments had begun to assemble on an all-Russian level, despite the lack of any national political forum. Statisticians, teachers, physicians, engineers, *zemstvo* workers, and a number of other professional groups began to hold congresses that strengthened their sense of professional identity and enabled them to view their professions and the problems they confronted in a national perspective. As Russia passed 1900 and turned toward the First World War and the revolutions of 1905 and 1917, *obshchestvo* thus had begun to think increasingly in national, as opposed to nationalist, terms. The sense of Russia's uniqueness and Russia's mission that once had led Dostoevskii to urge "the finding of an outlet for the anguish of Europe in the all-human and all-uniting Russian soul"[17] remained, but *obshchestvo* also had begun to focus its attention on Russian problems for which Russians must find practical solutions.

Although Russians had begun to search for practical, all-Russian solutions to national problems, Nicholas II, who had ascended the throne after Alexander III's death in 1894, was not prepared to enlarge the arena in which *obshchestvo* could exercise its growing concern for national welfare. The division between government and governed in Russia remained as rigid and starkly drawn as ever. "There exist two Russias, one quite different from the other," the great historian and soon-to-become leader of the Kadet party Pavel Miliukov wrote not long after the new century opened. "One is the Russia of the future, as dreamed of by members of the liberal professions; the other is an anachronism, deeply rooted in the past, and defended in the present by an omnipotent bureaucracy. The one spells liberty," he concluded, "the other, despotism."[18] Despotism and a modern market economy driven by the initiative of private citizens could not flourish together for very long.

Nicholas II and his advisers therefore remained hostile to public initiative and discouraged the continued broader involvement of *obshchestvo* in public affairs that the government of Alexander III had been forced to permit during the desperate days of famine and cholera at the beginning of the 1890s.[19] "We look forward, Sire, to its being possible and rightful for public institutions to express their views on matters concerning them, so that an expression of the . . . thought of representatives of the Russian people . . . may reach the heights of the throne," the representatives of Tver's provincial *zemstvo* wrote to Nicholas II at the beginning of his reign.[20] Any such hopes that *obshchestvo* might enter the national political arena were "senseless dreams," Nicholas replied a few weeks later. "I shall safeguard the principles of autocracy as firmly and as unflinchingly," he announced, "as did my late unforgettable father."[21]

By the principles of autocracy, Nicholas meant above all *proizvol*, a form of power that now stood in sharp contrast to the new social and political world that the industrial revolution had brought into being in Russia. "Autocracy," Lev Tolstoi concluded in 1902, "is an outmoded form of government that may still fit the needs of people isolated from the entire world somewhere in central Africa, but it no longer meets the needs of the Russian people."[22] Nicholas and his closest supporters continued to insist that that could not be so and that even *zakonnost'* must yield to state interests if called on to do so by the sovereign. "Justice itself yields to the demands of higher state interests," Nicholas's minister of internal affairs, Petr Durnovo, told the State Council at one point. "It is not for nothing," he concluded, "that according to the ideas of our people the tsar has to be terrible but gracious, terrible first and foremost and gracious afterwards."[23]

Durnovo's view did not meet the needs of the men who were shaping Russia's industrial revolution. Even when exercised by a gracious tsar, *proizvol* conflicted not only with *zakonnost'* as a moral force for social order and gradual progress but also with *zakonnost'* as the guarantee of private property that would permit entrepreneurs to operate safely in Russia's emerging market economy. Although obvious, the potential problems that lay in the conflict between *proizvol* and *zakonnost'* could remain muted so long as the autocrat supported Russia's industrialization and exercised *proizvol* to guarantee political and social order. But, should autocracy fail to maintain order, as it did in 1905, then the need to resolve the problem of *proizvol* would become more urgent. "The government has, in principle, capitulated to the principle of law, but has, in practice, so multiplied the exceptions that they altogether swamp the principle," one observer concluded. "Thus it has not yet been possible for the ordinary Russian to have any confidence in the principle of law as protecting him from arbitrary and exceptional chastisement."[24]

At the beginning of 1905, the time was not yet ripe for the transformation of autocracy in Russia, and the autocrat therefore still remained the key factor in Russian politics. The responsible citizen society that had begun to emerge in Russia at the beginning of the twentieth century thus was inevitably shaped by the conservative definition of the Great Reform society that had triumphed during Alexander III's reign and by the government's reluctance to permit that society to acquire a national perspective.[25] This continuing attempt to localize the interests of *obshchestvo*, Miliukov pointed out, had the awkward effect of politicizing those "fields of public life as might be expected, under more normal conditions of political life, to be free from party spirit."[26] Russia had followed the West decisively into the industrial revolution but had remained chronically unable to develop the political institutions that had formed such a central part of that process in the West. In 1905, Russia still had no national assembly and no institutionalized expression at the national level of the interests of those various economic and social groups that the industrial revolution had brought into being.

This created new tensions between government and *obshchestvo* that were destined to grow broader and more intensely political than they had been when the Russians had struggled to define the dimensions of the Great Reform society between 1861 and 1894. "Science and fiction, school and theater, learned societies and establishments for charity, universities and technical institutions, associations for self-help and self-culture, provincial councils and courts of justice," Miliukov wrote in February 1905, "none are free from party politics in a country where political parties are supposed not to exist at all."[27] Individual initiative, encouraged by state policy in economic affairs but denied all means of direct political expression, added new and very complex dimensions to Russian life as the empire entered the twentieth century. Politics was becoming the focus of Russians' attention with or without the autocrat's approval.

The limits of individual initiative without politics became very evident during the Russo-Japanese War, for neither Russia's government nor its new citizen society could meet the challenges of the war very easily or successfully. Certain that they would triumph over an enemy they disdained as racially inferior, the Russians had begun the war with confidence, with Minister of Internal Affairs Viacheslav Plehve proclaiming that a "small, victorious war" was exactly what Russia needed to distract public opinion that was becoming increasingly hostile to the government.[28] Despite their expectations for an early victory, the Russians suffered an uninterrupted series of military and naval disasters in the Far East between January 1904 and August 1905 while, at home, the government found it impossible to marshal support for war aims that focused on little-known and far distant lands. Responsible Russians therefore supported the war effort out of a sense of national obligation, not out of any belief that it could advance national interests. Such support took the form of supplying aid to disabled soldiers, war widows, and their families, often through local *zemstvo* offices. Then, when *obshchestvo* found its well-intentioned efforts at war relief opposed by the government itself, it turned against the war very sharply.[29]

No longer could the limited opportunities permitted by a reactionary government satisfy civic-minded citizens deprived of any opportunity for political action. "Is not every spontaneous action doomed? Is not every public initiative cut short? Is there any room left for conscious patriotism? Has not even the humble attempt of the self-governing assemblies [i.e. the *zemstva*] to unite in helping the sick and wounded been denounced as criminal, and forbidden by Plehve?" Miliukov reported hearing a young officer ask bitterly in 1904. "What wonder, then," the young man continued, "if the outward manifestations of our patriotism are not like those of other nations? How can it be otherwise, as long as real patriots are treated as traitors, while traitors are proclaimed patriots?"[30] Government and governed were moving onto a collision course. "Plehve's irritable and angry attitude toward the moderately liberal circles of society had the fatal effect of cementing together all elements of the opposition, including the extremes," Vladimir Gurko, a senior official in the Ministry of Internal Affairs, recalled in his memoirs. "Under these conditions," Gurko concluded, "every stern repression of revolutionary uprisings served only to widen the circle of those who were interested in politics and criticized the government."[31]

Such interests and criticisms already had begun to shape a national alliance against the *proizvol* of autocratic authority in which *obshchestvo* sought to use *zakonnost'* to control the sovereign in much the same way that earlier autocrats had tried to use it to control the *proizvol* of the bureaucracy. The first stirrings of this alliance had been seen in two semiclandestine all-Russian *zemstvo* congresses held in 1902 and 1903 and in the appearance of *Osvobozhdenie* (*Liberation*), a biweekly newspaper published in Stuttgart by a thirty-two-year-old émigré Russian Marxist-turned-liberal, Petr Struve. Proclaiming that "our task is not to divide but to unite," Struve in 1902 had urged that "the cultural and political liberation of Russia . . . become a national cause."[32] In response, a group of *zemstvo* politicians, university professors, and journalists met in Switzerland in the summer of 1903 to form a coalition of liberal elements in Russia. Then, at the beginning of 1904, they expanded their coalition into the Union of Liberation. Vowing to launch a broad assault against Nicholas II's autocratic regime, in which the ministerial structure continued to stand firmly against any form of political

accommodation with *obshchestvo*, they proclaimed that "the liqui-
dation of autocracy and the establishment in Russia of a constitutionalist regime" was their chief goal.[33]

The assassination of Plehve in the summer of 1904 and the
appointment of the moderate and conciliatory Prince Petr
Sviatopolk-Mirskii as his successor could not slow the confrontation that was building between *obshchestvo* and government.
A popular and charming man who, Witte remembered, was
"loved and respected" everywhere,[34] Sviatopolk-Mirskii sought
the desperately needed reconciliation with *obshchestvo* that
Plehve's repression had made so hopelessly impossible. Yet
Sviatopolk-Mirskii's promise that his policies would "conform
to the spirit of true and broad progress" so long as that "did
not conflict with the existing order"[35] was fraught with as many
dangers as Plehve's staunch conservativism had been. When
Russia's new minister of internal affairs spoke of "sincere benevolence and sincere confidence . . . toward the population in general,"[36] the expectations of *obshchestvo* soared to a level that no
ministerial servant of an autocratic master could hope to satisfy.
As *obshchestvo* demanded a meaningful and immediate place in
Russian politics, it became clear that Plehve's rigid bureaucrati-
zation of government and his confident use of police repression
had preserved order more easily than Sviatopolk-Mirskii's moderate policies ever could.

"The most dangerous moment for a bad government is when
it suddenly starts to yield to public opinion," Shmuel Galai once
wrote,[37] and that proved very much the case with Sviatopolk-
Mirskii's well-intentioned hope of granting the sorts of concessions that *obshchestvo* had never dared to imagine would be
possible under Plehve's strict regime. Demanding more concessions and greater freedom of political action than Sviatopolk-
Mirskii could possibly concede, *obshchestvo* turned against him
as quickly as it had against Plehve and, when he sought an
accommodation with the Union of Liberation at the end of 1904,
its leaders refused. Autocracy and *proizvol* now stood in stark
opposition to constitutionalism and *zakonnost'*. "There are no
intermediary positions between autocracy and constitutionalism,"
Miliukov announced grandly. Only "a formal abolition of autocracy," he insisted, would satisfy the Union of Liberation now.[38]
Unable to negotiate and unwilling to use force, Sviatopolk-Mirskii
resigned from office. "Everything has failed," he lamented as

he left a special meeting at which the emperor and his closest advisers rejected his proposals for further concessions to *obshchestvo* at the beginning of December. "Let us build jails."[39]

Sviatopolk-Mirskii's resignation only increased the clamor of civic-minded Russians for a voice in national affairs as the Union of Liberation organized almost forty public banquets in more than two dozen cities during late 1904 and early 1905 to marshal support for its campaign against autocracy. That summer, the politically active professional unions that emerged from this now famous "banquet campaign" merged into a powerful Union of Unions that claimed more than a hundred thousand members by the time that the tsar's government faced Russia's first effective nationwide general strike in October 1905.[40] As *obshchestvo* joined with Russia's surging revolutionary movement in the middle of that month to wrest the October Manifesto from Nicholas II, the citizen society that the Great Reforms had produced took on the role as the leading advocate for national transformation that Peter the Great had played so well and that Catherine II and Alexander I had gradually abandoned. Autocracy now stood firmly in the way of the political and social progress that Russia's economic modernization required in much the same way as the church and the conservative aristocracy had in the time of Peter the Great.

The wheel had come full circle. As the Revolution of 1905 came to an end, it was *obshchestvo*, a coalition of responsible social and professional groups not even imagined at the time of Peter the Great, that assumed the role as champion of Russia's transformation that the autocrat had played in the eighteenth century. Against it stood those autocratic institutions on which the forms of constitutional government had yet to be imposed, not the least of which was Russia's emperor himself. Certainly *obshchestvo* had won a larger space in which to work and, with it, was now obliged to shoulder larger and more complex tasks. The extent to which it would succeed in that undertaking and the degree to which it could resolve the dilemmas posed by building a society based on *zakonnost'* while the institutions that administered it continued to be drawn to the vagaries of *proizvol* would determine the fate of Russia's tardily begun experiment with constitutional government.

Russia's citizen society had scarcely more than a decade in which to achieve that transformation, and a large portion of that time would be filled with disruptions brought on by the greatest war that men and nations had ever fought. Overwhelmed by the demands of a conflict that was far beyond their strength to win, the Russians found that their nation's stumbling war effort undercut *zakonnost'* and legitimized *proizvol* in ways that life in peacetime never had. War introduced an urgency into natial politics that the opponents of autocracy had never envisioned a decade before and obliged *obshchestvo* to make choices that diverted it from its preferred path. That *obshchestvo* had not steered the Russians firmly along the course toward constitutional monarchy and a democratic polity that the West had taken in the wake of the industrial revolution became painfully clear well before the end of 1917, when the October Revolution hammered the last nails into the coffin that held the tattered remains of the Great Reform society. As Lenin and his successors elevated secrecy and *proizvol* above *glasnost'* and *zakonnost'*, the responsible citizen society that *obshchestvo* had struggled to create in Russia gave way to a new order in which the Russians conceded responsibility for civic affairs to the Bolshevik Party and its leaders. Those members of *obshchestvo* who did not perish in the course of the Civil War were driven into exile by it. Their disappearance from the turmoil of Russian politics left unanswered the question of how the Great Reform society would have fared in the complex world of the twentieth century.

# NOTES

## KEY TO ABBREVIATIONS

| | |
|---|---|
| *AHR* | *American Historical Review.* New York, 1895–. |
| *CMRS* | *Cahiers du monde russe et soviétique.* Paris, 1959–. |
| *CalSS* | *California Slavic Studies.* Berkeley and Los Angeles, 1960–. |
| *CSS* | *Canadian Slavic Studies.* Montreal and Pittsburgh, 1967–. |
| *EU* | *Ekonomicheskii ukazatel'.* St. Petersburg, 1857–58. |
| *GPB* | Gosudarstvennaia Publichnaia Biblioteka imeni M. E. Saltykova-Shchedrina. Otdel rukopisei. (Leningrad). |
| *HSS* | *Harvard Slavic Studies.* Cambridge, Mass, 1953–76. |
| *IA* | *Istoricheskii arkhiv.* Moscow, 1955–62. |
| *IstSSSR* | *Istoriia SSSR.* Moscow, 1957–. |
| *JfGOE* | *Jahrbücher für Geschichte Osteuropas.* Breslau. New Series, 1953–. |
| *JMH* | *Journal of Modern History.* Chicago, 1929–. |
| *KiS* | *Katorga i Ssylka.* Moscow, 1921–35. |
| *LN* | *Literaturnoe nasledstvo.* Moscow, 1931–. |
| *MG* | *Minuvshie gody.* St. Petersburg, 1908. |
| *MS* | *Morskoi sbornik.* St. Petersburg, Petrograd, Leningrad, 1852–. |
| *OC* | Osborn Collection. Sterling Memorial Library. Yale University. |
| ORGBL | Gosudarstvennaia Biblioteka S.S.S.R. imeni V. I. Lenina. Otdel rukopisei (Moscow). |

OSP        *Oxford Slavonic Papers.* New Series. Oxford, 1950–.

RA         *Russkii arkhiv.* Moscow, 1863–1917.

RBS        *Russkii biograficheskii slovar'.* 25 vols. St. Petersburg, 1896–1918.

RevS       Nechkina, M. V., ed. *Revoliutsionnaia situatsiia v Rossii v 1859–1861gg.* 8 vols. Moscow, 1960–79.

RH         *Russian History.* Pittsburgh, 1974–.

RM         *Russkaia mysl'.* Moscow, 1880–1918.

RS         *Russkaia starina.* St. Petersburg, 1870–1918.

RV         *Russkii vestnik.* Moscow-St. Petersburg, 1856–1906.

SEER       *Slavonic and East European Review.* London, 1922–.

SIRIO      *Sbornik imperatorskago russkago istoricheskago obshchestva.* St. Petersburg-Iur'ev-Moscow, 1867–1916.

SR         *Slavic Review.* Columbus, Ohio, 1945–.

TsGIAL     Tsentral'nyi Gosudarstvennyi Istoricheskii Arkhiv S.S.S.R. (Leningrad).

TsGAOR     Tsentral'nyi Gosudarstvennyi Istoricheskii Arkhiv Oktiabr'skoi Revoliutsii (Moscow).

VE         *Vestnik evropy.* St. Petersburg, 1866–1918.

VP         *Vestnik prava.* St. Petersburg, 1871–1906.

VS         *Voennyi sbornik.* St. Petersburg, 1858–1917.

ZhMIu      *Zhurnal Ministerstva Iustitsii.* St. Petersburg, 1859–68, 1894–1915.


**PREFACE**

1. Iu. I Gerasimova, "Krizis pravitel'stvennoi politiki v gody revoliutsionnoi situatsii i Aleksandr II," in *Revs* (1962), pp. 93–106. See also M. V. Nechkina, "Reforma 1861 goda kak pobochnyi produkt revoliutsionnoi bor'by (k metodologii izucheniia reformy)," in ibid., pp. 7–17.
2. P. A. Zaionchkovskii, *Otmena krepostnogo prava v Rossii*, 3rd ed. (Moscow, 1968), pp. 60–62.
3. Alfred J. Rieber, ed., *The Politics of Autocracy: The Letters of Alexander II to Prince A. I. Bariatinskii, 1857–1864* (Paris, 1966), pp. 24–27.
4. Terence Emmons, *The Russian Landed Gentry and the Peasant Emancipation of 1861* (Cambridge, 1968), p. 48.

5. Daniel Field, *The End of Serfdom: Nobility and Bureaucracy in Russia, 1855–1861* (Cambridge, Mass., 1976), p. 100.

6. "Zhurnaly komiteta uchrezhdennago Vysochaishim reskriptom 6 dekabria 1826 goda," *SIRIO*, LXXIV (1891): 264.

7. W. Bruce Lincoln, *In the Vanguard of Reform: Russia's Enlightened Bureaucrats, 1825–1861* (DeKalb, 1982).

8. V. V. Garmiza, *Podgotovka zemskoi reformy 1864 goda* (Moscow, 1957); S. Frederick Starr, *Decentralization and Self- Government in Russia, 1830–1870* (Princeton, 1972).

9. Richard Wortman, *The Development of a Russian Legal Consciousness* (Chicago, 1976); Friedhelm Berthold Kaiser, *Die russische Justizreform von 1864: Zur Geschichte der russischen Justiz von Katherina II bis 1917* (Leiden, 1972).

10. Daniel T. Orlovsky, *The Limits of Reform: The Ministry of Internal Affairs in Imperial Russia, 1802–1881* (Cambridge, Mass., 1981).

11. P. A. Zaionchkovskii, *Voennye reformy 1860–1870 godov v Rossii* (Moscow, 1952); P. A. Zaionchkovskii, *Provedenie v zhizn' krest'ianskoi reformy 1861g.* (Moscow, 1958); P. A. Zaionchkovskii, *Krizis samoderzhaviia na rubezhe 1870–1880 godov* (Moscow, 1964); P. A. Zaionchkovskii, *Pravitel'stvennyi apparat samoderzhavnoi Rossii v XIXv.* (Moscow, 1978); P. A. Zaionchkovskii, *Rossiiskoe samoderzhavie v kontse XIX stoletiia (Politicheskaia reaktsiia 80-kh—nachala 90-kh godov* (Moscow, 1970); L. G. Zakharova, *Zemskaia kontrreforma 1890g.* (Moscow, 1968); V. G. Chernukha, *Krest'ianskii vopros v pravitel'stvennoi politike Rossii* (Leningrad, 1972); V. G. Chernukha, *Vnutrenniaia politika tsarizma s serediny 50-kh do nachala 80-kh gg. XIX v.* (Leningard, 1978); N. M. Pirumova, *Zemskoe liberal'noe dvizhenie: Sotsial'nye korni i evoliutsiia do nachala XX veka* (Moscow, 1977); N. M. Pirumova, *Zemskaia intelligentsia i ee rol' v obshchestvennoi bor'be do nachala XXv.* (Moscow, 1986); I. V. Orzhekovskii, *Administratsiia i pechat' mezhdu dvumia revoliutsionnymi situatsiiami (1866–1878)* (Gorkii, 1973). In this connection, one also must add Zakharova's impressive recent work: *Samoderzhaviia i otmena krepostnogo prava v Rossii, 1856–1861* (Moscow, 1984).

12. Terence Emmons and Wayne S. Vucinich, eds., *The Zemstvo in Russia: An Experiment in Local Self-Government* (Cambridge, 1982); Harley Balzer, ed., *Professions in Russia at the End of the Old Regime* (Forthcoming, Cornell University Press); Edith Clowes and Samuel Kassow, eds., *Between Tsar and People* (Forthcoming, Princeton University Press, 1991).

13. Ben Eklof, *Russian Peasant Schools: Officialdom, Village Culture, and Popular Pedagogy, 1861–1914* (Berkeley and Los Angeles, 1986).

14. Nancy Mandelker Frieden, *Russian Physicians in an Era of Reform and Revolution, 1856–1905* (Princeton, 1981).

15. Richard G. Robbins, Jr., *The Tsar's Viceroys: Russian Provincial Governors in the Last Years of the Empire* (Ithaca, 1987).
16. Samuel D. Kassow, *Students, Professors, and the State in Tsarist Russia* (Berkeley and Los Angeles, 1989).
17. Scott Seregny, *Russian Teachers and Peasant Revolution: The Politics of Education in 1905* (Bloomington, 1988).
18. Allen Sinel, *The Classroom and the Chancellery: State Education Reform in Russia Under Count Dmitry Tolstoy* (Cambridge, Mass., 1973).
19. Heide W. Whelan, *Alexander III and the State Council: Bureaucracy and Counter-Reform in Late Imperial Russia* (Rutgers, 1982).
20. Thomas S. Pearson, *Russian Officialdom in Crisis: Autocracy and Local Self-Government, 1861–1900* (Cambridge, 1989).

**CHAPTER I:** AUTOCRACY, BUEAUCRACY, AND REFORM

1. Raymond H. Fisher, *The Russian Fur Trade, 1550–1700* (Berkeley and Los Angeles, 1943), pp. 108–22, 204–9; George V. Lantzeff, *Siberia in the Seventeenth Century: A Study of the Colonial Administration* (Berkeley and Los Angeles, 1943), pp. 33–46.
2. T. S. Willan, *The Early History of the Russia Company, 155–1603* (Manchester, 1956), pp. 55–56; Violet Barbour, *Capitalism in Amsterdam in the Seventeenth Century* (Ann Arbor, 1963), p. 119; Joseph T. Fuhrmann, *The Origins of Capitalism in Russia: Industry and Progress in the Sixteenth and Seventeenth Centuries* (Chicago, 1972), pp. 78, 248–50.
3. Richard Wortman, *The Development of a Russian Legal Consciousness* (Chicago and London, 1976), p. 9.
4. Michael Cherniavsky, *Tsar and People: Studies in Russian Myths* (New Haven and London, 1961), p. 72.
5. A. S. Pushkin, *Polnoe sobranie sochinenii v desiati tomakh* (Moscow, 1962–66), IV: 381–82.
6. Hans Rogger, *National Consciousness in Eighteenth-Century Russia* (Cambridge, Mass., 1960), pp. 48–54.
7. Robert E. Jones, *The Emancipation of the Russian Nobility, 1762–1785* (Princeton, 1973), pp. 79–82; Wilson R. Augustine, "Notes Toward a Portrait of the Eightenth-Century Russian Nobility," *CSS*, (Fall 1970): 381–85.
8. P. N. Miliukov, *Ocherki po istorii russkoi kul'tury* (St. Petersburg, 1901), III: 265–67; A. A. Kizevetter, *Istoricheskie ocherki* (Moscow, 1912), pp. 239–41.
9. Empress Catherine II, *Nakaz Imperatritsy Ekateriny II, dannyi kommissii o sochinenii proekta novago ulozheniia*, edited, with an introduction by N. D. Chechulin (St. Petersburg, 1907), p. 3, article 11.

10. Quoted in Wortman, *Development of a Russian Legal Consciousness,* p. 12.

11. *Nakaz Imperatritsy Ekateriny II,* p. 39, article 153.

12. Ibid., p. 4, articles 15, 13.

13. A. G. Dement'ev et al., eds., *Russkaia periodicheskaia pechat' (1702–1894gg): Spravochnik* (Moscow, 1959), pp. 14–49. On Catherine and the satirical journals of 1769–74, see also P. N. Berkov, "Satiricheskaia zhurnalistika 1769–1774gg.," in V. E. Evgen'ev-Maksimov, et al., eds., *Ocherki po istorii russkoi zhurnalistiki i kritiki* (Leningrad, 1950), I: 45–81.

14. N. I. Novikov, "Otryvok puteshestviia v*** I*** T***," in I. V. Malysheva, ed., *N. I. Novikov i ego sovremenniki: Izbrannye sochineniia* (Moscow, 1961), p. 100.

15. On Novikov and his satirical journals, see G. Gareth Jones, "Novikov's Naturalized *Spectator*," in J. E. Garrard, ed., *The Eighteenth Century in Russia* (Oxford, 1973), pp. 149–65; G. P. Makogonenko, *Nikolai Novikov i russkoi prosveshchenie XVIII veka* (Moscow and Leningrad, 1952), pp. 147–270; and Miliukov, *Ocherki istorii russkoi kul'tury,* III: 297–303.

16. "Smertnyi prigovor A. N. Radishchevu, 24 iiulia 1790g.," in D. A. Babkin, ed., *Protsess A. N. Radishcheva* (Moscow and Leningrad, 1952), p. 244.

17. G. P. Makogonenko, *Radishchev i ego vremia* (Moscow, 1956), pp. 39–54 and passim; L. B. Svetlov, *A. N. Radishchev: Kritiko-biograficheskii ocherk* (Moscow, 1958), pp. 31–57.

18. "Zamechaniia Ekateriny II na knigi A. N. Radishcheva," in Babkin, ed., *Protsess A. N. Radishcheva,* pp. 157–64.

19. Quoted in Emile Haumant, *La Culture Française en Russia (1700–1900)* (Paris, 1913), p. 176. See also A. M. Skabichevskii, *Ocherki istorii russkoi tsenzury, 1700–1863gg.* (St. Petersburg, 1892), p. 64.

20. Wortman, *Development of a Russian Legal Consciousness,* pp. 122, 129.

21. Iu. D. Levin, "Angliiskaia poeziia i literatura russkogo sentimentalizma," in M. D. Alekseev, ed., *Ot klassitsizma k romantizmu* (Leningrad, 1970), p. 233.

22. The first of these quotes is from Karamzin; the second from Uvarov. See Richard Pipes, ed. and trans., *Karamzin's Memoir on Ancient and Modern Russia: A Translation and an Analysis* (Cambridge, Mass., 1959), pp. 197–98; and Nicholas V. Riasanovsky, *Nicholas I and Official Nationality in Russia, 1825–1855* (Berkeley and Los Angeles, 1959), pp. 74–75.

23. *Nakaz Imperatritsy Ekateriny II,* p. 2, article 6.

24. M. P. Pogodin, *Istoriko-politicheskie pis'ma i zapiski v prodolzhenii Krymskoi voiny, 1853–1856* (Moscow, 1874), p. 254.

25. F. I. Tiutchev, "La Russie et la Revolution," *Polnoe sobranie sochienii F. I. Tiutcheva* (St. Petersburg, 1913), p. 344.
26. Martin Malia, *Alexander Herzen and the Birth of Russian Socialism, 1812–1855* (Cambridge, Mass., 1961), p. 43.
27. A. S. Pushkin, "Derevnia," *Polnoe sobranie sochinenii* (Moscow, 1962), I: 360–61.
28. A. D. Borovkov, "A. D. Borovkov i ego avtobiograficheskie zapiski," *RS*, No. 11 (November 1898): 353–54.
29. A. A. Kizevetter, "Vnutrenniaia politika Imperatora Nikolaia Pavlovicha," in Kizevetter, *Istoricheskie ocherki*, pp. 427–30.
30. "Zhurnaly komiteta uchrezhdennago Vysochaishim reskriptom 6 dekabria 1826 goda," *SIRIO*, LXXIV (1891): 264.
31. *Gosudarstvennyi sovet, 1801–1901gg.* (St. Petersburg, 1902), p. 64.
32. A. N. Filippov, "Istoricheskii ocherk obrazovaniia ministerstv v Rossii," *ZhMIu*, No. 9 (November 1902): 40.
33. S. M. Troitskii, *Russkii absoliutizm i dvorianstvo v XVIII v. Formirovanie biurokratii* (Moscow, 1974), pp. 169–176; P. A. Zaionchkovskii, *Pravitel'stvennyi apparat samoderzhavnoi Rossii v XIX v.* (Moscow, 1978), pp. 66–67; M. V. Klochkov, *Ocherki pravitel'stvennoi deiatel'nosti vremeni Pavla I* (Petrograd, 1916), pp. 95–108; D. F. Troshchinskii, "Zapiska Dmitriia Prokof'evicha Troshchinskago o Ministerstvakh," *SIRIO*, III (1868): 30–31.
34. Wortman, *Development of a Russian Legal Consciousness*, pp. 91–95; George L. Yaney, *The Systematization of Russian Government: Social Evolution in the Domestic Administration of Imperial Russia, 1711–1905* (Urbana, 1973), pp. 81–85.
35. Speranskii made this point as early as 1802. See M. M. Speranskii, "Otryvok o komissii ulozheniia," in S. N. Valk, ed., *M. M. Speranskii: Proekty i zapiski* (Moscow and Leningrad, 1961), p. 27.
36. "Otchety po Inspektorskomu Departamentu Grazhdanskago Vedomstva za 1847–1857gg.," TsGIAL, fond 1409, opis' 2, delo No. 6829; W. Bruce Lincoln, "A Profile of the Russian Bureaucracy on the Eve of the Great Reforms," *JfGOE*, XXVII (1979): 182–83; Zaionchkovskii, *Pravitel'stvennyi apparat*, p. 69.
37. The comparison between the total populations that Russian and European officials served is from Starr, *Decentralization and Self-Government*, p. 48. For statistics on the populations of nobles and merchants see A. G. Rashin, *Naselenie Rossii za 100 let (1811–1913): Statisticheskie ocherki* (Moscow, 1956), pp. 258–59. For the total numbers of civil servants in Russia at midcentury, see "Otchety po Inspektorskomu Departamentu Grazhdanskago Vedomstva za 1847–1857gg.," TsGIAL, fond 1409, opis' 2, delo No. 6829.
38. I. N. Borozdin, "Universitety v Rossii v pervoi polovine XIX veka," in *Istoriia Rossii v XIX veke*, III: 352–56.

39. I. Ia. Seleznev, *Istoricheskii ocherk Imperatorskago, byvshego tsarskosel'-skago, nyne Aleksandrovskago, litsei* (St. Petersburg, 1861), pp. 147–48; D. F. Kobeko, *Imperatorskii tsarskosel'skii litsei, 1811–1843gg.* (St. Petersburg, 1911), p. 16.

40. Wortman, *Development of a Russian Legal Consciousness*, p. 298, note 52.

41. M. E. Saltykov-Shchedrin, *Sobranie sochinenii* (Moscow, 1970), X: 271.

42. A. I. Artem'ev, "Dnevnik 1 ianvaria–31 iiulia 1856g.," GPB, fond 37, delo No. 158/8. Entry for January 11, 1856.

43. Lincoln, *In the Vanguard of Reform*, pp. 19–20; F. G. Terner, *Vospominaniia zhizni F. G. Ternera* (St. Petersburg, 1910), I: 68; A. A. Kharytonov, "Iz vospominanii A. A. Kharytonova," *RS*, LXXXI, No. 1 (January 1894): 116–17; P. I. Nebolsin, "Biudzhety peterburgskikh chinovnikov," *EU*, No. 11 (March 16 1857): 241–50.

44. N. V. Gogol, "Nevskii Prospekt," in N. V. Gogol', *Sobranie sochinenii N. V. Gogolia* (Moscow, 1959), III: 42.

45. See especially M. P. Veselovskii, "Zapiski M. P. Veselovskago s 1828 po 1882," GPB, fond 550.F.IV.861/420; S. I. Zarudnyi, "Pis'mo opytnago chinovnika sorokovykh godov mladshemu ego sobratu, postupaiushchemu na sluzhbu," A. S. Zarudnyi, ed., *RS*, C, No. 12 (December 1899): 543–46; A. I. Artem'ev, Dnevnik, 1 ianvaria–31 iiulia 1856g.," GPB, fond 37, delo No. 158/8. Entry for January 11, 1856.

46. A. I. Artem'ev, an agent of special commissions in the Ministry of Internal Affairs, filed a factual report in 1852 that is highly reminiscent of Gogol's work. See A. I. Artem'ev, "Dnevnik, iiun'–19 avgusta 1852g.," GPB, fond 37, delo No. 155/3.

47. "Vsepoddanneishii raport Kazanskago Voennago gubernatora o sdelannom im obozrenii vverennoi upravlenii ego gubernii," "Vsepoddanneishie raporty Saratovskago, Tul'skago, i Poltavskago Gubernatorov o sdelannom imi obozrenii vverennoi upravlenii ikh guberniiakh," TsGIAL, fond 1287, opis' 37, delo No. 120/1–2, 6–7.

48. Marc Raeff, "The Russian Autocracy and Its Officials," *HSS* IV (1957): 77–92; Starr, *Decentralization and Self-Government*, pp. 44–50; W. Bruce Lincoln, "The Genesis of an 'Enlightened' Bureaucracy in Russia, 1825–1856," *JfGOE*, XX, No. 3 (September 1972): 321–30.

49. See, for example, "Delo po otnosheniiu Khoziaistvennago Departamenta v statisticheskoe otdelenie o tom, kakie goroda i kogda imenno poluchili Vysochaishe utverzhdennye plany," sentiabr'–oktiabr', 1849g., TsGIAL, fond 1287, opis' 39, delo No. 824; "Donesenie chinovnika osobykh poruchenii Nadvornago Sovetnika A. K. Girsa Ego Vysokoprevoskhoditel'stvu Gospodinu Ministru Vnutrennikh Del," 17 avgusta 1844g., TsGIAL, fond 1287, opis' 39, delo No. 25/53–55; "Donesenie chinovnika khoziai-

212    Notes to Pages 20–23

stvennago departamenta Kollezhskago Assesora Veselovskago Ego Vysokoprevoskhoditel'stvu Gospodinu Ministru Vnutrennikh Del, 16 maia 1843g.," TsGIAL, fond 1287, opis' 39, delo No. 28/4–6, and several dozen similar files in this same collection.

50. Quoted in Wortman, *Development of a Russian Legal Consciousness*, p. 183.

51. See P. I. Liashchenko, *Istoriia narodnogo khoziaistva SSSR* (Moscow, 1956), I: 473; A. G. Troinitskii, *Krepostnoe naselenie Rossii po desiatoi narodnoi perepisi* (St. Petersburg, 1861), p. 45.

52. For some examples, see the service records of A. F. Shtakel'berg (TsGIAL, fond 1349, opis 3, delo No. 2535), A. K. Girs (TsGIAL, fond 1287, opis' 39, delo No. 52), K. K. Grot (TsGIAL, fond 1162, opis' 6, delo No. 154), N. P. Bezobrazov (TsGIAL, fond 1349, opis' 3, delo No. 171), K. A. Krizhivitskii (TsGIAL, fond 1349, opis' 3, delo No. 1157), A. K. Sivers (TsGIAL, fond 1284, opis' 75, delo No. 2), Count D. N. Tolstoi (TsGIAL, fond 1284, opis' 32, delo No. 192), and K. S. Veselovskii (TsGIAL, 1349, opis' 3, delo No. 391).

53. W. Bruce Lincoln, *Nicholas I: Emperor and Autocrat of All the Russias* (London, 1978), pp. 171–72.

54. P. A. Valuev, "Otryvok iz zamechanii o poriadke grazhdanskoi sluzhby v Rossii (1845g)," TsGIAL, fond 908, opis' 1, delo No. 24/26.

55. A. P. Zablotskii-Desiatovskii, "Statisticheskoe obozrenie gosudarstvennykh i obshchestvennykh povinnostei, dokhodov, i raskhodov v Kievskoi gubernii, 1850–1851gg.," TsGIAL, fond 940, opis' 1, delo No. 69/3.

56. Veselovskii, "Zapiski," GPB, fond 550.F.IV.861/389.

57. P. A. Valuev, "Duma russkago vo vtoroi polovine 1855g.," *RS*, LXX, No. 5 (May 1891): 355.

58. L. V. Tengoborskii, "Extraits du Mémoire secret du Conseiller Privé Actuel Tengoborski (janvier 1857)," TsGIAL, fond 851, opis' 1, delo No. 50/289–90.

59. L. A. Perovskii, "Dokladnaia zapiska o neobkhodimosti uluchshenii po gubernskim pravleniiam (1843g.)," TsGIAL, fond 1149, opis' 3 (1843), delo No. 94a/6–7, 12; L. A. Perovskii, "O prichinakh umnozheniia deloproizvodstva vo vnutrennem upravlenii (mart 1851g)," TsGIAL, fond 1287, opis' 36, delo No. 137/14.

60. Perovskii, "O prichinakh umnozheniia deloproizvodstva," TsGIAL, fond 1287, opis' 36, delo No. 137/14–15.

61. M. P. Veselovskii, "Zapiski M. P. Veselovskago," GPB, fond 550.F.IV. 861/390.

62. Ibid. See also, for example, "Obozrenie vsekh chastei gosudarstvennago upravleniia: Chast' tret'ia," (1831g.), GPB, fond 380, delo No. 67/1.

63. Letter of N. A. Miliutin to D. A. Miliutin, August 10, 1838, ORGBL, fond 169, kartonka 69, papka 6.
64. On this, see especially A. V. Golovnin, "Zapiski Aleksandra Vasil'-evicha Golovnina s marta 1867g.," TsGIAL, fond 851, opis' 1, delo No. 7/2.
65. Perovskii, "O prichinakh umnozheniia deloproizvodstva," TsGIAL, fond 1287, opis' 36, delo No. 137/16.
66. I. A. Blinov, *Gubernatory: Istoriko-iuridicheskii ocherk* (St. Petersburg, 1905), pp. 161–63.
67. "Zhurnaly komiteta uchrezhdennago Vysochaishim reskriptom 6 dekabria 1826 goda," p. 264.
68. Hans-Joachim Torke, "Das russische Beamtentum in der ersten Hälfte des 19. Jahrhunderts," *Forschungen zur osteuropäischen Geschichte,* XIII (1967): 214–15.
69. L. A. Perovskii, "O prichinakh umnozheniia deloproizvodstva," TsGIAL, fond 1284, opis' 36, delo No. 137/14–23; Tengoborskii, "Extraits du Memoire secret," TsGIAL, fond 851, opis' 1, delo No. 50/288–91.
70. Quoted in Wortman, *Development of a Russian Legal Consciousness,* p. 152.
71. N. P. Semenov, "Graf Viktor Nikitich Panin," *RA,* No. 3 (1887): 538, 546.
72. Lincoln, *In the Vanguard of Reform,* pp. 30–40, 62–67.
73. Ibid., pp. 43–51, 109–35.
74. P. A. Khromov, *Ekonomicheskoe razvitie Rossii v XIX–XX vekakh, 1800–1917* (Moscow, 1950), pp. 437–439; William L. Blackwell, *The Beginnings of Russian Industrialization, 1800–1860* (Princeton, 1968), pp. 390–92.
75. Khromov, *Ekonomicheskoe razvitie Rossii,* pp. 460–61; M. Tugan-Baranovskii, *Russkaia fabrika v proshlom i nastoiashchem* (Moscow, 1938), p. 65; M. P. Viatkin, "Ekonomicheskaia zhizn' Peterburga v period razlozheniia i krizisa krepostnichestva," in M. P. Viatkin et al., eds., *Ocherki istorii Leningrada* (Leningrad, 1955), I: 461–63; V. S. Virginskii, *Vozniknovenie zheleznykh dorog v Rossii do nachala 40-kh godov XIXv.* (Moscow, 1949), pp. 189–223.
76. A. E. Tsimmerman, "Vospominaniia Generala A. E. Tsimmermana," ORGBL, fond 325, kartonka 2, papka 1/243.
77. Baron M. A. Korf, "Dnevnik za 1840g.," TsGAOR, fond 728, opis' 1, delo No. 1817/iii/264.
78. A. V. Nikitenko, *Dnevnik* (Moscow, 1955), I: 421–22.
79. Quoted in A. V. Nikitenko, *Zapiski i dnevnik, 1826–1877* (St. Petersburg, 1893), I: 577.
80. Nikitenko, *Dnevnik,* I: 422.

81. Quoted in V. I. Semevskii, *Krest'ianskii vopros v Rossii v XVIII i pervoi polovine XIX stoletiia* (St. Petersburg, 1888), II: 138.
82. Nikitenko, *Dnevnik,* I: 338.
83. A. I. Artem'ev, "Dnevnik, 1 iiunia–31 dekabria 1855g.," GPB, fond 37, delo No. 157/83–84.
84. Valuev, "Duma russkogo," p. 355.
85. Quoted in Starr, *Decentralization and Self-Government,* p. 53.
86. Aleksandr Kamenskii, "Vsepoddanneishaia zapiska Kamenskago 1850 goda," *RS,* CXXII, No. 6 (June 1905): 629.
87. Lincoln, *In the Vanguard of Reform,* pp. 32–58.
88. "Pamiati A. P. Zablotskago," *RS,* XXXIII, No. 2 (February 1882): 540.
89. "Svedeniia o N. I. Vtorove za vremia sluzhby ego v Ministerstve Vnutrennikh Del s 1844 po 1862gg.," GPB, fond 163, delo No. 56/2.
90. N. A. Miliutin, "Obshchaia instruktsiia chinovnikam otriazhaemym dlia obozreniia gorodov," TsGIAL, fond 1287, opis' 39, delo No. 156/2–3. For a more thorough discussion of the way in which these men set out to learn about Russia and the sorts of data they assembled, see Lincoln, *In the Vanguard of Reform,* pp. 102–38.
91. A. D. Shumakher, "Pozdnie vospominaniia o davno minuvshikh vremenakh: Dlia moikh detei i vnuchat," *VE,* CXCVI, No. 3 (March 1899): 114.
92. K. S. Veselovskii, "Plan statisticheskago opisaniia Gosudarstvennykh Imushchestv i sosloviia sel'skikh zhitelei, sostoiashchago pod popechitel'stvom Ministerstva Gosudarstvennykh Imushchestv," 1847g., TsGIAL, fond 398, opis' 11, delo No. 3635/35–36.
93. Nikitenko, *Dnevnik,* I: 411.
94. P. A. Valuev, "Dnevnik grafa Petra Aleksandrovicha Valueva, 1847–1860gg.," *RS,* No. 4 (April 1891): 172–73.
95. "Otnoshenie Deistvitel'nago Tainago Sovetnika Dmitriia Buturlina 17-go marta 1849g., k Ministru Narodnago Prosveshcheniia Grafu S. S. Uvarovu," (konfidential'no), TsGIAL, fond 772, opis' 1, delo No. 2242/1–3.
96. Quoted in Cynthia H. Whittaker, *The Origins of Modern Russian Education: An Intellectual Biography of Count Sergei Uvarov, 1786–1855* (DeKalb, 1984), p. 237.
97. Lincoln, *Nicholas I,* pp. 303–11; N. Rodzianko, "Nabliudeniia za dukhom i napravleniem zhurnala *Biblioteka dlia Chteniia,*" (mai 1850), TsGIAL, fond 722, opis' 1, delo No. 2423/16; Pogodin, *Istoriko-politicheskiia pis'ma i zapiski,* p. 257.
98. Nikitenko, *Dnevnik,* I: 326.
99. These included the Moscow University professors Petr Redkin and Konstantin Kavelin, as well as the writers and publicists Ivan Aksakov, Iurii Samarin, Mikhail Saltykov-Shchedrin, and Ivan Turgenev.

100. P. S. Popov, ed., *Pis'ma k A. V. Druzhininu (1850–1863)* (Moscow, 1948), p. 10; A. E. Tsimmerman, "Vospominaniia Generala A. E. Tsimmermana," ORGBL, fond 325, kartonka 1, papka 2/7–8.
101. Quoted in Popov, ed., *Pis'ma k A. V. Druzhininu,* p. 11.
102. Quoted in A. G. Dement'ev, *Ocherki po istorii russkoi zhurnalistiki, 1840–1850gg* (Moscow and Leningrad, 1951), p. 106.
103. Quoted in ibid.
104. Quoted in Whittaker, *The Origins of Modern Russian Education,* p. 238.
105. M. Poggenpohl au Directeur de la Chancellerie de St. Petersbourg, 20 mars 1854, in Count K. V. Nesselrode, *Papiers et lettres du Chancelier Comte de Nesselrode, 1760–1850* (Paris, 1912), XII: 30–31.

#### CHAPTER II: THE IMPACT OF DEFEAT

1. Quoted from Harold Nicolson, *The Congress of Vienna: A Study in Allied Unity, 1812–1822* (New York, 1946), p. 250.
2. These quotes come from the memoirs of Count Beust, quoted in Constantin de Grunwald, *Tsar Nicholas I,* translated from the French by Brigit Patmore (London, 1954), p. 255.
3. P. A. Zaionchkovskii, "Dmitrii Alekseevich Miliutin: Biograficheskii ocherk," in P. A. Zaionchkovskii, ed., *Dnevnik D. A. Miliutina, 1873–1875gg.* (Moscow, 1947), I: 17.
4. For a brilliant discussion of the well-ordered police state, see Marc Raeff, *The Well-Ordered Police State: Social and Institutional Change through Law in the Germanies and Russia, 1600–1800* (New Haven, 1983), pp. 193–250.
5. Pis'mo K. D. Kavelina k T. N. Granovskomu, 5 sentiabria 1848g., in Sh. M. Levin, ed., "K. D. Kavelin o smerti Nikolaia I: Pis'ma k T. N. Granovskomu," *LN,* LXVII (1959): 596.
6. B. N. Chicherin, *Vospominaniia Borisa Nikolaevicha Chicherina: Moskva sorokovykh godov* (Moscow, 1929), p. 114.
7. Quoted in M. Lemke, *Nikolaevskie zhandarmy i literatura, 1826–1855gg.* (St. Petersburg, 1909), p. 303.
8. Tsimmerman, "Vospominaniia Generala Tsimmermana," ORGBL, fond 325, kartonka 1, papka No. 2/67.
9. Pis'mo N. A. Miliutina k P. D. Kiselevu, 4 marta 1858g., ORGBL, fond 129, kartonka 17, papka 55.
10. Lincoln, *In the Vanguard of Reform,* pp. 80–101, 148–62.
11. Ibid., pp. 86–90.
12. "Pis'mo K. D. Kavelina k T. N. Granovskomu, 5 sentiabria 1848g.," in Levin, ed., "K. D. Kavelin o smerti Nikolaia I," p. 596.
13. F. G. Terner, *Vospominaniia zhizni F. G. Ternera* (St. Petersburg, 1910), I: 169.
14. Lincoln, *In the Vanguard of Reform,* pp. 93–99.

15. I. S. Aksakov, *Izsledovaniia o torgovle na ukrainskikh iarmakakh* (St. Petersburg, 1858).

16. Of particular importance were Nikolai Miliutin's Provisional Section for the Reorganization of Municipal Government and Economy and the Provisional Statistical Section, both dominated by Nikolai Miliutin in the Ministry of Internal Affairs, and Zablotskii-Desiatovskii's Department of Rural Economy, especially its Academic Committee and its Statistical Section, in the Ministry of State Domains. See Lincoln, *In the Vanguard of Reform*, pp. 110–38.

17. "O prisuzhdennykh Uchennym Komitetom MGI po konkursu khoziaistvenno-statisticheskikh opisanii nagradakh," 10 noiabria 1850g., TsGIAL, fond 398, opis' 1, delo No. 4475/52.

18. A. P. Zablotskii-Desiatovskii, "Zapiska o nedostatkakh obshchestvennago i o vygodakh lichnago vladeniia krest'ian zemleiu," 1851g., TsGIAL, fond 940, opis' 1, delo No. 16/3.

19. A. P. Zablotskii-Desiatovskii, "Zapiska o roli Moskovskago i Peterburgskago obshchestv sel'skago khoziaistva v predstoiashchem osvobozhdenii krest'ian ot krepostnoi zavisimosti," 1856g., TsGIAL, fond 940, opis' 1, delo No. 17/9.

20. A. V. Golovnin, "Kratkii ocherk deistvii velikago kniazia Konstantina Nikolaevicha," GPB, fond 208, delo No. 2/269–71.

21. Quoted in A. F. Koni, "Velikii Kniaz' Konstantin Nikolaevich," in A. K. Dzhivelegov, S. P. Melgunov, and V. I. Picheta, eds., *Velikaia reforma* (Moscow, 1911), V: 38.

22. Quoted in ibid., pp. 37–38.

23. Golovnin, "Kratkii ocherk deistvii velikago kniazia Konstantina Nikolaevicha," GPB, fond 208, delo No. 2/269.

24. P. N. Glebov, "Morskoe sudoproizvodstvo vo Frantsii," *MS*, No. 11 (November 1859): 108–10.

25. Lincoln, *In the Vanguard of Reform*, pp. 146–47.

26. N. G. Chernyshevskii, *Polnoe sobranie sochinenii* (Moscow, 1939), II: 580.

27. A. F. Tiutcheva [Aksakova], *Pri dvore dvukh imperatorov: Vospominaniia, Dnevnik* (Moscow, 1928), entry for February 19, 1855, I: 179, 185.

28. Aleksandr Ivanovich Gertsen, *Polnoe sobranie sochinenii i pisem*, ed. M. K. Lemke (Petrograd, 1919), XIII: 616. On Herzen's financial dealings after he was obliged to leave Russia, see Malia, *Alexander Herzen*, pp. 389–90 and Judith Zimmerman, *Mid-Passage: Alexander Herzen and European Revolution, 1847–1852* (Pittsburg, 1989), p. 101.

29. Pis'mo K. D. Kavelina k T. N. Granovskomu, 4 marta 1855g., in Levin, ed., "K. D. Kavelin o smerti Nikolaia I," p. 607.

30. Chicherin, *Moskva sorokovykh godov*, p. 154.

31. Valuev, "Duma russkago," p. 355.

32. B. N. Chicherin, "Sovremennye zadachi russkoi zhizni," *Golosu iz Rossii: Sborniki A. I. Gertsena i N. P. Ogareva,* ed. M. V. Nechkina and E. L. Rudnitskaia (Moscow, 1975), IV: 86.

33. Chicherin, *Moskva sorokovykh godov,* p. 159.

34. Pis'mo K. D. Kavelina k T. N. Granovskomu, 4 marta 1855g., in Levin, ed., "K. D. Kavelin o smerti Nikolaia I," pp. 610–11.

35. N. Ia. Eidel'man, *Gertsen protiv samoderzhaviia: Sekretnaia politicheskaia istoriia Rossii XVIII–XIX vekov i vol'naia pechat'* (Moscow, 1973), p. 43.

36. Mikhail Lemke, *Ocherki osvoboditel'nago dvizheniia 'shestidesiatykh godov'* (St. Petersburg, 1908), pp. 43–44.

37. N. A. Dobroliubov, "Gubernskie ocherki," in N. A. Dobroliubov, *Sobranie sochinenii v deviati tomakh* (Moscow and Leningrad, 1962), II: 123.

38. Nikitenko, *Dnevnik,* II: 46.

39. Quoted in Starr, *Decentralization and Self-Government,* p. 61.

40. Iu. F. Samarin, "O krepostnom sostoianii i o perekhode iz nego k grazhdanskoi svobode," in Iu. F. Samarin, *Sochineniia* (Moscow, 1878), II: 18.

41. Nikitenko, *Dnevnik,* II: 46.

42. "Imperator Nikolai I i akademik Parrot," *RS,* No. 7 (July 1898): 145.

43. Quoted in Jacob W. Kipp and W. Bruce Lincoln, "Autocracy and Reform: Bureaucratic Absolutism and Political Modernization in Nineteenth-Century Russia," *RH,* VI, No. 1 (1979): 6. Speranskii identified five elites or "aristocracies" within any mature state: the hereditary nobility, the clergy, the industrial-commercial leadership, those in government service, and an intellectual-scholarly elite. See M. M. Speranskii, "O zakonakh: Besedy grafa M. M. Speranskago s Ego Imperatorskim Vysochestvom Gosudarem Naslednikom Tsesarevichem Velikim Kniazem Aleksandrom Nikolaevichem s 12 oktiabria 1835 po 10 aprelia 1837 goda," *SIRIO,* XXX (1880): 363–64.

44. Lincoln, *In the Vanguard of Reform,* pp. 172–74; *Materialy dlia istorii uprazdneniia krepostnago sostoianiia pomeshchich'ikh krest'ian v Rossii v tsarstvovanie Imperatora Aleksandra II* (Berlin, 1860), I: 116–17. See also Ia. A. Solov'ev, "Zapiski senatora Ia. A. Solov'eva," *RS,* XXXIV (1882): 110–11; P. P. Semenov-Tian-Shanskii, *Memuary* (Petrograd, 1916), III: 24–26.

45. N. Bakhtin, "Dopolnenie k zapiske zakliuchaiushchei v sebe soobrazheniia ob upravlenii otdel'nym vedomstvom," 20 noiabria 1856g., TsGAOR, fond 722, opis' 1, delo No. 605/2–3.

46. Theodore Taranovski, "The Aborted Counter-Reform: The Murav'ev Commission and the Judicial Statutes of 1864," *JfGOE,* XXIX, No. 2 (1981): 164.

47. V. A. Tsie, "Zapiska o merakh, neobkhodimykh dlia sokrashcheniia perepiski i uproshcheniia deloproizvodstva v gosudarstvennykh uchrezhdeniiakh," (1856g.), GPB, fond 833, delo No. 292/1–4.

48. Kniaz' P. A. Dolgorukov, "O vnutrennem sostoianii Rossii," noiabr', 1857g., TsGAOR, fond 647, opis' 1, delo No. 50/25.

49. *Kolokol*, No. 9 (15 fevralia 1859g.), in *Kolokol: Gazeta A. I. Gertsena i N. P. Ogareva* (Moscow, 1961), I: 67.

50. Quoted in Iu. I. Gerasimova, "Otnoshenie pravitel'stva k uchastii pechati v obsuzhdenii krest'ianskogo voprosa v periode revoliutionnoi situatsii kontsa 50-kh–nachala 60-kh godov XIXv.," in *RevS* (1974), p. 82.

51. Quoted in Nikitenko, *Dnevnik*, II: 16.

52. O. A. Przhetslavskii, "O glasnosti v russkoi zhurnal'noi literature," 20 ianvaria 1860g., TsGIAL, fond 772, opis' 1, delo No. 5129/1–27.

53. Quoted in Ulam, *In the Name of the People*, pp. 64–65.

54. *Kolokol*, No. 2 (1 avgusta 1857g.), and No. 9 (15 fevralia 1858g), in *Kolokol: Gazeta A. I., Gertsena i N. P. Ogareva*, I: 11, 67.

55. *Kolokol*, No. 13 (15 aprelia 1858g), in ibid., pp. 91, 98.

56. Ibid., p. 91.

57. Quoted in S. S. Tatishchev, *Imperator Aleksandr II: Ego zhizn' i tsarstvovanie* (St. Petersburg, 1911), I: 189.

58. "Pis'mo Imperatora Aleksandra Nikolaevicha k V. K. Elene Pavlovne, 26 oktiabria 1856g." Published in A. I. Levshin, "Dostopamiatnye minuty v moei zhizni: Zapiska Alekseia Iraklievicha Levshina," *RA*, No. 8 (1885): 489.

59. Quoted in Wortman, *Development of a Russian Legal Consciousness*, p. 163.

60. "Pis'mo Imperatora Aleksandra Nikolaevicha k V. K. Elene Pavlovne, 26 oktiabria 1856g," p. 489.

61. Quoted in L. G. Zakharova, *Samoderzhaviia i otmena krepostnogo prava v Rossii, 1856–1861* (Moscow, 1984), p. 65.

62. D. A. Obolenskii, "Moi vospominaniia o velikoi kniagine Elene Pavlovne," *RS*, CXXXVII, No. 3 (March 1909): 537.

63. Nikitenko, *Dnevnik*, I: 432.

64. "Pis'mo iz provintsii," *Kolokol*, No. 64 (1 marta 1860), in *Kolokol: Gazeta A. I. Gertsena i N. P. Ogareva* (Moscow, 1962), III: 534–35.

65. "Ot redaktsii," in Ibid., p. 533. See also 531–32.

**CHAPTER III:** BEGINNING RUSSIA'S RENOVATION

1. Quoted in Michael Florinsky, *Russia: A History and an Interpretation*, 2 vols. (New York, 1968), II: 896–97.

2. "Ot redaktsii," *Kolokol*, No. 64 (1 marta 1860), in *Kolokol: Gazeta A. I., Gertsena i N. P. Ogareva* (Moscow, 1962), III: 531.

3. "Pis'ma V. A. Zhukovskago k F. P Litke," *RA*, bk. 2 (1887): 335.
4. Quoted in A. P. Zablotskii-Desiatovskii, *Graf P. D. Kiselev i ego vremia* (St. Petersburg, 1882), II: 341.
5. Zakharova, *Samoderzhavie i otmena krepostnogo prava*, p. 89.
6. I. I. Ignatovich, *Pomeshchich'i krest'ian nakanune osvobozhdeniia* (Moscow, 1910), p. 62
7. Field, *The End of Serfdom*, pp. 31–32.
8. Ignatovich, *Pomeshchich'i krest'ian*, p. 62.
9. Field, *The End of Serfdom*, pp. 96, 100.
10. Quoted in Terence Emmons, *The Russian Landed Gentry and the Peasant Emancipation of 1861* (Cambridge, 1968), pp. 29–30.
11. Ibid., p. 33.
12. Quoted in Field, *The End of Serfdom*, p. 57.
13. See, for example, M. Poggenpohl au Directeur de la Chancellerie de St. Petersbourg, 20 mars 1854, in Nesselrode, *Papiers et lettres*, XII: 30-31.
14. A. I. Khodnev, *Istoriia Imperatorskago Vol'nago Ekonomicheskago Obshchestva s 1765 do 1865 goda* (St. Petersburg, 1865), p. 23.
15. A. N. Radishchev, "Puteshestvie iz Peterburga v Moskvu," in A. N. Radishchev, *Izbrannye filosofskie i obshchestvenno-politicheskie proizvedeniia*, ed. I. Ia. Shipanov (Moscow, 1952), p. 143.
16. For a discussion of these proposals, see N. M. Druzhinin, *Gosudarstvennye krest'iane i reforma P. D. Kiseleva* (Moscow and Leningrad, 1946), I: 154–93.
17. K. I. Lander, "Pribaltiiskii krai v pervoi polovine XIX veka," in *Istoriia Rossii v XIX veke* (St. Petersburg, 1907), II: 337–44; A. A. Kornilov, *Kurs istorii Rossii v XIX v.* (Moscow, 1918), I: 120–23.
18. Druzhinin, *Gosudarstvennye krest'iane*, I: 182–83, 480–81; V. I. Semenvskii, *Krest'ianskii vopros v Rossii v XVIII i pervoi polovine XIX stoletiia* (St. Petersburg, 1888), II: 22–37.
19. Quoted in Zakharova, *Samoderzhavie i otmena krepostnogo prava*, p. 71.
20. A. P. Zablotskii-Desiatovskii, "Zapiska o nedostatkakh," TsGIAL, fond 940, opis' 1, delo No. 16/1–5.
21. "O prisuzhdennykh Uchenym Komitetom MGI," TsGIAL, fond 398, opis' 1, delo No. 4475/52.
22. Field, *The End of Serfdom*, pp. 40–46; A. A. Kizevetter, "Vnutrenniaia politika Imperatora Nikolaia Pavlovicha," *Istoricheskie ocherki* (Moscow, 1912), pp. 475–94.
23. Kizevetter, "Vnutrenniaia politika Imperatora Nikolaia Pavlovicha," p. 478.
24. Quoted in Tatishchev, *Imperator Aleksandr II*, I: 278.
25. *Materialy dlia istorii uprazdneniia krepostnago sostoianiia pomeshchich'ikh krest'ian v Rossii v tsarstvovaniia Imperatora Aleksandra II* (Berlin, 1860), I: 116–17.

26. Orlovsky, *The Limits of Reform*, pp. 35–37; N. V. Varadinov, *Istoriia Ministerstva Vnutrennikh Del*, 8 vols. (St. Petersburg, 1858–63), III (Bk. 4): 22–43.

27. A. I. Levshin, "Dostopamiatnye minuty moei zhizni. Zapiska Alekseia Iraklievicha Levshina," *RA*, No. 8 (August 1885): 490–93.

28. Ibid., p. 492.

29. Zakharova, *Samoderzhavie i otmena krepostnogo prava*, pp. 54–60.

30. *Zhurnaly sekretnago i glavnago komitetov po krest'ianskomu delu s 10 oktiabria 1860 po 13 fevralia 1861 goda* (Petrograd, 1915), pp. 2–3.

31. Quoted in Zaionchkovskii, *Otmena krepostnogo prava*, p. 69.

32. Quoted in Field, *The End of Serfdom*, pp. 74–75.

33. Quoted in Zaionchkovskii, *Otmena krepostnogo prava*, p. 79. See also Field, *The End of Serfdom*, pp. 65–66; Zakharova, *Samoderzhavie i otmena krepostnogo prava*, pp. 61–71.

34. Quoted in Zaionchkovskii, *Otmena krepostnogo prava*, p. 77; Levshin, "Dostopamiatnye minuty moei zhizni," p. 537.

35. Quoted in Zaionchkovskii, *Otmena krepostnogo prava*, p. 80.

36. Emmons, *The Russian Landed Gentry and the Peasant Emancipation of 1861*, pp. 51–62; Field, *End of Serfdom*, pp. 77–83.

37. Zakharova, *Samoderzhavie i otmena krepostnogo prava v Rossii*, pp. 71–76; Emmons, *The Russian Landed Gentry and the Peasant Emancipation of 1861*, pp. 52–62; Field, *End of Serfdom*, pp. 77–83; Zaionchkovskii, *Otmena krepostnogo prava*, pp. 82–85.

38. On this point, see Zaionchkovskii, *Otmena krepostnogo prava*, p. 53.

39. *Materialy dlia istorii uprazdneniia krepostnago sostoianiia pomeshchich'ikh krest'ian v Rossii v tsarstvovaniia Imperatora Aleksandra II*, I: 140–41.

40. Ibid., p. 139.

41. Quoted in Zaionchkovskii, *Otmena krepostnogo prava*, p. 87.

42. Quoted in ibid.

43. Quoted in Field, *End of Serfdom*, p. 107.

44. "Iz otcheta Departamenta Politsii Ispolnitel'noi za 1858g. o krest'-ianskikh volneniiakh i merakh, priniatykh dlia ikh podavleniia," in S. B. Okun and K. V. Sivkov, eds., *Krest'ianskoe dvizhenii v Rossii v 1857–mae 1861gg. Sbornik dokumentov* (Moscow, 1963), p. 182.

45. *Materialy dlia istorii uprazdneniia krepostnago sostoianiia pomeshchich'-ikh krest'ian v Rossii v tsarstvovaniia Imperatora Aleksandra II*, I: 325–26.

46. Zakharova, *Samoderzhavie i otmena krepostnogo prava v Rossii*, p. 94.

47. Lincoln, *In the Vanguard of Reform*, pp. 109–38.

48. Among others, Nikolai Miliutin provided careful corrections and the Slavophile publicist Iurii Samarin prepared a lengthy commentary (much of it critical) about Solov'ev's work. Iu. F. Samarin, "Zamechaniia na 'Proekt plana rabot, predstoiashchikh dvorianskikh gubernskim komitetam, po ustroistvu krest'ianskago

byta'," in Samarin, *Sochineniia*, III: 56–71; Solov'ev, "Zapiski," *RS*, XXXIII (1881): 247–49; P. P. Semenov-Tian-Shanskii, *Memuary* (Petrograd, 1915–17), III: 64. For Solov'ev's proposal, see Samarin, *Sochineniia*, III: 58n–71n. For Miliutin's part in meetings of so-called reds held to discuss these questions see "Pis'mo N. A. Miliutina k D. A. Miliutinu," 19 aprelia 1858g., ORGBL, fond 169, kartonka 69, papka 10.

49. Pis'mo N. A. Miliutina k P. D. Kiselevu, 4 marta 1858g., ORGBL, fond 129, kartonka 17, papka 55.
50. Field, *The End of Serfdom*, p. 145.
51. A. I. Skrebitskii, *Krest'ianskoe delo v tsarstvovanie Imperatora Aleksandra II: Materialy dlia istorii osvobozhdeniia krest'ian* (Bonn, 1862), I: xxvi-xxxii.
52. Pis'mo N. A. Miliutina k D. A. Miliutinu, 19 aprelia 1858g., ORGBL, fond 169, kartonka 69, papka No. 10.
53. Semenov-Tian-Shanskii, *Memuary*, III: 57–67; "In re: Rostovtseva protiv Rossii," *Kolokol*, No. 22 (1 sentiabria 1858), in *Kolokol: Gazeta A. I., Gertsena i N. P. Ogareva*, I: 181.
54. Field, *The End of Serfdom*, p. 154.
55. Tatishchev, *Imperator Aleksandr II*, I: 310–11.
56. Skrebitskii, *Krest'ianskoe delo*, I: 382, 395. An abbreviated version of Rostovtsev's letters is to be found on pp. 382–97. See also, Solov'ev, "Zapiski," *RS*, XXXVII (1883): 265–69.
57. For just a few sources out of many that support this point, see Solov'ev, "Zapiski," *RS*, XXXVII (1883): 580–82; M. A. Miliutina, "Iz zapisok," *RS*, XCVII (1899): 49–50; Pis'mo N. A. Miliutina k D. A. Miliutinu, 19 aprelia 1858g., ORGBL, fond 169, kartonka 69, papka 10; Emmons, *The Russian Landed Gentry*, pp. 39–41.
58. *Sbornik pravitel'stvennykh rasporiazhenii po ustroistvu byta krest'ian, vyshedshikh iz krepostnoi zavisimosti* (St. Petersburg, 1869), I: 30–35.
59. Ibid., pp. 40–42.
60. For a discussion of the liberal program in the provincial committees, see Emmons, *The Russian Landed Gentry*, pp. 73–205.
61. Quoted in Field, *The End of Serfdom*, p. 162. For a discussion of the deliberations of the Main Committee that centered on the orders of October 26 and December 4, see Field, *The End of Serfdom*, pp. 159–64; Emmons, *The Russian Landed Gentry*, pp. 210–13; Zakharova, *Samoderzhavie i otmena krepostnogo prava*, pp. 124–34.
62. "In re: Rostovtseva protiv Rossii," *Kolokol*, No. 22 (1 sentiabria 1858), in *Kolokol: Gazeta A. I., Gertsena i N. P. Ogareva*, I,: 181; Pis'mo K. D. Kavelina k D. A. Miliutinu, 13 aprelia 1884g., ORGBL, fond 169, kartonka 64, papka 61.
63. Semenov-Tian-Shanskii, *Memuary*, III: 58–64; E. A. Egorov, "Iakov Ivanovich Rostovtsev," in S. A. Vengerov, ed., *Glavnye deiateli*

*osvobozhdeniia krest'ian* (St. Petersburg, 1903), pp 30–31; V. Ia. Bogucharskii, "Iakov Ivanovich Rostovtsev," in A. K. Dzhivelegov, S. P. Melgunov, and V. I. Picheta, eds., *Velikaia reforma: Russkoe obshchestvo i krest'ianskii vopros v proshlom i nastoiashchem* (Moscow, 1911), V: 62–63.

64. Quoted in Field, *The End of Serfdom*, p. 175.

65. G. A. Dzhanshiev, *A. M. Unkovskii i osvobozhdenie krest'ian* (Moscow, 1894), pp. 12–25; V. I. Semevskii, *Krest'ianskii vopros*, II: 347; Emmons, *Russian Landed Gentry*, pp. 80–88.

66. "Zapiska A. A. Golovacheva i A. M. Unkovskago" (1858g.), TsGAOR, fond 109, opis' 1, delo No. 1960. The latter part of this memorandum was published in *Kolokol*, No. 39 (1 aprelia 1859g), under the title "Proekt Un'kovskago," *Kolokol: Gazeta A. I. Gertsena*, II: 316–21; an English translation of excerpts from this memorandum is in Emmons, *Russian Landed Gentry*, pp. 427–43.

67. "Otzyvy chlenov gubernskikh komitetov," *Prilozhenie k trudam redaktsionnykh komissii* (St. Petersburg, 1859), II: 661, 682–98; *Pervoe izdanie materialov redaktsionnykh komissii dlia sostavleniia polozhenii o krest'ianakh, vykhodiashchikh iz krepostnoi zavisimosti* (St. Petersburg, 1859), XII: 1–4.

68. Quoted in Emmons, *Russian Landed Gentry*, pp. 341–42.

69. Ibid., p. 150.

70. Ibid., pp. 171–91; Kniaginia O. N. Trubetskaia, *Materialy dlia biografii kn. V. A. Cherkasskago* (Moscow, 1901), I: 229–309.

71. Emmons, *Russian Landed Gentry*, p. 204.

72. Solov'ev, "Zapiski," *RS*, XXXVII (1883): 279–81; K. D. Kavelin, "Mnenie ob luchshem sposobe razrabotki voprosa ob osvobozhdenii krest'ian," *Sobranie sochinenii K. D. Kavelina* (St. Petersburg, 1898), II: cols. 104–5.

73. W. Bruce Lincoln, *Petr Petrovich Semenov-Tian-Shanskii: The Life of A Russian Geographer* (Newtonville, Mass., 1980), pp. 22–41.

74. Semenov-Tian-Shanskii, *Memuary*, I: 190–91; D. A. Miliutin, "Moi starcheskie vospominaniia za 1816–1873gg., ORGBL, fond 169, kartonka 12, papka 4/96–99; "Delo o sluzhbe P. P. Semenova," TsGIAL, fond 1162, opis' 6, delo No. 496; Lincoln, *Semenov-Tian-Shanskii*, pp. 15–16.

75. Semenov-Tian-Shanskii, *Memuary*, I: 227–28, 214.

76. Ibid., III: 120–23.

77. *Sbornik pravitel'stvennykh rasporiazhenii po ustroistvu byta krest'ian*, I: 42.

78. Among the men he had known in the Geographical Society, Semenov nominated Miliutin, A. K. Giers, I. P. Arapetov, Iu. F. Samarin, Iu. A. Gagemeister, A. N. Popov, S. M. Zhukovskii, E. I. Lamanskii, N. V. Kalachev, Ia. A. Solov'ev, and M. Kh. Reitern. M. N. Liuboshchinskii and K. I. Domontovich (who did become members of the

Editing Commission) and D. P. Khrushchev and N. I. Stoianovskii (who did not) were men he had known during his student days. Among his nominees for "member-experts," Prince V. A. Cherkasskii, Iu. F. Samarin, A. N. Tatarinov, G. P. Galagan, N. I. Zheleznov, and N. Kh. Bunge (whose appointments Rostovtsev approved) and A. M. Unkovskii and A. I. Koshelev (whom he rejected) all were individuals whom Semenov had met in progressive salons or with whom he had become acquainted as a result of his friendships with St. Petersburg's enlightened bureaucrats. P. P. Semenov, *Istoriia poluvekovoi deiatel'nosti imperatorskago russkago geografhcheskago obshchestva, 1845–1895gg.* (St. Petersburg, 1896), I: 3–4, 143–54; Semenov, *Memuary,* III: 159–69.

79. Quoted in Zakharova, *Samoderzhavie i otmena krepostnogo prava,* p. 142. This bloc of eighteen included V. V. Taranovskii, Bunge, Zhukovskii, Giers, Arapetov, Kalachev, Solov'ev, Domontovich, Lamanskii, Semenov, Samarin, Cherkasskii, Popov, Zablotskii, Gagemeister, Reitern, N. N. Pavlov, and Miliutin; the satellite group included P. A. Bulgakov, Prince S. P. Golitsyn, Liuboshchinskii, B. F. Zalesskii, and A. D. Zheltukhin. Four times as many of this group had university educations as did the ministers of Alexander II. D. A. Miliuutin, "Moi starcheskie vospominaniia," ORGBL, fond 169, kartonka 12, papka No. 4/90–92; A. V. Golovnin, "Zapiski i primechaniia A. V. Golovnina," GPB, fond 208, delo No. 1/91; A. Ia. Panaeva, *Vospominaniia* (Moscow, 1956), pp. 188–201; Obolenskii, "Moi vospominaniia," *RS,* CXXXII, No. 3 (March 1909): 504–28; W. Bruce Lincoln, "The Ministers of Alexander II: A Brief Survey of Their Backgrounds and Service Careers," *CMRS,* XVII, No. 4 (October 1976): 469; W. Bruce Lincoln, "The Editing Commissions of 1859–1860: Some Notes on Their Members' Backgrounds and Service Careers," *SEER,* LVI, No. 3 (July 1978): 346–59.

80. Eventually two more sections were added: a financial section, organized in late April 1859, and a codification section in June 1860.

81. Semenov-Tian-Shanskii, *Memuary,* III: 135.

82. Ibid., p. 220.

83. Zakharova, *Samoderzhavie i otmena krepostnogo prava,* p. 142.

84. In support of these cursory generalizations, see Trubetskaia, *Materialy,* I, bk. 2: 7–72; Semenov-Tian-Shanskii, *Memuary,* III: 220–32; B. E. Nol'de, *Iurii Samarin i ego vremia* (Paris, 1926), pp. 125–31.

85. N. P. Semenov, *Osvobozhdenie krest'ian v tsarstvovanie Imperatora Aleksandra II: Khronika deiatel'nosti komissii po krest'ianskomu delu* (St. Petersburg, 1889), I: 146.

86. Ibid., p. 480.

87. See Stephen Hoch, "The Banking Crisis, Peasant Reform, and the Redemption Operation in Russia, 1857–1861," unpublished paper

224 Notes to Pages 83–89

to appear in *AHR*, 12–21, especially pp. 17–19. For the connection of these men in the Russian Geographical Society, see Lincoln, *In the Vanguard of Reform*, pp. 89, 100.

88. The other three men invited to the meeting were Petr Semenov, Domontovich, and S. M. Zhukovskii. Ibid., pp. 610–14; Trubetskaia, *Materialy*, I, bk. 2: 75–79; Skrebitskii, *Krest'ianskoe delo*, I: cxii–cxiv.

89. P. D. Stremoukhov, "Zametka odnogo iz deputatov pervago prizyva," *RS*, CII (April 1900): 143.

90. Miliutina, "Iz zapisok," *RS*, XCVII (1899): 49–50; Solov'ev, "Zapiski," *RS*, XXXVII (1883): 582; D. A. Obolenskii, "Moi vospominaniia," *RS*, CXXXIII, No. 4 (April 1909): 59; Trubetskaia, *Materialy*, I, bk. 2: 127, 148–66; M. A. Miliutina, "Zapiski M. A. Miliutiny," TsGIAL, fond 869, opis' 1, delo No. 1138/168–81; Semenov-Tian-Shanskii, *Memuary*, III: 426–34.

91. Semenov-Tian-Shanskii, *Memuary*, IV: 2–4.

92. Nikitenko, *Dnevnik*, II: 108.

93. Semenov-Tian-Shanskii, *Memuary*, III: 432–35.

94. Quoted in A. K. Dzhivelegov, "Graf V. N. Panin," *Velikaia reforma*, V: 148.

95. Quoted in Wortman, *Development of a Russian Legal Consciousness*, p. 168.

96. Field, *End of Serfdom*, p. 339.

97. N. P. Semenov, *Osvobozhdenie krest'ian*, III, pt. 1: 480–81.

98. Ibid., pp. 491–92. For the worries of Miliutin and his allies during Panin's tenure as chairman of the Editing Commission and an elaboration of the their efforts to deal with Panin, see the series of brief notes that Miliutin penned to Cherkasskii, July through September 1860 in ORGBL, fond Cherkasskago/III, kartonka 6, papka No. 1.

99. Semenov, *Osvobozhdenie krest'ian*, III, pt. 2: 753.

100. Quoted in Zaionchkovskii, *Otmena krepostnogo prava*, p. 122.

101. Ibid., p. 160.

102. Ibid., pp. 154–59.

103. The immensely complex provisions of the Emancipation Acts have been best summarized in English in Florinsky, *Russia*, II: 888–96 and P. I. Liashchenko, *History of the National Economy of Russia to the 1917 Revolution* (New York, 1970), pp. 379–97. These accounts, however, need to be revised in the light of Hoch, "Banking Crisis," pp. 16–20.

104. Quoted in P. A. Zaionchkovskii, *Provedenie v zhizn' krest'ianskoi reformy 1861g.* (Moscow, 1958), p. 64.

105. Ibid., passim, and Terence Emmons, "The Peasant and the Emancipation," in Wayne S. Vucinich, ed., *The Peasant in Nineteenth-Century*

Notes to Pages 89-94 225

Russia (Stanford, 1968), pp. 41–71.
106. Quoted in Zaionchkovskii, *Otmena krepostnogo prava*, p. 260.
107. Ibid., pp. 260–72.
108. Ibid., pp. 172–291.
109. G. T. Robinson, *Rural Russia Under the Old Regime: A History of the Landlord-Peasant World and a Prologue to the Peasant Revolution of 1917* (New York, 1957), p. 168.
110. Ibid., p. 290, note 24.
111. Quoted in Florinsky, *Russia*, II: 1223.
112. Raeff, *Well-Ordered Police State*, p. 229.
113. Ibid., pp. 228–31; Yaney, *Systematization of Russian Government*, pp. 63–74; Iu. V. Got'e, *Istoriia oblastnago upravleniia v Rossii ot Petra I do Ekateriny II*, 2 vols. (Moscow, 1913), passim.
114. A. D. Borovkov, "A. D. Borovkov i ego avtobiograficheskie zapiski," *RS*, No. 11 (November 1898): 353–55.
115. Torke, "Das russische Beamtentum," pp. 133–37; Starr, *Decentralization and Self-Government*, pp. 10–14.
116. Starr, *Decentralization and Self-Government*, pp. 27–28.
117. Ibid., p. 28.
118. "Perepiski po delam o poriadakh (mart 1851g)," TsGIAL, fond 1284, opis' 36, delo No. 137/24–27.
119. Starr, *Decentralization and Self-Government*, p. 31.
120. Perovskii, "Dokladnaia zapiska o neobkhodimosti uluchshenii po gubernskim pravleniiam" (1843g.), TsGIAL, fond 1149, opis' 3 (1843), delo No. 94a; "Delo po otnosheniiu Khoziaistvennago Departamenta v Statisticheskoe Otdelenie, o tom, kakie goroda i kogda imenno poluchii Vysochaishe utverzhdennye plany," 1849g., TsGIAL, fond 1287, opis' 39, delo No. 824; Donesenie chinovnika osobykh poruchenii Nadvornago Sovetnika A. K. Girsa Ego Vysokoprevoskhoditel'stvu Gospodinu Ministru Vnutrennikh Del," 17 avgusta 1844g., TsGIAL, fond 1287, opis' 39, delo No. 25/53–55; "Ofitsial'noe pis'mo N. A. Miliutina chinovniku osobykh poruchenii Nadvornomu Sovetniku Girsu," 30 oktiabria 1843g., TsGIAL, fond 1287, opis' 39, delo No. 25/34–37; "Ofitsial'noe pis'mo N. A. Miliutina chinovniku osobykh poruchenii Gospodinu Nadvornomu Sovetniku Shtakel'bergu ot Khoziaistvennago Departamenta, Vremennago Otdeleniia," 4 noiabria 1843g., TsGIAL, fond 1287, opis' 39, delo No. 22/48–51.
121. Starr, *Decentralization and Self-Government*, p. 35.
122. "Kratkii obzor deistvii Ministerstva Vnutrennikh Del s 1825 po 1850 god," TsGAOR, fond 722, opis' 1, delo No. 599/104.
123. K. N. Lebedev, "Iz zapisok senatora K. N. Lebedeva," *RA*, XLIX, No. 1 (January 1911): 109.
124. W. Bruce Lincoln, "Reform in Action: The Implementation of the

Municipal Reform Act of 1846 in St. Petersburg," *SEER*, LIII, No. 131 (April 1975): 202–9.

125. Starr, *Decentralization and Self-Government*, p. 43.
126. Quoted in Florinsky, *Russia*, II: 897.
127. "Formuliarnyi spisok A. K. Girsa," TsGIAL, fond 1284, opis' 31, delo No. 52 (and the materials in TsGIAL, fond 1287, opis' 39, dela Nos. 25 and 45); "Formuliarnyi spisok A. F. Shtakel'berga," TsGIAL, fond 1349, opis' 3, delo No. 2535 (and the materials in TsGIAL, fond 1287, opis' 39, dela Nos. 22 and 30, as well as his "Zapiska o prichinakh i sledstviiakh neurozhaev v Lifliandskoi gubernii i o sredstvakh preduprezhdeniia onym," [iiun' 1844g], in fond 1287, opis' 2, delo No. 970); "Formuliarnyi spisok grafa A. K. Siversa," TsGIAL, fond 1284, opis' 75, delo No. 2; and Formuliarnyi spisok grafa D. N. Tolstago," TsGIAL, fond 1284, opis' 32, delo No. 192; "Formuliarnyi spisok K. S. Veselovskago," TsGIAL, fond 1349, opis 3, delo No. 391.
128. For an example taken from real life in the provinces that illustrates this point in a striking fashion, see A. I. Artem'ev, "Dnevnik, iiun'–19 avgusta 1852g.," GPB, fond 37, delo No. 155/3.
129. Starr, *Decentralization and Self-Government*, p. 45.
130. On the difficulties that these officials of the central government had in receiving proper pay and allowances while they were serving in the provinces, see especially "Pis'mo ot komissii dlia revizii obshchestvennago i khoziaistvennago upravleniia goroda Rigi," 31 ianvaria 1847g., TsGIAL, fond 1287, opis' 39, delo No. 23.
131. Valuev, "Duma russkago," p. 355.
132. Perovskii, "O prichinakh umnozheniia deloproizvodstva," TsGIAL, fond 1287, opis' 6, delo No. 137/14.
133. Starr, *Decentralization and Self-Government*, pp. 124, 126.
134. *Materialy, sobrannye dlia Vysochaishei uchrezhdennoi komissii o preobrazovanii gubernskikh o uezdnykh uchrezhdenii* (St. Petersburg, 1870), I: section 3, p. 4.
135. Starr, *Decentralization and Self-Government*, pp. 128–36.
136. These two proposals are insightfully discussed in considerable detail in ibid., pp. 141–50. The following summary closely follows Starr's account, although it has been modified in light of Daniel Orlovsky's more recent conclusions. Orlovsky's treatment of Lanskoi's policies as minister of internal affairs is the best account yet written. See Orlovsky, *Limits of Reform*, pp. 52–63, 146–47, and passim.
137. See, for example, "Iz otcheta Departamenta Politsii Ispolnitel'noi za 1858g. o krest'ianskikh volneniiakh i merakh, priniatykh dlia ikh podavleniia," pp. 181–82.

138. P. A. Valuev, *Dnevnik P. A. Valueva. Ministra vnutrennikh del* (Moscow, 1961), I: 312.

139. Quoted in Anatole Leroy-Beaulieu, *Un homme d'état russe (Nicolas Milutine) d'après sa correspondance inédite: Etude sur la Russie et la Pologne pendant le regne d'Alexandre II (1856–1872)* (Paris, 1884), p. 24n; Solov'ev, "Zapiski," *RS*, XXXIII, No. 3 (March 1882): 562–79.

140. V. A. Artsimovich, *Viktor Antonovich Artsimovich: Vospominaniia-kharakteristika* (St. Petersburg, 1904), p. 74; TsGIAL, fond 982, opis' 1, delo No. 97/25–45.

141. The authorship of this memorandum has been attributed to Lanskoi (Solov'ev, "Zapiski," *RS*, XXV, No. 9 [September 1882]: 641–52), Miliutin (M. A. Miliutina, "Iz zapisok," *RS*, XCVII, No. 2 [February 1899]: 272), and Artsimovich (V. A. Artsimovich, *V. A. Artsimovich*, p. 159n). Starr, who is the most expert on this question, attributes it to Artsimovich. (*Decentralization and Self-Government*, p. 148).

142. TsGIAL, fond 982, opis' 1, delo No. 97/36.

143. G. A. Dzhanshiev, *Epokha velikikh reform* (St. Petersburg, 1905), p. 44; Orlovsky, *Limits of Reform*, pp. 59–60; Starr, *Decentralization and Self-Government*, pp. 145–49.

144. Quoted in Starr, *Decentralization and Self-Government*, p. 156.

145. V. V. Garmiza, *Podgotovka zemskoi reformy 1864 goda* (Moscow, 1957), p. 132; S. Ia. Tseitlin, "Zemskaia reforma," *Istoriia Rossii v XIX veke* III: 196–97.

146. Tseitlin, "Zemskaia reforma," p. 197; Garmiza, *Podgotovka*, p. 132.

147. Garmiza, *Podgotovka*, pp. 135–36; Starr, *Decentralization and Self-Government*, pp. 176–78; Tseitlin, "Zemskaia reforma," pp. 199–200; *Materialy sobrannye dlia Vysochaishei uchrezhdennoi komissii o preobrazovanii gubernskikh i uezdnykh uchrezhdenii* (Otdel administrativnyi) (St. Petersburg, 1870), I: section 4, 276–85.

148. Lettre de N. A. Milutine à D. A. Milutine, 11/3 decembre 1861, published in Leroy-Beaulieu, *Un homme d'état russe*, p. 120.

149. P. A. Valuev, "O vnutrennem sostoianii Rossii," 26 iiunia 1862, in Garmiza, ed., "Predpolozheniia i proekty," *IA*, III (January–February 1958): 141–43.

150. Kavelin, "Dvorianstvo i osvobozhdenie krest'ian," *Sobranie sochinenii*, II, col. 142; Lettre de N. A. Milutine á D. A. Milutine, 11/3 decembre 1861, published in Leroy-Beaulieu, *Un homme d'état russe*, p. 120.

151. Valuev, "O vnutrennem sostoianii Rossii," pp. 141–43; K. L. Bermanskii, "Konstitutsionnye proekty tsarstvovaniia Aleksandra II," *VP*, XXXV (November 1905): 225–33; L. G. Zakharova, *Zemskaia kontrreforma 1890g.* (Moscow, 1968), pp. 48–49.

228

Notes to Pages 101–106

152. Orlovsky, *Limits of Reform*, p. 70.
153. Quoted in Emmons, *Russian Landed Gentry*, p. 337.
154. Quoted in ibid., pp. 339, 342.
155. See ibid., pp. 350–93.
156. Quoted in Garmiza, *Podgotovka*, p. 166.
157. "Zhurnal obshchago prisutstviia kommisii o gubernskikh i uezd-nykh uchrezhdeniiakh," zasedaniia 10–12 marta 1862g. *Materialy po zemskomu obshchestvennomu ustroistvu (Polozhenie o zemskikh uchrezhdeniiakh)* (St. Petersburg, 1885), I: 182–85.
158. Starr, *Decentralization and Self-Government*, pp. 244–45.
159. Lettres de N. A. Milutine á M. A. Milutine, 19/31 janvier 1862, OC, p. 118; de A. V. Golovnine á N. A. Milutine, 25 decembre/6 janvier 1861/2, OC, pp. 122–23; de N. A. Milutine á A. V. Golovnine, 7/19 fevrier 1862, in Leroy-Beaulieu, *Un homme d'état russe*, p. 123; and du Grand Duc Constantine á N. A. Milutine, 25 fevrier/9 mars 1862, OC, pp. 128–129.
160. N. A. Miliutin, "Zapiska po voprosu o preobrazovanii zemskikh uchrezhdeniiakh," 22 maia 1862g., TsGIAL, fond 869, opis' 1, delo No. 397/28–30.
161. *Materialy po zemskomu obshchestvennomu ustroistvu*, I: 211–12.
162. Lincoln, *Nikolai Miliutin*, pp. 78–88.
163. Starr, *Decentralization and Self-Government*, pp. 275–77.
164. See Baron M. A. Korf, "Vzgliad na vnutrenniia preobrazovaniia poslednego desiatletiia," (aprel 1866g.), TsGAOR, fond 728, opis' 1, delo No. 2863/3.
165. Quoted in Garmiza, *Podgotovka*, p. 208. For a discussion of Korf's proposals, in addition to Garmiza, pp. 206–24, see N. N. Avinov, "Graf M. A. Korf i zemskaia reforma 1864g.," *RM*, No. 2 (February 1904): 94–111, and Starr, *Decentralization of Self-Government*, pp. 280–85.
166. Garmiza, *Podgotovka*, pp. 220–23.
167. N. Bakhtin, "Dopolnenie k zapiske zakliuchaiushchei v sebe soobrazheniia ob upravlenii otdel'nym vedomstvom," 20 fevralia 1856g., TsGAOR, fond 722, opis' 1, delo No. 605/2–10.
168. Starr, *Decentralization and Self-Government*, pp. 286–88.
169. Florinsky, *Russia*, II: 897–99, provides the best summary of how the new *zemstva* worked. For a history of the *zemstva* in action until the revolution of 1905, see V. V. Veselovskii, *Istoriia zemstva za sorok let*, 4 vols. (St. Petersburg, 1909–11).
170. I. I. Mikhailov, "Kazanskaia starina (iz vospominanii Iv. Iv. Mikhail-ova)," *RS*, C (October 1899): 102.
171. Wortman, *Development of a Russian Legal Consciousness*, p. 194.
172. D. Shubin-Pozdeev, "K kharakteristike lichnosti i sluzhebnoi deiatel'nosti S. I. Zarudnago," *RS*, LVII (February 1888): 481.

173. Lincoln, *In the Vanguard of Reform*, pp. 62–67; "Delo o sluzhbe S. I. Zarudnago," TsGIAL, fond 1405, opis' 528, delo No. 83. For Zarudnyi's oft-quoted and classic critique of the bureaucracy, see S. I. Zarudnyi, "Pis'mo opytnago chinovnika sorokovykh godov mladshemu ego sobratu, postupaiushchemu na sluzhbu," edited by A. S. Zarudnyi, *RS*, C, No. 12 (December 1899): 543–46; Shubin-Pozdeev, "K kharakteristike lichnosti," p. 481.

174. Zablotskii-Desiatovskii, "Vzgliad na istoriiu gosudarstvennykh imushchestv v Rossii," TsGIAL, fond 940, opis' 1, delo No. 12/66.

175. Wortman, *Development of a Russian Legal Consciousness*, p. 234; Lincoln, *In the Vanguard of Reform*, pp. 59–67; see also V. A. Tsie, "Zapiska o merakh, neobkhodimykh dlia sokrashcheniia perepiski i uproshcheniia deloproizvodstva v gosudarstvennykh uchrezhdeniiakh," (1856g), GPB, fond 833, delo No. 292/4.

176. G. Dzhanshiev, *Osnovy sudebnoi reformy* (Moscow, 1891), pp. 38–39.

177. I. A. Blinov, "Khod sudebnoi reformy 1864 goda," in *Sudebnye ustavy 20 noiabria 1864 goda za piat'desiat' let* (Petrograd, 1914), I: 105–21; Friedhelm Berthold Kaiser, *Die russische Justizreform von 1864: Zur Geschichte der russischen Justiz von Katherina II bis 1917* (Leiden, 1972), pp. 149–268.

178. "Delo o sluzhbe kn. D. A. Obolenskago," TsGIAL, fond 1162, opis' 6, delo No. 375; TsGAOR, fond 722, opis' 1, delo No. 460.

179. D. A. Obolenskii, "Zamechaniia na proekt novago poriadka sudoproizvodstva Rossii," TsGAOR, fond 647, opis' 1, delo No. 56/1, 5–6.

180. Ibid., delo No. 56/1.

181. A. F. Koni, *Ottsy i deti sudebnoi reformy (k piatidesiatiletiiu Sudebnykh Ustavov)* (Moscow, 1914), pp. 80–81.

182. See S. I. Zarudnyi, "O spetsial'nykh prisiazhnykh dlia osobago noda del v Anglii, Frantsii, i Italii," *ZhMIu* (November 1862): 267–83; S. I. Zarudnyi, "O reformakh sudoproizvodstva v Italii," *ZhMIu* (December 1862): 529–46.

183. Kaiser, *Die russische Justizreform von 1864*, pp. 190–94; Wortman, *Development of a Russian Legal Consciousness*, pp. 247–48.

184. Kaiser, *Die russische Justizreform von 1864*, p. 270; Wortman, *Development of a Russian Legal Consciousness*, p. 249; Tseitlin, "Zemskaia reforma," p. 197; Garmiza, *Podgotovka*, p. 132; "Sergei Ivanovich Zarudnyi," *RBS*, VII, p. 244.

185. Wortman, *Development of a Russian Legal Consciousness*, p. 252; G. A. Dzhanshiev, *Stranitsa iz istorii sudebnoi reformy: D. N. Zamiatnin* (Moscow, 1883), pp. 23–27; A. G. Dement'ev, et al., eds., *Russkaia periodicheskaia pechat'*, pp. 324, 373–74.

186. Wortman, *Development of a Russian Legal Consciousness*, pp. 252–57; Emmons, *Russian Landed Gentry*, pp. 80–83, 255–57.

187. V. Nabokov, "Raboty po sostavleniiu sudebnykh ustavov: Obshchaia kharakteristika sudebnoi reformy," in N. V. Davykov and N. N. Polianskii, *Sudebnaia reforma* (Moscow, 1915), pp. 304–6; Blinov, "Khod sudebnoi reformy 1864 goda," pp. 124, 126.
188. Koni, *Ottsy i deti sudebnoi reformy,* p. 145.
189. Ibid., pp. 98–102.
190. Ibid., 2–4; "Delo o sluzhbe D. A. Rovinskago," TsGIAL, fond 1349, opis' 3, delo No. 1899; Dzhanshiev, *Epokha velikikh reform,* pp. 682–86; A. F. Koni, "Dmitrii Aleksandrovich Rovinskii," in *Sobranie sochinenii A. F. Koni* (Moscow, 1968), V: 13–15; D. A. Rovinskii, "K sudebnym sledovateliam," *Vek,* No. 16 (1861): 545–47.
191. K. P. Pobedonostsev, "Vospominaniia o V. P. Zubkove," *RA,* bk. 1 (1904): 301–2.
192. K. P. Pobedonostsev, "Graf V. N. Panin," *Golosa iz Rossii,* No. 7 (1859): 137–38.
193. R. F. Byrnes, *Pobedonostsev: His Life and Thought* (Bloomington, 1968), pp. 25–26; Wortman, *Development of a Russian Legal Consciousness,* p. 216; A. E. Nol'de, *K. P. Pobedonostsev i sudebnaia reforma* (Petrograd, 1915), pp. 11–12; K. P. Pobedonostsev, "O reformakh v grazhdanskom sudoproizvodstve," *RV,* pp. 28–31.
194. *Gosudarstvennaia kantseliariia, 1810–1910* (St. Petersburg, 1910), primechaniia, p. xiii; Shubin-Pozdeev, "K kharakteristike lichnosti," pp. 481–82.
195. *Gosudarstvennaia kantseliariia,* primechaniia, pp. xii–xiii; M. Leonidov, "Aleksandr Mikhailovich Plavskii," *RBS,* vol. Plav-Prim, pp. 8–9; "Pii Nikodimovich Danevskii," ibid., vol. Dab-Diad, pp. 56–58; V. Nabokov, "Raboty po sostavleniiu sudebnykh ustavov," p. 306.
196. Wortman, *Development of a Russian Legal Consciousness,* pp. 258–59.
197. Quoted in Dzhanshiev, *Epokha velikikh reform,* p. 400.
198. Ibid., pp. 400–401.
199. On the experience of Hannover and the lessons the Russians drew from it, see especially A. A. Knirim, "O Gannoverskom grazhdanskom sudoproizvodstve," *ZhMIu,* No. 3 (March 1862): 545–608.
200. Dzhanshiev, *Epokha velikikh reform,* pp. 400–401.
201. Quoted in Wortman, *Development of a Russian Legal Consciousness,* pp. 260–1.
202. Nabokov, "Raboty po sostavleniiu sudebnykh ustavov," p. 338.
203. Nikitenko, *Dnevnik,* II: 298.
204. The biographical information on which this is based has been taken from *Gosudarstvennaia kantseliariia; Spisok chinam Pravitel'stvuiushchego Senata i Ministerstva Iustitsii;* and *Russkii biograficheskii slovar'.*
205. The others on the commission were A. F. Bychkov, G. K. Repinskii, Prince I. S. Volkonskii, O. O. Kvist, E. A. Peretts, N. G. Printts,

Professor N. I. Utin, Baron Vrangel, Shechkov, Gurin, Barshev-skii, Liubimov, Zheltukhin, Kreitzer, Brevern, M. Zarudnyi, and P. A. Zubov.

206. Dzhanshiev, *Epokha velikikh reform*, p. 406.
207. A detailed discussion of the provisions of these statutes can be found in Kaiser, *Die russische Justizreform von 1864*, pp. 340–406.
208. *Polnoe sobranie zakonov Rossiiskoi Imperii*, sobranoe 2-oe, No. 41473.
209. Przhetslavskii, "O glasnosti v russkoi zhurnal'noi literature," TsGIAL, fond 772, opis' 1, delo No. 5129/1–27.

## CHAPTER IV: THE GREAT REFORM ERA

1. Marc Raeff, *Imperial Russia, 1682–1825: The Coming of Age of Modern Russia* (New York, 1971), pp. 140–141.
2. B. E. Nol'de, *Peterburgskaia missiia Bismarka, 1859–1862* (Prague, 1925), p. 256.
3. Such an outlook underlay even the highly critical views of B. N. Chicherin, who once explained, "[Man] is not born as an abstract agent possessing unlimited liberty and knowing no duties, but as a member of a certain social organism, encompassing not just present generations but their ancestors and heirs." B. N. Chicherin, *O narodnom predstavitel'stve* (Moscow, 1866), p. 30, quoted in Gary M. Hamburg, "B. N. Chicherin and the Emergence of Russian Liberalism," unpublished book manuscript (chapter entitled "On Popular Representation," p. 5).
4. See Riasanovsky, *Nicholas I and Official Nationality*, p. 99; A. E. Presniakov, *Apogei samoderzhaviia: Nikolai I* (Leningrad, 1925), p. 13; and "Tsenzura v tsarstvovanie Imperatora Nikolaia I," *RS*, CVII, No. 9 (September 1901): 664.
5. On some of the beginnings of this process, see especially Frieden, *Russian Physicians*, pp. 87–96, 105–131; Kassow, *Students, Professors, and the State*, pp. 15–47; Christine Ruane, "Soul of the School: The Professionalization of Urban Schoolteachers of St. Petersburg and Moscow, 1860–1914," unpublished book manuscript, pp. 3–9; and Eklof, *Russian Peasant Schools*, pp. 194–206.
6. Robbins, *The Tsar's Viceroys*, pp. 8–17.
7. Sidney Monas, *The Third Section: Police and Society in Russia Under Nicholas I* (Cambridge, Mass., 1961), p. 145.
8. Quoted in ibid., p. 146.
9. Nikitenko, *Dnevnik*, I: 336.
10. Mikhail Lemke, *Ocherki po istorii russkoi tsenzury i zhurnalistiki XIX stoletiia* (St. Petersburg, 1904), p. 206.
11. Ibid, p. 239.

12. P. A. Valuev, "Dnevnik grafa Petra Aleksandrovicha Valueva," *RS*, LXX, No. 5 (May 1891): 340.
13. Lemke, *Ocherki*, p. 307.
14. K. K. Arsen'ev, *Zakonodatel'stvo o pechati* (St. Petersburg, 1903), pp. 5–6.
15. Nikitenko, *Dnevnik*, II: 16.
16. Iu. I. Gerasimova, "Otnoshenie pravitel'stva k uchastii pechati v obsuzhdenii krest'ianskago voprosa v period revoliutsionnoi situatsii kontsa 50-kh do nachala 60-kh godov XIX v," in *RevS* (1974), p. 82; A. M. Skabicheskii, *Ocherki istorii russkoi tsenzury (1700–1863)*, (St. Petersburg, 1892), pp. 430–33; Arsen'ev, *Zakonodatelstvo o pechati*, p. 7; Lemke, *Ocherki po istorii russkoi tsenzury*, p. 315.
17. Arsen'ev, *Zakonodatel'stvo o pechati*, pp. 7–8; N. P. Barsukov, *Zhizn' i trudy M. P. Pogodina*, 22 vols. (St. Petersburg, 1888–1906), XVI: 345–46.
18. *Materialy dlia istorii uprazdneniia krepostnago sostoianiia pomeshchich'-ikh krest'ian v Rossii*, I: 292n. See also Nikitenko, *Dnevnik*, II: 27.
19. Quoted in M. Lemke, *Epokha tsenzurnykh reform 1855–1865 godov* (St. Petersburg, 1905), p. 15.
20. Skabicheskii, *Ocherki istorii russkoi tsenzury*, p. 420; Gerasimova, "Otnoshenie pravitel'stva k uchastii pechati," p. 83; Levshin, "Dostopamiatnye minuty," pp. 540–41; Charles Ruud, "The Russian Empire's New Censorship Law of 1865," *CSS*, III, No. 2 (Summer 1969): 236.
21. Nikitenko, *Dnevnik*, II: 17.
22. Skabichevskii, *Ocherki istorii russkoi tsenzury*, pp. 440–41; Nikitenko, *Dnevnik*, II: 39; Lemke, *Ocherki po istorii russkoi tsenzury*, pp. 335–68.
23. Nikitenko, *Dnevnik*, II: 5–105; Skabichevskii, *Ocherki istorii russkoi tsenzury*, pp. 444–46.
24. Quoted in Lemke, *Ocherki po istorii russkoi tsenzury*, p. 335.
25. "Pis'mo grafa A. V. Adlerberga k F. I. Prianishnikovu, 25 ianvaria 1859g.," TsGIAL, fond 1288, opis' 21, delo No. 1/2.
26. Nikitenko, *Dnevnik*, II: 50.
27. Ibid., p. 71.
28. Ibid., pp. 64–66.
29. Ibid., p. 66.
30. Ibid., p. 86.
31. Ibid., pp. 102, 86.
32. Lemke, *Ocherki po istorii russkoi tsenzury*, p. 368; Charles A. Ruud, *Fighting Words: Imperial Censorship and the Russian Press, 1804–1906* (Toronto, 1982), pp. 111–12.

33. W. Bruce Lincoln, "Official Propaganda in Mid-Nineteenth-Century Russia: Baron M. A. Korf and *The Accession of Nicholas I*," *OSS*, XXI (1988): 123–25.

34. See especially M. A. Korf, "Dnevnik barona M. A. Korfa za 1840g.," TsGAOR, fond 728, opis' 1, delo No. 1817/iii/15–16, 84.

35. Lemke, *Ocherki po istorii russkoi tsenzury*, p. 307; Lemke, *Epokha tsenzurnykh reform*, p. 17. For one particular example of Korf's loyalty, see his carefully crafted account of the Decembrist revolt, published in Russian, French, German, and English editions. On this, see Lincoln, "Official Propaganda in Mid-Nineteenth-Century Russia," pp. 126–30; and M. A. Korf, "Istoricheskaia zapiska o proiskhozhdenii i izdanii knigi: Vosshestvie na prestol Imperatora Nikolaia I," GPB, fond M. A. Korfa, delo No. 50.

36. Lemke, *Epokha tsenzurnykh reform*, pp. 17–20.

37. Nikitenko, *Dnevnik*, II: 105.

38. Baron M. A. Korf, "Shestinedel'nyi epizod moei zhizni," TsGAOR, fond 728, opis' 1, delo No. 2612/26.

39. Hoch, "The Banking Crisis," pp. 16–19.

40. Quoted in Skabichevskii, *Ocherki istorii russkoi tsenzury*, p. 446. See also Lemke, *Epokha tsenzurnykh reform*, pp. 17–25.

41. Pis'mo A. G. Troinitskii k bratu," 15 dekabria 1859g., *Russkii arkhiv*, No. 6 (June 1896): 297.

42. Skabichevskii, *Ocherki istorii russkoi tsenzury*, p. 461; D. L. Mordovtsev, "Istoricheskie pominki po N. I. Kostomarove," *RS*, LXVI, No. 6 (June 1885): 624.

43. Pis'mo N. A. Dobroliubova k P. N. Kazanskomu, 18 (30) ianvaria 1861g., in N. A. Dobroliubov, *Sobranie sochinenii*, IX: 462.

44. Quoted in *Materialy dlia istorii uprazdneniia krepostnago sostoianiia pomeshchich'ikh krest'ian v Rossii v tsarstvovanie Imperatora Aleksandra II* (Berlin, 1861), II: 257.

45. Daniel R. Brower, *Training the Nihilists: Education and Radicalism in Tsarist Russia* (Ithaca, 1975), pp. 127–29.

46. Quoted in Gerasimova, "Krizis pravitel'stvennoi politiki," p. 103.

47. Nikitenko, *Dnevnik*, II: 210.

48. Valuev, *Dnevnik P. A. Valueva*, I: 118.

49. Nikitenko, *Dnevnik*, II: 237.

50. Valuev, *Dnevnik P. A. Valueva*, I: 67.

51. B. N. Chicherin, *Moskovskii universitet* (Moscow, 1929), p. 55.

52. A. V. Golovnin, "Raznitsa v napravlenii gosudarstvennoi deiatel'-nosti v pervoi i vo vtoroi polovine nyneshniago tsarstvovaniia," (mart' 1867g.), GPB, fond 208, delo No. 236/2; TsGIAL, fond 851, opis' 1, delo No. 7/3; A. V. Golovnin, "Kratkii ocherk deistviia Velikago Kniazia Konstantina Nikolaevicha," GPB, fond 208, delo

No. 2/269; A. V. Golovnin, "Materialy dlia zhizneopisaniia Velikago Kniazia Konstantina Nikolaevicha," TsGIAL, fond 851, opis' 1, delo No. 86/39–41.

53. A. V. Golovnin, "Zapiski A. V. Golovnina s 1861 po 1866gg.," TsGIAL, fond 851, opis' 1, delo No. 5/481.

54. Pis'mo A. V. Golovnina k v. k. Konstantinu Nikolaevichu, 30 maia 1862g., GPB, fond 208, delo No. 44/1.

55. "Delo tsentral'nago upravleniia po tsenzurnomu vedomstvu — po otchetu tsenzurnago vedomstva za 1863g.," TsGIAL, fond 775, opis' 1, delo No. 1–1864.

56. Charles A Ruud, "A. V. Golovnin and Liberal Russian Censorship, January-June 1862," *SEER,* L, No. 119 (April 1972): 203–08; Lemke, *Epokha tsenzurnykh reform,* pp. 100–111; A. V. Golovnin, "Doklad Imperatoru Aleksandru Nikolaevichu o polozhenii russkoi literatury i neobkhodimosti reorganizatsii tsenzury," 26 fevralia 1862g., TsGIAL, fond 772, opis' 1, delo No. 5977/148–156.

57. One hundred sixty two new periodicals came into existence between 1856 and 1861. By contrast, 17 appeared between 1850 and 1855. Dement'ev, et al., eds., *Russkaia periodicheskaia pechat' (1702–1894):* pp. 325–422.

58. This commission was composed of V. A. Tsie, K. S. Veselovskii, Major General Stürmer, F. F. Voronov (one of Golovnin's associates on the Central School Directorate), and I. E. Andreevskii, a professor of law at St. Petersburg University. Lemke, *Epokha tsenzurnykh reform,* p. 133.

59. "Delo o sluzhbe kn. D. A. Obolenskago," TsGIAL, fond 1162, opis' 6, delo No. 375; Golovnin, "Kratkii ocherk deistviia velikago kniazia Konstantina Nikolaevicha," GPB, fond 208, delo No. 2/271; Kniaz' D. A. Obolenskii, "Moi vospominaniia o velikoi kniagine Elene Pavlovne," *RS,* CXXXVII, No. 3 (March 1909): 508–10; W. Bruce Lincoln, "The Circle of Grand Duchess Yelena Pavlovna, 1847–1861," *SEER* 376–77

60. See, for example, V. A. Tsie, "Zapiska o merakh, neobkhodimykh dlia sokrashcheniia perepiski," GPB, fond 833, delo No. 292/4; W. Bruce Lincoln, "Reform and Reaction in Russia: A. V. Golovnin's Critique of the 1860s," *CMRS,* XVI, No. 2 (April-June 1975): 169–70; K. S. Veselovskii, "Vospominaniia," *RS,* CVIII, No. 12 (December 1901): 495–28; Veselovskii, "Otgoloski staroi pamiati," *RS,* C, No. 10 (October 1899): 5–23; Lemke, *Epokha tsenzurnykh reform,* p. 133.

61. Veselovskii, "Vospominaniia," pp. 516–18; Lemke, *Epokha tsenzurnykh reform,* pp. 204–7.

62. Quoted in A. M. Skabichevskii, *Ocherki istorii russkoi tsenzury,* pp. 494–95.

63. Quoted in Ruud, *Fighting Words*, p. 133.
64. P. A. Valuev, "O vnutrennem sostoianii Rossii," 26 iiunia 1862g., p. 143.
65. Orlovsky, *Limits of Reform*, p. 162.
66. Ruud, *Fighting Words*, pp. 133–35.
67. Quoted in Lemke, *Epokha tsenzurnykh reform*, pp. 260–63.
68. This commission included Nikitenko, V. K. Rzhevskii (from the editorial board of *Severniaia pochta*), and V. Ia. Fuchs as representatives of the Ministry of Internal Affairs; N. P. Giliarov-Platonov (a professor of philosophy from the Moscow Theological Seminary and a member of the Moscow Censorship Committee), I. E. Andreevskii (also a member of the first commission), and E. M. Feoktistov (whom Golovnin had assigned to prepare press digests for the emperor) from the Ministry of Public Instruction. A representative from the Ministry of Justice (Pogorel'skii) and the Second Section of His Majesty's Own Chancery (A. F. Bychkov) rounded out the commission. Nikitenko, *Dnevnik*, II: 617; Lemke, *Epokha tsenzurnykh reform*, p. 263.
69. Dzhanshiev, *Epokha velikikh reform*, pp. 355–59; Lemke, *Epokha tsenzurnykh reform*, pp. 380–89; Ruud, *Fighting Words*, pp. 137–49.
70. Nikitenko, *Dnevnik*, II: 514.
71. Ruud, *Fighting Words*, pp. 160–66.
72. Nikitenko, *Dnevnik*, II: 514–15.
73. N. A. Miliutin, "Zapiska o gubernskikh i uezdnykh uchrezhdeniiakh," TsGIAL, fond 1275, delo 33/105.
74. Michael F. Hamm, "Introduction," in Michael F. Hamm, ed., *The City in Late Imperial Russia* (Bloomington, 1986), pp. 2–3.
75. Ibid., p. 3.
76. Walter Hanchett, "Tsarist Statutory Regulations of Municipal Government in the Nineteenth Century," in Michael F. Hamm, ed., *The City in Russian History* (Lexington, 1976), p. 91.
77. *Gorodskie poseleniia v rossiiskoi imperii* (St. Petersburg, 1860), I: iv, vi; *Ekonomicheskoe sostoianie gorodskikh poselenii Evropeiskoi Rossii v 1861–1862gg.* (St. Petersburg, 1863), I: v.
78. *Ekonomicheskoe sostoianie gorodskikh poselenii Evropeiskoi Rossii v 1861–1862gg.*, I: vi.
79. "Pis'mo I. S. Aksakova k N. A. Miliutinu," 31 maia 1850g., TsGIAL, fond 869, opis' 1, delo No. 818/10.
80. See, for example, "Vsepoddanneishii raport Kazanskago Voennago gubernatora o sdelannom im obozrenii vverennoi upravlenii ego gubernii," and "Vsepoddanneishie raporty Saratovskago, Tul'skago, i Poltavskago Gubernatorov o sdelannom imi obozrenii vverennoi upravlenii ikh guberniiakh," TsGIAL, fond 1287, opis' 37, delo No. 120/1–7.

81. N. A. Miliutin, "Dokladnaia zapiska o blagoustroistve gorodov," TsGIAL, fond 869, opis' 1, delo No. 319/19.
82. "Sostoianie obshchestvennago upravleniia stolichnago goroda S.-Peterburga (iz revizii, proizvedennoi v 1843 godu Sanktpeterburgskim Grazhdanskim Gubernatorom)," TsGIAL, fond 1287, opis' 37, delo No. 738a/196–98.
83. A. I. Artem'ev, "Dnevnik, iiun'-19 avgusta 1852g.," GPB, fond 37, delo No. 155/3.
84. On this reform and its limited results, see W. Bruce Lincoln, "N. A. Miliutin and the St. Petersburg Municipal Act of 1864: A Study in Reform under Nicholas I," *SR*, XXXIII, No. 1 (March 1974): 55–68, and W. Bruce Lincoln, "Reform in Action: The Implementation of the Municipal Reform Act of 1846 in St. Petersburg," *SEER*, LIII, No. 131 (April 1975): 202–9.
85. *Ekonomicheskoe sostoianie gorodskikh poselenii Evropeiskoi Rossii v 1861–1862gg.*, I: vi.
86. Quoted in G. I. Shreider, "Gorod i gorodovoe polozhenie 1870 goda," *Istoriia Rossii v XIX veke*, IV: 15.
87. *Materialy otnosiashchiesia do novago obshchestvennago ustroistva v gorodakh imperii* (St. Petersburg, 1877), I: 1–2; Lester T. Hutton, "The Reform of City Government in Russia, 1860–1870" (Unpublished Ph. D. dissertation, University of Illinois, 1972), pp. 15–17.
88. *Materialy*, I: 3–30; Shumakher, "Pozdnye vospominaniia," *VE*, CXCVI (March 1899): 115–27; Dzhanshiev, *Epokha velikikh reform* (Moscow, 1907), p. 543.
89. N. I. Vtorov, "Dnevnik, 1842–1857gg.," GPB, fond 163, delo No. 83; M. de Pule, "Nikolai Ivanovich Vtorov," *RA*, Nos. 5–8 (1887): 428–30.
90. *Materialy*, I: 4–5.
91. Ibid., I: 33–173; Shreider, "Gorod i gorodovoe polozhenie 1870 goda," pp. 16–18.
92. See, for example, Valuev, "O vnutrennem sostoianii Rossii," p. 143.
93. *Materialy*, I: 173–467.
94. Ibid., pp. 304–19; Hutton, "Reform of City Government," pp. 28–29.
95. Ibid., pp. 308–10; N. I. Vtorov, *Sravnitel'noe obozrenie munitsipal'nykh uchrezhdenii Frantsii, Bel'gii, Italii, Avstrii, i Prussii, s prisovokupleniem ocherka mestnago samoupravleniia v Anglii* (St. Petersburg, 1864), pp. 286–94.
96. *Materialy*, I: 5.
97. P. M. Maikov, *Vtoroe otdelenie sobstvennoi e. i. v. kantseliarii, 1826–1882: Istoricheskii ocherk* (St. Petersburg, 1906), pp. 422–25.
98. *Materialy*, I: 469–94.
99. Shumakher, "Pozdnye vospominaniia," *VE*, CXCVI (April 1899): 711.

100. *Materialy,* II: 51–52.
101. *Otchet po Gosudarstvennomu Sovetu za 1869g.* (St. Petersburg, 1870), p. 17.
102. *Materialy,* II: 387–459.
103. Maikov, *Vtoroe otdelenie,* prilozhenie XIV, pp. 38–42; *Materialy,* III: 39–40. The other members of the commission were F. Brun', S. Shul'ts, and Zheleznov from the Second Section, Prince Aleksei Lobanov-Rostovskii (deputy minister of internal affairs); and Egor Peretts and Mikhail Mitkov (from the State Council's Department of Laws).
104. *Materialy,* III: 11–13.
105. Miliutin, "Zapiska po voprosu o preobrazovanii zemskikh uchrezhdeniia," TsGIAL, fond 869, opis' 1, delo No. 397/28.
106. *Materialy,* III: 296–300, 307–8.
107. Ibid., pp. 455–60.
108. Shreider, "Gorod i gorodovoe polozhenie 1870 goda," pp. 27–28.
109. Miliutin, "Zapiska o gubernskikh i uezdnykh uchrezhdeniiakh," TsGIAl, fond 1275, delo 33/105.
110. "Delo o sluzhbe D. A. Miliutina," TsGIAL, fond 1162, opis' 6, delo No. 334.
111. General Count F. V. Ridiger, "Pervaia zapiska general-ad"iutanta grafa Ridigera, predstavlennaia na blagovozzrenie Imperatora Aleksandra II-go, cherez voennago ministra, general-ad"iutanta kniaza Dolgorukova I-go," 4 iiunia 1955g., in N. A. Danilov, *Stoletie voennago ministerstva: Prilozheniia k istoricheskomu ocherku razvitiia voennago upravleniia v Rossii, 1802–1902gg.* (St. Petersburg, 1902), I: 20.
112. P. A. Zaionchkovskii, *Voennye reformy 1860–1870 godov v Rossii* (Moscow, 1952), pp. 45–46.
113. Ibid., p. 46.
114. Zaionchkovskii, "Dmitrii Alekseevich Miliutin," I: 17.
115. Quoted in Zaionchkovskii, *Voennye reformy,* p. 50.
116. Quoted in John L. H. Keep, *Soldiers of the Tsar: Army and Society in Russia, 1462–1874* (Oxford, 1985), p. 323.
117. Quoted in Zaionchkovskii, *Voennye reformy,* p. 50.
118. E. Willis Brooks, "Reform in the Russian Army, 1856–1861," *SR,* XLIII, No. 1 (Spring 1984): 71.
119. Quoted in ibid., p. 67.
120. Zaionchkovskii, "Dmitrii Alekseevich Miliutin," p. 18.
121. Brooks, "Reform in the Russian Army," p. 77.
122. Lincoln, *In the Vanguard of Reform,* pp. 43–58, 102–138.
123. A. J. Rieber, *The Politics of Autocracy,* pp. 62–68; Forrestt A. Miller, *Dmitrii Miliutin and the Reform Era in Russia* (Knoxville, 1968), pp. 29–32.

124. Zaionchkovskii, "Dmitrii Alekseevich Miliutin," p. 19.
125. "Delo o sluzhbe D. A. Miliutina," TsGIAL, fond 1162, opis' 6, delo No. 334; Zaionchkovskii, "Dmitrii Alekseevich Miliutin," p. 19.
126. Keep, *Soldiers of the Tsar*, pp. 353–54; I. Bliokh, *Finansy v Rossii XIX stoletiia* (St. Petersburg, 1882), II: 15–61; *Istoriia Ministerstva Finansov, 1802–1902* (St. Petersburg, 1902), I: 634–36.
127. V. G. Fedorov, *Vooruzhenie russkoi armii za XIX stoletie* (St. Petersburg, 1911), pp. 119–21; Zaionchkovskii, *Voennye reformy,* p. 137.
128. On the grand duke's policies and the beginnings of naval reform in Russia, see especially Jacob W. Kipp, "The Consequences of Defeat: Modernizing the Russian Navy, 1856–1863," *JfGOE,* XX, No. 2 (June 1972): 210–25.
129. Keep, *Soldiers of the Tsar,* pp. 357–58; Lincoln, *In the Vanguard of Reform,* pp. 146–48.
130. Quoted in Danilov, *Stoletie voennago ministerstva: Istoricheskii ocherk razvitiia voennago upravleniia v Rossii* (St. Petersburg, 1902), I: 381.
131. Ibid.
132. Brooks, "Reform in the Russian Army," pp. 68–76.
133. D. A. Miliutin, "Vsepoddanneishii doklad Voennago Ministra, 15 ianvaria 1862g.," in Danilov, *Stoletie voennago ministerstva: Prilozheniia,* I: 70–183.
134. Ibid., p. 71.
135. Ibid., p. 73.
136. "Vsepoddanneishii doklad Voennago Ministra, 15 ianvaria 1862g.," p. 78.
137. D. A. Miliutin, "Moi starcheskie vospominaniia," ORGBL, fond 169, kartonka 13, papka 1/32.
138. "Vsepoddanneishii doklad Voennago Ministra," 15 ianvaria 1862g., pp. 8890.
139. Quoted in Zaionchkovskii, *Voennye reformy,* p. 85.
140. Quoted in ibid., p. 88.
141. Of the 211 senior commanders to whom Miliutin sent his memorandum for comment, 117 supported the general lines of his proposals and only 10 resolutely opposed them. "R. V. O: Svod zamechanii na proekt na ustroistve voennago upravleniia po okrugam," *VS,* No. 3 (1863): 222. Most notable among the strongest opponents of Miliutin's proposals were senior cavalry officers who represented perhaps the most conservative branch of the Nicholaevan army.
142. Zaionchkovskii, *Voennye reformy,* p. 99.
143. [D. A. Miliutin], "Voennye reformy imperatora Aleksandra II," *VE,* XCIII, No. 1 (January 1882): 33.
144. Zaionchkovskii, *Voennye reformy,* p. 106; [Miliutin], "Voennye reformy Aleksandra II," p. 18.

145. John Bushnell, "The Tsarist Officer Corps, 1881–1914: Customs, Duties, Inefficiency," *AHR*, LXXXVI, No. 4 (October 1981): 767–69.

146. There are numerous examples to support this point. Among the most striking, see Perovskii's effort in the Ministry of Internal Affairs in the 1840s (see his "O prichinakh umnozheniia deloproizvodstva vo vnutrennem upravlenii [mart 1851g,]," TsGIAL, fond 1287, opis' 36, delo No. 137, and "Dokladnaia zapiska o neobkhodimosti uluchshenii po gubernskim pravleniiam," 1843g.; TsGIAL, fond 1149, opis 3 [1843], delo No. 94a), and the Committee on Reducing Correspondence that met between 1852 and 1857 (Starr, *Decentralization*, pp. 111–22).

147. M. Chubinskii, "Pamiati D. A. Miliutina," *VE*, No. 9 (September 1912): 324.

148. P. Bobrovskii, "Vzgliad na grammotnost' i uchebnye komandy (ili polkovye shkoly) v nashei armii," *VS*, LXXVI, No. 12 (December 1870): 281–84; Miller, *Dmitrii Miliutin*, pp. 88–90.

149. Quoted in Zaionchkovskii, *Voennye reformy*, p. 226.

150. Ibid., pp. 221–53; Miller, *Dmitrii Miliutin*, pp. 88–141.

151. Keep, *Soldiers of the Tsar*, pp. 370–71.

152. Bliokh, *Finansy v Rossii*, II: 200. When Miliutin became war minister, army expenditures accounted for 29 percent of Russia's budget. By 1874, they comprised 31 percent. *Istoriia Ministerstva Finansov*, I: 637–38.

153. Russia's reserves increased from 210,000 in 1862 to 553,000 in 1870. Zaionchkovskii, "Dmitrii Alekseevich Miliutin," pp. 26–27.

154. Ibid., pp. 37–44; Miller, *Dmitrii Miliutin*, pp. 213–225; Zaionchkovskii, *Voennye reformy*, pp. 289–93, 32431.

155. Grand Duke Konstantin Nikolaevich, "Dnevnik v. k. Konstantina Nikolaevicha za 19 ianvaria po 31 iiulia 1873g.," TsGAOR, fond 722, opis' 1, delo No. 104/44. Entry for April 14, 1873.

156. P. A. Zaionchkovskii, "Podgotovka voennoi reformy 1874g.," *IZ*, XXVII (1948): 173. The torturous history of the attacks launched against this proposed law and the tactics Miliutin used to defend it are best described in Zaionchkovskii, *Voennye reformy*, 254–337, and an English summary of much of Zaionchkovskii's discussion can be found in Miller, *Dmitrii Miliutin*, pp. 182–225.

157. W. Bruce Lincoln, *Passage Through Armageddon: The Russians in War and Revolution, 1914–1918* (New York, 1986), pp. 179–80.

158. P. A. Zaionchkovskii, *Samoderzhavie i russkaia armiia na rubezhe XIX–XX stoletii* (Moscow, 1973), p. 118.

159. Quoted in Major-General Sir Alfred Knox, *With the Russian Army, 1914–1917: Being Chiefly Extracts from the Diary of a Military Attaché* (London, 1921), II: 412.

160. Florinsky, *Russia*, II: 909.

**CHAPTER V:** TESTING THE GREAT REFORMS

1. Quoted in Florinsky, *Russia,* II: 896–97.
2. Aleksandr Kamenskii, "Vsepoddanneishaia zapiska Kamenskago 1850 goda," *RS* CXXII, No. 6 (June 1905): 629.
3. A. E. Tsimmerman, "Vospominaniia Generala A. E. Tsimmermana," ORGBL, fond 325, kartonka 2, papka 1/243.
4. Baroness M. P. Frederiks, "Iz vospominanii baronessy M. Frederiksa," *IV,* LXXI, No. 1 (January 1898): 455.
5. "Razbor novago krepostnago prava," *Kolokol,* No. 101 (June 15, 1861), in *Kolokol: Gazeta A. I. Gertsena,* IV: 848.
6. "Velikoruss," in *Kolokol,* No. 107 (September 15, 1861), in *Kolokol: Gazeta A. I. Gertsena,* IV: 900, 963. The authors of *Velikoruss* used the terms *obrazovannye klassy* and *obshchestvo* interchangeably. See also the same usage in "Otvet Velikorussu," in ibid., p. 895.
7. Przhetslavskii, "O glasnosti v russkoi zhurnal'noi literature," TsGIAL, fond 772, opis' 1, delo No. 5129/26.
8. Ibid.
9. Lincoln, *In the Vanguard of Reform,* pp. 59–67. See also, Zablotskii-Desiatovskii, "Vzgliad na istoriiu gosudarstvennykh imushchestv v Rossii," TsGIAL, fond 940, opis' 1, delo No. 12/66; V. A. Tsie, "Zapiska o merakh, neobkhodimykh dlia sokrashcheniia perepiski," GPB, fond 833, delo No. 292/4.
10. Quoted in Wortman, *Development of a Russian Legal Consciousness,* p. 266.
11. "Razbor novago krepostnago prava," *Kolokol,* No. 101 (June 15, 1861), in *Kolokol: Gazeta A. I. Gertsena,* IV: 845, 848.
12. "Chto nuzhno narodu?" *Kolokol,* No. 102 (July 1, 1861), in *Kolokol: Gazeta A. I. Gertsena,* IV: 853–54.
13. "Otvet Velikorussu," *Kolokol,* No. 107 (September 15, 1861), in *Kolokol: Gazeta A. I. Gertsena,* IV: 895.
14. Franco Venturi, *Roots of Revolution: A History of the Populist and Socialist Movements in Nineteenth Century Russia,* translated from the Italian by Francis Haskell, with an introduction by Isaiah Berlin (New York, 1966), p. 210.
15. The tragic Bezdna incident is best discussed in Daniel Field, *Rebels in the Name of the Tsar* (Boston, 1976), pp. 31–110. See also A. I. Iampol'skaia and D. S. Gutman, *Bezdenskoe vosstanie 1861g: Sbornik Dokumentov* (Kazan, 1948).
16. Zaionchkovskii, *Provedenie,* pp. 71–81. For a detailed discussion of peasant protests, see I. I. Ignatovich, "Volneniia pomeshchich'-ikh krest'ian ot 1854 po 1863gg.," *MG,* Nos. 5–6 (1908): 93–127; No. 7 (1908): 454–92; No. 8 (1908): 181–208; No. 9 (1908): 152–73; No. 11 (1908): 189–211.

17. Quoted in Venturi, *Roots of Revolution,* pp. 247–49.
18. "Velikoruss," in *Kolokol,* Nos. 107 (September 15, 1861) and 115 (December 8, 1861), in *Kolokol: Gazeta A. I. Gertsena,* IV: 900, 963.
19. R. G. Eimontova, *Russkie universitety na grani dvukh epokh: Ot Rossii krepostnoi k Rossii kapitalisticheskoi* (Moscow, 1985), pp. 254–65; Daniel Brower, *Training the Nihilists,* pp. 121–29. See also S. I. Gessen, *Studencheskoe dvizhenie v nachale shestidesiatykh godov* (Moscow, 1932), passim.
20. Quoted in Abbot Gleason, *Young Russia: The Genesis of Russian Radicalism in the 1860s* (Chicago and London), p. 141.
21. Ibid.
22. Quoted in ibid., p. 143.
23. Eimontova, *Russkie universitety na grani dvukh epokh,* pp. 300–20; Allen Sinel, *The Classroom and the Chancellery,* pp. 26–29.
24. Quoted in Gleason, *Young Russia,* p. 158.
25. Quoted in Brower, *Training the Nihilists,* p. 15.
26. D. I. Pisarev, "Bazarov," in *Sochineniia* (Moscow, 1955), II: 11.
27. Ibid., p. 50.
28. S. Reiser, "Peterburgskie pozhary 1862 goda," *KiS,* No. 10 (1932): 82–83; Gleason, *Young Russia,* p. 168.
29. Quoted in Gleason, *Young Russia,* p. 170.
30. P. Kropotkin, *Memoirs of a Revolutionist* (Boston and New York, 1899), pp. 165–66.
31. Quoted in Martin Katz, *Mikhail N. Katkov: A Political Biography, 1818–1887* (The Hague and Paris, 1966), p. 121.
32. Alexander Herzen, *My Past and Thoughts: The Memoirs of Alexander Herzen* (New York, 1968), p. 1310.
33. Ibid.
34. W. Bruce Lincoln, *In War's Dark Shadow: The Russians Before the Great War* (New York, 1983), pp. 140–41.
35. The bulk of these positions were created after 1881, but a beginning was made in the 1860s. On the first steps in the process of the development of *zemstvo* professionals, see Frieden, *Russian Physicians,* pp. 74–75; Samuel C. Ramer, "The Zemstvo and Public Health," in Terence Emmons and Wayne S. Vucinich, eds., *The Zemstvo in Russia: An Experiment in Local Self-Government* (Cambridge, 1982), pp. 282–87; and, most important, N. M. Pirumova, *Zemskaia intelligentsia i ee role' v obshchestvennoi bor'be do nachala XXv.* (Moscow, 1986), pp. 18–32.
36. Quoted in Emmons, *The Russian Landed Gentry,* p. 356. See also pp. 357–68.
37. K. D. Kavelin, "Iz pis'ma k A. L. Korsakovu," 16 maia 1865, *Sobranie sochinenii K. D. Kavelina,* 4 vols. (St. Petersburg, 1898–99), II: col. 161.

38. Ibid., col. 140.
39. Kavelin, "Dvorianstvo i osvobozhdenii krest'ian," col. 142.
40. Kavelin, "Iz pis'ma k A. L. Korsakovu," 16 maia 1865, col. 157.
41. Ibid., cols. 151–62.
42. Quoted in N. M. Pirumova, *Zemskoe liberal'noe dvizhenie: Sotsial'nye korni i evoliutsiia do nachala XX veka* (Moscow, 1977), pp. 29–30.
43. Quoted in ibid., p. 31.
44. Ibid., p. 30.
45. Sir Donald Mackenzie Wallace, *Russia*, 2nd ed. (London, Paris, New York, and Melbourne, 1905), pp. 237.
46. Kermit E. McKenzie, "Zemstvo Organization and Role Within the Administrative Structure," in Emmons and Vucinich, eds., *The Zemstvo in Russia*, pp. 44–46.
47. N. M. Korkunov, *Russkoe gosudarstvennoe pravo*, 4th ed. (St. Petersburg, 1903), II: 445–48. On the extent to which the bureaucracy gained strength in 1890, see Zakharova, *Zemskaia kontrreforma 1890g*, pp. 161–63.
48. Kavelin, "Iz pis'ma k A. L. Korsakovu," 16 maia 1865, col. 153.
49. Ibid., cols. 151–52.
50. Patrick L. Alston, *Education and the State in Tsarist Russia* (Stanford, 1969), p. 81.
51. Sinel, *The Classroom and the Chancellery*, p. 55
52. Pirumova, *Zemskoe liberal'noe dvizhenie*, p. 32.
53. Nikitenko, *Dnevnik*, III: 92.
54. Quoted in Theodore Dan, *The Origins of Bolshevism*, edited and translated from the Russian by Joel Carmichael (New York, 1964), p. 101.
55. A. N. Engel'gardt, *Iz derevni: 12 pisem*, quoted in Richard S. Wortman, *The Crisis of Russian Populism* (Cambridge, 1967), p. 58.
56. For a full discussion of Loris-Melikov's policies, the reader is referred to Orlovsky's insightful treatment. Orlovsky, *Limits of Reform*, pp. 170–96. See also Zaionchkovskii, *Krizis samoderzhaviia na rubezhe 1870–1880 godov* pp. 230–99.
57. Orlovsky, *Limits of Reform*, p. 191.
58. Quoted in ibid., p. 193.
59. Przhetslavskii, "O glasnosti v russkoi zhurnal'noi literature," 20 ianvaria 1860g., TsGIAL, fond 772, opis' 1, delo No. 5129/1–27.
60. Grand Duke Alexander [Mikhailovich], *Once A Grand Duke* (New York, 1932), p. 61.
61. Konstantin P. Pobedonostsev, *Reflections of a Russian Statesman*, translated from the Russian by Robert Crozier Long (Ann Arbor, 1965), p. 254.
62. E. A. Peretts, *Dnevnik E. A. Perettsa (1880–1883)* (Moscow and Leningrad, 1927), p. 60. See also "Pis'ma A. V. Golovnina k D. A.

Miliutinu," 9 oktiabria i 19 noiabria 1882g., 28 marta 1884g., ORGBL, fond 169, kartonka 61, papki 32, 38, 41; and "Prazdnovanie XXXVII godovshchinu osvobozhdeniia krest'ian," *RS*, XCIV (1898): 218–23.

63. Byrnes, *Pobedonostsev,* p. 106.
64. Jacob W. Kipp, "M. Kh. Reutern on the Russian State and Economy: A Liberal Bureaucrat During the Crimean Era, 1854–1860," *JMH*, XLVII, No. 3 (September 1975): 437–59, especially pp. 453 58.
65. Pobedonostsev, *Reflections,* p. 90.
66. Ibid., p. 245.
67. Ibid., p. 117.
68. Ibid., p. 90
69. Ibid., p. 37.
70. Quoted in Byrnes, *Pobedonostsev,* p. 154.
71. Whelan, *Alexander III and the State Council,* p. 62.
72. Quoted in Kipp, "M. Kh. Reutern on the Russian State and Economy," p. 457.
73. Pobedonostsev, *Reflections,* pp. 62, 35.
74. Quoted in P. A. Zaionchkovskii, *Rossiiskoe samoderzhavie v kontse XIX stoletiia (politicheskaia reaktsiia 80kh—nachala 90kh godov)* (Moscow, 1970), p. 60.
75. A. F. Koni, "Triumviry," in *Sobranie sochinenii,* II: 310.
76. S. Iu. Witte, *Vospominaniia* (Moscow, 1960), I: 369.
77. Quoted in Edward C. Thaden, *Conservative Nationalism in Nineteenth-Century Russia* (Seattle, 1964), p. 202.
78. Quoted in Alexander [Mikhailovich], *Once A Grand Duke,* p. 177.
79. Zaionchkovskii, *Rossiiskoe samoderzhavie,* p. 60.
80. A. A. Polovtsev, *Dnevnik gosudarstvennogo sekretaria A. A. Polovtsova,* edited by P. A. Zaionchkovskii (Moscow, 1966), II: 151.
81. Quoted in Sinel, *The Classroom and the Chancellery,* p. 53. See also Thomas S. Pearson, *Russian Officialdom in Crisis: Autocracy and Local Self-Government, 1861–1900* (Cambridge, 1989), pp. 168–169.
82. Whelan, *Alexander III and the State Council,* p. 70. See also pp. 64–79 for a particularly useful and sensitive discussion of the roles that Mershcherskii, Katkov, and Tolstoi played in shaping policy and opinion during the 1880s, as well as, of course, Zaionchkovskii's magisterial summary in *Rossiiskoe samoderzhavie,* pp. 66–81.
83. Quoted in ibid., pp. 65–66.
84. H. L. von Schweinitz, *Denkwürdigkeiten des Botschafters H. L. von Schweinitz* (Berlin, 1927), II: 203.
85. Quoted in Zaionchkovskii, *Rossiiskoe samoderzhavie,* pp. 64–65.
86. Pearson, *Russian Officialdom,* pp. 168–170.
87. Quoted in Zaionchkovskii, *Rossiiskoe samoderzhavie,* p. 65.
88. Quoted in Zakharova, *Zemskaia kontrreforma,* p. 72.

89. Pearson, *Russian Officialdom*, p. 246.
90. On the importance of fiscal concerns in imperial decision making, see A. J. Rieber, "Alexander II: A Revisionist View," *JMH*, XLIII, No. 1 (1971): 50–52; and Hoch, "Banking Crisis," pp. 12–21.
91. Pearson, *Russian Officialdom*, pp. 65–70, 75–79.
92. Zaionchkovskii, *Krizis samoderzhaviia*, pp. 238–44.
93. Quoted in Pearson, *Russian Officialdom*, p. 85.
94. "Vypiska iz zhurnala Uchenago Komiteta Ministerstva Gosudarstvennykh Imushchestv, ot 26 oktiabria 1854g.," TsGIAL, fond 398, opis' 16, delo No. 4852/68–70; and A. P. Zablotskii-Desiatovskii and Prince V. F. Odoevskii, eds., *Sel'skoe chtenie*, 4 vols (St. Petersburg, 1843–48), passim.
95. Pearson, *Russian Officialdom*, p. 85.
96. Ibid., p. 87. see also p. 86.
97. Yaney, *Systematization of Russian Government*, p. 338.
98. Pearson, *Russian Officialdom*, p. 125.
99. Ibid., pp. 121–35; Zaionchkovskii, *Rossiiskoe samoderzhavie*, pp. 217–33; Whelan, *Alexander III and the State Council*, pp. 173–75.
100. Quoted in Pearson, *Russian Officialdom*, p. 134.
101. Whelan, *Alexander III and the State Council*, p. 173.
102. Polovtsev, *Dnevnik*, I: 148.
103. Ibid.
104. Theodore Taranovski, "The Politics of Counter-Reform: Autocracy and Bureaucracy in the Reign of Alexander III, 1881–1894," Unpublished Ph. D. Dissertation, Harvard University, 1976, pp. 318–19, 442.
105. Quoted in Pearson, *Russian Officialdom*, p. 138.
106. Quoted in ibid., p. 148. see also pp. 135–47.
107. Ibid., p. 155.
108. Polovtsev, *Dnevnik*, I: 263.
109. On Pazukhin's background, the development of his views, and his relationship to Tolstoi, see Zakharova, *Zemskaia kontrreforma*, pp. 76–81; Whelan, *Alexander III and the State Council*, pp. 175–85; Pearson, *Russian Officialdom*, pp. 159–161; Seymour Becker, *Nobility and Privilege in Late Imperial Russia* (DeKalb, 1985), pp. 58–59; George Yaney, *The Urge to Mobilize: Agrarian Reform in Russia, 1861–1930* (Urbana, 1982), p. 73.
110. Pearson, *Russian Officialdom*, pp. 175–204; Whelan, *Alexander III and the State Council*, pp. 175–88; Zaionchkovskii, *Rossiiskoe samoderzhavie*, pp. 366–401; Yaney, *Systematization of Russian Government*, pp. 365–76.
111. Quoted in Pearson, *Russian Officialdom*, p. 170.
112. Yaney, *Systematization of Russian Government*, p. 363.
113. Ibid., pp. 369–76.

114. Quoted in Pearson, *Russian Officialdom*, p. 219.
115. Ibid., pp. 212-34; Whelan, *Alexander III and the State Council*, pp. 189–92; Zakharova, *Zemskaia kontrreforma*, pp. 91–117, Zaionchkovskii, *Rossiiskoe samoderzhavie*, 401–5.
116. Zakharova, *Zemskaia kontrreforma*, pp. 130–50; Pearson, *Russian Officialdom*, pp. 234–40; Whelan, *Alexander III and the State Council*, pp. 192–94.
117. On the achievements of the *zemstva* after 1890, see, briefly, Samuel C. Ramer, "The Zemstvo and Public Health," pp. 292, 307–8; Nancy M. Frieden, "The Politics of Zemstvo Medicine," in Emmons and Vucinich, eds., *The Zemstvo in Russia*, pp. 319–21; Jeffrey Brooks, "The Zemstvo and the Education of the People," in ibid., pp. 248–49, 263–25; Eklof, *Russian Peasant Schools*, pp. 97–102.
118. Zaionchkovskii, *Rossiiskoe samoderzhavie*, pp. 411–28.
119. Zaionchkovskii, *Pravitel'stvennyi apparat*, pp. 223–24.
120. Whelan, *Alexander III and the State Council*, pp. 159–70. See also Taranovski's very perceptive discussion of efforts to limit the tenure of judges in the 1890s and early 1900s. Theodore Taranovski, "The Aborted Counter-Reform: The Murav'ev Commission and the Judicial Statutes of 1864," *JfGOE*, No. 2, XXIX (1981): 161–84.
121. See especially Ryszard Kolodziejczyk, ed., *Gospodarka i finanse Królestwa Polskiego przed Powstaniem Styczniowym: Raport Joszefa Bossakowskiego z 1862r. dla Ministra Finansów M. Ch. Reuterna* (Warsaw, 1969), pp. 9–10, 363–65, and passim. I am indebted to Jacob W. Kipp for this citation.
122. Kipp, "M. Kh. Reutern on the Russian State and Economy," pp. 451–56.
123. Wortman, *Development of a Russian Legal Consciousness*, pp. 254–55.
124. Quoted in ibid., p. 257.
125. Joseph Bradley, "Voluntary Associations," pp. 1–5, 10–12, forthcoming in Edith Clowes and Samuel Kassow, eds., *Between Tsar and People* (Princeton, 1991).

**CHAPTER VI:** AT THE TURN OF THE CENTURY

1. Bradley, "Voluntary Associations," pp. 1–2.
2. See, for example, Jo Ann Ruckman, *The Moscow Business Elite: A Social and Cultural Portrait of Two Generations, 1840– 1905* (DeKalb, 1984), pp. 90–100; Joseph Bradley, *Muzhik and Muscovite: Urbanization in Late Imperial Russia* (Berkeley and Los Angeles, 1985), pp. 317–24, and, more generally, Thomas C. Owen, *Capitalism and Politics in Russia: A Social History of the Moscow Merchants, 1855–1905* (Princeton, 1981). For a slightly later period, see Adele Lindenmeyr, "A

Russian Experiment in Voluntarism: The Municipal Guardianships of the Poor, 1894–1914," *JfGOE*, XXX, No. 3 (1982): 429–51.

3. Florinsky, *Russia*, II: 1106.

4. Theodore von Laue, *Sergei Witte and the Industrialization of Russia* (New York and London, 1963), p. 106; P. I. Liashchenko, *Istoriia narodnago khoziaistva SSSR*, 3 vols. (Moscow, 1956), II: 180–81; Khromov, *Ekonomicheskoe razvitie Rossii*, pp. 384–86; Olga Crisp, *Studies in the Russian Economy Before 1914* (London, 1976), pp. 159–88.

5. Quoted in Richard G. Robbins, Jr., *Famine in Russia, 1891–1892* (New York, 1975), p. 6.

6. Ibid., pp. 5–8; P. Kh. Shvanebakh, *Nashe podatnoe delo* (St. Petersburg, 1903), pp. 11–15; Khromov, *Ekonomicheskoe razvitie*, pp. 468–469; A. P. Pogrebinskii, *Ocherki istorii finansov dorevoliutsionnoi Rossii* (Moscow, 1954), pp. 85–88; von Laue, *Witte and the Industrialization of Russia*, pp. 26–27, 30; Crisp, *Studies in the Russian Economy*, pp. 25–26.

7. L. Maress, "Pishcha narodnykh mass v Rossii," *RM* (October 1893): 66.

8. Quoted in Robbins, *Famine in Russia*, pp. 34–35.

9. Ibid., pp. 61–75.

10. V. A. Maklakov, *Vlast' i obshchestvennost' na zakate Staroi Rossii (Vospominaniia)* (Paris, 1936), p. 128.

11. Ibid., p. 131.

12. Frieden, *Russian Physicians*, pp. 138–60.

13. Eklof, *Russian Peasant Schools*, pp. 88–96; Brooks, "The Zemstvo and the Education of the People," pp. 262–65.

14. Sir Bernard Pares, *The Fall of the Russian Monarchy: A Study of the Evidence* (New York, 1961), p. 71.

15. Bradley, "Voluntary Associations," pp. 7–13.

16. A. P. Chekhov, *Anton Chekhov's Life and Thought: Selected Letters and Commentary*, translated by Michael H. Heim with Simon Karlinsky (Berkeley, 1975), p. 176.

17. Quoted in Marc Slonim, *The Epic of Russian Literature: From Its Origins Through Tolstoi* (New York, 1964), pp. 286–97.

18. Paul Miliukov, *Russia and Its Crisis* (Chicago and London, 1906), pp. vii–viii.

19. Zaionchkovskii, *Rossiiskoe samoderzhavie*, pp. 82–147; Pirumova, *Zemskoe liberal'noe dvizhenie*, pp. 158–74.

20. P. B. Struve, "My Contacts with Rodichev," *SEER*, XII, No. 35 (January 1934): 350.

21. Quoted in Edward Crankshaw, *The Shadow of the Winter Palace: Russia's Drift to Revolution, 1825–1917* (New York, 1976), p. 311.

22. L. N. Tolstoi, "Pis'mo Nikolaiu II," 16 ianvaria 1902," in L. N. Tolstoi, *Sobranie sochinenii*, 20 vols. (Moscow, 1960–65), XVIII: 293.

23. Quoted in Dominic Lieven, *Russia's Rulers Under the Old Regime* (New Haven and London, 1989), p. 217.

24. Sir Bernard Pares, *Russia Between Reform and Revolution: Fundamentals of Russian History and Character*, edited with an introduction by Francis B. Randall (New York, 1962), p. 305.

25. Leopold Haimson, "The Parties and the State: The Evolution of Political Attitudes," in Cyril Black, ed., *The Transformation of Russian Society: Aspects of Social Change Since 1861* (Cambridge, Mass., 1967) pp. 110–45.

26. Miliukov, *Russia and Its Crisis*, p. 221.

27. Ibid.

28. Witte, *Vospominaniia*, II: 292.

29. Edward H. Judge, *Plehve: Repression and Reform in Imperial Russia, 1902–1904* (Syracuse, 1983), pp. 208–13.

30. Miliukov, *Russia and Its Crisis*, p. xi.

31. V. I. Gurko, *Features and Figures of the Past: Government and Opinion in the Reign of Nicholas II*, translated by Laura Matveev (Stanford, 1939), pp. 245–46.

32. Quoted in Richard Pipes, *Struve: Liberal on the Left, 1870–1905* (Cambridge, Mass., 1970), p. 319. see also pp. 319–20; Pirumova, *Zemskoe liberal'noe dvizhenie*, p. 118; and D. N. Shipov, *Vospominaniia i dumy o perezhitom* (Moscow, 1918), pp. 215–20.

33. Quoted in Pipes, *Struve: Liberal on the Left*, p. 335. See also pp. 333–34; I. I. Petrunkevich, "Iz zapisok obshchestvennago deiatelia: Vospominaniia," in *ARR*, XXI (1934): 338–40; E. D. Chermenskii, "Zemsko-liberal'noe dvizhenie nakanune revoliutsii 1905–1907gg.," *IstSSSR*, No. 5 (1965): 50–52; Shmuel Galai, *The Liberation Movement in Russia, 1900–1905* (Cambridge, 1973), pp. 177–87.

34. S. Iu. Witte, *Vospominaniia*, 3 vols. (Moscow, 1960), II: 323.

35. Quoted in Florinsky, *Russia*, II: 1169.

36. Quoted in Terence Emmons, "Russia's Banquet Campaign," *CalSS*, X (1977): 47.

37. Galai, *Liberation Movement*, p. 208.

38. Quoted in ibid., p. 213.

39. Quoted in Gurko, *Features and Figures of the Past*, p. 304.

40. Emmons, "Russia's Banquet Campaign," pp. 48–49, 55–58, 81–82; Galai, *Liberation Movement*, pp. 232–37; V. Grinevich, *Professional'noe dvizhenie rabochikh v Rossii* (Moscow, 1923), pp. 45–66.

# WORKS AND SOURCES CITED

Because the sources and the secondary literature on the problems covered by this present study are immense, what follows makes no pretense at completeness. It does not even to list all the materials consulted in my research. It is, as the title indicates, *only* a list of the works and sources cited in the endnotes of this book.

Adlerberg, A. V., "Pis'mo grafa A. V. Adlerberga k F. I. Prianishnikovu, 25 ianvaria 1859g." TsGIAL, fond 1288, opis' 21, delo No. 1.

Aksakov, I. S. *Izsledovaniia o torgovle na ukrainskikh iarmakakh.* St. Petersburg, 1858.

———."Pis'ma k N. A. Miliutinu." TsGIAL, fond 869, opis' 1, delo No. 818.

Alexander II, Emperor. *The Politics of Autocracy: Letters of Alexander II to Prince A. I. Bariatinskii, 1857–1864.* Edited by A. J. Rieber. Paris and The Hague, 1966.

Alexander [Mikhailovich], Grand Duke. *Once a Grand Duke.* New York, 1932.

Alston, Patrick L. *Education and the State in Tsarist Russia.* Stanford, 1969.

Arsen'ev, K. K. *Zakonodatel'stvo o pechati.* St. Petersburg, 1903.

Artem'ev, A. I. "Dnevnik." GPB, fond 37, dela No. 155163.

Artsimovich, V. A. *Viktor Antonovich Artsimovich: Vospominaniia-kharakteristika.* St. Petersburg, 1904.

Augustine, Wilson R. "Notes Toward a Portrait of the Eighteenth-Century Russian Nobility," *CSS,* (Fall 1970): 374–425.

Avinov, N. N. "Graf M. A. Korf i zemskaia reforma 1864g.," *RM,* No. 2 (February 1904): 94–111.

Babkin, D. A., ed. *Protsess A. N. Radishcheva.* Moscow and Leningrad, 1952.

Bakhtin, N. "Dopolnenie k zapiske zakliuchaiushchei v sebe soobrazheniia ob upravlenii otdel'nym vedomstvom," 20 noiabria 1856g.
TsGAOR, fond 722, opis' 1, delo No. 605.

Barbour, Violet, *Capitalism in Amsterdam in the Seventeenth Century.* Ann
Arbor, 1963.

Barsukov, N. P. *Zhizn' i trudy M. P. Pogodina.* 22 vols. St. Petersburg,
1888–1906.

Becker, Seymour. *Nobility and Privilege in Late Imperial Russia.* DeKalb,
1985.

Bermanskii, K. L. "Konstitutsionnye proekty tsarstvovaniia Aleksandra
II," *VP,* XXXV (November 1905): 223–91.

Black, Cyril, *The Transformation of Russian Society: Aspects of Social Change
Since 1861* (Cambridge, Mass., 1967).

Blackwell, William L. *The Beginnings of Russian Industrialization, 1800–
1860.* Princeton, 1968.

Blinov, I. A. *Gubernatory: Istoriko-iuridicheskii ocherk.* St. Petersburg, 1905.

———. "Khod sudebnoi reformy 1864 goda," *Sudebnye ustavy 20 noiabria
1864 goda za piat'desiat' let,* I: 105–21.

Bliokh, I. *Finansy v rossii XIX stoletiia.* 2 vols. St. Petersburg, 1882.

Bobrovskii, P. "Vzgliad na grammotnost' i uchebnye komandy (ili polkovye shkoly) v nashei armii," *VS,* LXXVI, No. 12 (December
1870): 279–310.

Borovkov, A. D. "A. D. Borovkov i ego avtobiograficheskie zapiski," *RS,*
No. 11 (November 1898): 331–62; No. 12 (December 1898): 591–616.

Borozdin, I. N. "Universitety v Rossii v pervoi polovine XIX veka," in
*Istorii Rossii v XIX veke,* III: 349–79.

Bossakowski, Joszef. *Gospodarka i finanse Królestwa Polskiego przed
Powstaniem Styczniowym: Raport Joszefa Bossakowskiego z 1862r. dla
Ministra Finansów M. Ch. Reuterna.* Warsaw, 1969.

Bradley, Joseph. *Muzhik and Muscovite: Urbanization in Late Imperial Russia.*
Berkeley and Los Angeles, 1985.

———. "Voluntary Associations" Unpublished paper forthcoming in
Edith Clowes and Samuel Kassow, eds., *Between Tsar and People.*
Princeton, 1991.

Brooks, E. Willis. "Reform in the Russian Army, 1856–1861," *SR,* XLIII,
No. 1 (Spring 1984): 63–82.

Brooks, Jeffrey. "The Zemstvo and the Education of the People," in
Emmons and Vucinich, eds., *Zemstvo in Russia,* pp. 243–78.

Brower, Daniel R. *Training the Nihilists: Education and Radicalism in Tsarist
Russia.* Ithaca, 1975.

Bushnell, John. "The Tsarist Officer Corps, 1881–1914: Customs, Duties,
Inefficiency," *American Historical Review,* LXXXVI, No. 4 (October
1981), 767–69.

Byrnes, Robert F. *Pobedonostsev: His Life and Thought*. Bloomington, 1968.

Catherine II. *Nakaz Imperatritsy Ekateriny II, dannyi komissii o sochinenii proekta novogo ulozheniia*. Edited, with an introduction by N. D. Chechulin. St. Petersburg, 1907.

Chekhov, A. P. *Anton Chekhov's Life and Thought: Selected Letters and Commentary*. Translated by Michael H. Heim with Simon Karlinsky. Berkeley, 1976.

Chermenskii, E. D. "Zemsko-liberal'noe dvizhenie nakanune revoliutsii 1905–1907," *IstSSSR*, No. 5 (1965): 41–60.

Cherniavsky, Michael. *Tsar and People: Studies in Russian Myths*. New Haven and London, 1961.

Chernyshevskii, N. G. *Polnoe sobranie sochinenii*. 16 vols. Moscow, 1939–55.

Chicherin, B. N. "Sovremennye zadachi russkoi zhizni," *Golosa iz Rossii*, IV: 51–129.

————. *Vospominaniia Borisa Nikolaevicha Chicherina: Moskovskii universitet*. Moscow, 1929.

————. *Vospominaniia Borisa Nikolaevicha Chicherina: Moskva sorokovykh godov*. Moscow, 1929.

"Chto nuzhno narodu?" *Kolokol*, No. 102 (July 1, 1861), in *Kolokol: Gazeta A. I. Gertsena*, IV: 853–54.

Chubinskii, M. "Pamiati D. A. Miliutina," *VE*, No. 9 (September 1912): 316–38.

Crankshaw, Edward. *The Shadow of the Winter Palace: Russia's Drift to Revolution, 1825–1917*. New York, 1976.

Crisp, Olga. *Studies in the Russian Economy Before 1914*. London, 1976.

Dan, Theodore. *The Origins of Bolshevism*. Edited and translated from the Russian by Joel Carmichael. New York, 1964.

Danilov, N. A. *Stoletie voennago ministerstva: Prilozheniia k istoricheskomu ocherku razvitiia voennago upravleniia v Rossii, 1802–1902gg*. vol. I. St. Petersburg, 1902.

Davydov, N. V. and N. N. Polianskii, eds. *Sudebnaia reforma*. Moscow, 1915.

"Delo o sluzhbe D. A. Miliutina." TsGIAL, fond 1162, opis' 6, delo No. 334.

"Delo o sluzhbe kn. D. A. Obolenskago." TsGIAL, fond 1162, opis' 6, delo No. 375.

"Delo o sluzhbe D. A. Rovinskago." TsGIAL, fond 1349, opis' 3, delo No. 1899.

"Delo o sluzhbe P. P. Semenova," TsGIAL, fond 1162, opis' 6, delo No. 496.

"Delo o sluzhbe S. I. Zarudnago." TsGIAL, fond 1405, opis' 528, delo No. 83.

"Delo po otnosheniiu Khoziaistvennago Departamenta v statisticheskoe

otdelenie o tom, kakie goroda i kogda imenno poluchii Vysochaishe utverzhdennye plany," sentiabr'-oktiabr' 1849g. TsGIAL,
fond 1287, opis' 39, delo No. 824.

"Delo tsentral'nago upravleniia po tsenzurnomu vedomstvu—po otchetu
tsenzurnago vedomstva za 1863g." TsGIAL, fond 775, opis' 1, delo
No. 1–1864.

Dement'ev, A. G. *Ocherki po istorii russkoi zhurnalistiki, 1840–1850gg.* Moscow and Leningrad, 1951.

Dement'ev, A. G., et al., eds. *Russkaia periodicheskaia pechat' (1702–1894gg.):
Spravochnik.* Moscow, 1959.

Dobroliubov, N. A. *Sobranie sochinenii v deviati tomakh.* 9 vols. Moscow
and Leningrad, 1961–1964.

Dolgorukov, kniaz' P. A. "O vnutrennem sostoianii Rossii," noiabr'
1857g. TsGAOR, fond 647, opis' 1, delo No. 50.

"Donesenie chinovnika khoziaistvennago departamenta Kollezhskago
Assesora Veselovskago Ego Vysokoprevoskhoditel'stvu Gospodinu
Ministru Vnutrennikh Del, 16 maia 1843g." TsGIAL, fond 1287,
opis' 39, delo No. 28.

"Donesenie chinovnika osobykh poruchenii Nadvornago Sovetnika A. K.
Girsa Ego Vysokoprevoskhoditel'stvu Gospodinu Ministru Vnu-
trennikh Del," 17 avgusta 1844g. TsGIAL, fond 1287, opis' 39, delo
No. 25/53–55.

Druzhinin, N. M. *Gosudarstvennye krest'iane i reforma P. D. Kiseleva.* 2 vols.
Moscow and Leningrad, 1946, 1958.

Dzhanshiev, G. A. *A. M. Unkovskii i osvobozhdenie krest'ian.* Moscow,
1884.

———. *Epokha velikikh reform.* St. Petersburg, 1905.

———. *Osnovy sudebnoi reformy.* Moscow, 1891.

———. *Stranitsa iz istorii sudebnoi reformy: D. N. Zamiatnin.* Moscow,
1883.

Dzhivelegov, A. K., S. P. Melgunov, and V. I. Picheta, eds. *Velikaia
Reforma,* 6 vols. Moscow, 1911.

Eidel'man, N. Ia. *Gertsen protiv samoderzhaviia: Sekretnaia politicheskaia
istoriia Rossii XVIII-XIX vekov i vol'naia pechat'.* Moscow, 1973.

Eimontova, R. G. *Russkie universitety na grani dvukh epokh: Ot Rossii krepostnoi k Rossii kapitalisticheskoi.* Moscow, 1985.

Eklof, Benoit. *Russian Peasant Schools: Officialdom, Village Culture, and
Popular Pedagogy, 1861–1914.* Berkeley and Los Angeles, and London, 1986.

———. "Spreading the Word: Primary Education and The Zemstvo in
Moscow Province, 1864–1910." PhD dissertation. Princeton University, 1976.

*Ekonomicheskoe sostoianie gorodskikh poselenii Evropeiskoi Rossii v 1861–
1862gg.* 2 vols. St. Petersburg, 1863.

Emmons, Terence. *The Russian Landed Gentry and the Peasant Emancipation of 1861.* Cambridge, 1968.

——. "Russia's Banquet Campaign," *CalSS,* X (1977): 45–86.

Emmons, Terence, and Wayne S. Vucinich, eds. *The Zemstvo in Russia: An Experiment in Local Self-Government.* Cambridge, 1982.

Fedorov, V. G. *Vooruzhenie russkoi armii za XIX stoletie.* St. Petersburg, 1911.

Field, Daniel. *The End of Serfdom: Nobility and Bureaucracy in Russia, 1855–1861.* Cambridge, Mass., 1976.

——. *Rebels in the Name of the Tsar.* Boston, 1976.

Filippov, A. N. "Istoricheskii ocherk obrazovaniia ministerstv v Rossii," *ZhMIu,* No. 9 (November 1902): 39–72; No. 10 (December 1902): 1–26.

Fisher, Raymond H. *The Russian Fur Trade, 1550–1700.* Berkeley and Los Angeles, 1943.

Florinsky, Michael. *Russia: A History and an Interpretation* 2 vols. New York, 1968.

"Formuliarnyi spisok grafa A. K. Siversa." TsGIAL, fond 1284, opis' 75, delo No. 2.

"Formuliarnyi spisok grafa D. N. Tolstago." TsGIAL, fond 1284, opis' 32, delo No. 192.

"Formuliarnyi spisok A. K. Girsa." TsGIAL, fond 1284, opis' 31, delo No. 52.

"Formuliarnyi spisok A. F. Shtakel'berga." TsGIAL, fond 1349, opis' 3, delo No. 2535.

"Formuliarnyi spisok K. S. Veselovskago." TsGIAL, fond 1349, opis' 3, delo No. 391.

Frederiks, Baroness M. P. "Iz vospominanii baronessy M. P. Frederiksa," *IV,* LXXI, No. 1 (January 1898): 454–84.

Frieden, Nancy Mandelker. "The Politics of Zemstvo Medicine," in Emmons and Vucinich, eds., *Zemstvo in Russia,* pp. 315–43.

——. *Russian Physicians in an Era of Reform and Revolution, 1856–1905.* Princeton, 1981.

Fuhrmann, Joseph T. *The Origins of Capitalism in Russia: Industry and Progress in the Sixteenth and Seventeenth Centuries.* Chicago, 1972.

Galai, Shmuel. *The Liberation Movement in Russia, 1900–1905.* Cambridge, 1975.

Garmiza, V. V. *Podgotovka zemskoi reformy 1864 goda.* Moscow, 1957.

——. ed. "Predpolozheniia i proekty P. A. Valueva po voprosam vnutrennei politike (1862–1866gg.)," *IA,* III (January-February 1958): 138–53.

Gerasimova, Iu. I. "Krizis pravitel'stvennoi politiki v gody revoliutsionnoi situatsii i Aleksandr II," *RevS* (1962): 93–106.

——. "Otnoshenie pravitel'stva k uchastii pechati v obsuzhdenii krest'-

ianskago voprosa v periode revoliutsionnoi situatsii kontsa 50kh–nachala 60kh godov XIXv.," *RevS* (1974), pp. 81–105.

Gertsen, A. I. *Polnoe sobranie sochinenii i pisem Aleksandra Ivanovicha Gertsena.* Edited by M. K. Lemke. 22 vols. Petrograd, 1918–20.

———[Herzen]. *My Past and Thoughts: The Memoirs of Alexander Herzen.* New York, 1968.

Gessen, S. I. *Studencheskoe dvizhenie v nachale shestidesiatykh godov.* Moscow, 1932.

Gleason, Abbott. *Young Russia: The Genesis of Russian Radicalism in the 1860s.* Chicago and London, 1983.

Glebov, P. N. "Morskoe sudoproizvodstvo vo Frantsii," *MS*, No. 11 (November 1859): 101–11; No. 12 (1859): 344–69; No. 1 (1860): 47–63; No. 4 (1860): 318–52.

Gogol, N. V. *Sobranie sochinenii N. V. Gogolia.* 6 vols. Moscow, 1959.

*Golosa iz Rossii: Sbornik A. I. Gertsena i N. P. Ogareva.* 10 vols. London, 1856–60. Reprint edited by M. V. Nechkina and E. L. Rudnitskaia. 4 vols. Moscow, 1974–75.

Golovachev, A. A. and A. M. Unkovskii, "Zapiska A. A. Golovacheva i A. M. Unkovskago, (1858g.). TsGAOR, fond 109, opis' 1, delo No. 1960.

Golovnin, A. V. "Doklad Imperatoru Aleksandru Nikolaevichu o polozhenii russkoi literatury i neobkhodimosti reorganizatsii tsenzury," 26, fevralia 1862g. TsGIAL, fond 772, opis' 1, delo No. 5977.

———. "Kratkii ocherk deistviia Velikago Kniazia Konstantina Nikolaevicha." GPB, fond 208, delo No. 2.

———. "Materialy dlia zhizneopisaniia Velikago Kniazia Konstantina Nikolaevicha." TsGIAL, fond 851, opis' 1, delo No. 5.

———. "Pis'ma k v. k. Konstantinu Nikolaevichu." GPB, fond 208, delo No. 44.

———. "Pis'ma A. V. Golovnina k D. A. Miliutinu," 1882–1884gg. ORGBL, fond 169, kartonka 61, papki 32, 38, 41.

———. "Raznitsa v napravlenii gosudarstvennoi deiatel'nosti v pervoi i vo vtoroi polovine nyneshnego tsarstvovaniia," mart' 1867g. GPB, fond 208, delo No. 236.

———. "Zapiski i primechaniia A. V. Golovnina." GPB, fond 208, dela No. 1–7.

*Gorodskie poseleniia v rossiiskoi Imperii.* 7 vols. St. Petersburg, 1860–65.

*Gosudarstvennaia kantseliariia, 1810–1910.* St. Petersburg, 1910.

*Gosudarstvennyi Soviet, 1801–1901gg.* St. Petersburg, 1902.

Got'e, Iu. V. *Istoriia oblastnago upravleniia v Rossii ot Petra I do Ekateriny II.* 2 vols. Moscow, 1913.

Grinevich, V. *Professional'noe dvizhenie rabochikh v Rossii.* Moscow, 1923.

Grunwald, Constantin de. *Tsar Nicholas I.* Translated from the French by Brigit Patmore. London, 1954.

Gurko, V. I. *Features and Figures of the Past: Government and Opinion in the Reign of Nicholas II.* Translated by Laura Matveev. Stanford, 1939.

Haimson, Leopold. "Parties and the State: The Evolution of Political Attitudes," in Black, ed., *Transformation*, pp. 110–45.

Hamburg, Gary M. "B. N. Chicherin and the Emergence of Russian Liberalism." Unpublished book manuscript.

Hamm, Michael F., ed. *The City in Late Imperial Russia.* Bloomington, 1986.

——., ed. *The City in Russian History.* Lexington, 1976.

Hanchett, Walter. "Tsarist Statutory Regulations of Municipal Government in the Nineteenth Century," in Hamm, ed., *The City in Russian History,* pp. 91–114.

Haumant, Emile. *La Culture Française en Russie (1700–1900).* Paris, 1913.

Hoch, Stephen. "The Banking Crisis, Peasant Reform, and the Redemption Operation in Russia, 1857–1861." Unpublished paper forthcoming in *AHR*.

Hutton, Lester T. "The Reform of City Government in Russia, 1860–1870." Unpublished Ph. D. dissertation. University of Illinois, 1972.

Iampol'skaia A. I. and D. S. Gutman, *Bezdenskoe vosstanie 1861g: Sbornik Dokumentov.* Kazan, 1948.

Ignatovich, I. I. *Pomeshchich'i krest'ian nakanune osvobozhdeniia.* Moscow, 1910.

——. "Volneniia pomeshchich'ikh krest'ian ot 1854 po 1863gg.," *MG,* Nos. 5–6 (1908): 93–127; No. 7 (1908): 454–92; No. 8 (1908): 181–208; No. 9 (1908): 152–73; No. 11 (1908): 189–211.

"Imperator Nikolai I i akademik Parrot," *RS,* No. 7 (July 1898): 139–52.

*Istoriia Ministerstva Finansov, 1802–1902.* 2 vols. St. Petersburg, 1902.

*Istoriia Rossii v XIX veke.* 9 vols. St. Petersburg 1907–11.

"Iz otcheta Departamenta Politsii Ispolnitel'noi za 1858g. o krest'ianskikh volneniiakh i merakh, priniatykh dlia ikh podavleniia," in Okun and Sivkov, eds., *Krest'ianskoe dvizhenii,* pp. 180–84.

Jones, E. Gareth. "Novikov's Naturalized *Spectator,*" in Garrard, ed., *Eighteenth Century,* pp. 149–165.

Jones, Robert E. *The Emancipation of the Russian Nobility, 1762–1785.* Princeton, 1973.

Judge, Edward C. *Plehve: Repression and Reform in Imperial Russia, 1902–1904.* Syracuse, 1983.

Kaiser, Friedhelm Berthold. *Die russische Justizreform von 1864: Zur Geschichte der russischen Justiz von Katherina I bis 1917.* Leiden, 1972.

Kamenskii, Aleksandr. "Vsepoddanneishaia zapiska Kamenskago 1850 goda," *RS,* CXXII, No. 6 (June 1905): 629–57.

Karamzin, N. M. *Karamzin's Memoir on Ancient and Modern Russia: A Translation and an Analysis.* Edited and translated by Richard Pipes. Cambridge, Mass., 1959.

Kassow, Samuel D. *Students, Professors, and the State in Tsarist Russia.* Berkeley and Los Angeles, 1989.

Katz, Martin. *Mikhail N. Katkov: A Political Biography, 1818–1887.* The Hague and Paris, 1966.

Kavelin, K. D. "Pis'ma k D. A. Miliutinu." ORGBL, fond 169, kartonka 64, papka 61.

———. *Sobranie sochinenii K. D. Kavelina.* 4 vols. St. Petersburg, 1898–99.

Keep, John L. H. *Soldiers of the Tsar: Army and Society in Russia, 1462–1874.* Oxford, 1985.

Kharytonov, A. A. "Iz vospominanii A. A. Kharytonova," *RS,* LXXXI, No. 1 (January 1894): 101–32.

Khodnev, A. I. *Istoriia Imperatorskago Vol'nago Ekonomicheskago Obshchestva s 1765 do 1865 goda.* St. Petersburg, 1865.

Khromov, P. A. *Ekonomicheskoe razvitie Rossii v XIX–XX vekakh, 1800–1917.* Moscow, 1950.

Kipp, Jacob W. "The Consequences of Defeat: Modernizing the Russian Navy, 1856–1863," *Jahrbücher für Geschichte Osteuropas,* XX, No. 2 (June 1972): 210–25.

———. "M. Kh. Reutern on the Russian State and Economy: A Liberal Bureaucrat During the Crimean Era, 1854–1860," *JMH,* XLVII, No. 3 (September 1975): 437–59.

Kipp, Jacob W., and W. Bruce Lincoln. "Autocracy and Reform: Bureaucratic Absolutism and Political Modernization in Nineteenth-Century Russia," *RH,* VI, No. 1 (1979): 1–21.

Kizevetter, A. A. *Istoricheskie ocherki.* Moscow, 1912.

———. "Vnutrenniaia politika Imperatora Nikolaia Pavlovicha," in Kizevetter, *Istoricheskie ocherki,* pp. 419–502.

Klochkov, M. V. *Ocherki pravitel'stvennoi deiatel'nosti vremeni Pavla I.* Petrograd, 1916.

Knirim, A. A. "O Gannoverskom grazhdanskom sudoproizvodstve," *ZhMIu,* No. 3 (March 1862): 545–608.

Knox, Major-General Sir Alfred. *With the Russian Army, 1914–1917: Being Chiefly Extracts from the Diary of a Military Attaché.* 2 vols. London, 1921.

Kobeko, D. F. *Imperatorskii tsarskosel'skii litsei, 1811–1843gg.* St. Petersburg, 1911.

*Kolokol. Gazeta A. I. Gertsena i N. P. Ogareva.* 11 vols. Moscow, 1961–65.

Koni, A. F. *Ottsy i deti sudebnoi reformy (k piatdesiatiletiiu Sudebnykh Ustavov).* Moscow, 1914.

———. *Sobranie sochinenii A. F. Koni.* 8 vols. Moscow, 1966–69.

———. "Velikii kniaz' Konstantin Nikolaevich," in Dzhivelegov et al., eds., *Velikaia reforma,* V: 34–51.

Konstantin Nikolaevich, Grand Duke. "Dnevnik v. k. Konstantina Nikolaevicha." TsGAOR, fond 722, opis' 1, dela No. 74–124.

Korf, Baron M. A. "Dnevnik." TsGAOR, fond 728, opis' 1, delo No. 1817.

————. "Istoricheskaia zapiska o proiskhozhdenii i izdanii knigi: Vosshestvie na prestol Imperatora Nikolaia I." GPB, fond M. A. Korfa, delo No. 50.

————. "Shestinedel'nyi epizod moei zhizni." TsGAOR, fond 728, opis' 1, delo No. 2612.

————. "Vzgliad na vnutrenniia preobrazovaniia poslednego desiatletiia" (aprel 1866g). TsGAOR, fond 728, opis' 1, delo No. 2863.

Korkunov, N. M. *Russkoe gosudarstvennoe pravo.* 4th ed. 2 vols. St. Petersburg, 1903.

Kornilov, A. A. *Kurs istorii Rossii v XIX v.* 3 vols. Moscow, 1918.

"Kratkii obzor deistvii Ministerstva Vnutrennikh Del s 1825 po 1850 god." TsGAOR, fond 722, opis' 1, delo No. 599.

Kropotkin, P. *Memoirs of Revolutionist.* Boston and New York, 1899.

Lander, K. I. "Pribaltiiskii krai v pervoi polovine XIX veka," in *Istoriia Rossii v XIX veke,* II: 327–49.

Lantzeff, George V. *Siberia in the Seventeenth Century: A Study of Colonial Administration.* Berkeley and Los Angeles, 1943.

Laue, Theodore von. *Sergei Witte and the Industrialization of Russia.* New York and London, 1963.

Lebedev, K. N. "Iz zapisok Senatora K. N. Lebedeva," *RA,* bk. 1 (January 1888): 481–88, 617–28; bk. 2 (1888): 133–44, 232–43, 345–56; bk. 3 (1888): 248–70, 455–67; bk. 1 (1893): 284–97, 337–99; bk. 2 (1897): 633–55; bk. 3 (1900): 55– 70, 244–80; bk. 2 (1910): 333–408, 465–524; bk. 3 (1910): 183– 253, 353–76; bk. 1 (1911): 87–128, 216–34, 375–422, 534–66; bk. 2 (1911): 132–60, 224–60, 343–94, 465–511; bk. 3 (1911): 53– 107, 191–216, 321–52.

Lemke, M. *Epokha tsenzurnykh reform 1855–1865 godov.* St. Petersburg, 1905.

————. *Nikolaevskie zhandarmy i literatura, 1826–1855gg.* St. Petersburg, 1909.

————. *Ocherki osvoboditel'nago dvizheniia 'shestidesiatykh godov'.* St. Petersburg, 1908.

————. *Ocherki po istorii russkoi tsenzury i zhurnalistiki XIX stoletiia.* St. Petersburg, 1904.

Leonidov, M. "Aleksandr Mikhailovich Plavskii," *RBS,* vol. Plav-Prim, pp. 8–9.

Leroy-Beaulieu, Anatole. *Un homme d'état russe (Nicolas Milutine) d'après sa correspondance inédite: Étude sur la Russie et la Pologne pendant le regne d'Alexandre II (1856–1872).* Paris, 1884.

Levin, Iu. D. "Angliiskaia poeziia i literatura russkogo sentimentalizma," in Alekseev, ed., *Ot klassitsizma k romantizmu,* pp. 195–297.

Levin, Sh. M. "K. D. Kavelin o smerti Nikolaia I: Pis'ma k T. N. Granovskomu," *LN,* LXVII (1959): 596–612.

Levshin, A. I. "Dostopamiatnye minuty v moei zhizni: Zapiska Alekseia

Iraklievicha Levshina," *RA*, No. 8 (1885): 475–558.

Liashchenko, P. I. *Istoriia narodnago khoziaistva SSSR*. 3 vols. Moscow, 1956.

――――. *History of the National Economy of Russia to the 1917 Revolution*. New York, 1970.

Lieven, Dominic. *Russia's Rulers Under the Old Regime*. New Haven and London, 1989.

Lincoln, W. Bruce. "The Circle of Grand Duchess Yelena Pavlovna, 1847–1861," *SEER*, XLVIII, No. 112 (July 1970): 373–87.

――――. "The Editing Commissions of 1859–1860: Some Notes on Their Members' Backgrounds and Service Careers," *SEER*, LVI, No. 3 (July 1978): 346–59.

――――. "The Genesis of an 'Enlightened' Bureaucracy in Russia, 1825–1856," *JfGOE*, XX, No. 3 (September 1972): 321–30.

――――. *In the Vanguard of Reform: Russia's Enlightened Bureaucrats, 1825–1861*. DeKalb, 1982.

――――. *In War's Dark Shadow: The Russians Before the Great War*. New York, 1983.

――――. "The Ministers of Alexander II: A Brief Survey of Their Backgrounds and Service Careers," *CMRS*, XVII, No. 4 (October-December 1976): 467–83.

――――. "N. A. Miliutin and the St. Petersburg Municipal Act of 1846: A Study in Reform Under Nicholas I," *SR*, XXXIII, No. 1 (March 1974): 55–68.

――――. *Nicholas I: Emperor and Autocrat of All the Russias*. London, 1978.

――――. "Official Propaganda in Mid-Nineteenth Century Russia: Baron M. A. Korf and *The Accession of Nicholas I*," *OSP*, XXI (1988): 123–35.

――――. *Passage Through Armageddon: The Russians in War and Revolution, 1914–1918*. New York, 1986.

――――. "A Profile of the Russian Bureaucracy on the Eve of the Great Reforms," *JfGOE*, XXVII (1979): 181–96.

――――. "Reform and Reaction in Russia: A. V. Golovnin's Critique of the 1860s," *CMRS*, XVI, No. 2 (April–June 1975): 167–79.

――――. "Reform in Action: The Implementation of the Municipal Reform Act of 1846 in St. Petersburg," *SEER*, LIII, No. 131 (April 1975): 202–9.

Lindenmeyr, Adele. "A Russian Experiment in Voluntarism: The Municipal Guardianships of the Poor, 1894–1914," *Jahrbücher für Geschichte Osteuropas*, XXX, No. 3 (1982): 429–51.

McKenzie, Kermit E. "Zemstvo Organization and Role Within the Administrative Structure," in Emmons and Vucinich, eds., *Zemstvo in Russia*, pp. 31–78.

Maikov, P. M. *Vtoroe otdelenie sobstvennoi e. i. v. kantseliarii, 1826–1882:*

*Istoricheskii ocherk.* St. Petersburg, 1906.

Maklakov, V. A. *Vlast' i obshchestvennost' na zakate Staroi Rossii. Vospominaniia.* Paris, 1936.

Makogonenko, G. P. *Nikolai Novikov i russkoi prosveshchenie XVIII veka.* Moscow and Leningrad, 1952.

———. *Radishchev i ego vremia.* Moscow, 1956.

Malia, Martin. *Alexander Herzen and the Birth of Russian Socialism, 1812–1855.* Cambridge, Mass., 1961.

Malysheva, I. V., ed. N. I. *Novikov i ego sovremenniki: Izbrannye sochineniia.* Moscow, 1961.

Maress, L. "Pishcha narodnykh mass v Rossii," *RM* (October 1983): 43–67.

*Materialy dlia istorii uprazdneniia krepostnago sostoianiia pomeshchich'ikh krest'ian v Rossii v tsarstvovanie Imperatora Aleksandra II.* 3 vols. Berlin, 1860–62.

*Materialy otnosiashchiesia do novago obshchestvennago ustroistva v gorodakh Imperii.* 6 vols. St. Petersburg, 1877–83.

*Materialy po zemskomu obshchestvennomu ustroistvu (Polozhenie o zemskikh uchrezhdeniiakh).* 2 vols. St. Petersburg, 1885–86

*Materialy sobrannye dlia Vysochaishei uchrezhdennoi komissii o preobrazovanii gubernskikh o uezdnykh uchrezhdenii.* St. Petersburg, 1870.

Mikhailov, I. I. "Kazanskaia starina (iz vospominanii Iv. Iv. Mikhailova," *RS,* C, No. 10 (October 1899): 99–113; No. 11 (November 1899): 399–419.

Miliukov, P. N. *Ocherki po istorii russkoi kul'tury.* 3 vols. St. Petersburg, 1901.

———. *Russia and Its Crisis.* Chicago and London, 1906.

Miliutin, D. A. *Dnevnik D. A. Miliutina, 1873– 1875gg.* Edited by P. A. Zaionchkovskii. 4 vols. Moscow, 1947–50.

———. "Moi starcheskie vospominaniia za 1816–1873gg." ORGBL, fond 169, kartonki 12–16.

[———]. "Voennye reformy imperatora Aleksandra II," *VE,* XCIII, No. 1 (January 1882): 1–35.

———. "Vsepoddanneishii doklad Voennago Ministra, 15 ianvaria 1862g.," in Danilov, *Stoletie,* I: 70–183.

Miliutin, N. A. "Dokladnaia zapiska o blagoustroistve gorodov." TsGIAL, fond 869, opis' 1, delo No.319.

———. "Lettres à M. A. Miliutine." OC.

———. "Obshchaia instruktsiia chinovnikam otriazhaemym dlia obozreniia goroda." TsGIAL, fond 1287, opis' 39, delo No. 156.

———. "Ofitsial'noe pis'mo chinovniku osobykh poruchenii Gospodinu Nadvornomu Sovetniku Shtakel'bergu ot khoziaistvennago Departamenta, Vremennago Otdeleniia," 4 noiabria 1843g., TsGIAL, fond 1287, opis' 39, delo No. 22.

————. "Ofitsial'noe pis'mo chinovniku osobykh poruchenii Nadvornomu Sovetniku Girsu," 30 oktiabria 1843g., TsGIAL, fond 1287, opis' 39, delo No. 25.

————. "Pis'ma P. D. Kiselevu." ORGBL, fond 129, karton 17, papka 55.

————. "Pis'ma k D. A. Miliutinu." ORGBL, fond 169, karton 69.

————. "Zapiska po voprosu o preobrazovanii zemskikh uchrezhdeniiakh," 22 maia 1862g. TsGIAL, fond 869, opis' 1, delo No. 397.

Miliutina, M. A. "Iz zapisok Marii Ageevny Miliutinoi," *RS,* XCVII, No. 1 (January 1899): 39–65; No. 2 (February 1899): 265–88; No. 3 (March 1899): 575–601; XCVIII, No. 4 (April 1899): 105–17.

Miller, Forrestt A. *Dmitrii Miliutin and the Reform Era in Russia.* Knoxville, 1968.

Monas, Sidney. *The Third Section: Police and Society in Russia Under Nicholas I.* Cambridge, Mass., 1961.

Mordovtsev, D. L. "Istoricheskie pominki po N. I. Kostomarove," *RS,* LXVI, No. 6 (June 1885): 617–25.

Nabokov, V. "Raboty po sostavleniia sudebnykh ustavov: Obshchaia kharakteristika sudebnoi reformy," in Davydov and Polianskii, eds., *Sudebnaia reforma,* pp. 303–53.

Nechkina, M. V., ed. *Revoliutsionnaia situatsiia v Rossii v 1859–1861gg.* 8 vols. Moscow, 1960–79.

Nebolsin, P. I. "Biudzhety peterburgskikh chinovnikov," *EU,* No. 11 (March 16, 1857): 241–50.

Nechkina, M. V., ed. *Revoliutsionnaia situatsiia v Rossii v 1859–1861gg.* 8 vols. Moscow, 1960–79.

Nesselrode, Count K. V. *Papiers et lettres du chancellier Comte de Nesselrode, 1760–1850.* 12 vols. Paris, 1905–12.

Nicolson, Harold. *The Congress of Vienna: A Study in Allied Unity, 1812–1822.* New York, 1946.

Nikitenko, A. V. *Dnevnik.* 3 vols. Moscow, 1955.

————. *Zapiski i dnevnik, 1826–1877.* 2 vols. St. Petersburg, 1893.

Nol'de, A. E. *K. P. Pobedonostsev i sudebnaia reforma.* Petrograd, 1915.

Nol'de, B. E. *Iurii Samarin i ego vremia.* Paris, 1926.

————. *Peterburgskaia missiia Bismarka, 1859–1862.* Prague, 1925.

"O prisuzhdennykh Uchennym Komitetom MGI po konkursu khoziaistvenno-statisticheskikh opisanii nagradakh," 10 noiabria 1850g., TsGIAL, fond 398, opis' 1, delo No. 4475.

Obolenskii, D. A. "Moi vospominaniia o velikoi kniagine Elena Pavlovne," *RS,* CXXXVII, No. 3 (March 1909): 504–28; CXXXVIII, No. 4 (April 1909): 37–62.

————. "Zamechaniia na proekt novago poriadka sudoproizvodstva Rossii." TsGAOR, fond 647, opis' 1, delo No. 56.

"Obozrenie vsekh chastei gosudarstvennago upravleniia." Chast' tret'ia (1831g). GPB, fond 380, delo No. 67.

*Otchet po Gosudarstvennomu Sovetu za 1869g.* St. Petersburg, 1870.

"Otvet Velikorussu," *Kolokol,* No. 107 (September 15, 1861), in *Kolokol: Gazeta A. I. Gertsena,* IV: 895.

Okun, S. B. and K. V. Sivkov, eds. *Krest'ianskoe dvizhenie v Rossii v 1857–mae 1861gg: Sbornik dokumentov.* Moscow, 1963.

Orlovsky, Daniel T. *The Limits of Reform: The Ministry of Internal Affairs in Imperial Russia, 1802–1881.* Cambridge, Mass., 1981.

"Otchety po Inspektorskomu Departmentu Grazhdanskago Vedomstva za 1847–1857gg." TsGIAL, fond 1409, opis' 2, delo No. 6829.

"Otnoshenie Deistvitel'nago Tainago Sovetnika Dmitriia Buturlina 17-go marta 1849g., k Ministru Narodnago Prosveshcheniia Grafu S. S. Uvarovu," (konfidential'no). TsGIAL, fond 772, opis' 1, delo No. 2242.

Owen, Thomas C. *Capitalism and Politics in Russia: A Social History of the Moscow Merchants, 1855–1905.* Princeton, 1981.

"Pamiati A. P. Zablotskago," *RS,* XXXIII, No. 2 (February 1882): 531–60.

Panaeva, A. Ia. *Vospominaniia.* Moscow, 1956.

Pares, Sir Bernard. *The Fall of the Russian Monarchy: A Study of the Evidence.* New York, 1961.

———. *Russia between Reform and Revolution: Fundamentals of Russian History and Character.* Edited with an introduction by Francis B. Randall. New York, 1962.

Pearson, Thomas S. *Russian Officialdom in Crisis: Autocracy and Local Self-Government, 1861–1900.* Cambridge, 1989.

Peretts, E. A. *Dnevnik E. A. Perettsa (1880–1883).* Moscow and Leningrad, 1927.

Perovskii, L. A. "Dokladnaia zapiska o neobkhodimosti uluchshenii po gubernskim pravleniiam (1843g.)." TsGIAL, fond 1149, opis' 3 (1843), delo No. 94a.

———. "O prichinakh umnozheniia deloproizvodstva vo vnutrennem upravlenii (mart 1851g)." TsGIAL, fond 1287, opis' 36, delo No. 137.

*Pervoe izdanie materialov redaktsionnykh komissii dlia sostavleniia polozhenii o krest'ianakh, vykhodiashchikh iz krepostnoi zavisimosti.* 18 vols. St. Petersburg, 1859–60.

Petrunkevich, I. I. "Iz zapisok obshchestvennago deiatelia: Vospominaniia," in *ARR,* XXI (1934): 13–467.

"Pii Nikodimovich Danevskii," *RBS,* vol. Dab–Diad, pp. 56–58.

Pipes, Richard. *Struve: Liberal on the Left, 1870–1905.* Cambridge, Mass., 1970.

Pirumova, N. M. *Zemskaia intelligentsia i ee rol' v obshchestvennoi bor'be do nachala XXv.* Moscow, 1986.

———. *Zemskoe liberal'noe dvizhenie: Sotsial'nye korni i evoliutsiia do nachala XX veka.* Moscow, 1977.

Pisarev, D. I. *Sochineniia.* 4 vols. Moscow, 1955.

"Pis'mo ot komissii dlia revizii obshchestvennago i khoziaistvennago upravleniia goroda Rigi," 31 ianvaria 1847g., TsGIAL, fond 1287, opis' 39, delo No. 23.

Pobedonostsev, K. P. "Graf V. N. Panin," *Golosa iz Rossii*, No. 7 (1859): 3–142.

————. "O reformakh v grazhdanskom sudoproizvodstve," *RV*, XXI (1859): 541–80; XXII (1859): 5–34, 153–90.

————. *Reflections of a Russian Statesman.* Translated from the Russian by Robert Crozier Long. Ann Arbor, 1965.

————. "Vospominaniia o V. P. Zubkove." *RA*, bk. 1 (1904): 301–5.

Pogodin, M. P. *Istoriko-politicheskie pis'ma i zapiski v prodolzhenii Krymskoi voiny, 1853–1856.* Moscow, 1974.

Pogrebinskii, A. P. *Ocherki istorii finansov dorevoliutsionnoi Rossii.* Moscow, 1954.

Polovtsev, A. A. *Dnevnik gosudarstvennogo sekretaria A. A. Polovtseva.* Edited by P. A. Zaionchkovskii. 2 vols. Moscow, 1966.

Popov, P. S., ed., *Pis'ma k A. V. Druzhininu (1850–1863.* Moscow, 1948.

"Prazdnovanie XXXVII godovshchinu osvobozhdeniia krest'ian," *RS*, XCIV (1898): 218–23.

Presniakov, A. E. *Apogei samoderzhaviia: Nikolai I.* Leningrad, 1925.

*Prilozheniia k trudam Redaktsionnykh Komissii dlia sostavleniia polozhenii o krest'ianakh vykhodiashchikh iz krepostnoi zavisimosti.* 9 vols. St. Petersburg, 1859–60.

Przhetslavskii, O. Λ. "O glasnosti v russkoi zhurnal'noi literature," 20 ianvaria 1860g. TsGIAL, fond 772, opis' 1, delo No. 5129.

Pule, M. de. "Nikolai Ivanovich Vtorov, *RA*, Nos. 5–8 (1887): 420–35.

Pushkin, A. S. *Polnoe sobranie sochinenii v desiati tomakh.* Moscow, 1962–66.

"R. V. O: Svod zamechanii na proekt na ustroistve voennago upravleniia po okrugam," *VS*, No. 3 (1863): 218–30.

Radishchev, A. N. *Izbrannye filosofskie i obshchestvenno-politicheskie proizvedeniia.* Edited by I. Ia. Shipanov. Moscow, 1952.

Raeff, Marc. *Imperial Russia, 1682–1825: The Coming of Age of Modern Russia.* New York, 1971.

————. "The Russian Autocracy and Its Officials," *HSS*, IV (1957): 77–92.

————. *The Well-Ordered Police State: Social and Institutional Change Through Law in the Germanies and Russia, 1600–1800.* New Haven, 1983.

Ramer, Samuel C. "The Zemstvo and Public Health," in Emmons and Vucinich, eds., *Zemstvo in Russia*, pp. 279–314.

Rashin, A. G. *Naselenie Rossii za 100 let (1811–1913): Statisticheskie ocherki.* Moscow, 1956.

"Razbor novago krepostnago prava," *Kolokol*, No. 101 (June 15, 1861), in *Kolokol: Gazeta A. I. Gertsena*, IV: 845–48.

Reiser, S. "Peterburgskie pozhary 1862 goda," *KiS*, No. 10 (1932): 79–109.

Riasanovsky, Nicholas V. *Nicholas I and Official Nationality in Russia, 1825–1855.* Berkeley and Los Angeles, 1959.

Ridiger, General Count F. V. "Pervaia zapiska general-ad"iutanta grafa Ridigera, predstavlennaia na blagovozzrenie Imperatora Aleksandra II-go, cherez voennago ministra, general-ad"iutanta kniazia dolgorukova I-go," 4 iiunia 1855g., in Danilov, *Stoletiia Voennago Ministerstva: Prilozheniia,* I: 19–24.

Rieber, A. J. "Alexander II: A Revisionist View," *JMH,* XLIII, No. 1 (1971): 42–58.

———, ed. *The Politics of Autocracy: Letters of Alexander II to Prince A. I. Bariatinskii, 1857–1864.* Paris and The Hague, 1966.

Robbins, Richard G.,Jr. *Famine in Russia, 1891–1892.* New York, 1975.

———. *The Tsar's Viceroys: Russian Provincial Governors in the Last Years of the Empire.* Ithaca and London, 1987.

Robinson, G. T. *Rural Russia Under the Old Regime: A History of the Landlord-Peasant World and Prologue to the Peasant Revolution of 1917.* New York, 1957.

Rodzianko, N. "Nabludeniia za dukhom i napravleniem zhurnala *Biblioteka dlia Chteniia,*" (mai 1850). TsGIAL, fond 722, opis' 1, delo No. 2423.

Rogger, Hans. *National Consciousness in Eighteenth-Century Russia.* Cambridge, Mass., 1960.

Rovinskii, D. A. "K sudebnym sledovateliam," *Vek,* No. 16 (1861): 545–47.

Ruane, Christine. "The Soul of the School: The Professionalization of Urban Schoolteachers of St. Petersburg and Moscow, 1860–1914." Unpublished manuscript in progress.

Ruckman, Jo Ann. *The Moscow Business Elite: A Social and Cultural Portrait of Two Generations, 1840–1905.* DeKalb, 1984.

Ruud, Charles. "A. V. Golovnin and Liberal Russian Censorship, January–June 1862," *SEER,* L, No. 119 (April 1972): 191–219.

———. *Fighting Words: Imperial Censorship and the Russian Press, 1804–1906.* Toronto, 1982.

———. "The Russian Empire's New Censorship Law of 1865," *CSS,* III, No. 2 (Summer 1969): 235–45.

Saltykov-Shchedrin, M. E. *Sobranie sochinenii.* 20 vols. Moscow, 1970.

Samarin, Iu. F. *Sochineniia Iu. F. Samarina.* 8 vols. St. Petersburg, 1877–1911.

*Sbornik pravitel'stvennykh rasporiazhenii po ustroistvu byta krest'ian, vyshedshikh iz krepostnoi zavisimosti.* 3rd ed. St. Petersburg, 1869.

Shreider, G. I. "Gorod i gorodovoe polozhenie 1870 goda," *Istoriia Rossii v XIX veke.* IV: 1–29.

Schweinitz, H. L. von. *Denkwürdigkeiten des Botschafters H. L. von Schweinitz.* 2 vols. Berlin, 1927.

Seleznev, I. Ia. *Istoricheskii ocherk Imperatorskago, byvshego tsarskosel'skago, nyne Aleksandrovskago, Litsei.* St. Petersburg, 1861.

Semenov, N. P. "Graf Viktor Nikitich Panin," *RA*, No. 3 (1887): 537–66.

————. *Osvobozhdenie krest'ian v tsarstvovanie Imperatora Aleksandra II: Khronika deiatel'nosti komissii po krest'ianskomu delu.* 3 vols. in 5 parts. St. Petersburg, 1889–91.

Semenov-Tian-Shanskii, P. P. *Istoriia poluvekovoi deiatel'nosti imperatorskago russkago geograficheskago obshchestva, 1845–1895gg.* 3 vols. St. Petersburg, 1896.

————. *Memuary.* vols 3–4. t. Petersburg, 1915–17.

Semevskii, V. I. *Krest'ianskii vopros v Rossii v XVIII i pervoi polovine XIX stoletiia.* 2 vols. St. Petersburg, 1888.

Seregny, Scott J. *Russian Teachers and Peasant Revolution: The Politics of Education in 1905.* Bloomington, 1988.

Shipov, D. N. *Vospominaniia i dumy o perezhitom.* Moscow, 1918.

Shtakel'berg, A. F. "Zapiska o prichinakh i sledstviiakh neurozhaev v Lifliandskoi gubernii i o sredstvakh preduprezhdeniia onym," [iiun'1844g.], TsGIAL, fond 1287, opis' 2, delo No. 970.

Shubin-Pozdev, D. "K kharakteristike lichnosti i sluzhebnoi deiatel'nosti S. I. Zarudnago," *RS*, LVII (February 1888): 477–84.

Shumakher, A. D. "Pozdnie vospominaniia o davno minuvshikh vremenakh: Dlia moikh detei i vnuchat," *VE*, CXCCVI, No. 3 (March 1899): 89–128; No. 4 (April 1899): 694–728.

Shvanebakh, P. Kh. *Nashe podatnoe delo.* St. Petersburg, 1903.

Sinel, Allen, *The Classroom and the Chancellery: State Educational Reform in Russia Under Count Dmitry Tolstoi.* Cambridge, Mass., 1973.

Skabichevskii, A. M. *Ocherki istorii russkoi tsenzury, 1700–1863gg.* St. Petersburg, 1892.

Skrebitskii, A. I. *Krest'ianskoe delo v tsarstvovanie Imperatora Aleksandra II: Materialy dlia istorii osvobozhdeniia krest'ian.* 5 vols. Bonn, 1862–68.

Slonim, Marc. *The Epic of Russian Literature: From Its Origins Through Tolstoi.* New York, 1964.

Solov'ev, Ia. A. "Zapiski senatora Ia. A. Solov'eva," *RS* (February 1881–March 1884), XXX: 213–46, 721–56; XXXI: 1–32; XXXIII: 227–58, 561–96; XXXIV: 105–54, 389–426; XXXVI: 131–54, XXXVIII: 259–90, 579–614; XLI: 241–76, 575–608.

"Sostoianie obshchestvennago upravleniia stolichnago goroda S.-Peterburga (iz revizii, proizvedennoi v 1843 godu Sanktpeterburgskim Grazhdanskim Gubernatorom)." TsGIAL, fond 1287, opis' 37, delo No. 738a.

Speranskii, M. M. "O zakonakh: Besedy grafa M. M. Speranskago s Ego Imperatorskim Vysochestvom Gosudarem Naslednikom Tsesarevichem Velikim Kniazem Aleksandrom Nikolaevichem s 12 oktiabria 1835 po 10 aprelia 1837 goda," *SIRIO*, XXX (1880): 363–64.

Starr, S. Frederick. *Decentralization and Self-Government in Russia, 1830–1870.* Princeton, 1972.

Stremoukhov, P. D. "Zametka odnago iz deputatov pervago prizyva," *RS*, CII (April 1900): 139–44.

Struve, P. P. "My Contacts with Rodichev," *SEER*, XII, No. 35 (January 1934): 347–67.

*Sudebnye ustavy 20 noiabria 1864 goda za piat'desiat' let.* 2 vols. Petrograd 1914.

"Svedeniia o N. I. Vtorove za vremia sluzhby ego v Ministerstve vnutrennikh del s 1844 po 1862gg." GPB, fond 163, delo No. 56.

Svetlov, L. B. *A. N. Radishchev: Kritiko-biograficheskii ocherk.* Moscow, 1958.

Taranovskii, Theodore. "The Aborted Counter-Reform: The Murav'ev Commission and the Judicial Statutes of 1864," *JfGOE*, XXIX, No. 2 (1981): 161–84.

———. "The Politics of Counter-Reform: Autocracy and Bureaucracy in the Reign of Alexander III, 1881–1894." Unpublished Ph. D. Dissertation. Harvard University, 1976.

Tatishchev, S. S. *Imperator Aleksandr II: Ego zhizn' i tsarstvovanie.* 2 vols. St. Petersburg, 1911.

Tengoborskii, L. V. "Éxtraits du Mémoire secret du Conseiller Privé Actuel Tengoborskii (janvier 1857)." TsGIAL, fond 851, opis' 1, delo No. 50.

Terner, F. G. *Vospominaniia zhizni F. G. Ternera.* 2 vols. St. Petersburg, 1910.

Thaden, Edward C. *Conservative Nationalism in Nineteenth-Century Russia.* Seattle, 1964.

Tiutchev, F. I. *Polnoe sobranie sochienenii F. I. Tiutcheva.* St. Petersburg, 1913.

Tiutcheva [Aksakova], A. F. *Pri dvore dvukh imperatorov: Vospominaniia, Dnevnik.* Moscow, 1928.

Tolstoi, L. N. "Pis'mo Nikolaiu II," 16 ianvaria 1902g., in Tolstoi, *Sobranie sochinenii,* XVIII: 289–97

———. *Sobranie sochinenii.* 20 vols. Moscow, 1960–65.

Torke, Hans-Joachim. "Das russische Beamtentum in der ersten Hälfte des 19. Jahrhunderts," *Forschungen zur osteuropäischen Geschichte,* XIII (1967): 7–345.

Troinitskii, A. G. *Krepostnoe naselenie Rossii po desiatoi narodnoi perepisi.* St. Petersburg, 1861.

———. "Pis'mo A. G. Troinitskago k bratu," 15 dekabria 1859, *RA,* No. 6 (June 1896): 296–97.

Troitskii, S. M. *Russkii absoliutizm i dvorianstvo v XVIIIv: Formirovanie biurokratii.* Moscow, 1974.

Troshchinskii. D. F. "Zapiska Dmitriia Prokof'evicha Troshchinskago o Ministerstvakh," *SIRIO*, III (1868): 1–162.

Trubetskaia, Kniaginia O. N.*Materialy dlia biografii kn. V. A. Cherkasskago.* 2 vols. Moscow, 1901, 1904.

Tseitlin, S. Ia. "Zemskaia reforma," *Istoriia Rossii v XIX veke*, III: 179–231.

"Tsenzura v tsarstvovanie Imperatora Nikolaia I," *RS*, CVII, No. 8 (August 1901); 395–404; No. 9 (September 1901): 643–68; CXIII, No. 2 (February 1903): 305–28; No. 3 (March 1903): 571–91; CXIV, No. 4 (April 1903): 163–82; No. 5 (May 1903): 379–96; No. 6 (June 1903): 643–71.

Tsie, V. A. "Zapiska o merakh, neobkhodimykh dlia sokrashcheniia perepiski i uproshcheniia deloproizvodstva v gosudarstvennykh uchrezhdeniiakh." 1856g. fond 833, delo No. 292.

Tsimmerman, A. E. "Vospominaniia Generala A. E. Tsimmermana." ORGBL, fond 325, karton 1–2.

Tugan-Baranovskii. *Russkaia fabrika v proshlom i nastoiashchem.* Moscow, 1938.

Ulam, Adam. *In the Name of the People: Prophets and Conspirators in Pre-Revolutionary Russia.* New York, 1977.

Valk, S. N., ed. *M. M. Speranskii: Proekty i zapiski.* Moscow and Leningrad, 1961.

Valuev, P. A. "Dnevnik grafa Petra Aleksandrovicha Valueva, 1847–1860gg., *RS*, No. 4 (April 1891): 167–82; No. 5 (May 1891): 339–49; No. 6 (June 1891): 603–16; LXXI, No. 7 (July 1891): 71–82; No. 8 (August 1891): 265–78; No. 9 (September 1891): 547–602; LXXII, No. 10 (October 1891): 139–54; No. 11 (November 1891): 393–459.

———. *Dnevnik P. A. Valueva: Ministra vnutrennikh del.* Edited by P. A. Zaionchkovskii. 2 vols. Moscow, 1961.

———. "Duma russkago vo vtoroi polovine 1855g.," *RS*, LXX, No. 5 (May 1891): 348–59.

———. "O vnutrennem sostoianii Rossii," 26 iiunia 1862, in Garmiza, ed., "Predpolozheniia i proekty," pp. 138–53.

———. "Otryvok iz zamechanii o poriadke grazhdanskoi sluzhby v Rossii (1845g.)." TsGIAL, fond 908, opis' 1, delo No. 24.

Varadinov, N. V. *Istoriia Ministerstva Vnutrennikh Del.* 8 vols. St. Petersburg, 1858–63.

"Velikoruss," in *Kolokol*, Nos. 107 (September 15, 1861) and 115 (December 8, 1861), in *Kolokol: Gazeta A. I. Gertsena*, IV: 900, 963.

Vengerov, S. A., ed. *Glavnye deiateli osvobozhdeniia krest'ian.* St. Petersburg, 1903.

Venturi, Franco. *Roots of Revolution: A History of the Populist and Socialist Movements in Nineteenth Century Russia.* Translated from the Italian by Francis Haskell. With an introduction by Isaiah Berlin. New York, 1966.

Veselovskii, K. S. "Otgoloski staroi pamiati," *RS*, C, No. 10 (October 1899): 5–23.

—. "Plan statisticheskago opisaniia Gosudarstvennykh Imushchestv i sosloviia sel'skikh zhitelei, sostoiashchago pod popechitel'stvom Ministerstva Gosudarstvennykh Imushchestv," 1847g. TsGIAL, fond 398, opis' 11, delo No. 3635.

—. "Vospominaniia," *RS*, CVIII, No. 12 (December 1901): 495–528.

Veselovskii, M. P. "Zapiski M. P. Veselovskago s 1828 po 1882." GPB, fond 550.F.IV.861.

Veselovskii, V. V. *Istoriia zemstva za sorok let.* 4 vols. St. Petersburg, 1909–11.

Viatkin, M. P. "Ekonomicheskaia zhizn' Peterburga v period razlozheniia i krizisa krepostnichestva," in Viatkin, et al., eds., *Ocherki istorii Leningrada*, I: 447–505.

Viatkin, M. P., et al., eds. *Ocherki istorii Leningrada.* 2 vols. Leningrad, 1955.

Virginskii, V. S. *Vozniknovenie zheleznykh dorog v Rossii do nachala 40-kh godov XIXv.* Moscow, 1949.

Vtorov, N. I. "Dnevnik, 1842–1857gg." GPB, fond 163, delo No. 83.

—. *Sravnitel'noe obozrenie munitsipal'nykh uchrezhdenii Frantsii, Bel'gii, Italii, Avstrii, i Prussii, s prisovokupleniem ocherka mestnago samoupravleniia v Anglii.* St. Petersburg, 1864.

Vucinich, Wayne S., ed. *The Peasant in Nineteenth-Century Russia.* Stanford, 1968.

"Vsepoddanneishie raporty Saratovskago, Tul'skago, i Poltavskago gubernatorov o sdelannom imi obozrenii vverennoi upravlenii ikh guberniiakh." TsGIAL, fond 1287, opis' 37, delo No. 120/6–7.

"Vsepoddanneishii raport Kazanskago Voennago gubernatora o sdelannom im obozrenii vverennoi upravlenii ego gubernii." TsGIAL, fond 1287, opis' 27, delo No. 120/1–2.

"Vypiska iz zhurnala Uchenago Komiteta Ministerstva Gosudarstvennykh Imushchestv, ot 26 oktiabria 1854g." TsGIAL, fond 398, opis' 16, delo No. 4852.

Wallace, Sir Donald Mackenzie. *Russia.* 2nd ed. London, Paris, New York, and Melbourne, 1905.

Whelan, Heide W. *Alexander III and the State Council: Bureaucracy and Counter-Reform in Late Imperial Russia.* New Brunswick, 1982.

Whittaker, Cynthia H. *The Origins of Modern Russian Education: An Intellectual Biography of Count Sergei Uvarov, 1786–1855.* DeKalb, 1984.

Willan, T. S. *The Early History of the Russia Company, 1553–1603.* Manchester, 1956.

Witte, S. Iu. *Vospominaniia.* 3 vols. Moscow, 1960.

Wortman, Richard. *The Crisis of Russian Populism.* Cambridge, 1967.

—. *The Development of Russian Legal Consciousness.* Chicago and London, 1976.

Yaney, George L. *The Systematization of Russian Government: Social Evolution in the Domestic Administration of Imperial Russia, 1711–1905.* Urbana, 1973.

———. *The Urge to Mobilize: Agrarian Reform in Russia, 1861–1930.* Urbana, 1982.

Zablotskii-Desiatovskii, A. P. *Graf P. D. Kiselev i ego vremia.* 4 vols. St. Petersburg, 1882.

———. "Statisticheskoe obozrenie gosudarstvennykh i obshchestvennykh povinnostei, dokhodov i raskhodov v Kievskoi gubernii, 1850–1851gg." TsGIAL, fond 940, opis' 1, delo No. 69.

———. "Vzgliad na istoriiu gosudarstvennykh imushchestv v Rossii." TsGIAL, fond 940, opis' 1, delo No. 12

———. "Zapiska o nedostatkakh obshchestvennago i o vygodakh lichnago vladeniia krest'ian zemleiu," 1851g. TsGIAL, fond 940, opis' 1, delo No. 16.

———. "Zapiska o roli Moskovskago i Peterburgskago obshchestv sel'skago khoziaistva v predstoiashchem osvobozhdenii krest'ian ot krepostnoi zavisimosti," 1856g. TsGIAL, fond 940, opis' 1, delo No. 17.

Zablotskii-Desiatovskii, A. P., and Prince V. F. Odoevskii, eds., *Sel'skoe chtenie.* 4 vols. St. Petersburg, 1843–48.

Zaionchkovskii, P. A. "Dmitrii Alekseevich Miliutin: Biograficheskii ocherk," in Zaionchkovskii, ed., D. A. Miliutin, *Dnevnik,* I: 5–72.

———. *Krizis samoderzhaviia na rebezhe 1870–1880 godov.* Moscow, 1964.

———. *Otmena krepostnogo prava v Rossii.* 3rd ed. Moscow, 1968.

———. "Podgotovka voennoi reformy 1874g," *IZ,* XXVII (1948): 170–201.

———. *Pravitel'stvennyi apparat samoderzhavnoi Rossii v XIXv.* Moscow, 1978.

———. *Provedenie v zhizn' krest'ianskoi reformy 1861.* Moscow, 1958.

———. *Rossiiskoe samoderzhavie v kontse XIX stoletiia (politicheskaia reaktsiia 80kh—nachala 90kh godov).* Moscow, 1970.

———. *Samoderzhaviia i russkaia armiia na rubezhe XIX–XX stoletii.* Moscow, 1973.

———. *Voennye reformy 1860–1870 godov v Rossii.* Moscow, 1952.

Zakharova, L. G. *Samoderzhaviia i otmena krepostnogo prava v Rossii, 1856–1861.* Moscow, 1984.

———. *Zemskaia kontrreforma 1890g.* Moscow, 1968.

Zarudnyi, S. I. "O reformakh sudoproizvodstva v Italii," *ZhMIu* (December 1862): 529–46.

———. "O spetsial'nykh prisiazhnykh dlia osobago roda del v Anglii, Frantsii, i Italii," *ZhMIu,* (November 1862): 267–83.

———. "Pis'mo opytnago chinovnika sorokovykh godov mladshemu ego sobratu, postupaiushchemu na sluzhbu," A. S. Zarudnyi, ed., *RS,* C, No. 12 (December 1899): 543–46.

Zhukovskii, V. A. "Pis'ma V. A. Zhukovskago k F. P. Litke," *RA*, Nos. 5–8 (1887): 327–40.

*Zhurnaly sekretnago i glavnago komitetov po krest'ianskomu delu s 10 oktiabria 1860 po 13 fevralia 1861 goda.* Petrograd, 1915.

"Zhurnaly komiteta uchrezhdennago Vysochaishim reskriptom 6 dekabria 1826 goda," *SIRIO*, LXXIV (1891): 1–502.

Zimmerman, Judith E. *Mid-Passage: Alexander Herzen and European Revolution, 1847–1852.* Pittsburgh, 1989.

# INDEX

Adlerberg, Count Aleksandr, 125, 126
Adlerberg, Count Vladimir, 89
Administration. *See* Bureaucracy; Municipal reform; Provincial government
Agriculture, 134. *See also* Peasants, Russian; Serfs
Aksakov, Ivan, 43, 135, 168
Alexander I, Tsar, 15, 52, 202; administration under, 16–18; education of, 12–13; and emancipation issue, 65; and provincial reform, 92
Alexander II, Tsar, xiii–xiv, xvii, 33–60, 62, 116, 118, 121, 160–61, 179, 190; assassination of, 173–75, 192, 197; attempt on life of, 171–72; censorship under, 54, 122–32; coronation of, 47; and emancipation issue, 57, 67–90; and judicial reform, 57, 105–15, 163, 188; and military reform, 144–56; and municipal reform, 136–42; and provincial government, 96–105; radicals' rejection of, 58–59
Alexander III, Tsar, xvii, 194; coronation of, 175–76; and counterreforms, 176–89, 198; death of, 163; and military reform, 143
April Program, 72–73
Arakcheev, Count Aleksei, 13
Armaments, 37, 38, 147, 152
Army. *See* Military, Russian
Artem'ev, Aleksandr, 135–36
Artsimovich, Viktor A., 74, 96, 98–99
Austria, 27, 28, 100
Austria-Hungary, 157
Austro-Prussian War, 155
Autocracy, xii; and Alexander I, 12–13; and Alexander II, 39–60; and Catherine II, 8–12; in counterreform era, 176–77, 179–81, 185–86; and judicial reform, 105, 113, 115–17; and Loris-Melikov program, 174–75; and Nicholas I, 13–15, 160; and Nicholas II, 197–98; and Peter the Great, 5–6; radical rejection of, 172–73; and *zemstvo* laws, 101–2. *See also Proizvol*

Bakhtin, Nikolai, 52, 104